Contributions to Economics

The series *Contributions to Economics* provides an outlet for innovative research in all areas of economics. Books published in the series are primarily monographs and multiple author works that present new research results on a clearly defined topic, but contributed volumes and conference proceedings are also considered. All books are published in print and ebook and disseminated and promoted globally. The series and the volumes published in it are indexed by Scopus and ISI (selected volumes).

Jasper Ostle • Max Rangeley • James Lawson
Editors

Adam Smith's Wealth of Nations After 250 Years

Enduring Insights, New Challenges

Springer

Editors
Jasper Ostle
Adam Smith Institute
London, UK

Max Rangeley
The Cobden Centre
Plymouth, Devon, UK

James Lawson
Adam Smith Institute
London, UK

ISSN 1431-1933 ISSN 2197-7178 (electronic)
Contributions to Economics
ISBN 978-3-032-32298-2 ISBN 978-3-032-32299-9 (eBook)
https://doi.org/10.1007/978-3-032-32299-9

This Springer imprint is published by the registered company Springer Nature Switzerland AG
The registered company address is: Gewerbestrasse 11, 6330 Cham, Switzerland

Foreword

The year 2026 marks the 250th anniversary of the publication of Adam Smith's magnificent book, *An Inquiry into the Nature and Causes of the Wealth of Nations*. Few works have exerted such enduring influence while remaining so persistently contested. Smith has been presented in turn as the founder of economics, the philosopher of liberty, the theorist of capitalism, the defender of markets, the critic of empire, the apostle of self-interest and the moral psychologist of commercial society, or the "age of commerce". Yet, as I highlighted in my own book *Adam Smith: What he thought, and why it matters* (Allen Lane, 2018), no single description adequately captures the range, the depth or the ambition of Smith's ideas.

This multiplicity of intellectual identities is not accidental. Smith wrote at a moment of profound historical transformation. Eighteenth-century Scotland was emerging from political instability and economic backwardness into an age of commerce, improvement and intellectual ferment. The Scottish Enlightenment sought to understand, among much else, why some societies flourished while others stagnated; how commerce altered manners, morals and human institutions; and whether modern commercial society could sustain liberty and justice without dissolving into corruption or domination. Part of Smith's genius lay in recognising that these questions could not be answered in isolation from each other. Political economy, law, rhetoric, moral psychology, politics and history all formed part of a single inquiry into the nature and development of human society.

The essays collected in this volume seek to reflect that breadth. They return to Smith not as a museum piece embalmed within the history of economic thought, but as a living interlocutor whose thought continues to illuminate questions about morality, institutions, education, entrepreneurship, finance and political order that endure today. Taken together, they reveal both the underlying unity of Smith's project and the tensions that have made his work so fertile for subsequent interpretation.

The collection falls naturally into three broad movements of thought. The first reconstructs Smith in context, among his intellectual interlocutors, historical inheritances and institutional concerns. The second examines tensions within Smith's work and its reception, revisiting long-standing interpretive disputes while in places moving beyond them. The third explores the continuing practical application of Smith's ideas to issues relating to institutions, entrepreneurship, education and public policy.

The opening essays recover some of the remarkable scope of Smith's intellectual architecture. What emerges is not simply "the father of economics", but a thinker attempting to construct a comprehensive theory of commercial society—itself part of a still wider "science of man", as his unpublished works suggest. In *The Essence of Adam Smith*, Eamonn Butler provides an admirably clear and wide-ranging account of much of that larger project. Smith appears here as a philosopher working to integrate moral psychology, jurisprudence, rhetoric and political economy into a single explanatory framework. The essay is intentionally explanatory rather than revisionist, but it succeeds especially well in resisting the later fragmentation of Smith's thought into separate academic disciplines.

That wider framework is then extended through Michael Munger's stimulating essay on the "division of stock". This argues that Smith's treatment of capital allocation anticipates important elements of Walter Bagehot's highly influential later theory of the lender of last resort. Read in this light, Smith emerges not merely as a theorist of markets, but as a subtle analyst of liquidity, prudence and institutional stability. Munger's account is especially persuasive in showing that Smith understood a central tension of commercial society which remains today: the need to mobilise capital productively while restraining speculative excess and moral hazard, and the potential danger of a shift from lender to insurer of last resort.

A more historical and classical perspective follows in James Price's treatment of Smith and the ancients, which usefully reminds the reader of Smith's debts to Stoic and specifically Ciceronian traditions. Smith's language of virtue, sympathy, prudence and justice did not emerge from nowhere. On the contrary, as with Smith's deep reflection on Aristotelian and other traditions deriving from ancient Greece, Stoicism formed a crucial part of the several philosophical inheritances within which he worked.

The ideas of truck, barter and exchange are central to *The Wealth of Nations*, and Leonidas Montes offers a rich and sophisticated account of exchange as an organising principle of Smith's thought. Here, exchange is seen not merely as an economic transaction but as a fundamentally human practice rooted in persuasion, rhetoric, sociability and language itself. Montes succeeds especially well in reuniting dimensions of Smith's thought often artificially separated by modern scholarship. Moral psychology, rhetoric, jurisprudence and political economy become different aspects of the same unified, spare and elegant inquiry into how free individuals cooperate under conditions of liberty.

Jerry Evensky's contribution on "the liberal plan" closes the first section by foregrounding Smith's normative ambitions. Smith's defence of commercial society rested not merely upon efficiency or wealth creation, as he points out, but upon the hope that a system of "equality, liberty and justice" might allow human beings to escape relations of arbitrary dependence and flourish more fully. "Commercial society" in Smith's stadial theory may best be seen less as a final destination than as the latest product of a deep attempt to explain processes of social development whose future transformations Smith himself could not fully foresee.

If the first section establishes the breadth and ambition of Smith's system, the second explores its tensions and ambiguities. The old "Adam Smith Problem" may no longer dominate scholarship—something for which we can all be grateful—but the relationship between *The Theory of Moral Sentiments* and *The Wealth of Nations* remains central to understanding Smith's thought.

That issue is approached with care in Douglas Den Uyl's essay on Smith's "two moralities". Den Uyl resists attempts at easy harmonisation and instead subjects the differences between Smith's works to close scrutiny. He argues that the moral framework of *The Theory of Moral Sentiments* is rooted in sympathy, propriety and the judgement of the impartial spectator, whereas that of *The Wealth of Nations* relies more heavily upon prudence, justice, and what we now think of as the management of incentives within institutional life. The question, on this account, is how far Smith may have moved from a morality of character and mutual approbation towards a more impersonal account of social coordination within commercial society, and whether and how, with different emphases, a single unified morality can be reconstructed between Smith's two great published works.

A different but related tension appears in Maria Pia Paganelli's essay on self-interest and commercial society. Paganelli reminds the reader of Bart Wilson's distinction between "own interest" and "self-interest", arguing from it that Smith's commercial order functions harmoniously only when individuals pursue their interests within a framework of mutual recognition and restraint. This approach must be broadly right, but it needs to be handled with care. After all, the famous butcher-brewer-baker passage cited by Paganelli does not end with the reference to "own interest", but with a reference to "self-love". Smith is generally careful with terminology, but the "own interest"/"self-interest" distinction needs more exploration before we can be sure on this point.

The most unconventional contribution in the collection follows in Jack Russell Weinstein's "two overlapping readings" of *The Wealth of Nations*. At times both personal and methodologically idiosyncratic, the essay rightly resists the calcification of Smith into a static historical authority; instead, it treats *The Wealth of Nations* as a living text continually to be reinterpreted under changing historical conditions.

Craig Smith's account of pragmatism, optimism and improvement starts from a very different place, by asking what Smith himself hoped to achieve through publication of *The Wealth of Nations*. In so doing, he captures several central aspects of Smith's temperament and method. Smith emerges neither as a utopian theorist nor as a cynical realist, but as a "pragmatic optimist": deeply committed to improvement, yet acutely conscious of the dangers created by institutional fragility, unintended consequences and human imperfection.

The final section turns towards the continuing practical application of Smith's ideas. Here the focus shifts from interpretation to institutional and political use.

Jerry Muller's essay on "psychological institutionalism" explores how Smith understood institutions as mechanisms for channelling human motivations towards socially beneficial outcomes. Again, it does valuable service in showing how Smith avoids naïve optimism about virtue, remaining realistic about our distinctively moralised human world and resisting the often-crude reductionism of modern writers about incentives.

Questions of entrepreneurship and innovation are then explored by Max Rangeley and Daniel Lacalle. Smith himself possessed no developed theory of the firm, of technological transformation or of entrepreneurial creativity, and he remained deeply ambivalent about speculative "projectors" and large joint-stock enterprises outside limited domains. But although *The Wealth of Nations* does not furnish the materials for a developed theory of entrepreneurship or innovation, the authors usefully discuss the institutional and moral foundations of commercial society that we now see as entrepreneurship's enabling conditions: trust, exchange, specialisation and reputational order.

Constantine Yannelis carefully seeks to avoid anachronism in his treatment of human capital and education in *The Wealth of Nations*. Smith undoubtedly recognised that education, training and acquired abilities formed part of a nation's productive capital, but Yannelis's essay also again preserves Smith's broader moral and civic concerns. Education mattered for him not merely because it increased productivity, but because it helped to form capable and independent citizens—an important continuity between Smith's political economy and his wider philosophy of human flourishing.

The collection concludes with James Lawson's discussion of "micropolitics" and policy implementation. Drawing on modern public choice analysis, the essay tries to use Smith's thought to focus upon real-world difficulties of implementing reform within modern political systems, highlighting the effects of negative incentives, bureaucratic resistance and adverse unintended consequences.

As these remarks illustrate, 250 years after its publication, *The Wealth of Nations* continues to provoke disagreement because, in its intellectual fertility, depth and relevance, it addresses problems that remain fundamentally our own. The essays collected here differ widely in their method, emphasis and style. Yet together they reveal the enduring power of Smith's central focus: the question of how free societies achieve improvement—material, moral, institutional and human—without destroying the liberty upon which that improvement depends.

Hereford, UK
May 2026

Jesse Norman

Preface

Two hundred and fifty years ago, Adam Smith published the first edition of *An Inquiry into the Nature and Causes of the Wealth of Nations*. For £1 and 16 shillings, readers would encounter two volumes, five books, 31 chapters, a protracted digression on the price of silver, and 1097 pages meticulously addressing the sources, distributions, and uses of wealth and capital in eighteenth-century Britain and beyond. Smith's work would become as controversial as it was popular, warranting four further editions and the ire of mercantilist incumbents across British industry and commerce. Two years later, he would become Commissioner of Customs and Salt Duties for Scotland in recognition of his spearheading and then-heterodox contribution to economic thought. Today, this book earns him a prized place in the annals of economic and intellectual history and a deserved reverence as 'the father of modern economics'.

At the semiquincentennial anniversary of Smith's most well-known contribution to economics, scholars and institutions from across the world are paying homage. Conferences, articles, journals, lectures, and student parties are taking place to pay tribute to the Scottish economist at this historic milestone. Such sustained interest now and since attests to the continuing relevance of the *Wealth of Nations*, as its insights continue to provide explanations for how wealth is generated and how the custodianship of commerce can be exercised fruitfully.

This *festschrift* seeks to contribute to this body of celebrations. Our aim is to provide a holistic treatment of the *Wealth of Nations* as not just an historical artefact but as a living document that continues to guide academics, economists, statesmen, policymakers, and commentators. As is true of all great pieces of scholarship, its reception continues to be contested, renewed, and challenged by readers today. We and our fellow authors have sought to capture the ever-evolving nature of Smithian philosophy. This collection faces not just backwards but also forwards, towards new ideas, approaches, and applications.

Part I, 'Ideas and interlocutors in context', introduces and interrogates the works of Adam Smith in textual and contextual frameworks. What did Adam Smith really say, and who was he in conversation with? Dr. Eamonn Butler introduces this thread (and the book at large) by assessing the 'essence' of Smith as not just a philosopher of economics but one of morality, nature, psychology, and society, as well as how these polymathic fronts intersect. Professor Michael Munger situates Smith's theory of finance against Walter Bagehot's 'lender-of-last-resort' prescription of *Lombard Street*, grounding his revolutionary theory of capital reallocation in crises against Smith's 'division of stock' foundation.

James Price follows by contextualising Smith's philosophies of property and morality in his engagement with thinkers of antiquity such as Cicero, Aristotle, and the Stoics. Professor Leonidas Montes continues by grounding the psychology of persuasion as foundational to Smith's theory of exchange within an economy. Professor Jerry Evensky concludes this part by charting how Smith communicates the benefits of a liberal society to encourage readers to enact the ideals espoused in *The Wealth of Nations*.

Part II, 'Tensions in content and reception', reveals how divergent readings of Smith's oeuvre continue to clash. Professor Douglas Den Uyl reopens '*Das Adam Smith Problem*' to reveal a textual conflict between the moralities posited in *The Wealth of Nations* and the moral tools found in *The Theory of Moral Sentiments*, and how that may be resolved. Professor Maria Pia Paganelli reminds us of the tensions as well as the harmonies that Smith observed in market operations and how distinguishing 'own interest' from 'self-interest' can explain how these tensions arise.

Professor Jack Russell Weinstein deploys autobiography alongside exegesis to advance two readings of *The Wealth of Nations*, foregrounding Smith's diagnosis of 'character dysmorphia' and his commitment to 'fair play' as contestations to the text's scholarly fossilisation. Professor Craig Smith closes this part by reassessing Smith's legacy and vision of societal improvement by asking 'what did Smith himself hope to achieve in writing the book?'.

Part III, 'Smith in practice and applied', explores the different fronts through which Smith's philosophy and way of thinking can still find relevance and application today. Professor Jerry Muller argues how Smith's psychological formulations of passion and desire can inform institutional design in pursuit of societal betterment. Max Rangeley and Daniel Lacalle elaborate on how Smith's formulation of key pillars of commerce (trust, productivity, incumbency, value, exchange, and more) can explain the dynamics of modern entrepreneurialism.

Professor Constantine Yannelis follows by revealing how Smith's writing can be seen in parts as the forefather of modern human capital theory through his economisation of skills, learning, and training, carving a space for Smith's relevance in the provision of education. Finally, James Lawson concludes this part and *festschrift* by illustrating how the application of public choice theory to Smithian principles can build a model of public policy implementation called 'micropolitics', thus elaborating on how Smith's philosophies can have continuous application to governance and statecraft.

Taken apart, each article alone constitutes a meditated treatment of Smith's philosophy, context, and utility. But, together, they weave a story of a text and thinker whose ideas remain relevant, whose legacy is still being written, and whose tools can still be applied today.

Our warmest gratitude goes to all of the authors who have generously contributed their time, energy, and cognition to write the articles collated here. The Rt Hon Dr Jesse Norman MP, both a scholar of Smith in academia and a practitioner of his thought in Parliament, is also thanked for his kind foreword. Thanks are also warranted to Springer, without whom this work would not be published with the reach it would otherwise have. We would also like to thank the Adam Smith Institute for providing an organisation through which the classical economics and the philosophy of freedom espoused by their namesake can be personated. We thank Adam Smith for writing the work itself, a task of gargantuan scope that continues to inform and inspire people to this day. And, finally, our thanks go to you, dear reader, for opening this collection of articles. We hope it sparks interest.

London, UK — Jasper Ostle
Plymouth, UK — Max Rangeley
London, UK — James Lawson
May 2026

Contents

Abbreviations

LJ(A)	Lectures on Jurisprudence (1762–1763)
LJ(B)	Lectures on Jurisprudence (1766)
LRBL	Lectures on Rhetoric and Belles Lettres (1762–1763)
TMS	Theory of Moral Sentiments (1759)
WN/WoN	The Wealth of Nations (1776)

Ideas and Interlocutors in Context

The Essence of Adam Smith

Eamonn Butler

1 Adam Smith's Legacy

Adam Smith is one of the most important figures in intellectual history. Born in 1723 in Kirkcaldy, a trading port on Scotland's east coast, he would go on to become one of the leading figures of the Scottish Enlightenment. In some ways, he eclipsed even his most notable contemporaries, such as the philosophers Francis Hutcheson, Thomas Reid, and the celebrated David Hume (of whom he was a close friend), along with other prominent figures such as the historian and sociologist Adam Ferguson, and (in more practical fields) the geologist James Hutton, the physician Joseph Black and the engineer James Watt (Phillipson, 2010). Smith's ideas, steeped in the values of the Enlightenment—reason, observation, scientific method, and human improvement—continue to inform today's academic debates in economics, philosophy, and social and political science. And his major works, *The Theory of Moral Sentiments* (Smith, 1759) and *An Inquiry into the Nature and Causes of the Wealth of Nations* (Smith, 1776) continue to influence, not just academic debate, but the thoughts of practical policymakers, commentators, and businesspeople too (Norman, 2018).

1.1 Smith the Enlightenment Scholar

Though remembered chiefly as "the father of modern economics," Smith was much more of a polymath than that, perhaps better regarded as an early, pioneering social psychologist. He was fascinated by every dimension of human nature and the human mind. He read, debated, and wrote widely (it was said he could never resist buying

E. Butler (✉)
Adam Smith Institute, Cambridge, UK
e-mail: eamonn@adamsmith.or

J. Ostle et al. (eds.), *Adam Smith's Wealth of Nations After 250 Years*, Contributions to Economics, https://doi.org/10.1007/978-3-032-32299-9_1

and reading books), not just on economics and ethics but on politics, jurisprudence, science, arts, language, and the classics (Butler, 2007).

His education laid the foundation for this breadth of knowledge. He shone at school. And having entered the University of Glasgow at age 14, he was encouraged and influenced by the philosopher Francis Hutcheson. Later, as Snell Exhibitioner at Balliol College, Oxford, he immersed himself in classical literature. (Something he had to do on his own: he would complain in *The Wealth of Nations* that the Oxford professors, living on their guaranteed salaries, had "given up altogether even the pretence of teaching.") Returning to Scotland, he was invited by a family friend to give some public lectures in Edinburgh, which were received with great and widespread praise. He returned to Glasgow, this time as a teacher, his lectures covering a wide range of subjects that reflected the breadth of his learning: moral philosophy, logic, jurisprudence, language ('rhetoric'), politics, and economics ('political economy') (Ross, 2010).

As his life went on, he would discuss epistemology with Hume, politics with Voltaire, science with Hutton and Black, history with Ferguson, jurisprudence with Lord Kames, economics with Quesnay and Turgot. At the intellectual gatherings he loved—the Glasgow Literary Society, the Select Society, the Oyster Club, the Philosophical Society, the Royal Society of Edinburgh, and many more—he would develop and test his thoughts with other academics, and with merchants, artists, and scientists.

This lifetime of learning allowed Smith to integrate seemingly diverse ideas. Thus, his *impartial spectator* brought the Stoics' self-control into the development of conscience; he would broaden the physiocrats' focus on economics of agriculture into a comprehensive theory of wealth creation; his sociology would portray human societies as complex systems governed by natural laws, much like Newton's universe (Smith, 2006). (Indeed, he wrote an essay on Newton's scientific method, published posthumously).

Meanwhile, Smith's essays on literature and aesthetics would apply human psychology to explain our appreciation of beauty (Smith, 1795). He could trace the history of languages and analyse their role, not just in communication but for moral judgement too. He was, it has been said, "the last man to know everything." And even today, his holistic methodology prompts economists to reflect on the psychological, ethical, and political dimensions of economic life, informing economic movements such as the Public Choice School, Behavioural Economics (and "nudge" policies) along with many others (Butler, 2025).

1.2 Smith the Economist

Smith's impact on economics was of course particularly profound. His *Wealth of Nations* took ideas, observations, and facts from all around the world, fusing them with his own concepts to produce a new and comprehensive explanation of economic life. He developed concepts like GDP, specialisation, productivity, and capital that economists still use today. Being able to draw on a dazzling host of thinkers and examples from around the world, he systematised economics and gave it a recognisably modern form.

Smith realised that through specialisation, productivity could be increased dramatically, something he illustrated neatly in his pin factory example (Smith, 1776, Bk I Chap. 1). And he realised that specialisation between trades, and even between countries, could do the same, with (for example) countless specialists from many countries contributing to something as modest the "woollen coat…which covers the day-labourer, as coarse and rough as it may appear" (Smith, 1776 Bk I Chap. 1).

Smith also saw that exchange benefited both sides, not just the seller who ended up with money; but the buyer who ends up with the goods or services that they value more than the price. He recognised that, in voluntary transactions, buyers and sellers would not bother to trade unless they each thought themselves better by it. Such mutual gain from exchange explains why nearly all economists today support liberalisation of international trade, and perhaps why the market economy has proved so robust, however much political authorities have tried to suppress it.

Furthermore, Smith drew attention to capital accumulation and to innovation, both still seen as crucial for wealth creation and progress. His warnings on monopolies (especially government monopolies), on cronyism and on regulation still resonate in critiques of business and government. And his Invisible Hand metaphor has inspired economists, such as Friedrich Hayek, Milton Friedman, George Stigler, Thomas Sowell, and Deirdre McCloskey, to explore exactly how resources may be rationally allocated without central planning. Yet, focused always on the overall welfare of human society, Smith still saw roles for the state in infrastructure provision, education, financial regulation, and more.

Smith's modernity lies in his recognition that economics is about human flourishing, not money. And that same recognition continues to inform debates today on topics such as capitalism, sustainable development, global trade, and the social impact of emerging technologies (Norman, 2018).

1.3 Smith the Social Psychologist

As well as being a groundbreaking economist, Smith pioneered exploration of the human mind and social interactions. In *Moral Sentiments*, he examined how emotions, empathy, and social norms shape interpersonal behaviour, predating modern social psychology by a century (Smith, 1759). Humans, he realised, are inherently social beings, driven by a desire for approval by their peers. They have a natural empathy, and a conscience, that helps them regulate their actions in ways that benefit the whole species. All this long before Darwin, and even longer before psychology and bio-ethics became respectable disciplines.

Smith also analysed how society influences individuals, such as how virtues like prudence and justice develop from social interactions and how economic self-interest is tempered by the desire to be worthy of trust, something experimental economists are rediscovering today (Smith & Wilson 2015). To him, ethics and economics were but two parts of the human mind. Just as our economic self-interest creates a productive market, our self-interested desire for praise creates a harmonious society.

2 Smith's Contributions to Economics

2.1 *The Importance of* the Wealth of Nations

To a modern reader, Adam Smith's *Wealth of Nations* is a difficult book. Around 500 pages, it is written in flowery, rhetorical eighteenth century language. At points its abstract and theoretical arguments give way to polemics on trade policy or to facts and digressions on a diversity of subjects from colonial administration, through public debt and the history of taxation, to the price of silver. Yet, within this book lie some of the most revolutionary ideas in the history of social science.

It is true that not all the concepts that Smith weaves into his text were original. Though he was certainly inventive, his true genius was to synthesise his ideas together with those from other thinkers, disciplines, and countries, weaving them into a startlingly new, comprehensive, and modern-looking economic system that explained the facts and revealed the nature and principles of the industrial and commercial world that we still live in today.

The book's "infuriating" and "elephantine" sprawl is therefore part of its genius (Rosten, 1970). Smith's many digressions are not accidents. They illustrate his underlying recognition that economic phenomena cannot be understood in isolation from history, politics, law, and psychology, and that theory must be grounded in the observation and understanding of real-world facts and must account for them.

2.2 *Productive Capacity as the Key Measure of Wealth*

Perhaps Smith's most radical innovation is found in the opening line of the book. "The annual labour of every nation is the fund which originally supplies it with all the necessaries and conveniences of life." In that line, he identifies and indicates the importance of the concept of GDP that economists still use today as the index of a country's prosperity. In the next paragraph, GDP per capita. In the third, productivity. The wealth of a nation is not the money in its vaults but the productivity of its labour.

True, the idea of "national income" had been raised before, though in a limited context (Petty, 1662, 1691). But Smith's concept was of much wider application, and much more radical in terms of what he argued it meant for public policy. At the time, the prevailing, and seemingly commonsense, view was that a nation's economic (and therefore political and military) strength lay in the gold and silver it could hoard by securing a favourable balance of trade. Smith's insights overturned that whole approach and the entire regulatory edifice built upon it. He showed how both buyers and sellers benefited from voluntary exchange, and how it was not bullion, but the productive capacity of a nation to provide both the necessities of life and the surpluses that could be exchanged for other things that were its real strength and wealth. That would, in turn, lead him to propose instead a very different vision for public policy.

A nation's laws and regulations, he went on to argue, should not be aimed at accumulating gold and silver by means of subsidising exports and restricting imports. Rather, they should aim to augment the productive capacity of its land and people—particularly of "the labouring poor" who constituted "the great body of the people" (Smith, 1776, Bk V, Chap. 1, Pt III, Art. II) To do that would require policies of free trade, secure property rights, personal and economic liberty, limited regulation, and low taxes. When today's politicians pledge their commitment to economic growth, they are (often unwittingly) speaking the language of Adam Smith.

Even so, Smith was no slave to *laissez faire* non-intervention. He thought that raising a nation's productive capacity would also require public investment in human capital, in the form of support for education. And it would also require some of the same public support in infrastructure, such as the roads, bridges and harbours, that were needed to allow trade and commerce to flourish.

2.3 The Division of Labour

Another important insight in *The Wealth of Nations* is the enormous productivity that can be wrought from specialisation, what he called the "division of labour" and outlined in the first chapter of the book. As an example, he famously describes the different tasks being undertaken in a factory producing pins, where "one man draws out the wire, another straits it, a third cuts it, a fourth points it…" and so on (Smith, 1776, Bk I, Chap. 1).

Some observers complain that Smith probably never visited a pin factory and got the idea of it from a French encyclopaedia. But that is rather beside the point: Smith's genius lies in how he uses this example as a brilliant and easily grasped teaching tool from which he derives a very powerful principle, showing how there is a thousandfold gain in productivity from even this simple specialisation of tasks. And he understood that in more complex processes, such as those growing up in the industrialisation of his age, the productivity gain could be yet more still.

Such high levels of productivity, he went on to explain, came from first the increased dexterity and skill acquired by workers who repeated the same task many times. Another factor was the time saved in turning from one task to another. And a third was the use of specialist equipment that can help produce things better, faster, and cheaper. Today, the pin factory is eclipsed by assembly lines, semiconductor plants, and automated distribution centres. The productivity is even greater, but the specialisation principle remains the same foundation on which it rests.

Smith's views were, however, nuanced on the division of labour, as they were on much else. More than a century before Marx popularised the idea of alienation, Smith warned of the boredom and isolation that repetitive labour could produce among workers (Smith, 1776, Bk V, Chap. 1, Pt III). He considered this good reason to propose public investment in the antidote that was education. His dedication to boosting human productivity would never eclipse his commitment to human welfare.

2.4 The Invisible Hand and the Market Mechanism

No phrase of Adam Smith's is more famous, or more misunderstood, than the "invisible hand." It appears by name only once in *The Wealth of Nations* (and once more in *Moral Sentiments*), and, even then, in a very specific context.

When deciding where to invest, says Smith (Smith, 1776, Bk IV, Chap. 2) a person "intends only his own gain [but] is in this, as in many other cases, led by an invisible hand to promote an end which was no part of his intention." "By pursuing his own interest he frequently promotes that of the society more effectually than when he really intends to promote it" (a typically Adam Smith barb, aimed at officialdom).

Even if there are indeed "many other cases" as Smith suggests, he is not claiming that self-interest will always produce optimal outcomes. He was well aware of the limits of markets, as testified to by the existence of public goods (such as defence), monopolies (there were so many at the time), and externalities (he cites the nuisance to urban neighbours of trades such as butchers and tanners) (Smith, 1776 Bk V Chap. 1). But this "invisible hand," by which private self-interest rather unexpectedly produces a public benefit, is nevertheless a warning that we only scantily understand the relation between individual actions and societal outcomes. And Smith suggests that, under the right market conditions, individual self-interest may co-ordinate economic life far more effectively than any conscious central planner, a theme that Hayek would develop (Hayek, 1945).

In countless examples from around the world, Smith showed how the prices that emerge from market trading draw resources from less valued uses to more valued ones, and do so more quickly, more systematically and more thoroughly than could be matched by those he criticised as intending to promote the interest of society—like the interventionists and central planners of today. Prices, Smith explained, efficiently coordinate the work of countless specialists, from all over the globe, without any need for coercion or central direction. The task that remains for the economist is to discover how to steer our self-interest, and maximise our value-creating production, in ways that promote the welfare of the whole community.

3 Smith on Growth and Prosperity

The Wealth of Nations provided the first comprehensive explanation of how nations could (and did) become rich by accumulating capital and liberating markets from the over-regulation that vested interests foisted onto them. These policies, it argued, would unleash a self-reinforcing growth process that raised living standards, especially for the working poor. And that agenda has motivated every serious growth discussion since.

3.1 Capital Accumulation

Growth, explained Smith, is a long-term process, sustained by continuous investment in ever more and better tools, machines, buildings, and infrastructure. The more a society saves, the more it has available to invest. The more it invests, the more its productive capacity can be expanded. And the more that its productive capacity expands, the more prosperity and growth that it can generate.

Saving, then, is not about hoarding money, according to Smith. It is about accumulating resources that are available to be switched from financing immediate consumption into creating the means of future, more efficient production. Savings fund the investment that maintains workers and makes them more productive, while current extravagance (wasteful government spending in particular) destroys capital and so retards growth and future prosperity (Smith, 1776, Bk II, Chap. 3).

In surprisingly modern style, Smith goes on to explore the determinants of the savings and investment functions. Saving is difficult in poor countries because almost everything is spent on bare subsistence. But when a surplus appears, saving and thus investment become possible. Capital accumulation increases the quantity and quality of the tools that are available to workers, enabling them to create more and better products. It also finances infrastructure (e.g. roads, canals and harbours) that reduces trading costs.

It is a self-reinforcing cycle. Larger markets justify more specialisation and capital-intensive processes, which allow them to expand still further. So, when growth starts, it tends to accelerate, a scenario where the condition of the mass of the people "seems to be the happiest and the most comfortable" (Smith, 1776, Bk I, Chap. 8). While Smith recognised that rising growth may temporarily increase inequality, he argued that in the long run, competition would erode excessive profits and drive up the wages of the "labouring poor," producing a more equal outcome.

3.2 The Importance of Free Markets

Smith notes that the lure of profit draws capital investment to its most valued applications. The "obvious and simple system of natural liberty," where individuals (subject always to the rules of justice) are free to pursue their own interest in their own way, produces prosperity. And the freer that entrepreneurs are to experiment, to copy success, and to undercut competitors, the quicker and more easily does that happen.

By way of illustration, Smith points out the contrast between the heavily regulated but stagnant economies of continental Europe and the more free and growing economies of Britain and the Netherlands. Across the Atlantic too, he contrasts the North American colonies, where regulation was light, against the torpor of Latin America, crippled by bureaucracy.

Smith thought that the role of government in a free and prospering society was limited. It had three duties: national defence, the administration of justice, and certain public works and institutions that private enterprise cannot profitably undertake. Smith was no anarcho-capitalist: he supported regulations that protected public health, prevented fraud, restrained monopoly, and stabilised banking. But he argued that, beyond its proper functions, government should not try to direct the employment of labour and capital. Indeed, he believed that the prevailing regulation of prices, wages, apprenticeships, settlement laws, and colonial trade and much else did far more harm than good.

The last two centuries confirm Smith's insight. The growth unleashed by free markets has been a powerful engine of poverty reduction. The "hockey-stick" rise in living standards since 1800 occurred exactly where and when his policies of openness and liberty were adopted. The East Asian miracle of the late twentieth century, the rapid growth of India after 1991 and other examples all follow from his prescription: remove barriers to commerce, allow prices to guide resources, protect property, respect contracts, and the result is higher investment, growing productivity and rising wages for workers.

For Smith, then, growth and prosperity, and greater equality too, came through allowing individuals the maximum liberty to employ their labour and capital as they see fit. He knew that economic growth would not solve every ill. But he insisted (and more recent history has confirmed) that no other system has ever succeeded in generating sustained, broad-based prosperity on anything like the scale as those obvious and simple principles.

Today, amidst all the questioning of the legitimacy of the market system, Adam Smith's message remains strongly relevant. The patient accumulation of capital to boost productivity and economic growth is not a luxury. It is the only proven way of lifting the mass of humanity out of poverty.

4 Smith's Critique of Mercantilism

To Smith, the biggest enemies of this improvement were, paradoxically, the vested interests in commerce itself, aided (knowingly or not) by politicians. "People of the same trade seldom meet together, even for merriment and diversion," he observed, "but the conversation ends in a conspiracy against the public, or in some contrivance to raise prices"—before going on to note how official regulations made such conspiratorial meetings more likely (Smith, 1776, Bk I, Chap. 10).

But then, for almost two centuries, politicians, businesspeople, and economic thinkers had agreed that national wealth came from accumulating bullion by keeping out imports and boosting exports. Tariffs, bounties (i.e. subsidies), monopolies, and embargos had become the standard tools of policy. In *The Wealth of Nations*, which was as much of a polemic as it was an academic treatise, Smith ruthlessly demolished this entire intellectual system—mercantilism—and replaced it with something radically different.

Smith pointed out that trade and commerce are not zero-sum contests between the trading parties, but a positive-sum game in which each party gains something they value more than what they give up in exchange. Sellers might end up with more cash, but buyers end up with the goods they want. Preventing such exchanges necessarily reduces the value that is generated by them. Trade barriers do not enrich a country; they impoverish it.

This was a powerful and novel analysis that still resonates. Today, almost all economists accept the importance of greater freedom in international trade.

4.1 Challenging Mercantilist Ideas

Mercantilism rested on the beliefs that wealth is money and that the total quantity of money in the world is more or less fixed. So one nation can get richer only by taking money from others—through warfare, or by running trade surpluses. In this view, trade restrictions were perfectly rational.

Smith, though, redefined money. Money was not wealth, merely a medium of exchange. What people really want is not a pile of shiny metal, but the food, clothing, shelter, and comforts that it can buy. True wealth consists in affording the "necessaries, conveniences, and amusements of human life" (Smith, 1776, Bk I, Chap. 5). But a nation that piles up gold in its vaults remains poor, like a miser who goes hungry while being surrounded by a fortune in coin. The focus of trade policy, therefore, should not be to accumulate bullion but to pursue value. And when money is viewed in this way, trade is no longer a war in which one party can gain only if another loses. Trade occurs because both parties expect to benefit from it.

The implications of this for public policy were revolutionary. Trade policy, Smith explained, should facilitate the same specialisation and exchange that works in domestic commerce. Just as it is absurd for a tailor to grow his own wheat and a farmer to sew his own coat, it is equally absurd for Britain to produce grapes or Portugal to raise sheep in defiance of their climate. "What is prudence in the conduct of every private family, can scarce be folly in that of a great kingdom": instead of trying to make everything at home to avoid spending money abroad, we should buy in what we can get more cheaply from others (Smith, 1776, Bk IV, Chap. 2).

The mercantile system of controls on trade and commerce, Smith concluded, did not serve the interests of the public, only those of merchants and manufacturers. "The interest of the consumer," he noted acidly, "is almost constantly sacrificed to that of the producer" (Smith, 1776, Bk IV, Chap. 8). Producers lobbied fiercely to promote their self-interest, calling for tariffs and regulations to limit the threat of competition, both at home and abroad. But politicians should know better: "To hurt in any degree the interest of any one order of citizens, for no other purpose but to promote that of some other, is evidently contrary to that justice and equality of treatment which the sovereign owes to all the different orders of his subjects" (Smith, 1776, Bk IV, Chap. 8).

4.2 Specialisation, Trade Barriers, and the Wealth of Nations

In one of the longest sections in *The Wealth of Nations*, Smith explained why and how the labyrinthine mercantilist controls of his day were so deeply damaging to prosperity.

A key reason is climate. For instance, grapes grow easily in sunny France, and centuries of experience in viticulture and viniculture makes its wines cheap and high quality. Cold, rainy Scotland is a poor place to grow grapes, but it has ideal grazing for sheep, and centuries of perfecting the skills of sheep-rearing and weaving makes Scottish woollens cheap and high quality. This is an obvious basis for the specialisation and exchange that would benefit both countries.

But Britain's mercantilist policies, seeking to protect domestic industries and earn more from exports, subsidised the export trade in wool and restricted imports of other textiles, such as printed cotton, raising the cost of clothing to British consumers. Likewise, tariffs on wine imports, designed to raise revenues for the government and do down potential enemies, raised the price of those too, creating a thriving illegal smuggling industry into the bargain.

Meanwhile, mercantilist prohibitions on exporting machinery or preventing skilled artisans from working abroad aimed to preserve Britain's lead in technology. To Smith, these damaged the very industries they were meant to protect, since they prevented British manufacturers earning the foreign exchange they needed to buy raw materials. But they were also futile. Efforts to stop the export of machinery were "ineffectual," while attempts to stop the "emigration of artificers" were "undoubtedly impossible" (Smith, 1776, Bk IV, Chap. 8).

Smith was particularly scathing about colonial monopolies. He could see the political and defence justifications for the Navigation Acts, which forced the American colonies to buy European goods only through Britain and to ship their produce only in British ships. But he pointed out the serious economic damage that they did both sides. They enriched London merchants and ship-owners but raised prices for consumers in Britain and America. They were the "principal cause of the present commercial difficulties" and the resulting "troubles and disturbances" between Britain and America (i.e. the American War of Independence that had begun just a year before *The Wealth of Nations* was published) (Smith, 1776, Bk V, Ch 7, Pt III).

Trade barriers like these, argued Smith, have four pernicious effects. First, they divert capital and labour from more productive to less productive employments: resources are forced into protected industries where the country has no natural advantage. Second, they raise prices for consumers, reducing real incomes and the purchasing power of wages. Third, they encourage monopoly and retard innovation: sheltered from competition, domestic producers grow lazy and inefficient. And fourth, they provoke retaliation: when one country imposes tariffs, others reciprocate, shrinking the global market and injuring exporters.

Smith concedes that trade barriers might be necessary for national defence, even if their commercial effects were damaging. They might also be useful in countering foreign tariffs and thereby prompting other nations to reduce their barriers in pursuit of mutual free trade—but only as temporary measures: if they do not have this beneficial effect, a country should give up on them. And there was a case for gradualism where barriers had been in place a long time and their sudden removal could cause economic dislocation. But these were narrow exceptions. Smith's overwhelming conclusion was that "the mean rapacity, the monopolising spirit of merchants and manufacturers" (Smith, 1776, Bk I, Chap. 11) had perverted policy, and that the general interest lay in having the freest possible trade.

Smith's critique of mercantilism was one of the most successful demolitions in the history of ideas. Soon after, Britain would embark on free trade policies and enjoy a century of prosperity as a result. And academically, almost every subsequent advance in trade theory—Ricardo's comparative advantage theorem, terms-of-trade arguments, optimal tariff theory—has emerged from within the framework that Smith established.

Protectionism is still rife. But it is founded on fallacies that Smith exploded 250 years ago: the belief that exports are good and imports bad, that trade is a zero-sum game, and that domestic producers should be sheltered from foreign competition. When politicians suggest that tariffs will save jobs and stop jobs going overseas, it is the ghost of mercantilism speaking. As Smith explained, trade barriers do not create wealth; they merely redistribute it from consumers to producers, and from efficient producers to inefficient ones, sapping (not boosting) the prosperity of the nation. The more that the world has followed his advice, the richer it has become.

5 Smith's Moral Philosophy

It was not *The Wealth of Nations* but his first book, *The Theory of Moral Sentiments*, that made Smith internationally famous and which he regarded as his masterwork. He revised it continually until his death in 1790, adding new sections and polishing the prose. Together, the two form a single, ambitious project: to explain how a society of imperfect, self-interested human beings can nevertheless create a functioning social order, prosperity, and decency.

5.1 Sympathy and Moral Sentiments

At the heart of *The Theory of Moral Sentiments* is one of the most original concepts in ethics: "sympathy," or what we today would call empathy. To Smith, sympathy was the innate ability of humans to imagine themselves in another's situation and to understand their feelings. And it is from this, he argued (against all prevailing ideas) that our moral ideas emerge.

His opening sentence again says it all: "How selfish soever man may be supposed, there are evidently some principles in his nature, which interest him in the fortune of others, and render their happiness necessary to him, though he derives nothing from it except the pleasure of seeing it" (Smith, 1759, Pt I, Chap. 1).

To Smith, an empathic feeling for others is rooted deeply in our psychology as social creatures. We experience joy when others are joyful, grief when others grieve and indignation when we see injustice done to someone else. More than that, we feel sorrow and remorse when our actions distress others and earn their disapproval, and pleasure when our actions please others and earn their approval. And we approve of an action or a character when we can empathise with the motives behind it and disapprove when we cannot.

In this psychology lies the origin of our moral thinking. As we go through the years, facing countless occasions on which such sentiments arise, we gradually learn and develop ways of behaving in similar circumstances. We develop a behavioural code that we can apply to future situations that might arise, even hypothetical ones that we have never experienced before.

Even when nobody is there to judge us, this code of conduct has its effect. If we find a purse in an empty street, for example, do we steal the contents and carry on? No, says Smith. We judge our own actions as we believe others would, even if no others are around. "We endeavour to examine our own conduct as we imagine any other fair and impartial spectator would examine it" (Smith, 1759, Pt III, Chap. 1). This "impartial spectator" again resides in our psychology, constructed over years of social experience. Our desire to be worthy of praise becomes a motivator even more powerful than actual praise itself.

The philosophers of Smith's time were struggling to identify the source of our moral values. Were they the commands of a divine lawgiver? Or clerics' interpretation of those commands? Or perhaps a matter for reason? Smith's answer was simple but revolutionary: Our morality is a product of our social interaction. It emerges because it helps us to live alongside each other peaceably. Smith thanked Providence for this happy fact; today we might thank human evolution.

He was nevertheless very realistic about the limits of sympathy. We feel it more intensely for those close to us, less for strangers, and very little for distant millions. But institutions such as the theatre, literature, and the study of history could help us extend the range of our sympathy by allowing us to imagine ourselves in remote times and places.

Smith's ethical theory, therefore, is both descriptive and normative. It explains how moral standards emerge through our engagement in society. But it also prescribes how we might cultivate those standards in the future. For Smith, virtue was not a matter of heroic self-denial, but of propriety, calibrated by past experience alongside the imagined reactions of a well-informed and unbiased observer.

5.2 The Role of Justice and Institutions

Smith identified three key virtues—beneficence (kindness), prudence (self-care), and justice. But only justice can be enforced. Beneficence is admirable but cannot be compelled, as coercion would strip it of its value. Prudence is wise but again voluntary. Justice, however, can be enforced and "is the main pillar that upholds the whole edifice. If it is removed, the great, the immense fabric of human society … must in a moment crumble into atoms" (Smith, 1776, Pt II, Section II, Chap. 2).

Justice, to Smith, consists primarily in refraining from harm: respecting persons, property and contracts. Without these, cooperation fails. But enforcing justice requires institutions—the laws, courts, police, and ultimately the coercive power of the state needed to maintain the secure environment in which society can flourish.

Smith's discussion of justice is strikingly modern. He recognises that different rules evolve in different societies, but insists there are universal principles of justice, which emerge from how we feel when injury is visited on ourselves and others. Murder and theft, for example, provoke universal moral outrage because we all sympathise with the victims. And we codify this morality in enforceable rules of justice.

The institutions of justice must channel our sentiments in a functional way. Good laws align self-interest with social good; bad ones (e.g. those granting monopolies or oppressing the poor) corrupt morality and breed resentment.

Smith's moral philosophy is inseparable from his political economy. Free markets are not just economically desirable because they create wealth. They are morally desirable because they rest on non-coercive, voluntary exchange and on impartial rules of justice that promote the beneficial functioning of the whole society. Ethics and economics are simply two different aspects of the same human psychology.

6 Criticisms of Adam Smith

6.1 The Labour Theory of Value

Smith was a pioneer, and pioneers make mistakes. Many people think that his supposed acceptance of the labour theory of value is one of them. At one point in *The Wealth of Nations,* he comments: "If among a nation of hunters … it usually costs twice the labour to kill a beaver which it does to kill a deer, one beaver should naturally exchange for or be worth two deer." The critics point out that if a good's value is the labour invested in it, then something takes a great deal of labour but is essentially useless (like carrying water to the sea) must be of great value, which is absurd.

But we must remember that the labour theory had been the standard explanation of the value of different things for around two millennia before Smith wrote, and it would be nearly a century later before modern subjective theories, built on marginal utility and individual preferences would emerge to provide a better explanation (Jevons, 1871; Menger, 1871; Butler, 2025). So Smith's lapse into it is understandable. But Smith's example is limited to an imaginary world without capital, in which it might make some sense. And he is clearly unhappy with the labour theory, going on to explain the problems in measuring "labour" (e.g. skilled procedures that take little time to execute but take great time to learn, or the contribution of innovation in creating value), before going on to explain at much greater length the role of the "higgling and bargaining of the market" in setting prices (Smith, 1776, Bk V, Chap. 5).

6.2 The Invisible Hand

The "invisible hand" metaphor is criticised on three grounds. The first is that it suggests perfect market efficiency in which individual self-interest always leads to social benefit without the need for intervention, which is obviously overoptimistic. The second is that it was not original, having been identified a decade earlier by Adam Ferguson. The third is that it appears only once in *The Wealth of Nations*, and in a very limited context, so it is not as important as it is made out to be, and Smith should not be judged by it.

Yet, although the invisible hand is mentioned only once in the book, the principle behind it is what the entire work (and that of *Moral Sentiments* too) is about: namely, the complex relationship between individual actions and social outcomes. The idea that social institutions were "the result of human action, but not the execution of any human design" had indeed been expressed by Adam Ferguson 9 years earlier (Ferguson, 1767), and as Hayek notes, has even earlier roots (Hayek, 1960). But the point about Smith's treatment is that he showed, systematically and in detail, how widely the principle prevailed. Equally, he was far too shrewd to believe that private interest would always deliver public benefit, as his support for banking regulation and anti-monopoly measures demonstrates. As usual, he was not making any claim that markets were always perfect, and his focus was on the overall welfare of human society.

6.3 *Overoptimism and Complacency*

Smith is sometimes branded as an enthusiast for *laissez faire*, who downplayed problems like inequality, exploitation, environmental damage, and monopoly power. This is unfair, given his overt recognition of these problems—many of which he blamed on the collusion between businesspeople and the elites in power, and the inability of the authorities to see the long-term harmful consequences of their actions. Smith criticised vanity and indulgence and argued for progressive taxes and supported public education to raise the prospects of the poorest.

Nevertheless, some commentators still argue that Smith complacently accepted that economic growth requires significant wealth disparities. They argue that the large concentrations of wealth that result can be used to direct and distort markets. But Smith insisted that no society "can surely be flourishing and happy, of which the far greater part of the members are poor and miserable" (Smith, 1776, Bk I Chap. 8). Wealth and income differences, he thought, were indeed an inevitable fact in a growing economy. But happily, countries that were free were more likely to prosper, and as they prospered, it was the "labouring poor" who benefited most. Thus, wages had risen significantly in Britain, precisely when commercial restrictions were being relaxed. And in a growing economy, Smith argued, the competitive demand for labour rises faster than its supply expands, pushing up wages. All classes gain from economic growth, but the relative position of labour improves most. "The liberal reward of labour…is the natural symptom of increasing national wealth" (Smith, 1776, Bk I, Chap. 8). And to generate national wealth, you need economic freedom. Freedom and equality go together.

6.4 *Questions of Originality*

There is much criticism of Adam Smith on the grounds that many of his ideas were not original. Of course, if you go back long enough, and with determination enough, you can find antecedents for any idea, from Copernicus's heliocentric solar system, through Newton's physics and mathematics, to Darwin's evolutionary theory and Smith's economics. The important question, however, is how these great minds developed those ideas and what they made of them.

Thus, some critics argue that Sir William Petty identified GDP over a hundred years earlier than Smith. And Petty did indeed make the first systematic effort to estimate the national income and wealth of England and Ireland—though only as a way of calculating the realm's ability to finance wars through taxation, rather than as a theory of wealth creation (Petty, 1662, 1691). Smith would make it a concept of much wider application than a mere statistical measure. It would become the very target for economic policy. That made Smith's concept much more radical, implying policy changes that would end the protectionist measures prescribed by mercantilism and would promote the expansion of trade and commerce.

Likewise, it is argued that the Finnish-Swedish liberal thinker Anders Chydenius pre-empted many of the ideas attributed to Smith. Chydenius wrote widely on liberalism and economics, but it is his 1765 work, *The National Gain* that is cited as most obviously anticipating Smith. In that work, he argues that prosperity stems from economic freedom, allowing individuals to pursue their self-interest. This, he says, will lead to everyone finding their own niche, creating a harmonious economic society. He sees mercantilist policies (e.g. regulations, monopolies, subsidies, and trade barriers) as distorting that free system, and, like Smith, argues for their removal. He even mentions how nations gain by specialising in high-value activities rather than protecting inefficient ones. All very Adam Smith.

It is doubtful that Smith ever read *The National Gain*, a short pamphlet of around 20 pages, published in Swedish. But Smith was by no means unique among Enlightenment-era liberal thinkers in exploring the potential benefits of greater individual freedom and critiquing the damage done, particularly to the working poor, by the self-serving and protectionist policies of powerful political regimes. Many others were saying broadly similar things, and Smith, as we know, took ideas from many different sources (some, it is true, without attributing them) and from many different countries. But while Chydenius focuses his criticisms of trade restrictions (for instance) very specifically on the policies of a specific Swedish province, Ostrobothnia, Smith realises that the "system of natural liberty" is of very much wider, indeed universal, application, and not just in economic terms. In the course of a book 25 times longer than *The National Gain*, he builds all these ideas, and thousands of related facts, into a comprehensive explanation of economic and social psychology. It is in that, much wider, construction that Smith's genius and originality stand out.

6.5 Overreliance on Sympathy

There is no question about the originality of Smith's *Moral Sentiments*, replacing as it did a jumble of competing ideas about the source of human values with something completely new and based on the psychology of human beings as social creatures. But still there are questions and criticisms.

Critics argue, for instance, that the "impartial spectator" is too limited a way of guiding moral action, since conscience is biased by familiarity, custom, and social proximity. But for Smith, "sympathy" is a natural, empirical foundation for moral action, not limited by the biases of conscience, and capable of education. And it is helped along in different circumstances by the impartial spectator, whose limits Smith recognises, for example by noting how concerned we are for those nearest to us, while we care little for millions of distant others. But as social creatures, we have an intuitive feeling for justice. And though reason is not the basis of moral action as some of Smith's contemporaries thought, it can help us understand and curb our natural biases.

Nevertheless, critics argue that sympathy comes easier when those concerned are similar to us (say by class, status or race), and that this constrains social change, such as the accommodation of new or different cultures and practices. To Smith, however, sympathy fosters social bonds of all kinds. He warns against its neglect and corruption—in slavery and domination, for instance—and shows how sympathy extends beyond proximity when guided by virtue, education, and imagination.

Smith was highly innovative in basing ethics on sentiments rather than reason alone, but critics still question whether sympathy provides strong enough universal principles, especially compared to Kantian duty-based or Utilitarian utility-based ethics. In Smith's defence, it is clear that *Moral Sentiments* is both descriptive and normative. He accepts the practical limits of real-life sympathy, while offering broader principles of justice and virtue that stem from human nature itself. And this provides a flexible, intuition-led ethics that is stronger and more widely applicable than critics claim.

6.6 Resolving the Adam Smith Problem

Understandably, the unity in Smith's thought that has been described here has not always been obvious to everyone. While *Moral Sentiments* focused on empathy, *The Wealth of Nations* makes it plain that "it is not from the benevolence of the butcher, the brewer, or the baker, that we expect our dinner, but from their regard to their own interest" (Smith, 1776, Bk I, Chap. 2). Nineteenth-century German scholars labelled the apparent contradiction "Das Adam Smith Problem."

But the problem is easily answered. First, our social psychology has many parts. Even from the first sentence of *Moral Sentiments*, Smith recognises that self-interest coexists with empathy. The difference is one of context, not human nature. In close relationships, empathy dominates. In anonymous market exchanges with strangers, self-interest dominates. Through competition and the rules of justice, commercial society harnesses this very dependable motive to the benefit of everyone.

Second, the impartial spectator does not disappear when we enter the market. Even the most self-interested trader wants to be regarded as honest and reliable: not only is it natural to want to be worthy of praise, but being so is good for business too.

Third, Smith connects the two books explicitly. He contrasts the "man of system," the legislator who imagines that people can be manipulated like chess pieces, with the true legislator who works with the grain of human nature to channel self-interest into public good (Smith, 1776, Pt VI, Chap. 2). And the question of how individual action relates to social outcomes is an important theme of both works.

Fourth, as Ronald Coase pointed out, Smith's economic and moral thinking are both rooted in different forms of self-interest (Coase, 1976). The self-interest from pursuing commercial gain is obvious enough. But in moral contexts, Smith's view is that we act in moral ways because we want the approbation of others. As social creatures, we crave that approbation and seek to be worthy of their praise. It is in our self-interest to pursue these things.

Far from being contradictory, therefore, the two books are complementary. They both explain how rule-guided actions can produce harmony and coordination between millions of people, requiring neither direction from any authority nor heroic virtue from any individual.

Smith's unified vision is a realistic view of human beings as neither wholly benevolent nor wholly self-interested. In the appropriate contexts, they are capable of both empathy and egoism. The task of moral philosophers and political economists is to make these mixed motives work such that society flourishes. To do that, we do not need to transform human nature, only to channel it wisely. With the right institutions, justice, ethics, and markets can work together to transform private vices into public benefits: never perfectly, perhaps, but better than any known alternative.

The invisible hand of the market and the impartial spectator of conscience can and do work together. Morality and economics are not rivals, but partners in the great project of building a free and flourishing society.

7 Conclusion

Far from being merely the "father of modern economics," then, Adam Smith should be seen as a holistic thinker who understood the complexity of human social psychology and pulled its several aspects—moral, economic, political, aesthetic, and others—into a coherent whole. More than that, he showed how to focus these psychological elements into producing a harmonious and progressive social order, offering a realistic yet optimistic blueprint for a flourishing society. Two-and-a-half centuries later, as we grapple with technological change, social upheaval, and new moral challenges, Adam Smith's work continues to illuminate the path towards a free, prosperous and morally principled human world.

Bibliography

Butler, E. (2007). *Adam Smith—A primer*. Institute of Economic Affairs.
Butler, E. (2025). *An introduction to schools of economic thought*. Institute of Economic Affairs.
Chydenius, A. (1765). *The National Gain*. Lars Salvius.
Coase, R. H. (1976). Adam Smith's view of man. *Journal of Law and Economics, 19*(3), 529.
Ferguson, A. (1767). *An essay on the history of civil society*. Millar & Cadell.
Hayek, F. A. (1945). The use of knowledge in society. *American Economic Review, 35*(4), 519–530.
Hayek, F. A. (1960). *The constitution of liberty*. Routledge.

Jevons, W. S. (1871). *The theory of political economy*. Macmillan.
Menger, C. (1871). *Principles of economics. Originally published as Grundsätze der Volkswirtschaftslehre*. Wilhelm Braumüller.
Norman, J. (2018) Adam Smith: What he thought, and why it matters Allen Lane.
Petty, W. (1691). *Political Arithmetick*. R. Clavel & H. Mortlock.
Petty, W. (1662). *A treatise of taxes and contributions*. N. Brooke.
Phillipson, N. (2010). *Adam Smith: An enlightened life*. Yale University Press.
Ross, I. S. (2010). *The life of Adam Smith*. Oxford University Press.
Rosten, L. (1970) People have loved, known or admired. McGraw-Hill.
Smith, A. (1795). *Essays on philosophical subjects*. Cadell & Davies.
Smith, C. (2006). *Adam Smith's political philosophy: The invisible hand and spontaneous order*. Routledge.
Smith, A. (1759). *The theory of moral sentiments*. Millar, Kincaid & Bell.
Smith, A. (1776). *An inquiry into the nature and causes of wealth of nations*. Strahan & Cadell.

Adam Smith, "Division of Stock," and Lombard Street

Michael Munger

1 Introduction

Walter Bagehot's *Lombard Street* created the modern "lender of last resort" (LOLR). But read alongside Adam Smith's Book II account of "stock" (capital) in *The Wealth of Nations*, Bagehot's argument looks less like an innovation, and more like an elaboration. In fact, much of modern banking doctrine—and especially Bagehot's "LORL" doctrine—should be understood as being much more like an extension of Smith's highly original account of the political economy of capital allocation.

Or so it will be argued here. Smith's main focus in Book II of Wealth of Nations was that *financial rules had to accomplish one thing, but avoid another.*

- Society's stock should be employed productively, and be freed to move among productive uses to respond to changing conditions. Stock should not be immobilized as idle cash. To accomplish this, banks constantly run the risk of being caught short of cash on hand.
- On the other hand, the rules must always avoid creating incentives for reckless "projectors" to dissipate stock, pursuing investments that had poor prospects of success or that diverted focus away from production and further increases of stock.

Bagehot's conclusions were based on experience and are still the standard for central bank conduct (see, for discussion, Goodhart, 1988). It is impressive that Smith was able to anticipate, and lay out the foundations of that approach, with far less direct experience, and with not nearly the level of economic theory at his disposal. The four-part "Bagehot's Dictum" is not merely the operating manual for a central bank; the different parts together form a scaffolding for both supporting and

M. Munger (✉)
Duke University, Raleigh, NC, USA

J. Ostle et al. (eds.), *Adam Smith's Wealth of Nations After 250 Years*, Contributions to Economics, https://doi.org/10.1007/978-3-032-32299-9_2

constraining a system that limits panics without becoming a vending machine for bailout.

It is useful to summarize my version of "Bagehot's Dictum" at the outset, before I explore its roots in Adam Smith. Bagehot believed that the central bank should make iron-clad commitments to (1) always lend freely—in fact, without limit—to illiquid-but-solvent banks, (2) at a penalty rate, (3) only against good collateral, and (4) never do more. The problem is that this commitment to provide liquidity can easily become a trap, where the bank is called on to preserve solvency, especially in a setting where a cascade of insolvencies can result from a failure to act.

Illiquidity is an insufficiency of cash; *insolvency* is an insufficiency of value. If the "lender of last resort" crosses the line—lending against bad collateral, subsidizing losses, or even guaranteeing depositors of failed banks—the LOLR ceases to be an emergency liquidity backstop and becomes an *insurer* of last resort. That shift excuses depositor imprudence, erases incentives to monitor risk, and invites moral hazard. If depositors expect to be made whole regardless of bank behavior, there is no reason for depositors to care about excessive financial daring, because the suppliers of LOLR capital now shoulder the risk.

This same logic is present, but is underappreciated, in Book II of *Wealth of Nations*, a sustained meditation on how the division and deployment of stock determines a nation's productive capacity. Bagehot focuses on how the organization of credit can keep that stock continuously deployed during panics *without* encouraging misallocations and excessive risk taking before the panic. Still, without a clearly defined and credible boundary between liquidity aid and insolvency rescue, the very institution created to stabilize credit becomes the primary enabler for socializing losses and encouraging the next round of imprudence.

2 Adam Smith's "Division of Stock"

2.1 Stock

In Book II, Smith uses the term "stock" as the accumulated store of resources—goods, provisions, tools, materials, money—out of which people can maintain themselves and carry on work over time. At the level of an individual, the decisive conceptual point is Smith's distinction between stock for immediate consumption and stock used as capital. When someone has only a tiny stock, Smith says they consume it and rely on labor to get more for tomorrow. But once a person has enough stock to maintain them "for months or years," they will "derive a revenue from the greater part of it," reserving only what is needed for immediate consumption; that revenue-seeking part "is called his capital," while the remainder is the stock that supplies immediate consumption (including items like clothing and household furniture).

Where does stock come from? In Smith's account, it comes from production and saving—what is produced but not immediately consumed. Book II's treatment of accumulation makes this explicit: "Whatever a person saves from his revenue he adds to his capital," either employing it himself to maintain additional productive hands or lending it to someone else for interest (a share of profits). Smith generalizes the point from the individual to the society: since the capital of society is just the sum of individuals' capitals, the capital of society can be increased "only in the same manner," by saving out of annual revenue. In other words, stock is not a mysterious primitive endowment; it is the *result* of an intertemporal choice—producing now, and postponing some consumption so that the postponed portion becomes the means of employing labor and sustaining production.

2.2 Previous Accumulation

Smith's "previous accumulation" is introduced as a logical precondition for specialization. In the "rude state" with little exchange and little division of labor, Smith argues, there is no need for stock to be "stored up beforehand"; people can meet needs directly as they arise. But once the division of labor is "thoroughly introduced," the specialist cannot live off the direct product of his own labor while waiting for his output to be completed and sold; therefore, "a stock of goods of different kinds… must be stored up somewhere sufficient to maintain him, and to supply him with the materials and tools of his work" during the production-and-sale interval. Smith then states the conclusion in the strongest possible way: "This accumulation must, evidently, be previous" to sustained specialization, and as division of labor advances, the needed beforehand stock of provisions, materials, and tools must be larger. The argument is not (yet) a story about coercion or dispossession; it is primarily a structural claim about the time-lag between effort and market realization, and about the way accumulated stock makes continuous employment possible.

Marx explicitly seizes on this classical "prehistory" of capital in Chap. 26 ("The So-Called Primitive Accumulation")—but he flips its meaning. He criticizes political economy's tendency to tell an "idyllic" origin story, insisting that "conquest, enslavement, robbery, murder… force" play the "great part" in actual history. For Marx, the key isn't merely that stock had to be amassed somewhere so that specialization could proceed; rather, the central historical process is the creation of a labor force separated from independent access to means of production. His formulation is stark, even sarcastic: the "so-called primitive accumulation… is nothing else than the historical process of divorcing the producer from the means of production." In short: Smith's "previous accumulation" is a functional requirement for a complex commercial society; Marx's "primitive accumulation" is a historical explanation—often violent—for how the social conditions of capitalist production (capital owners on one side, wage-laborers on the other) came to exist.

2.3 Fixed and Circulating Capital

Smith's division of stock becomes most distinctive when he classifies capital by how it yields revenue. A capital can yield profit "only by means of… circulation," continually leaving and returning in different forms; this is "circulating capital." Or it can yield profit "without changing masters, or circulating any further"; this is "fixed capital."

He then gives a remarkably concrete taxonomy. The fixed capital of society is characterized by yielding "revenue or profit without circulating," and it consists chiefly of four articles: (i) useful machines and instruments of trade, (ii) "profitable buildings" used in production and commerce (shops, warehouses, workhouses, farm buildings), (iii) improvements of land (clearing, draining, enclosing, manuring), and (iv) the "acquired and useful abilities" of inhabitants—human capital embodied in trained skill, formed by maintenance during education or apprenticeship. Circulating capital, by contrast, yields revenue only by circulating and "changing masters," and it too has four parts: (i) money, (ii) provisions in the hands of sellers, (iii) materials for clothes, furniture, and building that are not yet finished goods, and (iv) completed work still held by merchants or manufacturers awaiting final sale.

Two further points matter for Smith's system. First, fixed and circulating capital are not independent: "Every fixed capital is… derived from, and requires to be continually supported by a circulating capital," because machines require materials and maintenance labor, and even improved land yields nothing without circulating advances that maintain the laborers who cultivate it. Second, this interdependence reveals the purpose of the whole classification, which is not merely technical bookkeeping but a theory of social provisioning.

2.4 What Is Wealth?

Smith never lets you forget that capital is instrumental. The "sole end and purpose both of the fixed and circulating capitals" is "to maintain and augment the stock which may be reserved for immediate consumption," because it is that consumption stock which "feeds, clothes, and lodges the people." On this view, capital is *means*—a way of organizing advances to productive labor so that the stream of consumables can be larger and more reliable.

That is why Smith's wealth concept is tied to the annual produce and to the capacity of a society to supply consumption. In Book II, when he turns to accumulation and the balance between capital and revenue, he states the macro implication: increases or decreases of capital tend to increase or diminish "the exchangeable value of the annual produce of the land and labour of the country, the real wealth and revenue of all its inhabitants." Wealth is therefore not simply "a big pile of stock" sitting idle; it is the flow of goods and services made possible by productive employment of stock—the annual produce (and its exchangeable value) available to sustain and improve people's lives, anchored in that stock reserved for consumption.

2.5 *Money*

Money is part of stock, and specifically part of circulating capital: it is "the money by means of which all the other three are circulated and distributed to their proper consumers." Yet, Smith repeatedly emphasizes that money is "dead stock," in the sense that, taken by itself, it produces nothing. The dealer's cash reserve is "so much dead stock" while it sits idle. And at the social level, the gold and silver money that circulates the annual produce is likewise "all dead stock," a valuable part of capital that "produces nothing" directly.

Why, then, is money useful? Precisely because money is an enabling instrument: it makes possible the circulation and distribution of the annual produce to "proper consumers." Smith's famous metaphor is that money is like a "highway" that carries goods to market while producing no "pile" of goods itself. Money is socially useful not as a generator of output but as a circulatory technology—a device that reduces the frictions of exchange, allowing the productive parts of stock (tools, materials, subsistence advances) to be coordinated and converted into consumable output.

2.6 *Banking*

Smith's discussion of banks (and especially paper credit) is strikingly modern in how clearly it frames the basic bank problem: banks allow merchants to hold fewer idle cash balances while still meeting "occasional demands." But that service is safe only under discipline. Smith offers a simple but powerful operational test: when banks advance on cash accounts, they must ensure that over a short horizon the repayments are at least equal to advances; otherwise, the outgoing stream exceeds the incoming stream and the bank's coffers are exhausted, even though the bank is not technically insolvent.

Smith is also explicit about a boundary condition: what a bank can properly advance is not the merchant's whole capital, but only that part of it the merchant would otherwise keep idle. When banks exceed that—when paper credit funds over-trading—Smith blames "bold projectors" for excessive circulation and instability.

This matters for the LOLR: the credit "system" is socially valuable because it frees stock from dead forms, but it also enables projectors to shift losses to others through fragile promises. Telling the difference is difficult, and if the costs of being wrong are covered by the central bank the number and size of the errors will explode.

Banking, for Smith, is an institutional method for economizing on dead stock—reducing the amount of idle money a commercial society must hold to keep exchange functioning. He is explicit that banking does not increase industry by magically "augmenting the capital of the country," but by making "a greater part of that capital active and productive than would otherwise be so." If merchants must hold large cash reserves to meet uncertain demands, that requirement immobilizes resources. The "judicious operations of banking" convert that immobilized reserve into "active and productive stock"—materials, tools, and provisions that can actually employ labor and generate output.

At the national scale, the same logic applies: by "substituting paper in the room of a great part" of gold and silver circulation, banking enables a country to transform part of its monetary "highways" into productive resources, thereby increasing the annual produce of land and labor. Smith is not naïve about risk, though: he concedes that commerce becomes "less secure" when suspended on the "wings of paper money" than when it travels on the "solid ground" of specie, and he discusses why certain precautions and constraints may be warranted.

So banks exist, in Smith's framework, because they are part of the machinery that allows a commercial society to run with less idle cash and more productive deployment of stock, while still meeting the liquidity needs of exchange.

2.7 Banks Optimize Division of Stock

Smith sees the social and commercial function of banks as discriminating and discerning, choosing good and rejecting bad investments. Without the shadow of state intervention, the system rewards keeping credit tied to short, self-liquidating commercial transactions. By constantly monitoring whether advances are being used to smooth liquidity or to fund speculative ventures, banks are the white blood cells of the system, fighting infection.

The basic rule is that what a bank can properly advance is "not… the whole capital" of an undertaker, nor "any considerable part," but only that portion the merchant would otherwise be forced to keep idle as ready money for "occasional demands." A bank stays within this boundary when it discounts "a real bill of exchange drawn by a real creditor upon a real debtor" that is "really paid" at maturity; then the bank is essentially substituting paper and discounting services for a cash buffer that would otherwise sit idle. When confined to such customers, the bank's inflows and outflows resemble a "water pond" with an outgoing stream matched by an incoming stream.

The imprudent "projector," by contrast, uses banking to obtain not a liquidity convenience but the project's whole fund—often through practices that mimic real trade while lacking real underlying settlement. Smith ties "excessive circulation of paper money" to the "over-trading of some bold projectors." His most detailed case is the system of "drawing and re-drawing," where A and B in different cities accept bills not because a real debt exists, but because each agrees to accept in order to raise money repeatedly; the apparent repayments are "altogether fictitious" because new discounted bills are required to pay the old ones, so the value first advanced is "never really returned" to the banks. This is precisely the kind of pseudo-liquidation that can finance "vast and extensive projects" on paper credit rather than on the projector's own capital.

How, then, can banks choose well? Smith gives two practical diagnostics. First, structure of paper: discounting "real bills" limits advances to commerce that clears through actual payment; "circulating bills" (or "fictitious" bills) are warning signs that paper is funding speculative projects rather than bridging routine demands. Second, behavior over time: banks should watch whether, over "four, five, six, or eight months," repayments are "fully equal" to advances; if repayments systematically fall short, the customer is not merely smoothing liquidity but drawing down bank capital, and the bank cannot "with any safety continue to deal" with them.

Finally, Smith notes that some schemes are easier to spot than others: if two parties discount continually with the same banker, he "must immediately discover" they are trading "not with any capital of their own, but with the capital which he advances." Yet, when projectors rotate among bankers in a wider circle, distinguishing real from fictitious bills becomes harder, and banks can find themselves trapped—discovering too late that refusing further discounts would bankrupt the projectors and possibly endanger the bank itself.

In Smith's system, then, the bank's "selection problem" is not solved by omniscience or moralizing. It is solved—imperfectly but systematically[1] —by insisting that credit remain tethered to short-term, verifiable commercial repayment, and by treating persistent, rolling reliance on new discounts to pay old claims as the signature of the imprudent projector.

3 Bagehot's Dictum: Smith, Only more So

3.1 Lombard Street

For Walter Bagehot, "Lombard Street" is both a place and a system: the London money-market world clustered around the Bank of England, private banks, joint-stock banks, and bill-brokers. He treats it as a *machine*—echoing Smith's "well-contrived machine" from *Theory of Moral Sentiments*—that continuously aggregates idle balances and re-deploys them, chiefly by discounting bills and moving "floating money" to the most profitable trades. This is precisely "division of stock."

He sees the entire system as an "organization of credit" (p. 11). "Organization" here means an *institutional arrangement*: a set of routines, markets, and counterparties that make borrowing/lending *systematic, scalable, and fast.* "Credit" means confidence (by the public), enforceable promises (by participants), and liquidity (an immediate capacity to pay). More specifically: Credit "means that a certain confidence is given, and a certain trust reposed." The key test is "soundness": *Is that*

[1] Lloyd Mints (1945) and other scholars have questioned the value of this "real bills" doctrine, but the correctness of the doctrine itself is beyond the scope of the present paper.

trust justified? (p. 11). Then he gives what we would now call an equilibrium condition: "Credit is a set of promises to pay; will those promises be kept?"

The difficulty for individual participants in the "system of credit" is that such promises can be deadly: liabilities can be huge, and payable on very short notice. Hence, the "cardinal excellence" is not elegance but immediacy: "an instant capacity to meet engagements" (p. 11). The modern word for this capacity is liquidity: the ability to convert assets into costless transferable values *fast enough to keep promises credible*.[2]

Bagehot adds an important nuance, one that explicitly echoes Adam Smith in Book II of *Wealth of Nations*: credit is *not* wealth. In later discussion of bills and bill-brokers, he distinguishes property from "pecuniary fidelity"—reputation for meeting engagements. The total value in a system is a snapshot of balance sheets; credit is an established habit of payment that creates commercial confidence that will increase the values on balance sheets over time. But credit is not reducible to balance sheet entries, and in fact inflated asset values are an indication that credit is fragile, because inflated assets are not liquid (p. 138).

The thesis of the book is that Lombard Street is not just a convenience; rather, a credit system is an essential aspect of commercial activity, a permanent intermediary between "accumulating" (saving) districts and "active employing" districts, moving funds from where they cannot be used well to where they can (from "Introductory," p. 7). This is the institutional machinery that fleshes out Smith's claim that capital flows without central plan or intention, toward higher social returns.

It is worth quoting Bagehot on this point at some length:

> This organisation is so useful because it is so easily adjusted. Political economists say that capital sets towards the most profitable trades, and that it rapidly leaves the less profitable and non-paying trades. But in ordinary countries this is a slow process, and some persons who want to have ocular demonstration of abstract truths have been inclined to doubt it because they could not see it. In England, however, the process would be visible enough if you could only see the books of the bill brokers and the bankers. Their bill cases as a rule are full of the bills drawn in the most profitable trades, and ceteris paribus and in comparison empty of those drawn in the less profitable. If the iron trade ceases to be as profitable as usual, less iron is sold; the fewer the sales the fewer the bills; and in consequence the number of iron bills in Lombard street is diminished. On the other hand, if in consequence of a bad harvest the com trade becomes on a sudden profitable, immediately 'com bills' are created in great numbers, and if good are discounted in Lombard Street. Thus English capital runs as surely and instantly where it is most wanted, and where there is most to be made of it, as water runs to find its level. (p. 6)

At the risk of oversimplifying, Smith had made a deeply perceptive observation, at a time when credit markets were relatively primitive, even in England. That point was that "stock" only had three employments: (a) productive use as investment; (b) non-productive use, either saved as cash or held in sterile assets, and (c) piled into defensive liquidity, a kind of earthworks erected against panics. In that context,

---

[2]This would generally mean cash, or fiat money, but it could mean transferrable bonds. The UK system designed and used "consols" for just this purpose.

Bagehot is arguing that the way Lombard Street had elaborated credit markets made (b) much more expensive, and (c) much less necessary. As a result, most stock can take the form of what Smith called "circulating capital" or productive "fixed capital" capable of being converted at short notice. The unity of understanding between Smith and Bagehot is actually remarkable.

3.2 *Unlimited Liquidity: A Commitment Device*

Bagehot did make a fundamental extension of Smith's "model," in a way that reflected a depth of understanding that is not fully appreciated even today. Bagehot's extension is simultaneously psychological (managing expectations) and mechanical (engineering a circuitry of transmission and "off" switches).

The strategic psychological claim addresses the impulse to hunker down in a financial storm, hoarding and rationing credit. But this is exactly the wrong signal to send, and the impulse is destructive because it ruins even the financially solvent firms that are caught short of liquidity. The shortage of cash creates the (false) impression of insolvency, leading to more hoarding of cash. The belief that cash is unattainable is autocatalytic; Bagehot's insight was that the opposite is also true. That is, if everyone believes that cash is plentiful, they have no reason to liquidate their assets so that they can hold cash, because they know they could get cash if they needed it.

He writes that discredit means an opinion that you "have not got any money," and therefore the remedy is to show that you have money by using it "for the public benefit" (pp. 23–24). Paradoxically, or so it might seem, the very availability of cash means that it will almost never be necessary, or desired, by the credit community. The central bank's lending is not a transfer; it is a *credible demonstration* that destroys the panic that would fuel a run.

Once a panic gains momentum, in Bagehot's view, private lending channels freeze. As George Selgin has recently demonstrated, this is precisely what happened between 1929 and 1932, in the United States. At first, the financial collapse—though severe—was not qualitatively different from other sharp "corrections" in asset prices. But the response of the Federal Reserve was to restrict, rather than expand, the availability of credit, and the result was that many technically solvent firms were unable to obtain the short-term cash needed to pay their obligations. As Bagehot pointed out, in a way that proved tragically prescient:

> …the Bank of England has in this respect no peculiar privilege; that it is simply in the position of a Bank keeping the Banking reserve of the country; that it must in time of panic do what all other similar banks must do; that in time of panic it must advance freely and vigorously to the public out of the reserve. (p. 96; emphasis added)… if securities, really good and usually convertible, are refused by the Bank, the alarm will not abate, the other loans made will fail in obtaining their end, and the panic will become worse and worse. (p. 97)

He also stresses that England's structure magnifies the strain: a system with many "dependent" institutions (banks and dealers holding no extra cash reserve) produces a stupendous collective demand for liquidity at the start of every panic (p. 28). Everyone tries to secure means of payment *all at the same time.*

3.3 The "Two Maladies"

Crises often combine an internal panic (domestic discredit) and an external drain (bullion export via adverse exchanges). This appears to rule out the "extend credit freely" solution, because the flight of capital, or trade deficits, calls for stringency (a rapid rise in the bank discount rate), while the internal panic calls for large, ready loans (p. 28). But this suggests the importance of the second part of Bagehot's dictum: "a penalty rate." The bank should raise the rate "as high as may be necessary" to stop the foreign export; otherwise, the bank "gets poorer and poorer," and domestic alarm persists. (pp. 27–28). However, though the interest charge is high, the amount of available loans must be effectively unlimited: "very large loans at very high rates" are the best remedy when the foreign drain is added to the domestic drain (p. 28). This solution, elegant in its simplicity, neatly solves both problems at once: few loans need to be made, precisely because credit is unlimited. But rates are high enough to stem the outflowing tide of currency, limiting the damage of the trade problems.

3.4 On Good Collateral

Bagehot's most explicit "dictum" appears as two rules for the holder of the ultimate reserve and is laid out on pages 96–97. The aim is not charity, nor the rescue of speculators; in fact, to insolvent speculators no mercy will be shown, and they will be singled out to be ruined, just as Smith had advocated. The only goal is to stop panic short, while protecting the reserve and safeguarding the vitality of the credit system.

Again, it is worth quoting from Bagehot at some length, to clarify the argument. There are, according to Bagehot, two rules:

> [T]hese advances, if they are to be made at all, should be made so as if possible to obtain the object for which they are made. The end is to stay the panic; and the advances should, if possible, stay the panic. And for this purpose there are two rules:—First. That these loans should only be made at a *very high rate of interest*. This will operate as a *heavy fine on unreasonable timidity*, and will prevent the greatest number of applications by persons who do not require it. The rate should be raised early in the panic, so that the fine may be paid early; that *no one may borrow out of idle precaution* without paying well for it; that the Banking reserve may be protected as far as possible. (pp. 96-97; emphasis added).

The high rate of interest conserves the central bank's reserves for true necessity, imposing a cost on the timid and discouraging idle precautions. So far, that sounds like austerity. But, no:

> Secondly. That at this rate these advances should be made on all good banking securities, and as largely as the public ask for them. The reason is plain. The object is to stay alarm, and nothing therefore should be done to cause alarm. But the way to cause alarm is to refuse someone who has good security to offer. The news of this will spread in an instant through all the money market at a moment of terror; no one can say exactly who carries it, but in half an hour it will be carried on all sides, and will intensify the terror everywhere. *No advances indeed need be made by which the Bank will ultimately lose. The amount of bad business in commercial countries is an infinitesimally small fraction of the whole business. That in a panic the bank, or banks, holding the ultimate reserve should refuse bad bills or bad securities will not make the panic really worse; the 'unsound' people are a feeble minority*, and they are afraid even to look frightened for fear their unsoundness may be detected. The great majority, the majority to be protected, are the 'sound' people, the people who have good security to offer. (p. 97, emphasis added)

So the "never bail out insolvency" element is not a moral aside, or throwaway. It is part of the *design*: lend to stop panic without socializing speculative loss.

3.5 Is the "Only on good collateral" Rule Enforceable?

Bagehot—and Smith before him—knew the temptations working on those who would operate the bank. Even in a large nation, the true insiders in the finance industry are all well known to each other. They may not be friends, but they fully recognize the importance of alliances and the need to take care of each other in bad times. One automatic stabilizer, of course, is the command to lend only at a penalty rate: even if loans are (mistakenly) made to an insolvent bank, the fact that the interest is high prevents the loan from providing any real help. In order to subvert Bagehot's dictum, the central bank would have to extend credit to an insolvent, and to do so at a rate that actually subsidizes and socializes that firm's debt exposure.

Bagehot suggests two additional safeguards: (i) an operational test (security) and (ii) a governance requirement (a known rule). Operationally, the "good collateral" must be "easily convertible" into cash, but only in "ordinary times." That means, of course, that in a crisis it may be impossible to convert assets into cash, and that is precisely why cash is needed, in large amounts and immediately. If the bank is known to be willing to advance on such collateral, the alarm of solvent merchants and bankers "will be stayed" (p. 97). Thus, the only safe plan is the "brave plan" (p. 98) to lend in a panic on every kind of current security on which money is generally lent in ordinary times. To act otherwise would be to create uncertainty, and creating certainty is the only thing that can calm fears in a crisis.

Any other rule, even if the discretion of the central bank could be trusted, the delay in announcing the "aid/no aid" decision case-by-case means the crisis proceeds beyond what can be controlled, even by massive bailouts. The loss of capital value in the first few days of a crisis dramatically raises the actual costs to the government; by contrast, acting immediately on certain principles limits the losses to firms that are actually insolvent, and could not be rescued with an infusion of liquidity in any case.

Bagehot's second requirement, a "known rule" rather than discretion, reinforces this logic.[3] If the first part of the rule says, "lend only on good credit;" the second part says "always and immediately lend on good credit, in amounts as large as requested." The reason is that, as noted above, refusing good security is much worse than lending over-generously, since good security ensures that the loans will be repaid.

The key point is what would now be called "signaling," since the one-way test—lend always, but only, on good credit—certifies the soundness of the institution. As a consequence, a "run" on the bank is far less likely, and in any case, the bank will be able to make good on its obligations because it has ready access to effectively unlimited amounts of liquidity. Central bank managers, who feel (plausibly) that prudence dictates the conservation, even hoarding, of reserves, are likely to lend too little, and much too late. Bagehot pointed out that the *signal* matters more than the marginal conservation of reserve. If a "good" borrower is refused, then their status as good is corrupted, and they will default for no good reason. If the bank waits until several good borrowers have defaulted, the amount of the reserves that must be committed to contain the contagion expands almost without limit.

Of course, the argument in favor of prudence has a point: the reserve may be insufficient to loan the full amounts requested, even if the loans are limited to "good" borrowers. Even then, lending is still the best expedient, because the alternatives are much worse. Making no loans and then belatedly making large loans ruins the bank; the same is true of making a few large loans at the outset and then suddenly stopping. The only strategy with a chance of succeeding is consistent lending on good security, defined as assets that in normal times would have enough value to more than cover the total amount of the loans.

[3] Bagehot's argument is later echoed and elaborated further by Milton Friedman, who advocated for rules over discretion in setting all of monetary policy, not just policy in a crisis. Friedman's reasons, cited in Dellas and Tavlas (2022, p. 11) will sound familiar: "First, discretion has had "unfortunate monetary consequences" since it "meant continued and unpredictable shifts in the immediate guides to policy and in the content of policy as the persons and attitudes dominating the authorities have changed" over time. Second, discretion exposed the authorities "to political and economic pressures and to the deceptive effects of short-lived ideas of events and opinions." Third, reliance on discretion in pursuing general goals "meant also the absence of any criteria for judging performance. The absence of clearly-defined rules and criteria for judging performance had been a serious defect of our present monetary arrangements.

3.6 *Harking Back: Bagehot's Dictum Solves Smith's Concern*

Bagehot's solvent-only lending is a direct institutional answer to Smith's worries about misallocation to "projectors" and the perversion of stock into unproductive uses. The bank's "crisis job" is to prevent a liquidity scramble from forcing solvent firms to sell off productive assets at fire-sale prices. But the bank must be forbidden from intervening to keep insolvent ventures from becoming zombie creatures, still alive only because of artificial and extraordinary life support. The collateral test is the mechanism that distinguishes "temporary inability to realize assets" from genuine insolvency (p. 97). The penalty rate helps keep the lending channel from becoming cheap support for speculators and projectors. These were precisely Smith's concerns, and though he hinted at the answer it was Bagehot who saw the solution clearly.

The different parts of Bagehot's architecture combine to prevent the Smithian nightmare scenario: panic drives everyone to convert assets into money, and the economy's "stock" is forced into the least productive form—idle hoards—right when it would have been most productively used to keep production and exchange going.

3.7 *Lombard Street, Again*

English credit markets, which Bagehot collectively styles "Lombard Street"—much as modern Americans call our version "Wall Street"—are the mechanism by which Smith's "division of stock" is accomplished. At the time, those financial institutions were by far the best managed and most efficient in the world. The concern about the central bank's policy is really secondary to Bagehot's explanation of how the Smithian "stock employed for future profit" is routed toward its best uses. Specifically, Lombard Street channeled savings from counties that could not efficiently or profitably employ that capital into the discount of bills from industrial districts (p. 7).

It might seem that the flow of wealth from rural counties to the center might be tribute, or taxation. But that is exactly backwards: most counties have wealth, but no fruitful employment for that stock. A "middleman" able to match up diverse sources of stock with the best investments is an enormous benefit for the rural counties. Furthermore, the directing of stock to profitable uses is rapidly self-adjusting: as profits shift, the composition of bills discounted shifts almost immediately (iron bills fall with new discoveries of ore; corn bills surge after a bad harvest). So credit is not merely a "veil."[4] It is the operating system that keeps circulating capital circulating in the lines of trade where it yields future profit.

---

[4] Karl Marx, in "A Contribution to the Critique of Political Economy" (1859), Part I, Chap. 1 "The Commodity", argued that commerce is "a relation hidden by a material veil…All the illusions of

Bagehot works to establish that there are really four rules, or courses of action, for the central bank. The three that are actually practiced are all disasters; the fourth rule, the one Bagehot proposes be adopted, is the best that could be done, but was rarely done in practice. The problem to be solved is to preserve and protect institutions that are solvent, but cash-strapped, and to mitigate the outflow of currency to other nations, while allowing—even hastening—the disappearance of institutions that are insolvent. The reason is not morality, but moral hazard: it is the decisions firms make that put them in one, or the other, of these categories. The sorting into "illiquid but sound" vs. "insolvent" is a function of the rule adopted.

The first rule, "never loan in a crisis," fails the first test, killing solvent firms without need. The second rule, "always loan in a crisis, with larger loans to the least sound firms," fails the second test, encouraging grandiose projectors. The third rule, "wait and see, and give no clear guidelines to shape expectations," may be the worst rule, and Bagehot notes that this seems to be the bank's actual chosen procedure. The problem is that waiting allows the solvent firms to die, but then belatedly acting saves the worst of the insolvent firms.

Bagehot's rule, of course, is the fourth: Lend freely, but only on good credit, short-term, at penalty rates, high enough to stem the external drain on currency moving abroad. In a panic, the normal allocation device seizes up: discounts vanish, bills can't be rolled, merchants must obtain "new loans to pay old debts" but can't (p. 29). Bagehot's argument should be taken to mean that the emergent institution of Lombard Street accomplishes Smith's "division of stock for future profit" framework, but that we might now call a "visible hand"—a central bank following Bagehot's Dictum—is necessary to buttress the system through institutional mechanisms. These mechanisms (bills, discounting, reserve centralization, and a crisis protocol) prevent panics from converting productive capital into defensive money hoards, which was precisely Smith's concern.

4 Implications for Today

4.1 Lender Vs. Insurer and "Minsky Moments"

The U.S. Federal Reserve was created in 1913; it appears that "abandon Bagehot's Dictum" was at the very top of their to-do list. The consequences of that insistence on privileging discretion over sensible rules have been causing catastrophes ever since. The most egregious example may be the actions of the Fed over the 1929–1933 period, where the monetary authority either did nothing, or actively contracted

the Monetary System arise from the failure to perceive that money … represents a social relation of production." It later became common to dismiss eighteenth century "classical" economics as holding that money is only a veil, but this conveniently ignores the notion that Bagehot believed the opposite. The "money is a veil" formulation is often also attributed (by Keynes, for example) to J. B. Say, but Say never said that they say Say said.

credit, killing thousands of solvent but cash-strapped firms, and resulting in a far deeper and longer financial crisis than should have happened.[5]

The difficulty is that the Fed has a variety of mandates, and some of these are directly in conflict. At present, by statute and practice, the Fed has no fewer than four obligations.[6]

(a) *Manage the currency* and *improve banking supervision* (original 1913 Act).
(b) *Maintain employment* (this and the next two are from the Fed Reform Act of 1977).
(c) *Maintain stable prices.*
(d) *Moderate long-term interest rates.*

Let us compare these mandates with Smith's statement of the problem, and Bagehot's recognition of the role of a central bank in managing the emergent financial order that solved the problem Smith identified. One sees immediately that the fact of multiple conflicting goals is a fatal flaw, ensuring that discretion rather than any one clear rule will be the way things get done. Rather than a lender of last resort, the American Fed sees itself, and is seen by Wall Street, as an "*insurer* of last resort" (IOLR). In practice, this cashes out as an imperative to "limit contagion." This obviously violates Bagehot's Dictum, and in a particularly perverse way: If the Fed promises to limit contagion, and act as the IOLR, then the degree of excessive risk-taking will explode.

It is important to understand what "contagion" means, in the financial context. It is useful here to take note of a contribution of the economist who taught me macroeconomic theory, Hyman Minsky. Minsky is remembered in the "Minsky Moment," the point in a credit boom when confidence flips suddenly—lenders and borrowers realize that a lot of debt that looked "safe" is only sustainable as long as asset prices keep rising or refinancing stays easy. When that realization hits, you get a rapid shift from risk-taking to credit hoarding. The conditions for a "Minsky Moment" to occur are (1) excessive leverage; (2) debt service barely matches cash flow, sometimes requiring new borrowing; (3) some setback, often apparently trivial, occurs and institutions all convert debt to cash at once.[7]

The "Minsky Moment" is the catalyst, or the spark; contagion is the rapid and extensive transmission of the initial failure, as it turns out that the soundness of debt instruments depended on a chain or network of connections to other debt. In such

[5] This "Fed worsened the Depression" thesis is well-documented, and is uncontroversially accepted by anyone who has read the history. A classic source is Friedman and Schwartz (1963); a recent and in-depth extension is Selgin (2024).

[6] The statute is US Code 12 § 225A. https://uscode.house.gov/view.xhtml?edition=prelim&num=0&req=granuleid%3AUSC-prelim-title 12-section225a&utm

[7] This "long period of false stability, followed by a short, wrenching correction" conception is reminiscent of Hemingway's *The Sun Also Rises,* where two characters are in Pamplona for the bullfights. Mike, a heavy-drinking and financially irresponsible member of the group, is talking to Bill about money. Bill asked: "How did you go bankrupt?" Mike replied: "Two ways. Gradually, then suddenly."

tightly connected and contingent networks, a failure anywhere can bring down other firms, even those whose link to the initial failure is quite distant.

The problem is that if "limiting contagion" involves bailing out insolvent firms—if they are large enough to be "SIFI" (systemically important financial institutions)—then there will be far more contagion to limit (Munger and Salsman, 2012). The results are just what Smith feared, and Bagehot sought to prevent: The Fed (and, in the U.S., the Treasury) have been ordered explicitly to care more about *large insolvent* firms than about *small, efficient, solvent, but cash-strapped*, firms.

If the purpose of the IOLR is to limit contagion, then insolvent institutions become *the* political priority—because their failures create what economists call "externalities," as the cascade of failures starts to take down institutions that would be solvent, if their debtors were able to make good on the claims owed. But then Bagehot's third rule (lend only on good collateral to solvent banks) becomes "not politically viable," since failing banks "that lack good collateral" may be precisely the most contagious.

If the LOLR is expected, by the financial network, to relax the key constraint of collateral quality, then the LOLR stops being a lender and becomes an IOLR—especially for depositors. That is the trap: an institution created to prevent self-fulfilling runs ends up underwriting the consequences of insolvency. This expectation of underwriting changes behavior ex ante and is "priced in" to the values of assets in the network. If the central bank or financial authority (i.e., the Treasury) tries to renege on the implied promise to rescue insolvents, as in the case of Lehman Brothers in September of 2008 (Sorkin, 2009), then there is the threat of catastrophic, mass insolvency, because all of the assets held as reserves are grossly overvalued.

4.2 Smith's "Projectors" (Reprise): Variations on the Theme

Smith's critique of "bold projectors" was not a costume drama or period piece. He argues that excessive debt instrument circulation and unsafe advances originate in "overtrading" by projectors. The mechanism is incentive-driven: if someone can gain upside value while shifting downside risk—through fragile credit promises that others must honor—then the division of stock will be perverse. Far too much stock will be directed by decisions of projectors, leaving little for legitimate investment.

Smith—and, for that matter, Bagehot—did not have the technical description we now use for this behavior, but they clearly understood the function of "moral hazard." Bagehot's system is explicitly and intentionally designed to limit adverse selection of investments, created by moral hazard in the risk distribution. By ignoring Bagehot's Dictum, the United States and other developed nations are actively creating the conditions for financial crises.

One key aspect of this system of regulation is the implementation of FDIC "deposit insurance." As most readers will know, this is a federally funded guarantee of bank deposits. Under the Smith–Bagehot system, a depositor would look at the riskiness of a bank's financial position and make deposit decisions accordingly. An unsound bank might attract deposits, but only if it paid a premium on rates. But under the FDIC regime, this safeguard is completely removed: One can invest literally anywhere without risk. But that means people choose where to deposit funds based not on soundness, but on small differences in the rates that are paid. This policy effectively props up the worst, weakest banks, because they are able to attract funds that should be denied.

If deposit insurance and emergency guarantees mean depositors expect reimbursement even when banks are insolvent, depositors stop monitoring risk—and banks can sneak along with insolvent balance sheets because their liability side no longer prices danger. In this world, the "dead stock" problem returns in a perverse way. The system may still economize on idle cash in normal times, but it does so by creating an implicit taxpayer backstop that encourages the holding of risky, opaque assets *as if they were safe*, and then making depositors whole when the assets turn out to have been fake. Smith's core aim—stock employed in ways "most likely to be employed with advantage" rather than wasted—is inverted, because those selling bad assets can afford to pay higher returns.

4.3 Penalty Rates and the "Routine Temptation"

Bagehot's "very high rates" prescription has a sorting and screening function: it deters all but genuine liquidity borrowers. If authorities instead provide funding at non-penalty rates (or protect depositors outright), then borrowing and risk-taking are no longer disciplined by cost. Thus, the demand for "insurance" precisely when it is most expensive to provide; Bagehot warns that if legal rates are set too high, lending will flow disproportionately to "prodigals and projectors," pulling capital away from safer, more productive hands. Bagehot's "penalty rate" is not an invitation to fund projectors; it is a temporary crisis tool paired with strict collateral. Break the pairing, and you get the worst of both worlds: high-risk borrowers and socialized losses.

There is a "moral hazard" problem in banking: The system only works because the banker's own capital is at risk, and not much of that. As Bagehot puts it:

> The main source of the profitableness of established banking is the smallness of the requisite capital. Being only wanted as a 'moral influence,' it need not be more than is necessary to secure that influence. Although, therefore, a banker deals only with the most sure securities, and with those which yield the least interest, he can nevertheless gain and divide a very large profit upon his own capital, because the money in his hands is so much larger than that capital. (p. 120)

The problem is that, if the LOLR becomes the IOLR, then that "moral influence" is provided not just by reputation but by explicit and implicit state guarantees. The public trust becomes an asset underwritten by policy. It is precisely the apparently routine and boring actions of a financial institution that lead to "Minsky Moments";

Bagehot is quite prescient on this point, anticipating Minsky's claim that long, boring calm is what heightens the sharpness of the eventual contraction:

> A Prime Minister, or a Chancellor of the Exchequer, or a Secretary of State must explain his policy and defend his actions in Parliament, and the discriminating tact of a critical assembly—abounding in experience, and guided by tradition—will soon discover what he is. But the Governor of the Bank would only perform quiet functions, which look like routine, though they are not, in which there is no immediate risk of success or failure; which years hence may indeed issue in a crop of bad debts, but which any grave persons may make at the time to look fair and plausible. A large Bank is exactly the place where a vain and shallow person in authority, if he be a man of gravity and method, as such men often are, may do infinite evil in no long time, and before he is detected. If he is lucky enough to begin at a time of expansion in trade, he is nearly sure not to be found out till the time of contraction has arrived, and then very large figures will be required to reckon the evil he has done. (p. 110)

The more the safety of the backstop expands, the more it is priced into Wall Street's daily operations and expectations. Large banks can accept the costs of compliance imposed by Sarbanes-Oxley or Dodd-Frank, while smaller institutions are driven from the market or prevented from entering in the first place. Overall, these modern violations of the Smithian ideal that capital should flow to its best uses rather than being steered by political privilege are getting worse, not better, as the decades pass.

5 Conclusion: The Smith–Bagehot Legacy

Read together, Smith and Bagehot offer a coherent doctrine. Smith argues conclusively that a nation's wealth depends on how its stock is divided and employed. Cash and currency are necessary but often unproductive "dead stock." Banking provides substantial social benefits by reducing idle cash balances—*if* banking firms do not become channels for overtrading and the ambitions of projectors.

Bagehot elaborates Smith's point, states the problem more clearly and proposes a clear solution in his "dictum." The problem is that when credit becomes a complex web of promises payable on demand, panics are crises of confidence and liquidity. The solution is the financial equivalent of the old military force-multiplier: the strategic reserve, a force that can immediately target a crisis and defuse it before it becomes a breakthrough, which is a much harder problem to solve. The dictum is that the reserve-holder must lend freely, immediately, at penalty interest rates, but on good security. If rates are low, the bank will risk subsidizing risk; if credit is given to the insolvent, the bank will risk its capital by creating zombie firms that cannot survive without continuous additional infusions of cash.

Unfortunately, Bagehot's insight is evergreen: modern regulators cannot credibly commit to Bagehot's boundary when their mission is defined as preventing Minsky's contagion. Once cast in the role of insurer, rather than lender, the central bank invites a carnival of risk subsidies. Banks seek excessive leverage, depositors stop caring about risk, moral hazard becomes "baked into expectations," and the system is pulled into the trap of repeated bailouts.

So the enduring lesson is not merely "lend freely in a panic," as some activist dirigistes have claimed. The deeper Smith–Bagehot lesson is that a credit system is an *allocation mechanism for society's stock*, and stability policy must be designed to preserve that allocation function under stress without converting the state into a standing guarantor of insolvency. Bagehot gave the rules; Smith gave the capital theory that explains why the rules matter; and recent events have illustrated and vindicated the modern public-choice diagnosis of why the rules are so hard to follow.

Bibliography

Bagehot, W. (1979 [1873]). *Lombard street: A description of the money market*. Hyperion Press.
Dellas, H., & Tavlas, G. S. (2022). Retrospectives: On the evolution of the rules versus discretion debate in monetary policy. *Journal of Economic Perspectives, 36*(3), 245–260.
Friedman, M. (1948). A monetary and fiscal framework for economic stability. In M. Friedman (Ed.), *Essays in positive economics* (pp. 133–156). University of Chicago Press.
Friedman, M. (1960). *A program for monetary stability*. Fordham University Press.
Friedman, M., & Schwartz, A. J. (1963). *A monetary history of the United States, 1867–1960*. Princeton University Press.
Goodhart, Charles. (1988). The Evolution of Central Banks. MIT Press.
Marx, K. (1919 [1867]). *Capital: A critique of political economy*. Charles Kerr. Translated by Ernest Untermann and Edward Aveling.
Marx, K. (2022 [1859]). In M. Dobb (Ed.), *A contribution to the critique of political economy*. International Publishing Company.
Mints, Lloyd. (1945). A History of Banking Theory. University of Chicago Press.
Munger, M. C., & Salsman, R. (2012). Too big to fail is too big. *Georgetown Journal of Law and Public Policy.*
Selgin, G. (2024). *False Dawn*. University of Chicago Press.
Smith, A. (1981 [1776]). *An inquiry into the nature and causes of the wealth of nations*. Liberty Fund.
Smith, A. (1982 [1759]). *The theory of moral sentiments*. Liberty Fund.
Sorkin, A. R. (2009). *Too big to fail*. Viking Press.

Adam Smith's Treatment of the Ancients

James Price

1 Introduction

The conventional narrative of Adam Smith's thought positions him as a radical innovator: the 'father of economics' who broke decisively with classical and medieval traditions to forge something entirely new.[1] Smith himself, seeking to demonstrate the originality of his moral philosophy, was keen to mark his distance from the systems that preceded him. And writers who were keen to laud Smith as a harbinger of modernity have often emphasised this. But Smith was profoundly engaged with the classical world, as all learned men of his age were, and the philosophers of ancient Greece and Rome (most prominently Aristotle and Cicero) shaped the structure of his moral and political thought. Acknowledging this helps relieve us of the burdensome view of Smith as a total novelty, and lets us see the continuity and discontinuity from the previous standard.

Smith had received the classical education standard for educated Scots of his era. From his youth, he was steeped in the texts of antiquity (not merely as historical artefacts, but as living sources for philosophical reflection). When he came to construct his own moral philosophy, when he wrestled with questions of justice and truth, the classical masters would have been, and clearly were, the natural starting point.

[1] Joseph A. Schumpeter, History of Economic Analysis, ed. Elizabeth Boody Schumpeter (New York: Oxford University Press, 1954), 184–194.

J. Price (✉)
Adam Smith Institute, London, UK

J. Ostle et al. (eds.), *Adam Smith's Wealth of Nations After 250 Years*,
Contributions to Economics, https://doi.org/10.1007/978-3-032-32299-9_3

He learned their arguments, and adapted them to address the challenges of the age that was being born around him. The result was thoughts that emerged from ancient ideas, remade for new purposes.

I should declare a bias at the outset. I have had a bust of Cicero on my shelf since studying him whilst reading ancient history at university. But I had never appreciated the impact he has had on many centuries of thinkers, not least Adam Smith. It was a pleasure to discover how deeply Cicero shaped Smith's own vision of human nature and social order. Cicero, as it turns out, is a far more important figure in Smith's thought than I had realised.

Behind Cicero stands the broader Stoic tradition, whose conception of natural providence Smith refigured within his moral psychology[2] and connected, suggestively, to the notion of an invisible hand guiding commercial society. Threading through both is the classical inheritance of virtue ethics: a tradition that Smith preserved, transformed, and deployed (perhaps most importantly, against the modern caricature of self-interest as mere greed).

From the opening line of the Theory of Moral Sentiments (TMS I.i.1.1):

> How selfish soever man may be supposed, there are evidently some principles in his nature, which interest him in the fortune of others, and render their happiness necessary to him, though he derives nothing from it except the pleasure of seeing it.

Smith is concerned, not with markets or prices in isolation, but with the broader question of what motivates human beings beyond self-interest: the same question that preoccupied the ancient moralists from whom he learned. Academic scholarship has benefited enormously from Gloria Vivenza; her two books remain indispensable,[3] and the contributions of Griswold,[4] Hanley,[5] and others have helped too. This chapter draws on their work to offer a broad survey for readers who may be less familiar with the classical dimension of Smith's thought.

2 Classical Education and Smith's Formation

Adam Smith was born at a moment when Scottish education was undergoing a profound change. The curriculum of both Scottish schools and universities maintained the classical tradition as central to intellectual formation, even as they incorporated

---

[2] Leonidas Montes, 'Smith and His Stoic Ancestry,' in New Voices on Adam Smith, ed. L. Montes and E. Schliesser (London: Routledge, 2006).

[3] Gloria Vivenza, Adam Smith and the Classics: The Classical Heritage in Adam Smith's Thought (Oxford: Oxford University Press, 2001); Gloria Vivenza, Adam Smith on the Ancients and the Moderns: Creating the Foundations of Commercial Society (London: Routledge, 2024).

[4] Charles L. Griswold, Adam Smith and the Virtues of Enlightenment (Cambridge: Cambridge University Press, 1999).

[5] Ryan Patrick Hanley, Adam Smith and the Character of Virtue (Cambridge: Cambridge University Press, 2009).

new philosophical currents from the Continent, and even, near-heretically for the Scots, from England.

From childhood, Smith encountered the texts of Greece and Rome to a degree that would embarrass even well-read undergraduate classicists today. Classical authors like Cicero, Livy, Sallust, Virgil, and Horace were the foundations of linguistic training and moral education. A student learned Latin and Greek not merely as languages but as portals to the accumulated wisdom of ancient civilisation.[6] Cicero held a special place. His rhetoric was studied as the model of eloquent prose; his philosophical works provided frameworks for thinking about ethics, politics, and the good life. Smith would have encountered, for example, *De Officiis*, or *On Duties* (cited directly in TMS), not as an obscure historical text but as a living manual for understanding proper conduct in public and private life. So thorough was his Latin education by the time he left school that Smith was allowed to skip the first-year remedial Latin course when he went up to Glasgow University.[7] And in his final year, he was described by the Greek professor as '*a very fine boy as any we have*'.[8]

At Glasgow, Smith studied under Francis Hutcheson, whom he later called 'the never-to-be-forgotten Hutcheson'. Hutcheson was himself deeply influenced by Cicero and the Stoics; his System of Moral Philosophy (1755) draws heavily on Ciceronian virtue. So Smith was heavily influenced by a teacher who had already begun the work of integrating classical ethics with modern concerns. Smith's personal library would eventually contain numerous editions of Cicero's works.[9]

Smith was not alone in his classical preoccupations. His contemporaries, including David Hume and Adam Ferguson, all engaged extensively with ancient moral philosophy. For example, Ferguson's *Essay on the History of Civil Society* (1767) drew on classical republican themes; Hume engaged extensively with ancient authors, often using them to attack the religious orthodoxies of the day.[10] But where others treated the ancients as a backdrop or a resource, Smith treated them as interlocutors. His method was to take a classical concept, test it against the evidence of modern experience, and reconstruct it within his own framework.

In his *Lectures on Rhetoric* and *Belles Lettres*, Smith analyses Cicero's style with the intimacy of someone who had spent years with the texts. He remarks on Cicero's emotional temperament, noting that Cicero 'seems to have been very easily

---

[6] James C. Hawley, 'Cicero's Duties and Adam Smith's Sentiments, 'in New Perspectives on Adam Smith's The Theory of Moral Sentiments, ed. Geoff Cockfield, Ann Firth, and John Laurent (Cheltenham: Edward Elgar, 2007).

[7] Jesse Norman, *Adam Smith: What He Thought and Why It Matters* (London: Penguin Books, 2018), 8.

[8] Ibid., 20.

[9] Vivenza (2001), 42. On the extent of Cicero in Smith's personal library, see Hiroshi Mizuta, Adam Smith's Library: A Catalogue (Oxford: Oxford University Press, 2000).

[10] Hume even admitted in a letter to secretly reading the classics when he was meant to be studying law 'while my Family fancyed I was poring upon Voet and Vinnius, Cicero and Virgil were the Authors which I was secretly devouring'.

depressed or elated by the misfortunes or prosperity of his friends'.[11] The feeling that Smith writes as though he *knows* Cicero, identifying in him precisely the capacity for sympathy that his own moral philosophy prizes, is understandable. This is something many have done over the centuries with Cicero, more than almost any other character in history, of course, because of the letters of his, passed down from antiquity, enabling us to see the inner thoughts and concerns of a 'great man' in a way almost without comparison in the ancient world.

When Smith returned to Glasgow as professor of Moral Philosophy, he based his lectures in part on Cicero's *De Officiis* and *De Finibus*. The Theory of Moral Sentiments grew directly from these lectures; Vivenza describes the work as a 'cultural seed-bed,' combining elements from classical philosophy with Smith's own empirical approach.[12] TMS, then, was not just influenced by Cicero; it was partly built on lectures *about* Cicero. For example, Smith's propriety concept, the idea that a feeling or action is virtuous when it is *fitting*,[13] draws directly on Cicero's *decorum*,[14] the notion of behaving in a way that is fitting to one's character.

3 Aristotle and Smith: 'Corresponds Pretty Exactly'

In Part VII of TMS, Adam Smith makes a helpful claim for those of us looking for his inspiration in antiquity. Having surveyed the ancient systems of moral philosophy, he states that his own system 'corresponds pretty exactly' with that of Aristotle (TMS VII.ii.1.12).

Aristotle (384–322 BC) was a Greek philosopher, and the founder of the Lyceum (a school for philosophy) in Athens. A student of Plato and later tutor to Alexander the Great, he was the first systematic thinker to treat ethics, politics, and what we would now (thanks in no small part to Smith) call economics, as connected subjects of empirical inquiry. There is no space here for more than the broadest sweep of Aristotle's works, nor even for the long and accomplished scholarship that links them to Smith. But the above quote is such a rare concession from a thinker who generally resists aligning himself with any single predecessor, that it is worth focusing on the debt Smith owes Aristotle. He does not, for example, also say this about Cicero, or about the Stoics, or about anyone else from the classical world.

Smith takes several ideas from Aristotle. First, and perhaps above all, the idea that virtue is a habit formed through practice. In the *Nicomachean Ethics* (II.1, 1103a-b), Aristotle writes:

[11] Smith, Lectures on Rhetoric and Belles Lettres [LRBL], Glasgow Edition, 29.ii.214 and 30.ii.236.

[12] Vivenza (2001), 41.

[13] TMS I.i.3.1–9.

[14] De Officiis I.93–96.

> We become just by the practice of just actions, self-controlled by exercising self-control, and courageous by performing acts of courage.

Smith agrees that moral education comes from the humble institutions of everyday social interaction (including the market), not from philosophical instruction.

Next, Smith also agrees with Aristotle that virtue lies between extremes: courage between cowardice and recklessness, generosity between stinginess and prodigality. Cicero and Cato illustrate this further, as we shall see later, with Smith consistently coming down on the side of pragmatism over obstinacy. Yet again, Smith 'consistently uses a classical concept, emphasising its similarity to his own but placing it within the framework of his theory and thereby modifying it to some extent'.[15]

Third, Aristotle's idea of '*phronesis*' (something like prudence, or pragmatic wisdom) is an empirical ability to judge what is right in particular situations, not through abstract rules but through experienced judgement. Smith's famous impartial spectator' uses something like *phronesis* in its observations.

Smith's treatment of self-command is perhaps his most Aristotelian virtue. The Greek idea of *enkrateia*[16] (self-command) denotes mastery over one's impulses. Aristotle treats it as the precondition of all other virtues, since without it no virtue can be reliably exercised. And Smith makes self-command central in Part VI of TMS, where it underpins prudence, justice, and beneficence alike. Hanley has described Smith as 'truly Aristotelian' in his insistence that self-knowledge is the foundation of this mastery (TMS VI.i.1–14).

Again, Aristotle's *megalopsychos*, the great-souled man, possesses a commanding indifference to fortune's accidents; I would argue that Smith's version of this figure is the man who, 'in danger, or in torture, upon the approach of death, preserves his tranquillity unaltered' (TMS III.iii.25). Aristotle grounds magnanimity in a reasonable estimation of one's own worth, Smith in his impartial spectator; but the portrait of the virtuous character, commanding respect through self-possession rather than display, has been argued to be recognisably the same.[17] The connection, whether it be a debt or just inspiration, goes deeper than individual ideas. Adam Smith and Aristotle share a conception of what moral philosophy should actually be for. In the *Nicomachean Ethics*, Aristotle warns that we should not expect the same precision in ethics as in mathematics; humans are too arbitrary, subjective, and human for such precise evaluation. Smith's conception of his moral system as 'practical' is again similar to Aristotle's; both thinkers insist that the aim of ethics is to make us better, not merely to satisfy our curiosity.[18] There are differences between

[15] Vivenza (2001), 47.

[16] Leonidas Montes, *Adam Smith in Context: A Critical Reassessment of Some Central Components of His Thought* (Basingstoke: Palgrave Macmillan, 2004).

[17] Hanley, 112–113.

[18] Aristotle, *Nicomachean Ethics* I.3 (1094b), where Aristotle warns that 'it is the mark of an educated man to look for precision in each class of things just so far as the nature of the subject admits.'

what 'better' looks like to them, of course. But they share an insistence that improvement requires proper action, as well as just thought.

After the *Nicomachean Ethics*, Aristotle turned to his *Politics*, developing his account of the political community growing out of his work on moral philosophy. So arguments on what the good life was, for both the individual and the good ordering of the city, are involved. He opens with the claim that the political community is the highest form of association because it aims at the highest good.[19]

I would argue that Smith does the same with his two great works, developing from the moral psychology of TMS to the political economy of the *Wealth of Nations*. The commercial order Smith describes is not a morally neutral mechanism; it is an arena in which the virtues analysed in TMS (prudence, justice, self-command) find their practical expression. Fleischacker has specifically made this comparison, saying that Smith 'developed his political concerns out of his moral philosophy, much as Aristotle did in moving from his *Ethics* to *The Politics*'.[20]

There are, of course, many differences between the two. By the eighteenth century, Newtonian physics had come to replace much of what Aristotle and the ancients thought about the natural world. It replaced the teleological universe in which Aristotle's ethics made intuitive sense—a universe where everything has a natural purpose, including human beings. As a result, Smith could no longer ground virtue in cosmic *telos* as Aristotle had. So his solution was to find an empirical foundation instead: the observable facts of human sympathy and spectatorial judgement.

But on questions of moral philosophy, and what it is for a person to live a good life, and how societies should behave, the wealth of ideas that Smith owes the classical inheritance is as clear as he has the good grace to admit, always used to productive and often novel ends.

4 Cicero and Smith

4.1 The Sentiment of the Heart

Marcus Tullius Cicero (106–43 BC) was a Roman statesman, orator, and philosopher. He served as consul of the Roman Republic and was its most eloquent defender, ultimately murdered on the orders of Mark Antony for his opposition to autocratic rule. He was a man who died for republican liberty.

During an enforced retirement from public life under the so-called Triumvirate, Cicero turned to the consolations of philosophy. He was strongly influenced by Stoic ideas, blending them with Roman traditions, but tried to cover the sweep of thought in many of his works. Most important for Smith, perhaps, was *De Officiis*

[19] Politics I.1, 1252a.

[20] Samuel Fleischacker, *On Adam Smith's Wealth of Nations: A Philosophical Companion* (Princeton: Princeton University Press, 2004), 34.

(On Duties), written in 44 BC as a letter to his son Marcus, then studying philosophy in Athens. It is organised into three books. The first concerns what is morally honourable (*honestum*), discussing the four cardinal virtues (wisdom, justice, courage, temperance) and the concept of *decorum* (best thought of as propriety). The second concerns what is expedient or useful (*utile*). The third, and most original, reconciles the two, arguing that whatever is morally upright must also be genuinely useful:

> Nothing more destructive could have been introduced into human life than the separation of expediency from moral uprightness.[21]

Cicero was not the inventor of these ideas. He drew eclectically on Stoic, Platonic, and Aristotelian thought, synthesising the Greek schools for a Roman audience.[22] He describes his own method with characteristic self-awareness: he follows the Stoics 'not as a translator, but... drawing from their wells as I see fit, using my own judgement and discretion'.[23] The description fits Smith at least as well as it fits Cicero. He surveys the field of ideas, working through each school in turn (propriety systems in TMS VII.ii.1, prudence systems in VII.ii.2, benevolence systems in VII.ii.3, then his critique of all of them in VII.ii.4), taking what he wants from each. Smith dined on philosophy a la carte, rather than being stuck on the *prix fixe* menu.

4.2 Propriety

Smith's moral concept of propriety comes in part from Cicero. Cicero's *decorum* (translating the Greek *prepon*) denotes the morally fitting action; one that takes account of character, circumstances, audience, and timing. In *De Officiis* (I.93–96), Cicero writes:

> There is a form of goodness which relates to propriety, and from which an orderly approach to things of this kind can be derived... propriety is a concordance with nature, in which moderation and self-control are apparent, together with a certain distinguished bearing.

Cicero transmits and transforms these Aristotelian ideas. In Part VII of TMS, where Smith surveys the ancient moral systems, he places Plato, Aristotle, and the Stoics together as those who 'place virtue in propriety', that is, in 'the suitableness of the affection from which we act to the object which excites it'.[24] He then declares his own allegiance: while propriety is not the 'sole ingredient' in every virtuous action, 'there is no virtue without propriety'. By self-identifying with the propriety tradition, Smith makes the inheritance clear.

---

[21] Cicero, De Officiis III.101.

[22] There is a wonderful, if embellished, story in Plutarch's Life of Cicero (4.7) of a Roman who, upon hearing a young Cicero declaiming in Greek, remarked: 'Greece I pity for her sad fortune, since I see that even the only glories which were left to us, culture and eloquence, are through thee to belong also to the Romans.'

[23] Cicero, De Officiis I.6, trans. P. G. Walsh (Oxford: Oxford University Press. 2000).

[24] TMS VII.ii.1.

4.3 The Race Metaphor: Justice and Self-Interest

Cicero offers a metaphor for justice that Smith adopts almost verbatim. In *De Officiis* (III.42), drawing on an example from the Stoic philosopher Chrysippus, Cicero writes:

> When a man runs in the stadium, he ought to strive and compete to the greatest possible extent in order to win, but he ought in no way to trip his fellow-competitor or to push him over; thus, in life, it is not unjust for anyone to pursue whatever he finds useful, but to despoil another is a violation of justice.

Smith's version, in TMS (II.ii.2.2):

> In the race for wealth, and honours, and preferments, he may run as hard as he can, and strain every nerve and every muscle, in order to outstrip all his competitors. But if he should justle, or throw down any of them, the indulgence of the spectators is entirely at an end. It is a violation of fair play, which they cannot admit of.

Smith takes Cicero's metaphor and its moral lesson almost whole.[25] What he adds is the psychological mechanism: where Cicero offers a principle of justice, Smith adds the 'indulgence of the spectators'; his impartial spectator framework. Cicero gives the content of justice (compete but do not despoil); Smith gives the psychology that enforces it (spectatorial disapproval). The synthesis between their views goes both ways, because Cicero himself was personally disgusted by the cruelty and violence meted out in animal hunts and gladiatorial arenas. He expressed spectatorial disapproval of what were, to his mind, unvirtuous acts.[26]

The market, let alone life more broadly, should be seen *not as* a war of all against all, as Hobbes might have called it. Instead, it is a race with rules. This pushes back clearly on the caricatures of Smith as advocating for selfishness above all, and the origin of this concept goes back thousands of years. It also addresses what some scholarship calls Das Adam Smith Problem'—a dispute alleging that his two great works read so differently. By seeing Smith in this classical tradition and seeing the root of many of his thoughts, it becomes clear that he sees the impossibility of having pure self-interest without the moral rules he takes from the likes of Aristotle and Cicero.

---

[25] He describes them as a cruel and inhumane spectacle "*crudele gladiatorum spectaculum et inhumanum*" Marcus Tullius Cicero, Tusculan Disputations 2.41, trans. J. E. King, Loeb Classical Library 141 (Cambridge, MA: Harvard University Press, 1927).

[26] Cicero, *De Officiis* II.73–85, trans. Walsh.

4.4 *Ancestor of Commercial Liberty*

Cicero's political philosophy contains further arguments that reinforce and inform Smith's defence of commercial society. In *De Officiis* (I.20–21), Cicero articulates what is essentially a principle of negative justice:

> The first office of justice is that no man should harm another unless he has been provoked by wrongdoing; the next, that one should treat common goods as common and private goods as one's own.

Cicero uses this to defend private property rights from a century of political violence instigated by the reforming Gracchi brothers, Tiberius and Gaius. Without going into historical debates, Cicero saw them as responsible for so much of the instability and breakdown in the *concordia ordinum* of his day. In *De Officiis* (II.73–85), he mounts a sustained attack on what today we might call populist redistribution[27]:

> Those who wish to be regarded as friends of the people, and who for that reason either attempt agrarian legislation, so that occupiers are driven from their homes, or propose that money lent should be remitted to borrowers, are undermining the foundations of the commonwealth. They are destroying concord, which cannot exist when money is taken from some and bestowed on others; and they are destroying equity, which is utterly subverted if everyone is not allowed to keep what belongs to him.

The statesman's duty, for Cicero, is to protect private property, not to redistribute it. The state exists to secure the conditions under which citizens can pursue their own interests justly.

Here can be found classical foundations for many Smithian ideas, not least his criticism of mercantilism. The mercantile system granted privileges to some at the expense of others and restricted market entry, using the state as an instrument for private advantage. Cicero would call that a violation of justice: using political power to 'destroy concord', preventing others from competing fairly in the race.

On this foundation, Smith builds his 'system of natural liberty':

> Every man, as long as he does not violate the laws of justice, is left perfectly free to pursue his own interest his own way, and to bring both his industry and capital into competition with those of any other man, or order of men. The sovereign is completely discharged from a duty, in the attempting to perform which he must always be exposed to innumerable delusions, and for the proper performance of which no human wisdom or knowledge could ever be sufficient; the duty of superintending the industry of private people, and of directing it towards the employments most suitable to the interest of the society.[28]

And justice, for Smith, is not merely a virtue of the individual heart; it is the prerequisite for any functioning commercial society:

> Justice… is the main pillar that upholds the whole edifice. If it is removed, the great, the immense fabric of human society, that fabric which to raise and support seems in this world,

---

[27] Ibid.

[28] WN IV.ix.51.

> if I may say so, to have been the peculiar and darling care of Nature, must in a moment crumble into atoms.[29]

And further: 'Society may subsist, though not in the most comfortable state, without beneficence; but the prevalence of injustice must utterly destroy it'.[30] Without justice, commerce is impossible.[31]

Smith's own observation that even robbers and murderers must observe justice among themselves derives directly from Cicero (*De Officiis* II.40).[32]As Haakonssen has shown, the lineage of property rights runs from Cicero through Grotius and Pufendorf to Smith, and Smith's natural jurisprudence is best understood as an attempt to complete this project on empirical foundations.[33] In his *Lectures on Jurisprudence*, Smith traces the development of property rights through Roman legal categories.[34]

4.5 'Dregs of Romulus'

Temperament and pragmatism matter here too, as they did with Aristotle. Cato the Younger was a contemporary of Cicero, an arch-Stoic who committed suicide rather than submit to Caesar. This is presented in TMS as an act of great courage (TMS I.iii.1.13). But Vivenza argues that Smith does not celebrate Cato's greatness as a politician beyond this.[35]

Cicero himself complained that 'our friend Cato… behaves as though he were living in Plato's Republic rather than in the dregs of Romulus'.[36] The pragmatic, engaged philosopher-statesman is, for Smith, a more admirable figure than the rigid republican martyr. Active engagement with imperfect reality (Cicero's approach) is preferable to principled withdrawal from it (Cato's approach).

Classical liberalism, one might say, is Ciceronian rather than Catonian. It works with messy reality rather than demanding philosophical perfection. This has certainly been the author's own experience in government. Regardless, Cicero's life and thought, blending human reality with ideal virtue, blending principle and pragmatism, and trying to do good whilst being realistic about the world as it is, are clear

---

29 TMS II.ii.3.4.

30 Vivenza (2001), 66–68.

31 Vivenza (2001), 52–53.

32 Knud Haakonssen, *The Science of a Legislator* (Cambridge: Cambridge University Press, 1981).

33 Vivenza (2001), 97–107.

34 Vivenza (2024), 103–107.

35 Cicero, *Epistulae ad Atticum* II.1.8, trans. D. R. Shackleton Bailey, Loeb Classical Library (Cambridge, MA: Harvard University Press, 1999).

36 Leonidas Montes, 'Smith and His Stoic Ancestry,' in New Voices on Adam Smith, ed. L. Montes and E. Schliesser (London: Routledge, 2006).

inspirations for Smith. I will feel comfortable allowing my busts of the two men to sit near one another on my shelf.

5 The Stoic Inheritance: Providence, Self-Command, and the Invisible Hand

5.1 The Stoic Framework

The Stoic school, founded by Zeno of Citium around 300 BC, taught that the universe is governed by a rational principle (*logos*) or Providence, and that human beings, as rational creatures, are part of this cosmic order.[37] From the outset, there are clear differences, as Smith's empirical moral psychology replaces that metaphysical foundation with something more human and observable: human beings feel sympathy and develop moral rules from accumulated social experience, not a divine rational principle.

Nonetheless, there were Stoics who were important to Smith. These include Epictetus (c. 50–135 AD), the former slave whose *Discourses* emphasised what is 'up to us' and what is not; Marcus Aurelius (121–180 AD), the philosopher-emperor; and Seneca (c. 4 BC–65 AD), the statesman and essayist. Smith reserves his highest praise for Marcus Aurelius, calling him 'the mild, the humane, the benevolent Antoninus'.[38] He also embodied the Ciceronian 'active life': philosophy applied to statecraft, not withdrawal from it. In the *Meditations*, he wrote:

> Everything is interwoven, and the web is holy; none of its parts are unconnected. They are composed harmoniously, and together they compose the world. One world, made up of all things. One divinity, present in them all.[39]

Epictetus, too, is praised as 'The independent and spirited, but often harsh Epictetus' who may 'be considered as the great apostle' for the Stoic school.

5.2 Admiration and Critique

Smith was both attracted to and sceptical of Stoicism. He deeply admired Stoic self-command: the need to moderate expressions of feeling so that others can enter into them sympathetically is present at the start of TMS, which owes something both to the Aristotelian *enkrateia* (discussed above) and Stoic discipline, which Smith repurposes for his system to build on sympathy.

---

[37] TMS VII.ii.1.15.

[38] Marcus Aurelius, Meditations VII.9.

[39] Vivenza (2001), 73–77.

But Smith explicitly rejects Stoic *apatheia*, the elimination of the passions. He sides with the Peripatetics (Aristotelians): we should feel emotions but in the right degree and at the right time.[40] In fact, complete elimination of feeling would destroy the very capacity for sympathy on which his system depends. His critique of Stoic moral perfectionism highlights the unhelpfulness of ideas taken to their logical extremes:

> As all the actions of the wise man were perfect, and equally perfect; so all those of the man who had not arrived at this supreme wisdom were faulty, and as some Stoics pretended, equally faulty... the man who had killed a cock, for example, improperly and without a sufficient reason, was as criminal as him who had murdered his father.[41]

Smith's verdict is blunt: this doctrine 'is evidently too absurd to deserve any serious consideration' (TMS VII.ii.1.41). He also offers a broader critique of ancient moral philosophy that reveals his own commitments:

> The ancient systems, which place virtue in propriety, seem chiefly to recommend the great, the awful, and the respectable virtues, the virtues of self-government and self-command; fortitude, magnanimity, independency upon fortune, the contempt of all outward accidents, of pain, poverty, exile, and death. It is in these great exertions that the noblest propriety of conduct is displayed. The soft, the amiable, the gentle virtues, all the virtues of indulgent humanity are, in comparison, but little insisted upon, and seem, in those ancient moralists, to have been extorted from them rather against their will. They seem to have been apprehensive that to acknowledge these softer virtues might give occasion to suspect that they meant to recommend effeminate indulgence.[42]

His is a thoroughly humane classicism—reflective of a desire to be lovely as well as loved, perhaps.

5.3 *Providence and the Invisible Hand*

More usefully, the connection between Stoic Providence and Smith's invisible hand runs deep. The Stoics taught that Providence governs the universe: apparent evils are parts of a larger, beneficent design. Smith inherits this framework and, as always, turns it to his own ends.

Critics often point out that the metaphor of the invisible hand appears only twice in Smith's major works: in TMS IV.1.10, the rich 'are led by an invisible hand to make nearly the same distribution of the necessaries of life, which would have been made, had the earth been divided into equal portions among all its inhabitants'. And in the *Wealth of Nations*:

---

[40] TMS VII.ii.1.40.

[41] TMS VII.ii.4.2.

[42] WN IV.ii.9.

> [The individual] intends only his own gain, and he is in this, as in many other cases, led by an invisible hand to promote an end which was no part of his intention. Nor is it always the worse for the society that it was no part of it.[43]

But the structure is very similar to Stoic Providence more broadly: unintended beneficial order arising from individual actions within a larger system.[44] Smith's innovation is that he does not require the reader to believe in literal *divine* Providence. The mechanism works regardless,[45] perhaps through psychology (self-interest channelled by sympathy and the impartial spectator) or through institutions and ideas (property rights, rule of law, and competition).

The invisible hand is more prevalent in his works than those two specific mentions suggest. In TMS, he writes of 'the all-wise Author of Nature' who arranges things so that individual actions produce social benefits beyond anyone's intention:

> The administration of the great system of the universe… the care of the universal happiness of all rational and sensible beings, is the business of God and not of man. To man is allotted a much humbler department, but one much more suitable to the weakness of his powers, and to the narrowness of his comprehension: the care of his own happiness, of that of his family, his friends, his country.[46]

It has been argued that Smith's 'Author of Nature' is closer to the Stoic *logos* than to the Christian God; the impartial spectator replaces divine judgement as the moral tribunal.[47] Regardless, Stoic Providence, Smith's invisible hand, and Hayek's 'spontaneous order' all express the same insight that complex, beneficial social structures can emerge from human action but not from human design, and that attempts to impose structures from the top down can have negative consequences for society.

My argument is not that Smith secretly believed in Stoic theology or that the invisible hand is simply Providence by another name. But Smith inherited from the Stoics a way of thinking about unintended order, how individual actions within a system can produce outcomes that no individual intended or foresaw, that allowed Smith to explain how a decentralised system of exchange, in which each person pursues their own interest, can produce the co-ordinated allocation of resources that serves the common good. Crucially, the argument does not require benevolent motivation. Famously, the butcher, the brewer, and the baker provide our dinner not from benevolence but from self-interest (WN I.ii.2).

---

[43] Vivenza (2001), 64–67.

[44] Echoing Laplace's famous response to Napoleon.

[45] TMS VI.ii.3.6.

[46] Vivenza (2024), 36–45.

[47] TMS III.v.1.

6 Commercial Virtue

This is where all the ideas discussed above—propriety, providence, self-command, *enkrateia,* and the idea that these virtues can be improved through practice in the real world—come together in Smith. These are not just relevant for individuals, but are virtues that make the burgeoning commercial society of the eighteenth century possible. Smith follows Cicero in aiming moral teaching not at sages but at ordinary decent people:

> The coarse clay of which the bulk of mankind are formed, cannot be wrought up to such perfection. There is scarce any man, however, who by discipline, education, and example, may not be so impressed with a regard to general rules, as to act upon almost every occasion with tolerable decency.[48]

Commercial society does not require saints; it requires 'tolerable decency'. Hanley has argued that Smith's account of self-command is not merely a concession to human weakness but a positive account of how character is formed through the discipline of commercial life.[49] This is like Cicero's 'middle duties' (*officia media*) applied to the marketplace. Vivenza highlights the concept of *fides* (trustworthiness, good faith) as central: it is both a Ciceronian virtue and a commercial necessity.[50]

In fact, the ancients made no particular distinction between ethics and economics. Cicero's *De Officiis* discusses property, commerce, and duties alongside virtue. Aristotle's *Politics* treats household management as inseparable from the good life. The Greek word for this? *Oikonomia*, the origin of our word 'economics'.

Because without trust, trade collapses. In a market, self-command means restraining the urge to cheat or defraud, bearing losses without seeking political remedy through special privileges, and maintaining reputation through consistent behaviour, because the alternative is a greater calamity or the system irrevocably breaking down. Whether it is Stoic Providence or human self-command, the discipline born of both virtue and self-interest allowed for the explosion of capitalism that still does such good in the world today.

7 Classical Philosophy and the Foundations of Political Economy

As this is a book for the Adam Smith Institute, I would be remiss not to dwell on some classical origins of political economy. In *De Officiis* (II.78), Cicero attacks the agrarian reforms of the Gracchi brothers, arguing that redistributive confiscation of property undermines the very foundations of civic order. The state exists, Cicero

48 Hanley, *Adam Smith and the Character of Virtue*, 112–113.

49 Hanley, 112–113.

50 Vivenza (2024), 27–35.

insists, precisely to protect what people have acquired through honest industry; a government that seizes private property to buy popular support destroys the trust on which commerce depends.

Smith's argument in Book IV of the *Wealth of Nations* against mercantile monopolies and government-granted privileges follows a recognisably Ciceronian logic. The objection is not abstract but political: interference rewards faction and punishes honest industry. The free market, for both thinkers, is defended not merely as efficient but as just.[51]

To meddle in this consenting exchange, then, is unjust. The villain for Cicero was the rabble-rouser, the Gracchi brothers, or in his own time a *popularis* like Julius Caesar; those who would upset the natural order (the order of the classes—the *concordia ordinum*) by giving in to the mob. Smith worried about those who would suppress human behaviour, those we might now think of as central planners. But their crimes are similar.

There is a favourite passage of TMS at the Adam Smith Institute, used as a summary of all that it believes to be wrong in modern political economy—the infamous 'man of system':

> The man of system ... seems to imagine that he can arrange the different members of a great society with as much ease as the hand arranges the different pieces upon a chess-board. He does not consider that the pieces upon the chess-board have no other principle of motion besides that which the hand impresses upon them; but that, in the great chess-board of human society, every single piece has a principle of motion of its own, altogether different from that which the legislature might chuse to impress upon it.[52]

The man of system is, in classical terms, the anti-*phronimos*. Where Aristotle's man of practical wisdom judges each situation on its merits, attending to particulars and adjusting to circumstance, the man of system reasons entirely from abstract principle. The man of system thinks he knows what the ideal arrangement looks like and tries to impose it wholesale, ignoring the fact that each piece on his chessboard has a will of its own. In this passage, Smith uses classical ideas to predict the rise of socialists who will commit Hayek's fatal conceit of thinking they could be smart enough to plan ahead of time what the invisible hand allows for in real time.

8 Ancient Precedents for the Division of Labour

Ancient thought runs through a great many of the ideas that Smith espouses. Take the division of labour as one example. Smith's famous illustration: 'One man draws out the wire, another straights it, a third cuts it, a fourth points it' (WN I.i.3) has ancient forebears like Plato (Republic II.369b-c) and Xenophon (Cyropaedia VIII.

[51] Cicero, De Officiis II.78.

[52] TMS VI.ii.2.17–18.

ii).[53] The latter describes how in large cities craftsmen specialise in making one type of shoe, while in small towns one man does everything.

There are always differences; Plato assumes that people have different natural aptitudes and that specialisation reflects this; Smith argues the opposite, that differences between individuals arise largely from the division of labour itself. The philosopher and the street porter, Smith claims, were almost identical at birth (WN I.ii.4). In fact, Smith's most radical departure from classical thought is his identification of labour as a source of value. The ancients viewed manual labour with suspicion, associating it—quite literally—with slavery. Smith inverts this: the 'propensity to truck, barter, and exchange' is natural, labour is productive, and it is the basis of national wealth.[54]

Smith did recognise the dark side. The division of labour could make workers 'as stupid and ignorant as it is possible for a human creature to become' (WN V.i.f.50). His solution—public education and moral formation—draws again on classical resources: the ancient emphasis on cultivating complete citizens, not narrow specialists.[55]

Finally, what I believe ultimately distinguishes Smith's political economy from later utilitarian accounts is its classical grounding in human flourishing. The *Wealth of Nations* is not just a manual for maximising aggregate output. Smith's repeated concern is with the condition of 'the labouring poor' (WN I.viii.36), with whether ordinary people can live with dignity, feed their families, and participate in social life without shame. This is closer to Aristotle's *eudaimonia* than to Bentham's 'felicific calculus'. Hanley has argued that Smith cultivates the classical virtues (prudence, magnanimity, beneficence) as remedies for the psychological ills that commercial society may engender: anxiety, restlessness, and inauthenticity. The economy Smith describes is not an end in itself but the material precondition for the Aristotelian good life.[56]

Fundamentally, Smith appreciated what the ancients had (civic virtue, the formation of character through public life) but recognised that commercial society as it had come into being would require different institutional arrangements. His criticisms of the 'man of system' were to recognise that the new world that was being born around him, with its opportunities and complexity, would require a deeply human understanding at its centre. He took that insight from the classical world and turned it into something that informs us to this day.

[53] Vivenza (2024), 124–126.

[54] Vivenza (2001), 134–135.

[55] Vivenza (2001), 180–181.

[56] Vivenza (2001), 189.

9 Conclusion

Adam Smith was a classical thinker in the deepest sense. This does not mean he was a mere imitator of ancient wisdom. Smith was decidedly original, and his originality consisted in part in the way he brought classical philosophical concepts into dialogue with modern empirical psychology and the realities of commercial society. He took the classical vocabulary of virtue, propriety, justice, and beneficence, and he reconstructed it for a modern age.

Vivenza captures this with a memorable formulation: the classics provided Smith with 'forms, not carrier pigeons'; conceptual structures to adapt, not conclusions to repeat.[57] Smith's thought is a composite: Stoic universal harmony, Aristotelian practical virtue, Epicurean realism about self-interest, and Ciceronian practical wisdom, all held together by his modern, personal insights into the moral sentiments and sympathy, and by an institutional framework of justice. His four cardinal virtues (prudence, justice, self-command, beneficence) are explicitly classical in structure but adapted for commercial society: courage is subsumed under self-command, reflecting the shift from martial to commercial life.[58]

This recovery of Smith's classical inheritance can do a number of beneficial things in this anniversary year, and beyond. Most obviously, it corrects the notion that Smith was an amoral advocate of unbridled self-interest. Smith's vision of human flourishing is rooted in a classical conception of virtue. He believed that private interest, properly channelled through justice and refined by beneficence, could generate public good. But this vision depends entirely on a robust account of virtue, education, and the moral sentiments. The 'invisible hand' only works in a society where people play by the rules of justice; where, as in Cicero's race, they strain every nerve to win but do not trip their competitors. Critics of commercial society often argue that markets corrode virtue, that the pursuit of profit is incompatible with the good life. Smith's classical inheritance suggests otherwise. Markets, properly regulated by justice, can be arenas for the exercise of virtue: prudence in managing one's affairs, self-command in bearing losses and resisting temptation, and justice in fair dealing. These are not modern inventions; they have their birth in classical virtues adapted for modern commercial conditions.

Then there is the Stoic insight that individual actions within a well-ordered system can produce collective benefits beyond anyone's intention. As the world gets ever more dizzyingly complicated and interconnected, the worth of this idea becomes more precious. And Cicero's warning that using political power to redistribute wealth undermines the very foundations of the commonwealth retains its force in an age increasingly dissimilar to his own.

Smith's engagement with the ancients also offers a methodological lesson. He read them not as unimpeachable gospel, but looking for insights that survive translation into a different context, testing ancient claims against modern evidence,

---

[57] Vivenza (2024), 145–185.

[58] Ibid.

preserving what works and discarding what does not. We should read Smith himself in the same spirit. The *Wealth of Nations* and the *Theory of Moral Sentiments* are not sacred texts to be quoted as authorities; they are works of philosophical argument to be engaged with, tested, and, where necessary, revised.

Finally, the tradition of commercial liberty has deeper philosophical roots than is ordinarily acknowledged. As capitalism continues to attract scepticism, Smith's philosophy demonstrates that defenders of commercial society cannot rest solely on arguments of economic efficiency. Just as vital is the human side, the philosophical account of human nature: an understanding of what human beings are capable of, what virtues they can develop, what forms of community they can build. Cicero knew this; Smith knew it too. The defence of property, the rule of law, the priority of justice, the limits of state power, the value of self-command: these are not recent innovations. They are the inheritance of a philosophical tradition stretching back through Smith and Cicero to the Athens of Aristotle and the Stoa of Zeno. The bust of Cicero on my shelf looks out at a world that still needs reminding of these things. Two hundred and fifty years after Smith gave them systematic expression, they remain as urgent as ever.

Bibliography

Ancient

Aristotle. (1932). *Politics* (H. Rackham, Trans.). Loeb Classical Library. Harvard University Press.
Aristotle. (2009). *Nicomachean ethics* (David Ross, Trans., revised by Lesley Brown). Oxford University Press.
Aurelius, M. (2006). *Meditations* (Martin Hammond, Trans.). Penguin.
Cicero. (1913). *De Officiis* (Walter Miller, Trans.). Loeb Classical Library. Harvard University Press.
Cicero. (1927). *Tusculan disputations* (J. E. King, Trans.). Loeb Classical Library. Harvard University Press.
Cicero. (1999). *Epistulae ad Atticum* (D. R. Shackleton Bailey, Trans.). Loeb Classical Library. Harvard University Press.
Plato. (1992). *Republic* (G. M. A. Grube, Trans., revised by C. D. C. Reeve). Hackett.
Plutarch. (1919). Cicero. In *Lives* (Vol. VII, B. Perrin, Trans.). Loeb Classical Library. Harvard University Press.
Xenophon. (1914). *Cyropaedia* (Walter Miller, Trans.). Loeb Classical Library. Harvard University Press.

Modern

Fleischacker, S. (2004). *On Adam Smith's wealth of nations: A philosophical companion*. Princeton University Press.
Forman-Barzilai, F. (2010). *Adam Smith and the circles of sympathy*. Cambridge University Press.
Griswold, C. L. (1999). *Adam Smith and the virtues of enlightenment*. Cambridge University Press.

Haakonssen, K. (1981). *The science of a legislator: The natural jurisprudence of David Hume and Adam Smith*. Cambridge University Press.

Hanley, R. P. (2009). *Adam Smith and the character of virtue*. Cambridge University Press.

Hawley, J. C. (2007). Cicero's duties and Adam Smith's sentiments. In G. Cockfield, A. Firth, & J. Laurent (Eds.), *New perspectives on Adam Smith's the theory of moral sentiments* (pp. 234–265). Edward Elgar.

Mizuta, H. (2000). *Adam Smith's library: A catalogue*. Oxford University Press.

Montes, L. (2004). *Adam Smith in context: A critical reassessment of some central components of his thought*. Palgrave Macmillan.

Montes, L. (2006). Smith and his stoic ancestry. In L. Montes & E. Schliesser (Eds.), *New voices on Adam Smith*. Routledge.

Norman, J. (2018). *Adam Smith: What he thought and why it matters*. Penguin Books.

Nussbaum, M. C. (1994). *The therapy of desire: Theory and practice in Hellenistic ethics*. Princeton University Press.

Schumpeter, J. A. (1954). *History of economic analysis* (E. B. Schumpeter, Ed.). Oxford University Press.

Smith, A. (1976a). *The theory of moral sentiments [1759, rev. 1790]. (Glasgow edition, A. L. Macfie & D. D. Raphael (Eds.))*. Clarendon Press.

Smith, A. (1976b). *An inquiry into the nature and causes of the wealth of nations [1776, rev. 1789] (Glasgow edition, R. H. Campbell, A. S. Skinner, & W. B. Todd (Eds.))*. Clarendon Press.

Smith, A. (1980). In W. P. D. Wightman & J. C. Bryce (Eds.), *Essays on philosophical subjects (Glasgow edition)*. Clarendon Press.

Smith, A. (1983). In J. C. Bryce (Ed.), *Lectures on rhetoric and belles Lettres (Glasgow edition)*. Clarendon Press.

Vivenza, G. (2001). *Adam Smith and the classics: The classical heritage in Adam Smith's thought*. Oxford University Press.

Vivenza, G. (2024). *Adam Smith on the ancients and the moderns: Creating the foundations of commercial society*. Routledge.

Exchange, Persuasion, and the Liberal Order

Leonidas Montes

1 Introduction: Exchange in Context

Adam Smith's intellectual legacy is regularly partitioned by modern disciplinary boundaries that were foreign to his own self-understanding. *The Theory of Moral Sentiments* (1759) is treated as a work of "ethics," *An Inquiry into the Nature and Causes of the Wealth of Nations* (1776) as a foundational treatise in "economics," his *Lectures on Jurisprudence* and would be about "law" and *Lectures on Rhetoric and Belles Lettres*, "communication." The interpretive result is predictable: Smith becomes either the philosopher of sympathy and moral approbation or the economist of markets and self-interest. When the two sides of the corpus are compared, the conversation tends to revolve around a familiar dilemma—the so-called "Adam Smith Problem"—as if Smith had to choose between sympathy and self-interest, between moral sentiments and the pursuit of gain.[1]

That dilemma is poorly posed. Smith's inquiry is, from the beginning, an inquiry into social coordination among free and imperfect agents. His intellectual legacy seeks to explain how order arises, how it is sustained, and how it degenerates. The moral question is not whether human beings sometimes act sympathetically and sometimes act prudently; it is whether social interaction can be organized so that ordinary motives—mixed, partial, often vain, and yet capable of self-command—can produce cooperation rather than conflict. The economic question is not whether markets encourage self-interest; it is whether exchange among strangers can be

[1] For the origins, development and intellectual context of the Adam Smith Problem, see (Montes, 2003).

L. Montes (✉)
Universidad Adolfo Ibañez, Santiago, Región Metropolitana, Chile
e-mail: lmontes@cepchile.cl

J. Ostle et al. (eds.), *Adam Smith's Wealth of Nations After 250 Years*, Contributions to Economics, https://doi.org/10.1007/978-3-032-32299-9_4

rendered productive and legitimate without the replacement of liberty by coercion, privilege, or domination. The political question is not whether the state is useful; it is whether political power can be confined to a framework of justice compatible with the agency of citizens.

A large literature has explored these connections. Some readings emphasize Smith's role in the Scottish Enlightenment and the emergence of the concept of "commercial society" (Berry, 2013; Winch, 1978).[2] Other readings stress the philosophical foundations of Smith's political economy in his moral theory and epistemology (Fleischacker, 2004; Schliesser, 2017). Still others have highlighted the unity of Smith's system through the idea of a marketplace of moral, social, and economic interaction (Otteson, 2002). My contribution sits at an adjacent angle: it foregrounds exchange as a rhetorical practice of persuasion among agents, and it reconstructs the liberal order as an institutional strategy for keeping "sympathetic persuasion" rather than coerciveness (Montes, 2019).

Smith's road to a classical liberal society appears at the outset of WN. Already in the first page of WN, Smith refers to the "savage nations of hunters and fishers" that are "miserably poor." In the savage nations—the first stage of civilization—they have: "the necessity sometimes of directly destroying, and sometimes of abandoning their infants, their old people, and those afflicted with lingering diseases, to perish with hunger, or to be devoured by wild beasts" (WN, Intro and Plan.4: 10). Yet, Smith compares this situation with the final stage of "commercial society":

> Among civilized and thriving nations, on the contrary, though a great number of people do not labour at all, many of whom consume the produce of ten times, frequently of a hundred times more labour than the greater part of those who work; yet the produce of the whole labour of the society is so great, that all are often abundantly supplied, and a workman, even of the lowest and poorest order, if he is frugal and industrious, may enjoy a greater share of the necessaries and conveniences of life than it is possible for any savage to acquire. (WN, Intro and Plan.4: 10)

This contrast is evocative and insightful. The father of economics envisioned modernity and the benefits of progress in society. For that purpose, he compared civilized society with the "savage nations of hunters and fishers" of our ancestors. But the lively and moving image of the kids and elderly abandoned "with lingering diseases, to perish with hunger, or to be devoured by wild beasts" is more than eloquent. The reader even feels a call for sympathy. In sum, since the first page of WN, the road to progress is morally drawn.

The first chapter of Book I of WN is "Of the Division of Labour." Smith analyzes and explains the exponential productive impact of "a very trifling manufacture" (WN, I.i.3: 14). It is the pin factory that he could see while working on WN in Kirkcaldy.[3] He then argues how "great multiplication of the productions of all the different arts" promotes the "universal opulence which extends itself to the lowest

---

[2] Recently Sagar has persuasively argued that we should not speak of "commercial society" as the fourth and final stage. The correct term would be "the age of commerce" (2022: 48). Actually "commercial society" appears only two times in Smith's published legacy.

[3] He states "I have seen a small manufactory of this kind" (WN, I.i.3: 15).

ranks of the people" (WN, I.i.10: 22). The division of labor, the principal engine of opulence, is not the result of any "human wisdom" aimed at general prosperity. It is the "slow and gradual consequence" of a propensity to exchange. Yet, Smith immediately complicates the matter: the propensity is more plausibly the consequence of "the faculties of reason and speech." In other words, exchange is rooted in communicative capacities and thus belongs to the moral and rhetorical dimensions of social life. It is not a morally neutral mechanism; it is a practice that presupposes norms and institutions—especially justice—without which it collapses.

But he closes the first chapter of WN comparing, in a very suggestive and provocative Rawlsian manner, the "extremely simple and easy" condition of a poor person with a European prince. The difference is enormous. However, this difference

> Does not always so much exceed that of an industrious and frugal peasant, as the accommodation of the latter exceeds that of many an African king, the absolute master of the lives and liberties of ten thousand naked savages. (WN, I.i.11: 24)

This is another suggestive and evocative example that inclines the reader to rationally sympathize with progress and civilization. Both early comparisons evince Adam Smith's pragmatism and realism. The contrast between savage society and the age of commerce, and between the European king and the "industrious and frugal peasant" leads to a defense of progress and civilization. It is not a normative call, nor a romantic ideal about the present for the future. Both examples are about facts. And both have one aim: progress and civilization. After underlining the importance and purpose of these two contrasts, now we need to uncover the "nature and causes" of progress. Exchange is the key to understanding economics.

The brief Chap. 2, "Of the Principle which gives occasion to the Division of Labor," is perhaps the most important in WN. It begins with this paragraph:

> "This division of labor, from which so many advantages are derived, is not originally the effect of any human wisdom, which foresees and intends that general opulence to which it gives occasion. It is the necessary, though very slow and gradual, consequence of a certain propensity in human nature, which has in view no such extensive utility; the propensity to truck, barter, and exchange one thing for another. (WN I.ii.1: 25)

No one invented the division of labor. There is no "human wisdom" behind this "slow and gradual" social process. The division of labor is the necessary consequence of "the propensity to truck, barter, and exchange one thing for another." And no idea of generating "such extensive utility" lies behind this propensity either. The invisible hand and Hayek's spontaneous order is present at the very beginning of WN.

We have seen that the cause of a nation's wealth is the division of labor. And the cause of the division of labor is the propensity to exchange. But Smith wants to go deeper and wonders about the cause of exchange:

> Whether this propensity be one of those original principles in human nature, of which no further account can be given, or whether, as seems more probable, it be the necessary consequence of the faculties of reason and speech, it belongs not to our present subject to enquire. (WN, I.ii.2: 25)

Exchange is not something that falls from the heavens, or an instinct, but rather a human propensity that has evolved along with "reason and speech." Smith delves deeply into economics and observes the ultimate cause of the wealth of nations. Simply put, we trade because we think and communicate. Thus, the market is a complex system of millions of exchanges, a manifold catallaxy that facilitates commerce and goes to form the economy. He then makes the startling observation:

> Nobody ever saw a dog make a fair and deliberate exchange of one bone for another with another dog. Nobody ever saw one animal by its gestures and natural cries signify to another, this is mine, that yours; I am willing to give this for that. When an animal wants to obtain something either of a man or of another animal, it has no other *means of persuasion* but to gain the favour of those whose service it requires. A puppy fawns upon its dam, and a spaniel endeavours by a thousand attractions to engage the attention of its master who is at dinner, when it wants to be fed by him. (WN I.ii.2: 26, italics added)

Smith sees humans as distinguished from animals by "reason and speech." We can imagine and even observe one dog exchanging a bone with another. But that exchange will not be "fair and deliberate": it will involve biting rather than reason or speech. Exchange between us humans is fair, and we employ persuasion.

The Anglosaxon word "fair" cannot be translated into other languages (Wierzbicka, 2006). It is not about justice or the law, or an ethics relating to honesty alone. Closely linked in sport to the idea of "fair play," the word has a deeply embedded social meaning. Suppose a player is fouled so badly in a soccer match that he has to be taken off the pitch. The ball goes out, and under the rules, a player from the opposing team has to throw in. What does he do? He gives the ball to the goalkeeper of the team that is a player down. The rules did not call for this, but the spectators applaud. The word "fair," an essentially social and moral concept, is bound up with that approval from others, and with sympathy, or the way others perceive our conduct.

This is very important because Smith, a careful writer who was scrupulous in his choice of words, argues that human beings trade in a "fair and deliberate" way. We ponder our own interests but also think about the approval of others. Now, since exchange is the foundation of the entire economy and the market, this is an important condition. The market, like any sport or game, has an underlying morality.

Free market systems ideally rests on fairness. The law is very necessary, but it is not enough. In market competition, the sympathy of a "fair and impartial spectator" helps to mold behavior. The approval of others, and of society, also plays a role vis-à-vis self-interest, making the market seem less of a cold, cruel place. Following the Stoics, Smith adds that human life seems to be "a game of great skill" in which chance plays a major role, with the pleasure of the game arising "from playing well, from playing fairly, and playing skillfully."

Smith insists that in a civilized society, we are "at all times in need of the co-operation and assistance" of others. But if we need others' help, "to expect it from their benevolence" or goodwill alone would be futile. "Give me that which I want, and you shall have this which you want," is the essence of every bargain. Ultimately, exchange is a reciprocal benefit to both parties. In economic terms, there is a surplus for the producer and another for the consumer. He continues with a famous phrase that has so often led to self-interest being confused with selfishness:

> It is not from the benevolence of the butcher, the brewer, or the baker that we expect our dinner, but from their regard to their own interest. (WN, I.ii.2: 26–7)

Smith's examples are deliberately ordinary. People buy dinner from butchers, brewers, and bakers, and in such transactions we appeal "not to their humanity, but to their self-love … and never talk to them of our own necessities but of their advantages" (WN I.ii.2: 26–7). Even the beggar, living on charity, must still enter the market with the coins he receives.

The fundamental importance of trade, the basis of the economy understood as catallaxy, has social and moral implications. Besides fairness, there is also the idea of "persuasion." Smith tells us that a dog has no "means of persuasion" other than fawning on its master to get what it wants. Human beings, though, can use "reason and speech" to trade through "persuasion." The sweet or gentle commerce (*doux commerce*) of the catallaxy operate through persuasion. Economics as catallaxy can also be understood as persuasive trading.

Smith also speaks of persuading rather than merely convincing. Persuasion, in Smith's usage, is not the conquest of an opponent but the attempt to secure assent by addressing the other's standpoint.[4] Because exchange is conducted through language, bargaining is inseparable from rhetoric; this is the background against which Smith's idea of "sympathetic persuasion" should be read. Smith even remarks that in government "management and persuasion are always the easiest and safest instruments of government as force and violence are the worst and the most dangerous" (WN, V.i.g.19: 799).

He ends this concise and profound second chapter with an optimistic note: our "disposition to truck, barter, and exchange" means that everything we produce by the division of labor ends up in "a common stock." In sum, we all benefit.

A key implication about the importance of exchange is that Smith's celebrated account of markets is not an amoral tale of self-interest replacing sympathy. Rather, it is a theory of how cooperation among strangers becomes possible when exchange is embedded in a moral and legal framework. This is why Smith's political economy continuously returns to jurisprudence, public goods, education, and the dangerous influence of privileges and monopolies. Commercial society is productive only under conditions that keep exchange "fair and deliberate." Those moral conditions —underpinned by self-command, praiseworthiness, and propriety— to the rule of law.[5]

Exchange for Smith is not merely a market transaction. It is a fundamental human propensity, intimately tied to reason and speech, and therefore inseparable from persuasion. If humans are "the animals who bargain," then bargaining is already a social practice of influence, justification, and mutual recognition. That single move—reading the propensity to exchange as a rhetorical and

[4] To convince someone is to prevail over the other (the word "convince" comes from the Latin *convinco*, meaning "to conquer" or "to win"). The word "persuade" has a different etymology and meaning, being connected to what is soft and sweet.

[5] On the uniqueness and importance of Smith's self-command, see Montes (2020).

anthropological claim— explains Smith's corpus. It links ethics to political economy and political economy to liberal politics.

The aim is to show why exchange explains how a liberal order can emerge. But it also explains why that order is fragile, always threatened by the capture of institutions, the vanity of the powerful, and the rhetoric of organized interests. To read Smith through exchange is, therefore, to recover a liberalism as simultaneously persuasive and realistic, as an institutional strategy for enabling cooperation among free agents while restraining the moral and political pathologies that those same agents can generate.

On this basis, I will develop three connected claims. First, exchange is anthropological and rhetorical: it is rooted in reason, speech, and persuasion. Second, exchange is moral: fair exchange presupposes justice, so the architecture of TMS is a condition of commercial society rather than an alternative to it. Third, exchange is political: it underwrites a liberal order by disciplining power, and it illuminates Smith's critique of mercantilism as a political economy of privilege and extraction. Some brief conclusions wrap up this chapter.

2 The Propensity to Exchange: From Persuasion to Sympathetic Persuasion

Smith begins WN with a concrete scenario—the pin factory—and only then excavates the underlying principle that "gives occasion" to the division of labor. What appears as a story about productivity is, more deeply, a story about social coordination. Specialization presupposes exchange; exchange presupposes predictability; predictability presupposes norms and institutions that stabilize expectations. A society cannot develop extensive division of labor where property is insecure, violence common, or political power arbitrary. In this sense, the economic argument is already a moral and political argument.

The anthropological core of Smith's analysis lies in his brief discussion of the "nature and causes" of the propensity to exchange. If exchange is a consequence of the faculties of reason and speech, it implies that exchange is also a practice of justification and agreement. It depends on symbolic capacities: the capacity to represent claims ("this is mine, that is yours"), to imagine counterfactuals ("if you give me this, I will give you that"), and to form expectations about future behavior. Exchange therefore belongs to the domain of social meaning.

Smith's comparison with animals is instructive precisely because it is concrete. Animals can "gain the favour" of others; they can even cooperate. But they cannot make a "fair and deliberate exchange." The phrase is not accidental. A "deliberate" exchange is one that can be considered, refused, and negotiated; it presupposes a sphere of reason and liberty. A "fair" exchange presupposes norms of reciprocity and an expectation that others will not take advantage by force or fraud. By placing fairness and deliberation into the basic definition of exchange, Smith signals that commercial society is a rule-governed order.

The rhetorical character of exchange follows immediately. We need to persuade, to present reasons, and anticipate objections. It is to adapt one's proposal to the other's standpoint. Modern economics often describes this interaction as the meeting of supply and demand; Smith describes it as the interaction of persons whose claims must be intelligible and whose agreements must be credible. The practice of exchange thus requires the mutual recognition of agency. Even when motives are prudential, the act of exchanging is relational and communicative.

This is why Smith's emphasis on speech is so important. Speech is the instrument through which exchange becomes possible, but it is also the instrument through which moral standards evolve. Through speech we praise and blame, excuse and condemn; we narrate intentions and evaluate consequences; we form reputations. Commercial society cannot function without these practices, because repeated exchanges depend on trust and credibility. The market is therefore not merely an aggregation of transactions; it is a practice sustained by reputational mechanisms and by the expectation of justice.

Scholars of Smith have emphasized different dimensions of this point. Some have read Smith primarily as the theorist of commercial society, emphasizing the civilizing and emancipatory potential of commerce (Berry, 2013). Others have stressed the philosophical foundations of Smith's political economy in his moral theory and epistemology (Fleischacker, 2004; Schliesser, 2017). My emphasis complements these readings by highlighting the role of exchange and persuasion. If exchange is grounded in speech, then persuasion is not an accidental feature of markets; it is their anthropological basis. The market is, in this sense, a vast arena of persuasion among strangers.

Understanding exchange as persuasion also clarifies Smith's insistence that the division of labor is not the result of design. In a world of persuading agents, coordination cannot be achieved by commanding a plan. It emerges from dispersed proposals, acceptances, refusals, and revisions. The structure of commercial society is thus produced through innumerable acts of speech and agreement. That is the deeper unity between the "science of man" and political economy: both are theories of interaction under conditions of limited knowledge and mixed motives. Hayek's spontaneous generation is a very good way to understand these phenomena.

Finally, the anthropological reading helps explain why Smith's economic liberalism is not merely technical. If exchange presupposes liberty and justice, then the political protection of those preconditions is fundamental. This is why Smith can simultaneously defend a system of natural liberty and assign the state extensive duties of justice, defense, and public works. The market is not a substitute for the state; it is a practice that requires a particular kind of state—one that secures the rule of law.

Smith's interest in persuasion was an early concern. In LJA, lecture notes from 1762 to 1763, delivered the same academic year as the *Lectures on Rhetoric and Belles Lettres*, Smith more clearly reflects on the propensity to exchange and its close relationship with persuasion:

> If we should enquire into the principle in the human mind on which this disposition of trucking is founded, it is clearly the naturall inclination every one has to persuade. The offering of a shilling, which to us appears to have so plain and simple a meaning, is in reality offering an argument to persuade one to do so and so as it is for his interest. Men always endeavour to persuade others to be of their opinion even when the matter is of no consequence to them. If one advances any thing concerning China or the more distant moon which contradicts what you imagine to be true, you immediately try to persuade him to alter his opinion. And in this manner every one is practising oratory on others thro the whole of his life. (LJA, vi.56: 352)

Here, Smith is more direct and precise: exchange is "founded" in the "natural inclination every one has to persuade." Moreover, exchange is an act of communication that appeals to self-interest. In a way, exchange requires persuasion, justice, morality, and rational deliberation.

In LJB, lecture notes that correspond to the academic year 1763–1764, we find another very important passage that advances and develops the "nature and causes" of exchange and the between the philosopher and the street porter (WN, I.ii.4: 28–9). But right after this fundamental distinction that has important political and economic implications, and after explaining the unintended cooperation of the street porter and philosopher due to exchange, Smith insists on the relationship between persuasion and exchange. He argues:

> The real foundation of [division of labor] is that principle to perswade which so much prevails in human nature. When any arguments are offered to perswade, it is always expected that they should have their proper effect. If a person asserts any thing about the moon, tho' it should not be true, he will feel a kind of uneasiness in being contradicted, and would be very glad that the person he is endeavouring to perswade should be of the same way of thinking with himself. We ought then mainly to cultivate the power of perswasion, and indeed we do so without intending it. Since a whole life is spent in the exercise of it, a ready method of bargaining with each other must undoubtedly be attained. (LJB, 222: 493–494)

In this passage from LJB, Smith claims that we ought to "cultivate the power of persuasion." In society, we are constantly exercising this "power," and we even exercise it "without intending it." In fact, according to Smith, we spend our "whole life" persuading. Smith closes the above quoted passage arguing that "[s]ince a whole life is spent in the exercise of it," persuasion is "a ready method of bargaining with each other [that] must undoubtedly be attained" (LJB, 222: 494). From this sentence, it seems that the continuous exercise of persuasion would necessarily lead to a "ready method" of exchange. The relationship between persuasion and the market is clear. Persuasion, for Smith, is just another trade, another form of exchange.

Smith's treatment of persuasion reinforces the consistency of his social project. The father of economics had a clear and realistic understanding of human nature, the risks of unbounded persuasion, and the need of sympathy to harness persuasion and protect individual freedom. In sum, Smith's development of persuasion, from rhetoric to ethics, politics, and economics, underpins his idea of a civilized and free society. And the condition of "fair" exchange reinforces the morality of economics.

If exchange depends on persuasion, then persuasion becomes the moral pivot of commercial society. Persuasion is a method of influence, and influence is morally ambivalent. Adam Smith was aware of the centrality of persuasion and its dangers as a natural human instinct or desire. He knew that "[t]he desire of being believed, the desire of persuading, of leading and directing other people, seems to be one of the strongest of all our natural desires," but he also knew that "speech is the great instrument of ambition, of real superiority, of leading and directing the judgments and conduct of other people" (TMS, VII.iv.25: 336). The risks of "leading and directing other people" demand a framework to protect individual liberty against the perils of the human desire to persuade, control, and even dominate other people. In this sense, Smith's persuasion is also another warning and a call for liberty, tolerance, and human dignity.

Persuasion can be exercised through reasons or through manipulation; through respect or through domination; through sympathy or arrogance. Smith is acutely aware of this ambivalence because his moral theory relies on the social desire for approval and recognition. Human beings are not merely self-preserving; they are evaluative and social. They seek to be seen, accepted, and morally recognized.

The opening of TMS proposes that sympathy is a basic principle of human nature: we can enter, imaginatively, into the sentiments of others. But Smith's sympathy is not only sentimental harmony. It is a mechanism of social calibration that joins "the best heart with the best head." Through sympathy, we learn what kinds of passions others can go along with, and we moderate our own passions accordingly. Social life is thus an ongoing process of adjustment between agents and spectators. Moral order emerges as a fragile equilibrium between sentiments, reason, and approval.

At the center of this equilibrium stands a second-order moral demand: we seek not only praise but praiseworthiness (TMS III.2.1: 113–114); not only belief but beliefworthiness (TMS VII.iv.25: 336). This distinction is fundamental. It introduces the impartial spectator, an internalized standpoint from which we evaluate ourselves. The impartial spectator is not an abstract deity; it is a social standpoint made internal through habituation. It disciplines vanity by asking whether admiration is deserved. And it disciplines persuasion by asking whether agreement has been secured through legitimate means.

In this reconstruction, Smith's foundational idea is best described as sympathetic persuasion: persuasion becomes socially productive and morally legitimate when it is constrained by sympathy and guided by the impartial spectator. The act of influencing others must remain responsive to their perspective and must be disciplined by a concern for praiseworthiness and beliefworthiness. Sympathetic persuasion is therefore not only a sentiment; it is a demanding moral discipline applied to the ubiquitous desire to influence.

Sympathetic persuasion has three components that matter for exchange. First, it requires the capacity to take the other's standpoint seriously. Bargaining is not mere assertion; it is adjustment. Second, it requires self-command. To bargain fairly, one must restrain the temptation to exploit temporary advantage, the temptation to deceive, and the temptation to use coercion where persuasion would suffice. Third, it requires a moralized concern for the legitimacy of agreements. Even if the law permits opportunism, the impartial spectator can condemn it as unworthy of esteem.

This reading also helps us to overcome the so-called Adam Smith Problem. The apparent tension between TMS and WN arises only if we assume that WN is a theory of "economic man" driven by a narrow self-interest alone. But Smith's account of exchange presupposes moral and juridical constraints, while his account of morality presupposes prudence and self-interest as ordinary motives. The marketplace for sympathetic persuasion presuppose free agents coordinating through persuasion within constraints that preserve mutual recognition.

Smith's attention to rhetoric reinforces the point. In the LRBL, he treats persuasion as a general human affair exercised in ordinary life, not only in politics or. Rhetoric, properly understood, is not manipulation but the adaptation of speech to audience and purpose, and therefore a discipline of mutual intelligibility. A commercial society is, in effect, a society of rhetorical interaction: price and contract are not the only means; reputation, narrative, and credibility.

But Smith is realistic: persuasion is always vulnerable to corruption. Individuals may become skilled in deception; factions may learn to mobilize the public through misleading rhetoric; the wealthy may attract admiration and thus distort moral judgment. Yet, Smith does not infer that persuasion should be replaced by coercive "truth." He infers the opposite: because persuasion is inevitable, it must be disciplined by moral education and institutional design. The impartial spectator is one disciplinary mechanism; the rule of law is another. Competition, when open and privilege-free, can also discipline market persuasion.

Sympathetic persuasion therefore becomes a key to Smith's classical liberalism. Liberal order is not the absence of influence; it is the institutionalization of influence under constraints that respect agency. Exchange is legitimate because it is a practice among persons who are equal in juridical standing. Where exchange is backed by privilege or force, exchange degenerates into extraction. This provides the moral bridge to Smith's critique of mercantilism and his defense of natural liberty.

3 Political Economy as Social Coordination

Smith's political economy is often read as a celebration of self-interest understood as part of prudence. But it can also be read as a theory of social order emerging from exchange among free agents. The distinctive Smithian claim is not that people pursue their own advantage—an observation as old as moral philosophy itself—but that a system of exchange can coordinate dispersed information, motives, and efforts in ways that increase opulence and, under certain conditions, improve the condition of the poor.

The mechanism begins with division of labor. Individuals discover that they can produce more effectively. But they need to trade and that trade requires an enlarged market, an enlarged market that depends on the propensity to exchange. The entire process is cumulative and spontaneous, not designed. Smith's repeated insistence that opulence is an unintended consequence is therefore a methodological statement about commercial society. It emerges from innumerable local adjustments rather than from a single plan.

To emphasize unintended order requires limits on political design and limits on coercive coordination. Here, Smith anticipates themes later developed by Hayek, but Smith's route is distinctly moral and sociological. Because human beings have their own "principles of motion" and because social interaction is mediated by persuasion, a political attempt to arrange society as a plan will collide with the autonomy of agents and the complexity of their local circumstances (Hayek, 1960).

Yet, exchange is not a free-floating mechanism. It presupposes a framework of justice. If property is insecure, contracts unenforced, or political favor arbitrary, the cost of transacting rises. This is why Smith treats the administration of justice as one of the core duties of the sovereign. Political economy, in Smith's hands, is inseparable from jurisprudence (Haakonssen, 1981; Fleischacker, 2004).

The rhetorical character of exchange again matters. Exchange is an interactional achievement among strangers (Otteson, 2002). It requires persuasion, but persuasion must be credible. Credibility depends on reputation, which in turn depends on moral norms and on enforcement. A market of strangers functions only when a background of trust exists—trust that agreements will be honored, or that violations will be punished. Even in anonymous markets, intermediaries, legal standards, and reputational signals supply this background.

Smith's famous remark that we obtain our dinner not from benevolence but from regard to our own self-interest should therefore be interpreted carefully. Smith is not saying that sympathy is absent from social life. Commercial society needs justice and commutative justice is the minimal moral condition without which commerce cannot subsist. Smith is explicit in TMS that without justice society becomes a "den of lions," because resentment makes peaceful coexistence impossible.

Moreover, Smith's picture of market interaction is richer than the caricature suggests. Market participants do not merely calculate; they cultivate reputation, adapt to customers, and respond to competition. Their prudence is embedded in social expectations. This is why Smith devotes so much attention to institutional pathologies that distort competition: monopolies, exclusive companies, and regulations designed to serve particular interests. When such distortions arise, market persuasion is displaced by arbitrary political persuasion. The discipline of consent is weakened, and the moral conditions of exchange deteriorate.

Smith's political economy does not require moral perfection from market participants. Commercial society allows cooperation among strangers with mixed motives. It does not require benevolence as a precondition for exchange. But it does require justice, honesty, and self-restraint sufficient to sustain credibility and peaceful interaction.

The foundational character of "fair and deliberate exchange" implies that market transaction is legitimate only where parties can deliberate and refuse. The freedom to refuse is not an option; it is constitutive of exchange. Where refusal is impossible—because of violence, legal coercion, or monopolistic privilege—the transaction becomes extraction. This is why Smith's defence of natural liberty is inseparable from his condemnation of mercantilism, monopolies, and privileges that eliminate competition and genuine choice.

The institutional corollary follows: a liberal commercial society must invest in the public conditions of credibility. Impartial courts, predictable enforcement, and a public ethos that condemns fraud are not external add-ons to the market. They are part of the market's preconditions. When public institutions are corrupt or arbitrary, opportunism becomes rational; the cost of contracting increases; and exchange retracts. But Smith's realism appears in his recognition that a liberal order is fragile. Commercial society can degrade the virtues it presupposes if it encourages admiration of wealth above virtue or if it erodes civic education. This is why Smith is attentive to the education of citizens.

Exchange, because it requires consent, has a disciplinary effect on power. In ordinary interactions, one cannot simply command; one must persuade. The satisfaction of one's wants becomes tied to the recognition of others' agency. This is a structural reason why Smith associates commercial society with freedom. Individuals can pursue their ends, but they must do so through cooperation rather than coercion.

This argument should not be confused with the claim that markets eliminate power. They do not. Power can exist in markets through wealth, information asymmetries, or monopoly. Smith's point is rather conditional: where competition is open and privileges absent, the need to persuade customers and partners creates constraints. Commercial society thus tends, though imperfectly, to replace personal dependence with impersonal relations mediated by rules. It can reduce the scope for arbitrary domination.

This logic extends beyond economics. Commercial society habituates individuals to negotiation, compromise, and reciprocal advantage.[6] It creates interdependence that raises the cost of conflict and makes peaceful cooperation valuable. Hirschman's classic account of early modern arguments for capitalism emphasizes precisely this civilizing expectation: that "interests" could tame destructive passions (Hirschman, 1977). Smith shares a version of this thought, though he is more alert than many of his predecessors to the moral ambivalence of commercial life.

The political implication is that a society of exchange develops an aversion to authoritarian planning. Exchange produces a plurality of projects and occupations; it disperses knowledge and initiative. As Friedrich Hayek later emphasized, dispersed knowledge cannot be aggregated by a single mind, and rules are superior to commands for coordinating that knowledge (Hayek, 1960). Smith anticipates the anti-hubris conclusion, but he grounds it in moral and social psychology: the "man of system" fails because he treats persons as pieces rather than as agents. It is worth reproducing this paragraph in full for its beauty, depth, and continuing relevance:

[6] Garsten (2006) argues that democratic judgment depends on a defense of persuasion rather than its suppression, because public life cannot escape disagreement and therefore cannot escape rhetorical contestation.

> The man of system, on the contrary, is apt to be very wise in his own conceit; and is often so enamored with the supposed beauty of his own ideal plan of government, that he cannot suffer the smallest deviation from any part of it. He goes on to establish it completely and in all its parts, without any regard either to the great interests, or to the strong prejudices which may oppose it. He seems to imagine that he can arrange the different members of a great society with as much ease as the hand arranges the different pieces upon a chess-board. He does not consider that the pieces upon the chess-board have no other principle of motion besides that which the hand impresses upon them; but that, in the great chess-board of human society, every single piece has a principle of motion of its own, altogether different from that which the legislature might choose to impress upon it. If those two principles coincide and act in the same direction, the game of human society will go on easily and harmoniously, and is very likely to be happy and successful. If they are opposite or different, the game will go on miserably, and human society must be at all times in the highest degree of disorder. (TMS VI.ii.2.17: 233–234)

The "man of system" is a dogmatist, one who thinks he knows what is best for society and is not willing to listen to or accept any criticism or improvement. In his arrogance, he believes he can move the pieces on the board of society at will, but forgets that each piece, that is, each of us, has its own movement, its own plans for life, its own freedom. If what the politician tries to do matches what society wants, the social game will go "easily and harmoniously." But if they do not coincide, the game will go "miserably, and human society must be at all times in the highest state of disorder."

Smith's critique of the "man of system" is among the most memorable passages of TMS. It is also the most illuminating for a theory of liberal order grounded in exchange. The passage is often quoted as an anti-utopian warning about policy design. That is part of its meaning, but the deeper claim concerns the moral and political implications of a society constituted by exchange among agents. If individuals coordinate through persuasion and agreement, then politics must respect their agency. The "man of system" refuses this respect and therefore threatens liberty.

The foundational character of exchange is structural. A commercial society is a society of trading and bargaining. Its members do not merely obey; they negotiate, respond, and adapt. Their plans are plural and their knowledge local. To impose a comprehensive plan from above is not only epistemically presumptuous; it is also a moral violation of agency. It replaces free exchange with command. In this sense, Smith's liberalism is not merely a preference for markets. It is an ethic of respect for persons as choosing agents.

Here, exchange becomes a political model. Exchange is a form of coordination that acknowledges the other as a partner rather than an object. It is, under conditions of justice, a practice of reciprocal recognition. Liberal politics generalizes this principle: it seeks to coordinate social life through general rules rather than through discretionary direction, and it seeks to legitimate coercion only as necessary to protect justice. The political analogue of "fair and deliberate exchange" is a constitution order that prevents domination.

Smith's liberalism also has implications for toleration. In a society of exchange, disagreement is normal. Individuals differ in projects, tastes, and beliefs.

Coordination therefore requires a framework within which disagreement can persist without violence. Markets provide one mechanism by which plural desires can coexist; rule of law provides another. Free exchange becomes the normal mode of social influence; coercion becomes exceptional. This is a central liberal insight: the goal is not unanimity but peaceful coexistence under general rules.

The danger, for Smith, is that persuasion can be captured by faction. The mercantile system is a paradigmatic example. Organized interests mobilize rhetoric to secure privileges, and the public becomes vulnerable. Smith's solution is not the abolition of politics but its restraint. General rules, transparency, and civic education are needed to reduce the informational advantage of factions. The impartial spectator provides a moral ideal; institutions provide practical constraints.

This reading also clarifies Smith's relation to classical liberalism. Hayek's critique of central planning emphasizes knowledge problems and Buchanan's constitutional political economy emphasizes incentives and the dangers of rent-seeking (Buchanan, 1975). Smith anticipates both themes, but he grounds them in a moral psychology of persuasion and vanity. Factions form not only because of incentive structures, but because human beings seek domination, admiration, and influence. Institutional design must therefore address both the incentives and the moral culture of public life.

Exchange, finally, also provides a practical reason for humility in politics. Because social order emerges from countless acts of bargaining and adjustment, the legislator cannot "make" society; he can only set conditions. The wise legislator aims to remove unjust restraints and to protect justice, not to arrange industry in detail. The Smithian liberal order is therefore an order of rules rather than rulers: it protects individual liberty of movement and enterprise, restrains privilege and monopoly, and invests in the public institutions that sustain credibility and judgment. In a society of exchange, legitimacy depends on respecting the autonomy of agents. The "man of system" is the opposite: he embodies the temptation to replace persuasion with command.

This does not mean that exchange replaces politics. It means that politics must respect the conditions that make exchange possible. Policies that grant privileges, restrict entry, or manipulate markets in favor of particular interests or concentrated interests, weakens the discipline of consent. The result is not merely inefficiency but political corruption: the public learns that success depends not on free exchange but on securing favor.

Hence, Smith's hostility to monopolies and exclusive companies. They are not only economically distortive; they are politically and morally corrupting. They create a class that treats the state as an instrument of private gain and treats the public as a means. Thus, the analysis of markets becomes a critique of power. In sum, exchange disciplines power only when power does not capture exchange.

For Smith, then, the market entails liberal implications. It does not guarantee virtue, but it can cultivate habits of reciprocity and provide structural reasons to respect others' agency. Under a framework of justice and open competition, exchange becomes a practical school of non-domination.

4 Mercantilism: Liberalism Without Naïveté

Smith's critique of mercantilism is often reduced to "free trade." Although accurate, the deeper Smithian indictment is that the mercantile system institutionalizes a form of anti-exchange. It replaces open-ended bargaining under general rules with privilege, coercion, and the political allocation of opportunity. It converts commerce into an instrument of privileges.

The mercantile system rests on a set of false ideas: that wealth consists in bullion, that trade is a zero-sum contest among nations, and that national prosperity requires systematic restriction of imports and promotion of exports. But Smith's critique is not only epistemic. It is also political. These false ideas become the rhetoric through which organized interests secure privileges. Tariffs, exclusive trading companies, colonial monopolies, and navigation acts do not serve the public; they serve those who can influence legislation.

Mercantilism is the darker side of persuasion. Concentrated interests convince legislators and the public. They frame their demands as patriotic necessity. The public, dispersed and less informed, becomes vulnerable to manipulation. This is precisely where Smith's emphasis on free exchange matters. Persuasion, when not disciplined by sympathetic constraint and by general rules, becomes a tool of faction. The mercantile system is not merely a set of bad policies; it is a regime for distortion embedded in institutions of privilege.

Smith's alternative is the system of natural liberty: individuals should be left free to pursue their interests, so long as they do not violate the laws of justice, and they should be free to bring their industry and capital into competition with others. It is a vision of free exchange under law. The wrongness of mercantilism lies precisely in its violations of general justice: it grants privileges, restricts entry, and turns the state into an instrument for the advantage of some at the expense of others.

Paganelli has recently underscored the moral dimension of Smith's argument, showing that Smith regarded mercantilist policies as not only inefficient but immoral—inefficient because they distort allocation and create perverse incentives, immoral because they produce unjust burdens and often brutal treatment of those without political power (Paganelli, 2024). This reading is faithful to Smith's own emphasis on the burdens placed on consumers and on the ways in which colonial policies impose costs on subjects who lack political voice.

The imperial dimension deserves explicit emphasis. Mercantilism is a doctrine of empire as much as a doctrine of trade. Exclusive companies and colonial monopolies are justified as instruments of national enrichment, but they typically operate as mechanisms of extraction from colonized populations and as mechanisms of privilege for metropolitan elites (Rothschild, 2001). Smith's skepticism about imperial arrangements is therefore an extension of his defense of voluntary cooperation under general rules.

If mercantilism is anti-exchange, its characteristic mechanisms become clearer. First, it restricts entry and competition, thereby making exchange less deliberate and more coercive: the consumer faces fewer alternatives, and the producer faces fewer competitors. Second, it shifts persuasion from market to politics: success comes from lobbying rather than serving. Third, it converts the state into an enforcer of asymmetry: legal privileges guarantee gains to some while socializing costs on others. In this way, mercantilism corrodes both economic efficiency and the rule of law.

Smith's critique is therefore inseparable from his liberal politics. Mercantilism is a regime in which power captures exchange. On the contrary, classical liberalism is a regime in which exchange disciplines power by requiring that gains be obtained through voluntary transactions under general rules. To defend free exchange is, in this sense, to defend a political constitution that resists privilege, faction, and the manipulation of public rhetoric.

The anti-privilege orientation is also why Smith's position is more demanding than a narrow laissez-faire caricature. The liberal task is institutional: dismantle privileges, ensure the impartial administration of justice, and create a framework within which bargaining can be fair and deliberate. In this respect, Smith's liberalism is closer to a jurisprudential project.

To place exchange at the center of Smith's system is to recognize that the market is a juridical institution. Exchange depends on the security of possession, the enforceability of agreements, and the predictability of adjudication. These are not optional conveniences; they are constitutive conditions of commercial society. Smith's LJ, and the structure of Book IV of WN, show that political economy is a branch of the science of a legislator (WN, IV.Intro.1: 428).

Haakonssen's interpretation of Smith as a theorist of natural jurisprudence captures the point well: Smith's moral and economic reasoning is framed by a theory of justice and the institutions that sustain it (Haakonssen, 1981). Justice is, in Smith's moral philosophy, the minimal and indispensable virtue. Society can survive without beneficence but it cannot survive without justice. The reason is structural: injustice generates resentment and retaliation; it dissolves trust; it makes cooperation costly. Commercial society intensifies this dependence on justice because it multiplies interactions among strangers.

The rule of law is the institutional expression of this presupposition. Under this liberal framework, rules are general, publicly known, and predictably enforced. Generality matters because exchange requires stable expectations. If property and contract are subject to discretionary favor, bargaining becomes uncertain and costly. In this sense, the rule of law is not a moral luxury but an economic precondition and a political guarantee of liberty.

Smith's system also implies a sharp distinction between exchange and extraction. Exchange is voluntary transfer under general rules; extraction is appropriation through force, fraud, or privilege. Mercantilism is extraction disguised as commerce. Slavery is extraction without disguise. Monopoly privilege is extraction legalized. Understanding these distinctions clarifies why Smith's liberalism is also a moral project: it aims to enlarge the sphere of voluntary cooperation.

A liberal state, therefore, is not simply a minimal state. It has substantial duties: defense, the administration of justice, and the provision of public works and institutions that private exchange cannot supply efficiently such as basic education. But these duties are enabling duties. They create and maintain the framework within which exchange can coordinate social life. They do not direct exchange toward a comprehensive plan. This is the Smithian meaning of natural liberty: a framework in which individuals may pursue their projects under rules that secure the person and property of others.

Smith's institutional argument can be read as an early form of constitutional political economy. James Buchanan later formalized the idea that liberal order depends on constitutional constraints that limit rent-seeking and protect generality. Smith anticipates the same concern in his critique of privileges and in his insistence that general rules are necessary to prevent the state from becoming an instrument of faction. What Smith adds is a deeper moral argument: rent-seeking is not only an incentive problem; it is an expression of vanity and the desire to dominate. Constitutional restraint is therefore not merely a technical fix; it is also a moral safeguard.

The juridical dimension also reinforces the role of moral psychology. Because exchange relies on persuasion, it is vulnerable to persuasion's abuse. Smith's moral theory provides internal constraints—praiseworthiness, propriety and self-command—while jurisprudence provides external constraints—rules against fraud, violence, and breach of contract. Together they stabilize expectations and make bargaining deliberate rather than coercive. In this way, morality and law converge on the preconditions of commercial society.

Smith's attention to education further confirms this jurisprudential structure. In Book V of WN, Smith worries that extensive division of labor can render workers "as stupid and ignorant as it is possible for a human creature to become," undermining their civic and moral capacities (WN V.i.f.50: 782). His remedy is public education. This is not a departure from liberalism; it is a defense of liberal order. A citizenry without judgment is vulnerable to manipulation by factional rhetoric. If exchange depends on persuasion, then a liberal polity requires citizens able to judge persuasion.

A reconstruction of Smith around exchange must resist two temptations: the apologetic temptation to treat commerce as automatically virtuous, and the cynical temptation to treat commerce as automatically corrupting. Smith is neither naïve celebrant nor romantic critic. He is a realist of social tensions. Commercial society improves material conditions and can enlarge the sphere of personal independence. Yet, it also generates risks: vanity, dependence, inequality of influence, and the distortion of moral judgment.

These risks follow from the same human psychology that makes exchange possible. Because exchange is mediated by persuasion, and because persuasion is linked to the desire for approval, commercial society can amplify status competition. Individuals may come to admire wealth as a sign of success and to neglect virtue. The impartial spectator is the moral remedy, but it is imperfect. Moral judgment can be socially distorted when spectators themselves are captivated by riches. Smith recognizes this distortion and treats it as a danger for moral culture.

The question for liberal politics is therefore how to preserve the benefits of exchange while mitigating its moral and political dangers. Smith's answer is institutional and educational rather than utopian. He does not propose to control commerce. He proposes to secure justice, dismantle privileges, and provide public education to strengthen citizens' judgment. In other words, he seeks to correct the conditions under which exchange becomes corrupted.

This correction is necessary because commercial society can produce political turmoil. Wealth can translate into influence. Influence can translate into privileges. Privileges can undermine competition. Smith's critique of mercantilism is in part a critique of these risks. The mercantile system is precisely the mechanism through which economic power captures political power and turns it into privilege. Liberalism, in Smith's sense, is an anti-privilege project aimed at breaking these risks and restoring the rule of law.

Finally, Smith's liberalism is a demanding project. It does not promise that commerce will automatically yield virtue. It promises that, under conditions of justice and non-privilege, exchange can coordinate social life peacefully and productively while protecting individual liberty. The task is to sustain those conditions against constant temptations: vanity, faction, the admiration of power, and the desire to direct others.

5 Conclusion: Exchange as the Foundation of Smith's System

Exchange is the primary hidden unity of Smith's project. It is the principle that connects the moral psychology of sympathy and judgment with the political economy of markets and the liberal politics of restrained government. At the anthropological level, exchange is grounded in reason and speech and therefore presupposes persuasion. At the moral level, exchange requires fairness and deliberation and therefore presupposes sympathetic persuasion, praiseworthiness, and self-command (Montes, 2020). At the political level, exchange underwrites a liberal order because it depends on justice and because it constrains coercive plans: it teaches reciprocity, raises the cost of domination, and demands institutions that secure liberty under law.

Smith's formidable critique of mercantilism is fierce. Mercantilism is a political economy of unfree exchange: it privileges the few, restrains the many, and corrupts persuasion into manipulation. It is inefficient, but more importantly it is unjust—often brutal toward those without political power (Paganelli, 2024). Smith's liberalism, by contrast, is a political economy of anti-privilege and rule-governed liberty.

To place exchange at the center of Smith's thought is therefore not to reduce Smith to economics. It is to restore the unity of his social theory: political economy, morality, and jurisprudence are different aspects of a single problem—how free persons can coordinate their lives through rules, persuasion, and mutual recognition, without surrendering their liberty to faction, privilege, or the "man of system."

Smith's invisible hand today can seem strangely elusive. Contemporary societies are vulnerable to mercantilist temptations—regulatory capture, rent-seeking, and the manipulation of public rhetoric by concentrated interests—and to the moral pathologies of admiration and status anxiety. Smith offers no simple remedy, but he offers a classical liberal framework: protect the rule of law, dismantle privileges, cultivate judgment, and organize social coordination around voluntary exchange rather than legalized extraction. On the 250th anniversaries of both *The Wealth of Nations* (1776) and U.S. independence, recovering Smith's legacy is timely—and challenging.

Bibliography

Berry, C. J. (2013). *The idea of commercial society in the Scottish enlightenment*. Edinburgh University Press.

Buchanan, J. M. (1975). *The limits of liberty: Between anarchy and leviathan*. University of Chicago Press.

Fleischacker, S. (2004). *On Adam Smith's wealth of nations: A philosophical companion*. Princeton University Press.

Garsten, B. (2006). *Saving persuasion: A defense of rhetoric and judgment*. Harvard University Press.

Griswold, C. L. (1999). *Adam Smith and the virtues of enlightenment*. Cambridge University Press.

Haakonssen, K. (1981). *The science of a legislator: The natural jurisprudence of David Hume and Adam Smith*. Cambridge University Press.

Hayek, F. A. (1960). *The constitution of liberty*. University of Chicago Press.

Hirschman, A. O. (1977). *The passions and the interests: Political arguments for capitalism before its triumph*. Princeton University Press.

McCloskey, D. N. (2006). *The bourgeois virtues: Ethics for an age of commerce*. University of Chicago Press.

McKenna, S. J. (2006). *Adam Smith: The rhetoric of propriety*. SUNY Press.

Montes, L. (2019). Adam Smith's foundational idea of sympathetic persuasion. *Cambridge Journal of Economics, 43*(1), 1–15. https://doi.org/10.1093/cje/bex090

Montes, L. (2020). The relevance of propriety and self-command in Adam Smith's theory of moral sentiments. *Social Philosophy and Policy, 37*(1), 118–137. https://doi.org/10.1017/S0265052520000072

Montes, L. (2003). Das Adam Smith problem: Its origins, the stages of the current debate, and one implication for our understanding of sympathy. *Journal of the History of Economic Thought, 25*(1), 63–90. https://doi.org/10.1080/1042771032000058325

Montes, L. (2004). *Adam Smith in context: A critical reassessment of some central components of his thought*. Palgrave Macmillan.

Otteson, J. R. (2002). *Adam Smith's marketplace of life*. Cambridge University Press.

Paganelli, M. P. (2024). Adam Smith and the inefficient immorality of mercantile policies. *Estudios Públicos, 2*, 89–105. https://doi.org/10.38178/07183089/1441240502

Rothschild, E. (2001). *Economic sentiments: Adam Smith, Condorcet, and the enlightenment*. Oxford University Press.

Sagar, P. (2022). *Adam Smith reconsidered: History, liberty, and the foundations of modern politics*. Princeton University Press.

Schliesser, E. (2017). *Adam Smith: Systematic philosopher and public thinker*. Oxford University Press.

Smith, A. (1976a). In R. H. Campbell, A. S. Skinner, & W. B. Todd (Eds.), *An inquiry into the nature and causes of the wealth of nations*. Oxford university press. (Original work published 1776).

Smith, A. (1976b). In D. D. Raphael & A. L. Macfie (Eds.), *The theory of moral sentiments*. Oxford University Press. (Original work published 1759).
Smith, A. (1978). In R. L. Meek, D. D. Raphael, & P. G. Stein (Eds.), *Lectures on jurisprudence*. Oxford University Press.
Smith, A. (1983). In J. C. Bryce (Ed.), *Lectures on rhetoric and belles Lettres*. Oxford University Press.
Wierzbicka, A. (2006). *English: Meaning and culture*. Oxford University Press.
Winch, D. (1978). *Adam Smith's politics: An essay in historiographic revision*. Cambridge University Press.

Adam Smith and the Liberal Plan

Jerry Evensky

1 Introduction[1]

Adam Smith believed that there is a natural order, a design to the universe.[2] While we have no direct access to the blueprints of the design, based on the careful, dispassionate observation and analysis of philosophers, humankind has imagined a representation of the design that seems consistent with what we observe on the face of nature. Smith cites Sir Issac Newton as greatest of these philosophers.[3]

---

[1] For a more detailed analysis of Smith's vision of humanity's past and its prospect see *Adam Smith's Moral Philosophy* (Evensky, Cambridge University Press, 2005). For a more detailed analysis of his Liberal Plan see *Adam Smith's Wealth of Nations—A Readers Guide* (Evensky, Cambridge University Press, 2015)

[2] For the mature Smith the deity was about faith, not proof. As Philo, the skeptic in Hume's Dialogues *Concerning Natural Religion*, expresses it:

> [T]here is no view of human life, or of the condition of mankind, from which, without the greatest violence, we can infer the moral attributes, or learn that infinite benevolence, cojoined with infinite power and infinite wisdom, which we must discover by the eyes of faith alone (Hume, 201–2).

This faith is the source of Smith's hope for humankind and it is that hope that motivated his life as a moral philosopher, a life committed to representing the invisible connecting principles that can lead humankind toward that benevolent prospect with which the deity has endowed humankind: "the liberal plan of equality, liberty and justice" (*WN*, 664).

[3] "And even we, while we have been endeavouring to represent all philosophical systems as mere inventions of the imagination … have insensibly been drawn in, to make use of language express-

---

J. Evensky (✉)
Syracuse University, Syracuse, NY, USA
e-mail: jevensky@syr.edu

J. Ostle et al. (eds.), *Adam Smith's Wealth of Nations After 250 Years*, Contributions to Economics, https://doi.org/10.1007/978-3-032-32299-9_5

One element of the design is, however, not purely represented on the face of nature. This element, distorted and unnatural, is humankind. In humankind, there is a "vile rust" (*TMS*, 316), vice, that impedes the ideal design from being realized. This distortion due to "human frailty"[4] (Correspondence, 221) (unbridled self-interest) makes it difficult to discern the natural (ideal) order of humankind based on what we see.

It is this distinction between humankind and the rest of nature that, in Smith's day, distinguished Moral Philosophy and from Natural Philosophy.[5] Adam Smith was a Moral Philosopher. He sought to imagine the invisible connecting principles, the undistorted design, that represents the ideal constitution of humankind. His vision of Moral Philosophy has three dimensions: social/moral, political/legal, economic/market. *The Theory of Moral Sentiments* represents his analysis of the moral dimension. His vision of the legal dimension is reflected in the lecture notes of students in his jurisprudence classes. *The Wealth of Nations* is his analysis of the economic forces that determine the material well-being of society, thus the title: *An Inquiry into the Nature and Causes of the Wealth of Nations*. If we want to approach the ideal society, and thereby achieve the greatest wealth for the nation, these three dimensions must align in an environment of perfect justice. "Justice … is the main pillar that upholds the whole edifice" (*TMS*, 86).

Smith believed that the ideal is a limit. We can approach it but never realize it. The history of humankind is a story of progress toward the ideal. Progress comes from the constructive co-evolution of the three dimensions of society toward a more just, more productive society. Individual societies emerge and grow as their moral and legal infrastructure approximates perfect justice. To the degree that a given society approximates the ideal, that society enjoys the potential for sustained material growth.

Societal evolution is a natural selection process. Every society is a natural experiment. *Ceteris paribus*, material progress provides a society with the means to defend itself. Thus, the justice of a society's moral and legal infrastructure determines the sustainability of each societal experiment.

No society can be perfectly just because human frailty gives rise to vice. The best we can hope for is a society that nurtures a largely ethical citizenry and establishes

---

ing the connecting principles of this one [(Newton's)], *as if* they were the real chains which Nature makes use of to bind together her several operations." (*HA*, 105, emphasis added)

[4] Smith says in his eulogy for his dearest friend, David Hume, "I have always considered him, both in his lifetime and since his death, as approaching as nearly to the idea of a perfectly wise and virtuous man, as perhaps the nature of *human frailty* will permit" (Correspondence, 221, emphasis added).

[5] "The beauty of a systematical arrangement of different observations, connected by a few common principles, was first seen in the rude essays of those ancient times towards a system of natural philosophy. Something of the same kind was afterwards attempted in morals. The maxims of common life were arranged in some methodical order, and connected together by a few common principles, in the same manner as they had attempted to arrange and connect the phenomena of nature. The science which pretends to investigate and explain those connecting principles, is what is properly called Moral Philosophy." (*WN*, 769)

just structures of jurisprudence that determine the standards for contracts and to deal with those citizens who do not have the self-command to eschew the perceived benefits of vice.

The progress of humankind is not monatomic. Vice and immoral behavior infect every society. Thus, every society includes behaviors that can undermine justice. These behaviors are the limiting factors of a society's progress. They lead to stagnation (China) or decline (Bengal).[6] Smith believed that Great Britain was in his day the society that had made the greatest progress toward the ideal. But he feared that the vice of Mercantilists' greed was undermining the British experiment making him progressively less sanguine about Britain's prospect. In Book 4 of *The Wealth of Nations,* Smith exposes the vices of Mercantilist policies calling them out as designed to line the pockets of the Mercantilists with no consideration for the greater good of the citizenry of Great Britain.[7]

Justice is a central theme of Smith's *Wealth of Nations*: Material progress goes hand-in-hand with progress of justice.

> It is the great multiplication of the productions of all the different arts … which occasions, *in a well-governed society*, that universal opulence which extends itself to the lowest ranks of the people. (*WN*, 22, emphasis added)

> Note the phrase "well governed society." It seems like a sidebar observation. In fact, it is the linchpin of Smith's analysis of the wealth of nations. I will return to this "well governed society" and how Smith envisioned it being realized below.

For now, I will assume society is "well governed" and analyze how Smith imagines this ideal liberal society will realize the greatest wealth for the nation.

With this model of the ideal in mind, I will examine Book III of the *WN* wherein Smith examines an historical case: the emergence of Europe from the chaos after the fall of Rome to the emergence of the vastly more productive nation states of his day—Britain being the leader in this achievement. This case is Smith's empirical demonstration that his model is consistent with the assertion that progress toward the ideal is possible. While the path to progress can be convoluted, progress can be made as a significant portion of the general population escapes the fetters of dependence and achieves independence and security.

With Smith's model of progress in place, I will examine the limitations in Smith's model that made government intervention necessary for the well-being of a liberal society (e.g., the need for trust in Banking, provision of Public Goods, addressing the stupefying effect of too fine a Division of Labor).

Then there is Mercantilism. The case the Mercantilists make is that trade is a zero-sum game. It is a war. To the degree that I win, you lose. Winning the trade war is the

---

[6] China is rich but it is stationary. Bengal is declining. Its population is being immiserated.

[7] The initial Mercantilist policy goal was to win at trade in order to accrue the largest holdings of gold and silver. This evolved so that by the 1770s, while the goal was still to win at trade, winning was not measured by the holdings of precious metals, it was measured by the size of the trade surplus. Tariffs, bounties, restrictions on trade, colonies, a strong navy, were some of the tools Mercantilists supported to achieve their goal.

source of a nation's wealth. Smith says this is not the way trade works. Trade is potentially a positive sum game. When it is free and fair, there are mutual gains from trade. It is these gains from trade (domestic and international) that increase a nation's wealth.[8]

Mercantilism is the bane of Smith's existence. He sees Mercantilism as a self-serving policy agenda, disguised as a pseudo-philosophy. His dismissal of that policy agenda evolves significantly in a series of revised editions of *WN* from disdain to a visceral disgust as he addresses the challenges of these policies. The source of this evolution in his thinking is his growing perception that Mercantilism represents a clear and present danger to Britain's success at pursuing the liberal vision he holds dear.

This evolution in his perception transforms his voice. He was, prior to his growing concern about Mercantilism, a committed classical liberal—one who sees citizenship as a badge of freedom and government as instrumenetally essential for national security, personal security, and the security of contracts. The central theme of the liberal plan is laissez-faire. Individuals seeking to better their condition do not need the government to tell them how to do that.

The classical liberal doesn't believe in active citizenship. Every citizen is naturally and appropriately committed first and foremost to his own well-being. Government is simply a tool for facilitating individuals' objectives. The smaller the government, the better. It has no claim on citizens' souls. For example, classical liberals believed that it is not a citizen's duty to defend the nation. The government should establish a professional standing army to do that. Soldiering is a profession, not a calling.

In contrast, the civic humanist believes that citizenship is an active duty. For example, the civic humanist rejects the idea that individuals, following their own self-interest, should be recruited into a standing army that has as its job the protection of *the* state. That protection should be the responsibility of citizen soldiers organized as a militia to defend *their* state.

In his last revisions to *The Theory of Moral Sentiments* published in 1790, Smith creates a hybrid of these. The classical liberal model he presents in *The Wealth of Nations* remains intact (including his endorsement of a standing army), but below this superstructure is a civic humanist foundation.[9] Smith believed that in order to

---

[8] "Nothing … can be more absurd than this whole doctrine of the balance of trade, upon which, not only these restraints, but almost all other regulations of commerce are founded. When two places trade with one another, this doctrine supposes that, if the balance be even, neither of them either looses or gains; but if it leans in any degree to one side, that one of them loses and the other gains in proportion to its declension from the exact equilibrium. Both suppositions are false. A trade which is forced by means of bounties and monopolies, may be, and commonly is disadvantageous to the country in whose favour it is meant to be established.… But that trade which, without force or constraint, is naturally and regularly carried on between any two places is always advantageous, though not always equally so, to both." (*WN*, 488–9).

[9] "Men of republican principles have been jealous of a standing army, as dangerous to liberty. It certainly is so, wherever the interest of the general, and that of the principal officers, are not necessarily connected with the support of the constitution of the state. … But where the … military force is placed under the command of those who have the greatest interest in the support of the civil

resist the growing power of Mercantilism, society needs civic humanist citizenship and leadership, leaders who are willing to place the well-being of the commonwealth above the interests of themselves and the factions they represent, and citizens who do the same.

Finally, we come back to that *sine qua non* for the success of liberal society, that it be "well governed." Where does Smith believe this good government will come from? To address this question, we will turn to the *Theory of Moral Sentiments*.

That is where we are going. We begin with Smith's vision of the classical liberal ideal.

2 Adam Smith's Classical Liberal Story: How a Simple System of Natural Liberty Realizes the Greatest Wealth for the Nation (in a Well Governed Society)

> All systems, either of preference or of restraint, therefore, being thus completely taken away, the obvious and simple system of natural liberty establishes itself of its own accord. Every man, ***as long as he does not violate the laws of justice***, is left perfectly free to pursue his own interest his own way, and to bring both his industry and capital into competition with those of any other man, or order of men [(i.e., faction)]. The sovereign is completely discharged from a duty, in the attempting to perform which he must always be exposed to innumerable delusions, and for the proper performance of which, no human wisdom or knowledge could ever be sufficient; the duty of superintending the industry of private people, and of directing it towards the employments most suitable to the interests of the society. (***WN***, 687–688, emphasis added)

---

authority … a standing army can never be dangerous to liberty. On the contrary, it may, in some cases, be favourable to liberty. The security which it gives to the sovereign renders unnecessary that troublesome jealousy, which, in some modern republics, seems to watch over the minutest actions, and to be at all times ready to disturb the peace of every citizen. … To a sovereign … who feels himself supported … by a well regulated standing army … [t]hat degree of liberty which approaches to licentiousness, can be tolerated … It is in such countries only, that the public safety does not require that the sovereign should be trusted with any discretionary power, for suppressing even the impertinent wantonness of this licentious liberty." (*WN*, 706–707)

2.1 *The Dynamic of Growth in* The Wealth of Nations*: The Division of Labor, the Extent of the Market, and Competition*

A healthy society is growing in its production. If Smith is to represent *The Nature and Causes of the Wealth of Nations,* he must offer an analysis of the conditions that make growth possible. He begins that analysis with these opening words of *The Wealth of Nations*:

> The greatest improvements in the productive powers of labour, and the greater part of the skill, dexterity, and judgment, with which it is anywhere directed, or applied, seem to have been the effects of the division of labour. (*WN*,13)

If the division of labor is the key to productive power, what determines the degree to which the labor can be divided? The division of labor is limited by the extent of the market. This helps explain why China became so rich and Great Britain was doing so well in 1776. Both countries enjoy a geography that lends itself to trade—inland waterways and an extensive coast.

Trade is crucial to Smith's analysis. The division of labor is very productive, but what each individual has at the close of the day is a surplus of whatever he was producing. He has none of the other products he needs or wants. Trade gives an individual the opportunity to vent his surplus in return for the other commodities he did not make but needs or wants. Smith asserts that individuals will participate in trade because we all have a "propensity to truck, barter, and exchange one thing for another." (*WN*, 25).

When trade is free and fair (recall the "well governed society"), those who participate in the market exchange face competition from others who come to the market with the same purpose. Every one of them wants to do as well as possible in the market process, so they are all looking for an advantage. But a free and fair market makes securing an advantage impossible.

> The whole of the advantages and disadvantages of the different employments of labour and stock, must, in the same neighbourhood, be either perfectly equal, or continually tending to equality. If, in the same neighbourhood, there was any employment evidently either more or less advantageous than the rest, so many people would crowd into it in the one case, and so many would desert it in the other, that its advantages would soon return to the level of other employments. This, at least, would be the case in a society where things were left to follow their natural course, where there was perfect liberty, and where every man was perfectly free both to choose what occupation he thought proper, and to change it as often as he thought proper. Every man's interest would prompt him to seek the advantageous, and to shun the disadvantageous employment. (*WN*,116)

The "neighborhood" is the space within which trade can be carried on without great impediments.[10] Difficult geography (e.g. impenetrable mountain ranges) or

[10] "Good roads, canals, and navigable rivers, by diminishing the expense of carriage, put the remote parts of the country more nearly upon a level with those in the neighbourhood of the town." (*WN*, 163)

hostile groups (e.g., bandits or an enemy nation) can significantly limit the size of the neighborhood thereby limiting the extent of the market. Access to navigable waterways extends the available market. This is an advantage that Britain enjoys.

2.2 *How Growth Unfolds: Productive Vs. Unproductive Labor, Capital Accumulation and the Circuits of Capital*

In Smith's analysis, not all labor produces a vendable commodity. Smith distinguishes between productive and unproductive labor—the former reproduces itself in the process of production, the latter leaves no trace of itself that can be used in further production.

Examples of productive labor include agricultural workers, manufacturers, blacksmiths, etc. Unproductive labor includes soldiers, representatives, barbers, etc. Smith is not saying that unproductive labor is not useful, soldiers, representatives, and barbers may be useful, but their labor is unproductive, because it does not contribute to growth. "[T]he work of all of them [(unproductive laborers)] perishes in the very instant of its production." (*WN*, 331).

Productive labor generates a stock that can be used to support further labor. It alone provides the means to invest in further production to grow the wealth of the nation. The share of the stock committed to further production is capital.

Note the phrase "the share of stock." The stock generated by a given cycle of production can be allocated in one of two ways. It can be used for immediate consumption, or it can be used as capital to invest in refining the division of labor making the next cycle of production more fruitful. Prudent individuals save and accumulate stock from each cycle and reinvest it as capital in subsequent cycles. That is the cause of the growth in wealth of the nation.

> In the midst of all the exactions of government, this capital has been silently and gradually accumulated by the private frugality and good conduct of individuals, by their universal, continual, and uninterrupted effort to better their own condition. It is this effort, protected by law, and allowed by liberty to exert itself in the manner that is most advantageous, which has maintained the progress of England towards opulence and improvement in almost all former times, and which, it is to be hoped, will do so in all future times. (*WN*, 345)

Beyond the immediate neighborhood market, Smith identifies three circuits of trade: "the home trade, the foreign trade of consumption [(trade between the investor's nation and another nation)], and the carrying trade" (facilitating trade between two alien nations). (*WN*, 368) In order to better their own condition, individuals' capital will naturally flow to the most advantageous investment opportunity first. That is the home trade. Trading near home has the advantages of a quick turnaround so capital can be reinvested in short order and a lower risk than the other circuits because it remains under the investor's watchful eye. The second and third circuits are successively longer turnarounds and involve more risk.

But as capital deepens in that first circuit, the rate of profit on capital diminishes. At some point, the rate of profit from the foreign trade of consumption becomes competitive and capital will spill into that second circuit. Then as capital deepens in that second circuit, the rate of profit on capital diminishes yet further. At some point, the rate of profit from the facilitating of trade between two alien nations becomes competitive, and capital will spill into this third circuit. Each expanding circuit represents an extension of the market.

It is this dynamic to which Smith is referring when he writes:

> By preferring the support of domestic to that of foreign industry, he intends only his own security; and by directing that industry in such a manner as its produce may be of the greatest value, he intends only his own gain; and he is in this, as in many other cases, led by an *invisible hand* to promote an end which was no part of his intention. Nor is it always the worse for the society that it was no part of it. By pursuing his own interest, he frequently promotes that of the society more effectually than when he really intends to promote it. I have never known much good done by those who affected to trade for the public good. It is an affectation, indeed, not very common among merchants, and very few words need be employed in dissuading them from it. (*WN*, 456, emphasis added)

This dynamic has another benefit as Smith sees it. While the deepening of capital diminishes the rate of profit, it raises the wages of labor.[11] In a growing economy, where the circuits of trade (and thus the extent of the market) are expanding, capital deepens more quickly than the pool of productive labor expands. This competition for productive labor raises wages.[12] This is a central benefit of the liberal plan:

> Is this improvement in the circumstances of the lower ranks of the people to be regarded as an advantage, or as an inconveniency, to the society? The answer seems at first abundantly plain. Servants, labourers, and workmen of different kinds, make up the far greater part of every great political society. But what improves the circumstances of the greater part, can never be regarded as any inconveniency to the whole. No society can surely be flourishing and happy, of which the far greater part of the members are poor and miserable. It is but equity, besides, that they who feed, clothe, and lodge the whole body of the people, should have such a share of the produce of their own labour as to be themselves tolerably well fed, clothed, and lodged. (*WN*, 96)

In a well governed society, individuals reinvest a growing pool of capital. That is the fuel for growth and that growth increases the well-being of the working class. This is Smith's vision of an ideal liberal order: Capital holders constrained by competition to a tolerable, modest return and the working class tolerably well fed, clothed, and lodged.

---

[11] "When profit diminishes, merchants are very apt to complain that trade decays, though the diminution of profit is the natural effect of its prosperity, or of a greater stock being employed in it than before." (WN, 108)

[12] "It is the stock that is employed for the sake of profit, which puts into motion the greater part of the useful labour of every society. The plans and projects of the employers of stock regulate and direct all the most important operation of labour, and profit is the end proposed by all those plans and projects. But the rate of profit does not, like rent and wages, rise with the prosperity, and fall with the declension of the society. On the contrary, it is naturally low in rich, and high in poor countries, and it is always highest in the countries which are going fastest to ruin." (*WN*, 266)

Is it realistic to imagine that an approximation of such a society could emerge from the chaotic past? Smith believed it is, and he cites Britain as, to date, the best approximation to emerge from the messy evolution of humankind.

3 Power of the Invisible Hand: WN Book III

Productive labor is essential to growth, and there is one form of productive labor that is the key that starts the engine of growth. That is the farmer:

> No equal capital puts into motion a greater quantity of productive labour than that of the farmer. … In agriculture … Nature labours along with man … No equal quantity of productive labour employed in manufactures, can ever occasion so great reproduction. In them Nature does nothing; man does all; and the reproduction must always be in proportion to the strength of the agents that occasion it. The capital employed in agriculture, therefore, not only puts into motion a greater quantity of productive labour than any equal capital employed in manufactures … it adds a much greater value to the annual produce of the land and labour of the country, to the real wealth and revenue of its inhabitants. Of all the ways in which a capital can be employed, it is by far the most advantageous to society. (*WN*, 363–364)

> If individuals are going to allocate their capital to its initial best advantage the place to invest that capital is in agriculture. "According to the natural course of things, therefore, the greater part of the capital of every growing society is, first, directed to agriculture …" (*WN*, 380)

Once agriculture is realizing the surpluses generated by these agricultural investments, those surpluses can support the growth of productive labor in the nearby towns. The tradesmen who undertake "some sort of coarse industry of the manufacturing kind [that] must have been carried on in those towns, [are focused on their small neighborhood] before they could well think of employing themselves in foreign commerce" (*WN*, 380). Smith's model would predict that this is the natural order of things: Growth starts in agriculture, and the surpluses of agriculture provide the sustenance for towns to emerge. "But though this natural order of things must have taken place in some degree in every such society, it has, in all the modern states of Europe, been in many respects entirely inverted" (*WN*, 380).

Smith seizes on this inversion of the natural order to demonstrate that his model can explain this apparent anomaly.[13] He makes his case by demonstrating that the history of Europe from the fall of Rome to the emergence of productive nation states (e.g., Britain) is an evolutionary story of chance, circumstance, and the intended and unintended consequences of human action leading to progress. Progress was not inevitable, but in this case, it was realized as the model suggests despite the convoluted evolutionary path it took due to the foibles of "human frailty."

---

[13] With respect to those who "dismiss ["'irregularities' and 'corruptions'" (Campbell, 55)] … as interesting irrelevances … far from being irrelevant, these irregularities are, for Smith, crucial tests for his theory, and the more of them he can explain the more secure he regards its empirical basis" (Campbell, 55).

After the fall of Rome, there was chaos. Chaos makes the world unpredictable, insecure. Insecurity shuts down trade. If one cannot feel confident that the products he would bring to the market will be safe from theft or onerous taxes, he will not participate in the market. If he thinks he can get to the market, but the treasure he will receive for his wares is at risk from theft or onerous taxes, that too will discourage him from going to market.[14] Absent a reasonable expectation of safe market participation, the market collapses. When the market collapses, the town has no venue for exchanging its goods at which point the town collapses. Without a town to which it can vent its surpluses, croplands were largely left untilled. This contraction of trade due to the pervasive insecurity of the times left countless individuals destitute. The inhabitants of the towns were "in the same state of villanage" (*WN*, 397) as those in the country.

In the midst of this chaos, a few privileged individuals seized the opportunity to bring some semblance of order by engrossing the lands and pronouncing themselves landlords over their parcels and over the inhabitants who happened to populate that land. The quid pro quo was: You stand with me and I will organize you into a force that will provide all of us protection. Smith asserts that this might have been a necessary "transitory evil" (*WN*, 382) to create some measure of stability, but this transitory evil was made permanent by the laws of entail and primogeniture. These ensured that the power of the lord would be sustained whole across generations (*WN*, 382–383).

Those who remained in the towns paid a tax to the king in return for security. This was paid by the individual traders to representatives of the king. The numerous transactions required a large number of king's agents to collect these payments, an onerous process for individual tradesmen. Individual payments were ultimately replaced by a collective payment on behalf of all the town's traders. In time, the payment became a fixed amount that the burghers of the town conveyed to the king.

"Along with this grant, the important privileges were generally bestowed upon the burghers of the town to whom it was given … [T]he principal attributes of villanage and slavery being thus taken away from them, they now at least became really free, in our present sense of the word freedom" (400). In this independent free space, the burgers built nascent institutions for self-government.

> Why would the king willingly allow the creation of semi-autonomous states within his realm? Because there was another player in this realm that had the resources to be formidable to the king.

> The lords despised the burghers, whom they considered not only as a different order, but as a parcel of emancipated slaves, almost of a different species from themselves. The wealth of the burghers never failed to provoke their envy and indignation, and they plundered them upon every occasion without mercy or remorse. The burghers naturally hated and feared the

[14] "They seem, indeed, to have been a very poor, mean set of people, who seemed to travel about with their goods from place to place, and from fair to fair…. [T]axes used to be levied upon the persons and goods of travellers, when they passed through certain manors, when they went over certain bridges, when they carried about their goods from place to place in a fair, when they erected in it a booth or stall to sell them in." (*WN*, 397)

> lords. The king hated and feared them too; but though, perhaps, he might despise, he had no reason either to hate or fear the burghers. Mutual interest, therefore, disposed them to support the king, and the king to support them against the lords. They were the enemies of his enemies, and it was his interest to render them as secure and independent of those enemies as he could. By granting them magistrates of their own, the privilege of making bye-laws for their own government … he gave them all the means of security and *independency* of the barons which it was in his power to bestow. (*WN*, 410-412, emphasis added)

This opened up opportunities for towns with access to water carriage to trade in more distant markets. There they could "derive their subsistence" (*WN*, 405) in return for their wares. This is Smith's explanation for why progress began in the towns before the country, an inversion of the natural course of things.

As the towns grew, the inhabitants of the country remained in villanage, under the watchful eye of the lord. "The great Earl of Warwick is said to have entertained every day, at his different manors, 30,000 people …." (*WN*, 412–413).

The progress of the towns generated a growing pool of capital in the towns that made possible greater division of labor. Some of this capital spilled into the countryside bringing improvements to production there. The increasing agricultural output in the country supported a larger population and further division of labor in the towns. But the villanage, the total dependency of the people of the country, was an impediment to this growth. Enter the invisible hand to realize progress. That is the promise of the liberal plan.

> [W] hat all the violence of the feudal institutions could never have effected, the silent and insensible operation of foreign commerce and manufactures, [the dynamics of Smith's liberal plan,] gradually brought about. These gradually furnished the great proprietors with something for which they could exchange the whole surplus produce of their lands, and which they could consume themselves, without sharing it either with tenants or retainers. All for ourselves, and nothing for other people, seems, in every age of the world, to have been the vile maxim of the masters of mankind. As soon, therefore, as they could find a method of consuming the whole value of their rents themselves, they had no disposition to share them with any other persons. For a pair of diamond buckles, perhaps, or for something as frivolous and useless, they exchanged the maintenance, or, what is the same thing, the price of the maintenance of 1000 men for a year, and with it the whole weight and authority which it could give them. … [And] thus, for the gratification of the most childish, the meanest, and the most sordid of all vanities they gradually bartered their whole power and authority. (*WN*, 418–419)

When producing for the market "[e]ach tradesman or artificer derives his subsistence from the employment, not of one, but of a hundred or a thousand different customers. Though in some measure obliged to them all, therefore, he is not absolutely dependent upon any one of them." (*WN*, 420) Thus, this dynamic moved society toward the liberal ideal of workers gaining more independence.

The landlord wants the maximum rent from his land so that he can maximize his buying power in the market.[15] In order to achieve this, he needs to shed the expense

---

[15] "The desire of food is limited in every man by the narrow capacity of the human stomach; but the desire of the conveniencies and ornaments of building, dress, equipage, and household furniture, seems to have no limit or certain boundary." (*WN*, 181)

of most of his previous retainers. Those who remain to work the land need incentives to be as productive as possible by making improvements on the land. The farmers need stability for their leases if they are to make improvements. That means they require long leases. These long leases give the farmers much more independence from the landlord.[16] Again we see the invisible hand of the liberal plan realizing increased independence of the working class.

> A revolution of the greatest importance to the public happiness, was in this manner brought about by two different orders of people, who had not the least intention to serve the public. To gratify the most childish vanity was the sole motive of the great proprietors. The merchants and artificers, much less ridiculous, acted merely from a view to their own interest .... Neither of them had either knowledge or foresight of that great revolution which the folly of the one, and the industry of the other, was gradually bringing about. (*WN*, 424)

In Book III, Smith lays out his case that realizing the liberal plan is the objective of the invisible hand. Smith makes this case by demonstrating that the liberal plan empowered by the invisible hand can emerge from what seemed to be a hopeless, chaotic environment. Smith finds hope in this dynamic, but he understands that there are some obstacles to progress that can potentially stymie the invisible hand.

4 Smith on Limitations of the Invisible Hand's Ability and the Role of Government

The classical liberal recognizes roles that the government must play. Among them: It has to provide for the common defense. It must also set up a judicial system to adjudicate competing understandings of contracts and to hold accountable those who do not follow the law. There are some roles that the government is called upon to undertake that seem to violate the principles that represent the bedrock of the liberal plan. For example:

4.1 Banking

"Where the issuing of bank notes for such very small sums is allowed, and commonly practised, many mean people are both enabled and encouraged to become bankers. A person whose promissory note for £5, or even for 20 s, would be rejected by every body, will get it to be received without scruple when it is issued for so small a sum as a sixpence. But the frequent bankruptcies to which such beggarly

[16] "The relationship evolved from serfdom, to tenancy, to rental tenancy with long leases. Each step encouraged the tenant to invest more heavily in improving the land, and each step made the tenant's relationship with the landlord more contractual and less arbitrary" (Muller, 122)

bankers must be liable, may occasion a very considerable inconveniency, and sometimes even a very great calamity, to many poor people who had received their notes in payment." (*WN*, 323)

> [T]hose exertions of the natural liberty of a few individuals, which might endanger the security of the whole society, are, and ought to be, restrained by the laws of all governments; of the most free, as well as or the most despotical. The obligation of building party walls, in order to prevent the communication of fire, is a violation of natural liberty, exactly of the same kind with the regulations of the banking trade which are here proposed. (*WN*, 324)

4.2 Too Fine a Division of Labor

"In the progress of the division of labor, the employment of the far greater part of those who live by labor, that is, of the great body of the people, comes to be confined to a few very simple operations; frequently to one or two. But the understandings of the greater part of men are necessarily formed by their ordinary employments. The man whose whole life is spent in performing a few simple operations, of which the effects, too, are perhaps always the same, or very nearly the same, has no occasion to exert his understanding, or to exercise his invention, in finding out expedients for removing difficulties which never occur. He naturally loses, therefore, the habit of such exertion, and generally becomes as stupid and ignorant as it is possible for a human creature to become."

> … But in every improved and civilized society, this is the state into which the labouring poor, that is, the great body of the people, must necessarily fall, unless government takes some pains to prevent it. (*WN*, 781–782)[17]

Smith proposes that …

> [f]or a very small expense, the public can facilitate, can encourage and can even *impose* upon almost the whole body of the people, the necessity of acquiring those most essential parts of education. (*WN*, 785, emphasis added)

To this end, Smith envisions "little schools" for the children of the working class where they would learn to read and write at a basic level as well as being "instructed in the elementary parts of geometry and mechanics" (*WN*, 785). This intervention would, Smith supposes, ameliorate the perverse effect of too fine a division of labor. These competencies are valuable in all but the lowest ranking jobs. The children could be encouraged to apply themselves to their studies with the promise of "little

[17] "In some cases, the state of society necessarily places the greater part of individuals in such situations as naturally form in them, without any attention of government, almost all the abilities and virtues which that state requires, or perhaps can admit of. In other cases, the state of the society does not place the greater part of individuals in such situations; and some attention of government is necessary, in order to prevent the almost entire corruption and degeneracy of the great body of the people." (*WN*, 781)

badges of distinction" (*WN*, 786) or of the likelihood of success on examinations that provide access to trades.

It is the case, however, Smith seems to be overly optimistic. The lowest order of workers, given their lack of marketable skills, cannot escape this mind-numbing work. If the economy dictates that these jobs are an essential part of the production nexus, some workers will either be trapped in them by powerful forces that limit their options (the most likely case) or, in a fair and free market, the wages will compensate for the disagreeableness of the work seducing workers to choose sustaining their body over expanding their mind. No "little schools" or "badges" will change this.

4.3 Infrastructure

"That the erection and maintenance of the public works which facilitate the commerce of any country, such as good roads, bridges, navigable canals, harbors, etc. must require very different degrees of expense in the different periods of society, is evident without any proof [...] It does not seem necessary that the expense of those public works should be defrayed from that public revenue, as it is commonly called, of which the collection and application are in most countries, assigned to the executive power. The greater part of such public works may easily be so managed, as to afford a particular revenue, sufficient for defraying their own expense without bringing any burden upon the general revenue of the society." (*WN*, 724).

Given the very high start-up costs, the initial provision of "public works" such as high roads and canals is often done by government. However, financing the upkeep of this infrastructure is not necessarily a burden the government must bear. Maintenance of canals can be trusted to private individuals because the alignment of incentives ensures that revenue from the canal will be used for its maintenance. "In several different parts of Europe, the toll or duty upon a canal is the property of private persons, whose private interest obliges them to keep up the canal. If it is not kept in tolerable order, the navigation necessarily ceases altogether, and, along with it, the whole profit which they can make by the tolls" (*WN*, 725).

Not so the highroads:

> The tolls for the maintenance of a high-road cannot, with any safety, be made the property of private persons. A high-road, though entirely neglected, does not become altogether impassable, though a canal does. The proprietors of the tolls upon a high-road, therefore, might neglect altogether the repair of the road, and yet continue to levy very nearly the same tolls. It is proper, therefore, that the tolls for the maintenance of such a work should be put under the management of commissioners or trustees (*WN*, 726).

It is the responsibility of governments to assess the alignment of incentives for any public works project and to arrange the financing of the project accordingly.

4.4 *Monopoly*

When a company of merchants undertake, at their own risk and expense, to establish a new trade with some remote and barbarous nation, it may not be unreasonable to incorporate them into a joint-stock company, and to grant them, in case of their success, a monopoly of the trade for a certain number of years. It is the easiest and most natural way in which the state can recompense them for hazarding a dangerous and expensive experiment, of which the public is afterwards to reap the benefit. A temporary monopoly of this kind may be vindicated, upon the same principles upon which a like monopoly of a new machine is granted to its inventor, and that of a new book to its author. [...] [But once enjoying the advantage of a monopoly, the beneficiary will lobby to make that arrangement permanent.] By a perpetual monopoly, all the other subjects of the state are taxed very absurdly in two different ways: first, by the high price of goods, which, in the case of a free trade, they could buy much cheaper; and, secondly, by their total exclusion from a branch of business which it might be both convenient and profitable for many of them to carry on. (*WN*, 754-755)

To develop this point, Smith examines the decision of the Parliament to establish monopolies for the African trade and the Indian trade. In each of these cases, Smith found that the merchants were mismanaging the artificial advantages Parliament afforded them, the enterprises inevitably started failing, and the merchants returned to Parliament, hat in hand, pleading for a bailout. Initially, the Parliament was the leading player in determining the course of trade policy. The mercantilists were beholden to the Parliament. This is where things stood when Smith left in 1763 for a tour of Europe as the tutor of the Duke of Buccleuch (Ross, 196).[18]

That year, 1763, was a pivotal year in the relationship between Parliament and the Mercantilists.

> [Starting in] 1763 ... [mercantile] interests ... so dominated politics that men observed that mercantilism had changed from the control of trade in the interest of national policy, to the control of national policy in the interest of trade. ... The increasing importance of Parliament [and its "factionalized and undisciplined party system" (Kammen, 97)] seemed to encourage efforts by powerful groups seeking to influence regulation by political pressure. (Kammen, 75, 95)

Smith returned from his travels with the Duke in the fall of 1766. In early 1767, he returned to his mother's house in Kirkcaldy where he settled in to write *The Wealth of Nations*.

[18] It was a common rite of passage among the elite to have their young boys escorted by a scholar on a tour to Europe, tutoring the young lad along the way. See (Ross, 196)

5 Smith's Growing Awareness that Britain's Experiment with the Liberal Plan Is in Danger: The Threat of Monopoly

From early 1767 to 1772, Smith lived with his mother in Kirkcaldy as he worked on *The Wealth of Nations*.

In Kirkcaldy, he was out of the loop, only remotely aware of the growing Mercantilist power.[19] He writes of the remoteness of Kirkcaldy to Lord Fitzmaurice in London on February 21, 1759:

> This country is so barren of all sorts of transactions that can interest anybody that lives at a distance from it that little entertainment is to be expected from any correspondence on this Side of the tweed. Our epistles to our friends at the capital commonly consist more in enquiries than in information. I must therefore put your Lordship in mind of the promise you was so good as to make to me of some times letting me hear from you of what passes in the Great World, either at home or abroad. (*Correspondence*, 28)

On September 3, 1772, he writes to Sir William Pulteney that "[m]y book would have been ready for the Press by the beginning of this winter; but for interruptions … [that] will oblige me to retard its publication for a few months longer" (*Correspondence*, 164). He did not finish it in a few months. It took years. His arrival in London confronted him with the reality of a new political dynamic that had unfolded in his absence. The mercantilists were taking control of government policies.

Upon his return to London, Smith was welcomed by many dear friends and admirers, and he quickly became active in the intellectual and political life of the city. "He was admitted to the Royal Society in May 1773, attended Lord Wedderburn's weekly dining club, and was admitted to Johnson's Literary Club" (Steven, 202). He arrives in London in 1773 ready to publish the *WN*, but it is not finally published until March 9, 1776 (Campbell and Skinner, "The Text and Apparatus," *WN*, 61). Given what he saw in London, he had a lot more to say about the Mercantile system:

> This monopoly has so much increased the number of some particular tribes of them, that, like an overgrown standing army, they have become formidable to the government, and, upon many occasions, intimidate the legislature. The member of parliament who supports every proposal for strengthening this monopoly, is sure to acquire not only the reputation of understanding trade, but great popularity and influence with an order of men whose numbers and wealth render them of great importance. If he opposes them, on the contrary, and still more, if he has authority enough to be able to thwart them, neither the most acknowledged probity, nor the highest rank, nor the greatest public services, can protect him from the most infamous abuse and detraction, from personal insults, nor sometimes from real

[19] Chatbox informs me that "In 1776, traveling from Kirkcaldy, Scotland, to London by horse would have been quite a journey. The distance is approximately 400 miles (about 640 kilometers). On horseback, travelers could cover around 25 to 30 miles per day on average, depending on the terrain, weather, and the condition of the horse and rider.

"Given these conditions, the journey might have taken approximately 13 to 16 days. This estimation assumes consistent daily travel without lengthy stops or interruptions." (accessed 12/08/25) danger, arising from the insolent outrage of furious and disappointed monopolists. (*WN*, 471)

The Mercantilists were much more keenly aware of their own interests, than the country gentlemen were of their interests.[20] It was in the Mercantilists' interest to protect and preserve their monopoly trade with the American colonies. Citing Locke as their philosophical guiding star, they concocted a pseudo-philosophy to persuade the country gentlemen that their policy proposals were in the nation's interest. Smith has no use for the self-serving policy proposals of the Mercantilists.

The monopoly of the American colonial trade that the Mercantilists achieved served them well, but it cost Britain dearly. The artificially high monopoly returns attracted capital away from more socially productive allocations. This enhanced the Mercantilists' wealth, but it also channeled the nation's assets into a more tenuous allocation. Rather than capital flowing into many channels thereby spreading the risk by diversifying the nation's portfolio, it disproportionately sent capital into a favored channel: trade with the American colonies.[21] This serves the interest of the Mercantilists at the expense, both literally and figuratively, of the consumers who have to pay more for monopoly priced goods, are taxed more to deal with the huge debt the Mercantilists' policy created (debt from wars fought to protect the Mercantilists' interest) and bear the risks that these policies impose on the British economy.

The first edition of *The Wealth of Nations* reflected Smith's dismay with Mercantilism as of 1776. But he was not done with the Mercantilists. He wanted to know more about the depth of Mercantilists influence on trade. To that end, when he

[20] "As during their whole lives they are engaged in plans and projects, they have frequently more acuteness of understanding than the greater part of country gentlemen. As their thoughts, however, are commonly exercised rather about the interest of their own particular branch of business than about that of the society, their judgment, even when given with the greatest candour (which it has not been upon every occasion), is much more to be depended upon with regard to the former of those two objects, than with regard to the latter. Their superiority over the country gentleman is, not so much in their knowledge of the public interest, as in their having a better knowledge of their own interest than he has of his. It is by this superior knowledge of their own interest that they have frequently imposed upon his generosity, and persuaded him to give up both his own interest and that of the public, from a very simple but honest conviction, that their interest, and not his, was the interest of the public. The interest of the dealers, however, in any particular branch of trade or manufactures, is always in some respects different from, and even opposite to, that of the public." (*WN*, 266–267)

[21] "The industry of Great Britain, instead of being accommodated to a great number of small markets, has been principally suited to one great market. Her commerce, instead of running in a great number of small channels, has been taught to run principally in one great channel. But the whole system of her industry and commerce has thereby been rendered less secure; the whole state of her body politic less healthful than it otherwise would have been. In her present condition, Great Britain resembles one of those unwholesome bodies in which some of the vital parts are overgrown, and which, upon that account, are liable to many dangerous disorders, scarce incident to those in which all the parts are more properly proportioned. A small stop in that great blood-vessel, which has been artificially swelled beyond its natural dimensions, and through which an unnatural proportion of the industry and commerce of the country has been forced to circulate, is very likely to bring on the most dangerous disorders upon the whole body politic. The expectation of a rupture with the colonies, accordingly, has struck the people of Great Britain with more terror than they ever felt for a Spanish armada, or a French invasion." (*WN*, 604–605)

finished *The Wealth of Nations*, he actively sought a position as a Commissioner of Customs.

He did not need the job. He had a very comfortable pension from the Duke of Buccleuch. Indeed, he offered to give up that pension when he got the trade position.[22] The attraction of this position was that it gave him access to the inner workings of Mercantilists' effectiveness in shaping the government's trade policy.

In 1784, having served as a Commissioner of Customs for several years, Smith returns to *The Wealth of Nations* project with "Additions and Corrections," the most significant addition being a new chapter in Book IV titled *Conclusion of the Mercantile System.*[23]

That chapter begins with a lengthy review of examples that reflect special interests' influence on trade policy and the self-serving objectives of those lobbyist inspired policies. Smith feels that the draconian punishments built into these policies unmask the power of the lobbyists like the Mercantilists. For example he cites: "By the 8th of Elizabeth, chap. 3, the exporter of sheep, lambs, or rams, was for the first offence, to forfeit all his goods for ever, to suffer a year's imprisonment, and then to have his left hand cut off in a market town, upon a market day, to be there nailed up; and for the second offence, to be adjudged a felon, and to suffer death accordingly" (*WN*, 648).[24]

The Evolution of Smith's Thinking on The Wealth of Nations: Post-1773

Smith's Moral Philosophical vision was framed by the four stages theory (Meek, 1971). This theory held that humankind has evolved through four stages (ergo the name): hunting and gathering, pasturage, agriculture, and finally commercial society. These stages represented progress with each stage embodying a more complex production and distribution system realizing ever greater wealth for the nation. The final stage, commerce, is the pinnacle of humankind's progress. The ideal of the liberal plan represents perfection of the commercial stage, but this is unattainable due to human frailty. The most we can hope for is an approximation of the ideal. With a mind's-eye vision of what the invisible connecting principles of the liberal

---

[22] "Financial inducement could not have been a strong factor … [since] he offered to give up the pension … he held from [the Duke of] Buccleuch on receiving the Customs appointment…." (Ross, 306)

[23] With respect to the "famous chapter of *Wealth*, 'Conclusion of the Mercantile System' … [Anderson, Shughart, and Tollison] suggest two simple links between Smith's customs experience and this added material. First, Commissioner Smith must have acquired a detailed knowledge of the various statutes it was his job to enforce, given his evident diligence; the chapter is based on direct knowledge of relevant laws rather than on secondary sources. Second, Smith may have had ample opportunity as commissioner to observe interest group behavior at first hand as a determinant of economic policy" (Anderson, Shughart, and Tollison, 755).

[24] "It is the industry which is carried on for the benefit of the rich and the powerful, that is principally encouraged by our mercantile system. That which is carried on for the benefit of the poor and the indigent is too often either neglected or oppressed." (WN, 644) "[T]he cruellest of our revenue laws, I will venture to affirm, are mild and gentle, in comparison to some of those which the clamour of our merchants and manufacturers has extorted from the legislature, for the support of their own absurd and oppressive monopolies. Like the laws of Draco, these laws may be said to be all written in blood." (*WN*, 648)

plan are, Smith wrote to identify policies that he believed would facilitate progress toward that perfect condition.

When Smith set about writing *The Wealth of Nations,* he was sanguine about England's successes to date and its prospects for the future. This bears repeating:

"In the midst of all the exactions of government, … capital has been silently and gradually accumulated by the private frugality and good conduct of individuals, by their universal, continual, and uninterrupted effort to better their own condition. It is this effort, protected by law, and allowed by liberty to exert itself in the manner that is most advantageous, which has maintained the progress of England towards opulence and improvement in almost all former times, and which, it is to be hoped, will do so in all future times." (*WN*, 345)[25]

> "In Great Britain industry is perfectly secure; and though it is far from being perfectly free, it is as free or freer than in any other part of Europe." (*WN*, 540)

These quotations reflect the essence of the optimism that fueled Smith's faith in the liberal plan. Individuals exercising frugality and good conduct, who are seeking to better their own condition protected by law and secure in their liberty, will be guided by the invisible hand to make choices that lead society toward opulence and the approximation of the ideal liberal plan.

Upon Smith's return to London in 1773, his growing awareness of the power of Mercantilism to undermine the Liberal Plan diminished his assessment regarding Britain's prospects.[26] We have seen this as the central theme of his 1784 addition to

[25] "England, on account of the natural fertility of the soil, of the great extent of the sea-coast in proportion to that of the whole country, and of the many navigable rivers which run through it, and afford the conveniency of water carriage to some of the most inland parts of it, is perhaps as well fitted by nature as any large country in Europe to be the seat of foreign commerce of manufactures for distant sale, and of all the improvements which these can occasion. From the beginning of the reign of Elizabeth, too, the English legislature has been peculiarly attentive to the interest of commerce and manufactures. … But what is of much more importance than all of them, *the yeomanry of England are rendered as secure, as independent, and as respectable, as law can make them.* … It is now more than two hundred years since the beginning of the reign of Elizabeth, a period as long as the course of human prosperity usually endures." (*WN*, 424–425, emphasis added)

[26] The rulers of Great Britain have, for more than a century past, amused the people with the imagination that they possessed a great empire on the west side of the Atlantic. This empire, however, has hitherto existed in imagination only. It has hitherto been, not an empire, but the project of an empire; not a gold mine, but the project of a gold mine; a project which has cost, which continues to cost, and which, if pursued in the same way as it has been hitherto, is likely to cost, immense expense, without being likely to bring any profit; for the effects of the monopoly of the colony trade, it has been shewn, are to the great body of the people, mere loss instead of profit. It is surely now time that our rulers should either realize this golden dream, in which they have been indulging themselves, perhaps, as well as the people; or that they should awake from it themselves, and endeavour to awaken the people. If the project cannot be completed, it ought to be given up. If any of the provinces of the British empire cannot be made to contribute towards the support of the whole empire, it is surely time that Great Britain should free herself from the expense of defending those provinces in time of war, and of supporting any part of their civil or military establishment in time of peace; and endeavour to accommodate her future views and designs to the real mediocrity of her circumstances." (*WN*, 946–947)

The Wealth of Nations. In his 1790 revised version of *The Theory of Moral Sentiments*. Smith addresses this challenge.

6 A Classical Liberal Superstructure with a Civic Humanist Foundation

The 1790 edition of *The Theory of Moral Sentiments* includes a new Part VI titled, *Of the Character of Virtue*. This new part begins with a reflection on prudence. Prudence is the care and commitment to one's own well-being. It is enlightened self-love (self-interest).

It is the prudent individual who saves. That savings is thrown into the circuit of production where it supports productive labor. That productive labor not only replaces the resources that sustained it; it also generates added revenue that can be reinvested in the circuit of productive labor. Each cycle increases the wealth of the nation. The prudent person, as a saver, is essential to Smith's analysis of *The Wealth of Nations*.

The prudent man is not interested in getting into other people's business or in the business of governing other people. Prudence is not about the community, it is about oneself. "Prudence … when directed merely to the care of the health, the fortune and of the rank and reputation of the individual … commands a certain cold esteem but seems not entitled to any very ardent love or admiration" (*TMS*, 216).

Further down the same page (*TMS*, 216), we see Smith introduce the civic humanist individual's commitment to the wellbeing of the commonwealth and his fellow citizens as enabled in part by his practice of prudence[27]:

> Wise and judicious conduct, when directed to greater and nobler purposes than the care of the health, the fortune, the rank and reputation of the individual, is frequently and very properly called prudence. (*TMS*, 216)
>
> Smith embellishes on this by identifying "superior prudence," as a characteristic of actors who are clearly to be esteemed for their strong and noble commitment to the commonwealth.
>
> We talk of the prudence of the great general, of the great statesman, of the great legislator. Prudence is, in all these cases, combined with many greater and more splendid virtues, with valour, with extensive and strong benevolence, with a sacred regard to the rules of justice, and all these supported by a proper degree of self-command. This *superior prudence*, when carried to the highest degree of perfection, necessarily supposes the art, the talent, and the habit or disposition of acting with the most perfect propriety in every possible circumstance and situation. It necessarily supposes the utmost perfection of all the intellectual and of all the moral virtues. It is the best head joined to the best heart. It is the most perfect wisdom combined with the most perfect virtue. (*TMS*, 216, emphasis added)

[27] In order to inspire this "motivation … [for] the common interest" Smith turns to a progressively more civic humanist voice extolling "citizenship … as an active virtue" (Pocock, 1983, 235).

In this quotation, Smith introduces a subtle but profound expansion of the connotation of prudence. There is "prudence" and now we have "superior prudence." This "superior prudence" is, as the name implies, prudence with the power to reach beyond enlightened self-interest. It is an enabler of noble or heroic action. The simply prudent individual would never sacrifice personal tranquility for power to improve the constitution of the state, and he would certainly not sacrifice his life for the well-being of the commonwealth. Smith is expanding the use of "prudence" beyond self-directed interests to a more noble realm. This broader connotation is only possible when wrapped in the civic humanist arms of "many greater and more splendid virtues, with valour, with extensive and strong benevolence, with a sacred regard to the rules of justice, and all these supported by a proper degree of self-command." It gives us a superior version of human nature, *homo economicus* becomes *homo communitas*.

The lesson Smith learns from his analysis of Mercantilism is that a faction with significant market power (e.g., lucrative natural or artificial monopoly or collusion) has the resources to "intimidate the legislature." It will effectively bully the legislature into defending and expanding that power.

Where does Adam Smith see the antidote to this intimidation coming from? He sees it in a civic humanist leadership that refuses to be intimidated and that is committed first and foremost to the wellbeing of the commonwealth and of every citizen of that commonwealth.

> The leader of the successful party ... if he has authority enough to prevail upon his own friends to act with proper temper and moderation (which he frequently has not), may sometimes render to his country a service much more essential and important than the greatest victories and the most extensive conquests [of the patriot]. He may re-establish and improve the constitution, and from the very doubtful and ambiguous character of the leader of a party, he may assume the greatest and noblest of all characters, that of the reformer and legislator of a great state; and, by the wisdom of his institutions, secure the internal tranquility and happiness of his fellow-citizens for many succeeding generations. (*TMS*, 231-2)

Extolling the virtues of the civic humanist statesman in 1790, Smith cites Solon, "one of the leading figures in the republican 'myth'" (Winch,160), as a model: "The man whose public spirit is prompted altogether by humanity and benevolence, will ... like Solon, when he cannot establish the best system of laws, he will endeavour to establish the best that the people can bear" (*TMS*, 233).

Then, apropos of his own enterprise and his own role in civil society, Smith reminds the leader that a system of philosophy can a valuable tool for policy, but only when it is applied with humility:

> Some general, and even systematical, idea of the perfection of policy and law, may no doubt be necessary for directing the views of the statesman. But to insist upon establishing, and upon establishing all at once, and in spite of all opposition, everything which that idea may seem to require, must often be the highest degree of arrogance. [...] It is to fancy himself the only wise and worthy man in the commonwealth, and that his fellow-citizens should accommodate themselves to him and not he to them. (*TMS*, 234)[28]

[28]This is what Smith refers to as the "man of system ... wise in his own conceit". (*TMS*, 233)

7 Takeaways from *The Wealth of Nations*

In Smith's analysis of *The Wealth of Nations,* the regular citizens who work hard to give their family a tolerable life are the focus of his concern.[29] They are the source of the productive labor that drives the wealth of nations. Smith believed that they deserve a fair share of the fruits of that productivity.

When a nation is on the path to progress, we should observe:

- wages rise,
- profits fall,[30]
- the ranks of society becoming less divided as wages rise and return to capital falls,
- labor becoming more independent from individual or factional capital holders,
- labor becoming more productive, and
- transgenerational control of assets diminishing, and wealth diffused, as reflected in his opposition to laws of entail and primogeniture.

The power of self-serving factions turns that outcome on its head. For example, Mercantilist policies were designed to raise profits, which they did while lowering wages. These policies made workers more dependent because the number of firms with which they could find work diminished.

The Mercantilist's focus on self leads him to undermine the realization of a well-governed society, that prerequisite for the liberal plan to succeed. The Mercantilist is a poster child for the human characteristic that undermines the good government of civil society: human frailty … unbridled self-love.[31]

If we are all motivated only by self-interest (self-love), how can we approximate the liberal plan? We can't. The freedom which the liberal plan requires is an invitation to chaos, the Hobbesian abyss, as factions seek sustained advantages. For freedom to flourish, there needs to be bridles on individuals'/factions' self-interests. Citizens must be "well governed."

Where does Smith believe this well-governed society will come from? It comes from "government" and "Government." The lower case "government" represents socially constructed norms. Each society has sets of norms. These norms may vary among the different factions within a society. The norms are generally tacit

[29] "Their welfare [that of the working class] is the prime concern of economic policy, as Smith conceived it." (Muller, 75)

[30] "In a country which had acquired its full complement of riches, where, in every particular branch of business, there was the greatest quantity of stock that could be employed in it, as the ordinary rate of clear profit would be very small, so the usual market rate of interest which could be afforded out of it would be so low as to render it impossible for any but the very wealthiest people to live upon the interest of their money." (*WN*, 113)

[31] "It cannot be difficult to determine who have been the contrivers of this whole mercantile system; not the consumers, we may believe, whose interest has been entirely neglected; but the producers whose interest has been so carefully attended to; and among this latter class our merchants and manufacturers have been by far the principal architects" (*WN*, 661).

knowledge, seemingly timeless and broadly accepted by the citizenry whose factions they serve. The norms of those with power are reinforced by the visible power of institutional "Government." Thus, there is a price to be paid for challenging the norms of those in power. But social norms can and do change. "Government" can and does so too.

Smith envisioned progress as being made possible by the co-evolution of "government," "Government," and the economic system. The trajectory of that evolution depends on the degree to which more refined standards of inclusive justice are adopted as a common element in the norms (shared values) of all existing factions, affording more and more of the citizens, the independence, security, and opportunities that come with justice. There is a natural selection bias toward those societies that most closely approximate the ideal of justice for all, but even the most advanced society is constantly at risk because human frailty is always present. Individuals with no commitment to the norms of justice pursue their unbridled self-interest and in doing so they undermine the "main pillar" of the liberal plan, justice. Smith sees that as the consequence of Mercantile policies that undermined the British experiment.

To address this challenge, Smith adds a civic humanist voice to provide a foundation to his classical liberal tome, *An Inquiry into the Nature and Causes of the Wealth of Nations*. Sustaining progress toward the liberal ideal, "the liberal plan of equality, liberty and justice" (*WN*, 664)) requires citizens and leaders who are actively committed to the well-being of the community pursuing liberty and justice for all.

Bibliography

Anderson, G. M., Shughart, W. F., II, & Tollison, R. D. (1985). Adam Smith in the custom house. *Journal of Political Economy., 93*(4), 740–759.

Campbell, R. H., & Skinner, A. (1976). "General Introduction." *An inquiry into the nature and causes of the wealth of nations*. In R. H. Campbell & A. Skinner (Eds.), *The Glasgow edition of the works and correspondence of Adam Smith* (Vol. 2, pp. 1–60). Clarendon Press.

Campbell, T. D. (1971). *Adam Smith's science of morals*. George Allen & Unwin Ltd.

Chatbox. n.d. In 1776, traveling from Kirkcaldy, Scotland, to London by horse … Accessed 12August 2025.

Evensky, J. (2005). *Adam Smith's moral philosophy: A historical and contemporary perspective on markets, law, ethics, and culture*. Cambridge University Press.

Evensky, J. (2015). *Adam Smith's wealth of nations: A readers guide*. Cambridge University Press.

Harpham, E. (1984). Liberalism, civic humanism, and the case of Adam Smith. *American Political Science Review., 78*(3), 764–774.

Hont, I., & Ignatieff, M. (1983). *Wealth and virtue: The shaping of political economy in the Scottish enlightenment*. Cambridge University Press.

Hume, D. (1947). *Dialogues concerning natural religion*. Bobbs-Merrill.

Kammen, M. (1970). *Empire and interest: The American colonies and the politics of mercantilism*. J.B. Lippincott Company.

Meek, R. L. (1971). Smith, Turgot, and the 'four stages' theory. *History of Political Economy, 3*(1), 9–27.

Muller, J. (1993). *Adam Smith in his time and ours: Designing the decent society*. The Free Press.

Pocock, J. G. A. (1975). *The Machiavellian moment: Florentine political thought and the Atlantic republican tradition*. Cambridge University Press.

Pocock, J. G. A. (1983). Cambridge paradigms and Scotch philosophers: a study of the relations between civic humanist and the civil jurisprudential interpretation of eighteenth-century social thought. In I. Hont & M. Ignatieff (Eds.), *Wealth and virtue* (pp. 235–252). Cambridge University Press.

Ross, I. (1995). *The life of Adam Smith*. Clarendon Press.

Smith, A. (1976a). The theory of moral sentiments. In D. D. Raphael & A. L. Maefie (Eds.), *The Glasgow edition of the works and correspondence of Adam Smith* (Vol. 1). Clarendon Press.

Smith, Adam. 1976b. *An inquiry into the nature and causes of the wealth of nations*.

Campbell, R. H., & Skinner, A. S. (n.d.). *The Glasgow edition of the works and correspondence of Adam Smith* (Vol. 3). Clarendon Press.

Smith, A. (1977). The correspondence of Adam Smith. In E. C. Mossner & I. S. Ross (Eds.), *The Glasgow edition of the works and correspondence of Adam Smith* (Vol. 6). Clarendon Press.

Smith, A. (1980a). Essays on philosophical subjects. In W. P. D. Wightman & J. C. Bryce (Eds.), *The Glasgow edition of the works and correspondence of Adam Smith* (Vol. 3). Clarendon Press.

Smith, A. (1980b). The principles which lead and direct philosophical enquiries; illustrated by the history of astronomy. In W. P. D. Wightman & J. C. Bryce (Eds.), *Essays on philosophical subjects, the Glasgow edition of the works and correspondence of Adam Smith* (Vol. 3, pp. 33–105). Clarendon Press.

Stevens, D. (1975). Adam Smith and the colonial disturbances. In A. Skinner & T. Wilson (Eds.), *Essays on Adam Smith* (pp. 202–217). Clarendon Press.

Todd, W. B. (1976). "Text and Apparatus." *An Inquiry into the nature and causes of the wealth of nations*. In R. H. Campbell & A. Skinner (Eds.), *The Glasgow edition of the works and correspondence of Adam Smith* (Vol. 2, pp. 61–66). Clarendon Press.

Winch, D. (1978). *Adam Smith's politics: An essay in historiographic revision*. Cambridge University Press.

Tensions in Content and Reception

Adam Smith's Two Moralities

Douglas Den Uyl

1 The Problem

> "Nothing but exemplary morals can give dignity to a man of small fortune." (WN.V.i.g.38)
>
> "The good temper and moderation of contending factions seem to be the most essential circumstances in the public morals of a free people." (WN.V.i.f.40)

One would expect that an author who commands a certain subject area with depth and nuance, as demonstrated through published work on the subject, would display some of the main aspects of that expertise in other works. Such does not seem to be the case with Adam Smith's *Theory of Moral Sentiments* (henceforth TMS) in relation to the latter *An Inquiry into the Nature and Causes of the Wealth of Nations*[1] (henceforth WN).[2] The term "morals" itself appears in a number of places in WN, though most prominently in only two sections of Book V (WN V.i.f—WN V.i.g). The same can be said for the term "morality." These two sections of Book V are the only places in the WN that one finds a "sustained" discussion of

[1] The editions of TMS and WN being used here are: *The Theory of Moral Sentiments,* (Oxford University Press/Liberty Classics: 1982), and *An Inquiry into the Nature and Causes of the Wealth of Nations,* (Oxford University Press/Liberty Classics: 1981).

[2] That there is something different with respect to morality when considering the relationship between TMS and WN has been noted by virtually every sustained commentary on Smith. Simplistically there seem to be two moralities that express two views of human nature and human activity. The WN has one take, and TMS another. For a particularly excellent discussion of the two different looks, see Smith, Vernon L. 1998. "The Two Faces of Adam Smith." Southern Economic Journal 65, no. 1 (July): 1–19.

D. Den Uyl (✉)
Liberty Fund, Indianapolis, IN, USA
e-mail: ddenuyl@libertyfund.org

J. Ostle et al. (eds.), *Adam Smith's Wealth of Nations After 250 Years*, Contributions to Economics, https://doi.org/10.1007/978-3-032-32299-9_6

morals and morality. Several issues connected to morality are brought up in these sections, including discussions of casuistry, the problem of "little sects," and the problem of the "two moralities." It is the last of these that I want to give some attention to here.

> In every civilized society, in every society where the distinction of ranks has, once, been completely established, there have been always two systems of morality current at the same time; of which the one may be called the strict or austere; the other, or, if you will, the liberal or **loose** system. The former is generally admired and revered by the common people; The latter is commonly more esteemed and adopted by what are called people of fashion. The degree of disapprobation with which we ought to mark the vices of levity, the vices which are apt to arise from great prosperity, and from the excess of gaiety and good humour, seems to constitute the principal distinction between those two opposite schemes or systems. In the liberal or loose system, luxury, wanton and even disorderly mirth, the pursuit of pleasure to some degree of intemperance, the breach of chastity, at least in one of the two sexes, &c. provided they are not accompanied with gross indecency, and do not lead to falsehood or injustice, are generally treated with a good deal of indulgence, and are easily either excused or pardoned altogether. In the austere system, on the contrary, those excesses are regarded with the utmost abhorrence and detestation. The vices of levity are always ruinous to the common people, and a single week's thoughtlessness and dissipation is often sufficient to undo a poor workman for ever, and to drive him through despair upon committing the most enormous crimes. The wiser and better sort of the common people, therefore, have always the utmost abhorrence and detestation of such excesses, which their experience tells them are so immediately fatal to people of their condition. The disorder and extravagance of several years, on the contrary, will not always ruin a man of fashion, and people of that rank are very apt to consider the power of indulging in some degree of excess as one of the advantages of their fortune, and the liberty of doing so without censure or reproach, as one of the privileges which belong to their station. In people of their own station, therefore, they regard such excesses with but a small degree of disapprobation, and censure them either very slightly or not at all. (WN V.i.g 10)

This description of moral conduct is missing some of the key elements found in TMS. There is no consultation with the impartial spectator; no activity in the correspondence of sentiments; no sense of concern for what is praiseworthy; no benevolent sociality; and so on. If TMS were an actual description of the sociology of morality (among other things), would we not expect to find some of those central tenets from TMS deployed here, at least to some extent?

What seems to be driving conduct in the WN world, depicted in the foregoing passage, are simply pursuits of self-interest which manifest themselves in various degrees of pursuing personal pleasure, depending on one's circumstances. If there are any central elements of TMS (such as impartial spectating) connected to the description just provided above, they would be found in the third person observer and commentator—in this case, Adam Smith himself. It is possible that the central processes of moral activity described in TMS may exist here as remnants of some original functional guiding principles. Such remnants of active moral norms may allow one to censure "very slightly" some forms of conduct, though without much concern or effect in the cases of persons of rank. And the norms that functionally do exist for persons of rank might be said, in some situations, only to rule in extreme cases—extremes being actions that violate principles of simple justice. In short, not much of the normative world described in TMS seems to be present in the moral world of WN that is depicted in our cited passage.

2 The First Solution

Perhaps, however, we are moving a bit too quickly here. The "common people" do seem to have rather strict functional norms to which they adhere. Going against these norms is wrong because of the potential, even likely, consequences. The consequences would not only be detrimental to the individual but to others in his or her social sphere, such as family members. The "ruin" spoken of in the passage is largely financial ruin, but that alone affects other aspects of one's life and the lives of those around one. True, there does not seem to be any references to the impartial spectator here, but there do seem to be two virtues manifested in the behavior of the common people. Those virtues are justice and prudence.

Besides concerning itself with moral development and the processes involved in moral action, TMS is said to focus on three—possibly four—main virtues. These virtues are justice, prudence, and beneficence. Some add a fourth, namely, self-command.[3] We will stay with the first three just mentioned. I have argued elsewhere[4] that WN is concerned with the first two of these virtues—justice and prudence. Given that the WN is focused upon wealth and commerce, there is little to say about benevolence and beneficence. Justice, it turns out, is needed in every social situation as its very grounding. So the virtue *especially* associated with commerce—and thus WN—would be, and is, prudence. Let us accept this characterization for now. If so, one can see immediately that prudence is the dominant virtue in the rendition of moral activity in our passage above, at least for the common people, again, with justice always in the background. Smith defines prudence as follows:

> The care of the health, of the fortune, of the rank and reputation of the individual, the objects upon which his comfort and happiness in this life are supposed to principally to depend, is considered as the proper business of that virtue which is commonly called Prudence. (TMS VI.i.5)[5]

[3] Smith himself says self-command is a virtue (e.g., TMS III.3.37). However to my way of thinking it supports the other three virtues and in itself is not always a good. An evil doer with great self-command might do more harm than another with less or none. If the term virtue is used simply to mean "a good thing to have," then of course it is a virtue. Something similar can be said about propriety which Smith considers in TMS VII.II.1. Similar to self-command, propriety is found in all virtues and impropriety all vices, but neither stands alone. When they are made to do so absurdity, not virtue, is the result.(TMS VII.ii.1.50)

[4] See my, "Sympathy, Sentiment and Commerce: Prudence, Exchange, and Correspondence in the Wealth of Nations," forthcoming in the *Independent Review*.

[5] The word "supposed" is interesting, and we shall say something about it below.

The possible ruin of fortune among the common people would certainly affect health and rank if one suffers such ruin. It might be objected that the concerns and actions of the common people, exhibited in our passage, are not instances of moral virtue because the adherence to norms of sobriety, etc. are being followed for the wrong reason. The norms of prudence are not being followed because they are right, but simply because they are in one's own interest and for one's own well-being. As it turns out, that is exactly what prudence demands—that we take care of our interests and thus our health, fortune, and reputation. Self-interest is just what is required in such circumstances; hence, the objection turns out to be no real objection at all.

For persons of rank, the issue is a bit more complicated. It does seem that Smith is using the same standards of prudence as he does for the common people, as we see from his commentary on the excesses of persons of rank. Moreover, Smith is judging from a third-person perspective, measuring the actions of those persons of rank as an "impartial spectator" would. Even if the person of rank is not harmed by the likes of "disorderly mirth," that person has nonetheless crossed a line for Smith. This negative judgment on line crossing employs the same prudential norms used for the common people. Hence, those norms apparently still apply, even if negative consequences for particular persons of rank are not dire or are non-existent. That is because moral norms are embedded socially for Smith; norms discouraging excessive mirth are generally more desirable overall to have socially extant than not having them.[6]

Our conclusion then is that with prudence being the primary virtue and motivator in a commercial order, we have an answer to our opening "problem." That answer is that there is no inconsistency here with TMS, only a narrowing of focus. Instead of worrying about all categories of virtue and their particular norms, WN, when it considers virtue at all, focuses on the one most relevant to the subject matter at hand, namely, prudence. There is no claim that prudence is the only virtue, or that it is "better" than the others, or even that one must prioritize it over all other virtues at all times in the commercial world. It is simply the case that for the very most part, prudence is the predominant virtue in commerce. This narrowing of focus is not a sign of inconsistency but of special attention. And this narrowing is even more narrow than first appearances might suggest, for there is a "superior" form of prudence Smith discusses in TMS that does not show up here at all. We shall mention this superior form later, but for now we seem to have shown that TMS is not ignored so much as it is truncated in WN.

[6] Of course, culture may change some of this, although there would be limits that would not be culturally relative. See, for example, the discussion of natural justice below.

3 The Second "Solution"

We could end our query here if it was not for the fact that Smith uses parallel language of the strict and the loose morality in TMS itself. Here, the two modalities are represented in moral theorizing, rather than moral practice. The following is what Smith says about this division in moral theorizing:

> ...the rules of justice are the only rules of morality which are precise and accurate; that those of all other virtues are loose, vague, and indeterminant; that the first may be compared to the rules of grammar; the others to those which critics lay down for the attainment of what is sublime and elegant in composition, and which present us rather with a general idea of the perfection we ought to aim at, than afford us any certain and infallible directions for acquiring it.
>
> As the different rules of morality admit such different degrees of accuracy, those authors who have endeavored to collect and digest them into systems have done it in two different manners; and one set has followed through the whole that loose method to which they were naturally directed by the consideration of one species of virtues; while another has as universally endeavored to introduce into their precepts that sort of accuracy of which only some of them are susceptible. (TMS VII.iv.1-2)

The second school mentioned—the precise group—no doubt refers to the casuists and casuistry of which Smith is highly critical (TMS VII.iv.7ff; WN V.i.30–36). The first set of moral theorists (ones dealing with looseness) includes "all the ancient moralists" (WN VII.iv.3). "All the ancient moralists" might be a bit too sweeping, but it is largely accurate. The ancients were predominantly concerned with what we today would call "virtue ethics." The norms of virtue ethics take the form of principles or practices exercised through certain traits of character. A norm like avoiding excessive mirth would call for a seriousness of character, but how much mirth is too much is loose indeed. Persons of rank exploit that openness. By contrast, the casuists treat all moral norms as if they were rules of justice, not only by trying to carefully make them into precise rules, but also by supposing that this is both necessary and desirable for true moral conduct. What interests us here is that a Smithean moral philosophy seeks to incorporate both the loose and the strict.

As we have already noticed, rules of justice must be precise and specifically functional. This is because rules of justice define the context for permissible actions as well as serving to adjudicate claims made by some against others. Looseness here would spell chaos. Moreover, justice is the controller of a very negative but necessary sentiment—resentment.[7] Resentment arises when it is perceived that one person has injured or offended another. Resentment compels precision because acting from resentment alone can easily become excessive in its response. But without it, the motivation to abide by the rules would be virtually non-existent, because of too loose a commitment to them.

[7] For a fine discussion of resentment see: Michelle Schwarze, *Recognizing Resentment: Sympathy, Injustice, and Liberal Political Thought,* Cambridge University Press, 2020. David Hume and Adam Smith are the main thinkers discussed in this work.

It should be noted that Smith tends to use "justice" most of the time in a certain way that does not include what the term itself often covers. He is perfectly aware of the alternatives, but for his purposes—namely, purposes which are social and political—one use is most appropriate. His sticking to this one form helps explain his constant assertions about the strictness of justice. He says,

> The word, it is to be observed, which expresses justice in the Greek language, has several different meanings; and as the correspondent word in all other languages, so far as I know, has the same,...In one sense we are said to do justice to our neighbour when we abstain from doing him any positive harm, and do not directly hurt him, either in his person, or in his estate, or in his reputation. This is that justice which I have treated of above, the observance of which may be extorted by force, and the violation of which exposes to punishment. In another sense we are said not to do justice to our neighbour unless we conceive for him all that love, respect, and esteem, which his character, his situation, and his connexion with ourselves, render suitable and proper for us to feel, and unless we act accordingly. It is in this sense that we are said to do injustice to a man of merit who is connected with us, though we abstain from hurting him in every respect...(TMS VII.ii.1.10)

Smith makes the same main point much earlier in TMS: "we may often fulfill all the rules of justice by sitting still and doing nothing" (TMS II.ii.1.10). He points out that the sort of justice which is fulfilled by "doing nothing" is often labeled "commutative" justice, whereas the other form goes by "distributive" justice. Smith almost always is supposing commutative justice when he speaks of justice. That is certainly the case in this famous passage from the WN:

> All systems, either of preference or of restraint, therefore, being thus completely taken away, the obvious and simple system of natural liberty establishes itself of its own accord. Every man, as long as he does not violate the laws of justice, is left perfectly free to pursue his own interest his own way...(WN IV.ix.51)

The commutative justice referred to here is "natural" justice which may not always be reflected in practice, as we note below. Still, commutative justice is the model of justice Smith is working with which also explains why strictness is called for. Social order could not be maintained with looseness about what injures or not because we respond to those injuries with coercion, namely, punishment. It would be unjust in itself to respond to any alleged injury with whatever level of coercion the responder desired. Smith's predominant use of commutative justice may have influenced the future of an understanding of what government should do. For perhaps a way of thinking about what so-called "classical liberalism" is, is to say that the state is to limit itself predominantly to concerns of commutative justice.

So, while the rules of justice need to be well-defined, and corrected if they are not well defined, other moral norms—even ones expressing strong obligations—are much more open ended. For example, the virtue of prudence allows one to act for oneself only, but to what degree, and is that degree the same for all persons? We all concur that there can be excessive self-interest, but we likely differ on the degree in which excess is manifest. We may also be held to obligations of benevolence and charity, but here also to what degree? It is possible, in other words, that by ignoring the virtue of prudence, one can exceed an otherwise appropriate level of giving to others. We are familiar with those who put their own circumstances in jeopardy while acting for others. But that level of jeopardy may be different for one person and another. We might also come up with a precise number—say 10% of one's income—that some religions or churches have adopted as the "right" amount of giving. But this sort of precision is a generalization, and does not answer the question of whether 9% or 11% might be better, and better for whom. It is probably the "right" number with respect to the convenience of having some number as a guide, but not necessarily with respect to the act of benevolence itself.

What then is ethics beholden to, and what may call for some open endedness and variations in ethical judgments? The answer in Smith's case is experience. Experience here refers, largely but by no means exclusively, to the outcome, or how things turned out, and whether these results are favorable, good, or pleasing, or whether they are unfavorable, bad, or displeasing. Smith allows our sentiments to vary in both ways. Smith says,

> Fortune has in this, as well as in some other respects already mentioned, great influence over the moral sentiments of mankind, and, according as she is either favourable or adverse, can render the same character the object, either of general love and admiration, or of universal hatred and contempt. This great disorder in our moral sentiments is by no means, however, without its utility…(TMS VI.iii,30)

Hence,

> That the world judges by the event, and not by the design, has been in all ages the complaint, and is the great discouragement of virtue. Everybody agrees to the general maxim, that as the event does not depend on the agent, it ought to have no influence upon our sentiments,…But when we come to particulars, we find that our sentiments are scarce in any one instance exactly conformable to what this equitable maxim would direct.(TMS II.iii.3.1)

Smith is claiming that the results matter significantly in how we judge an action. If, for example, you stumble into something and create a positive effect of some sort—even though there was no intention on your part to do so—you are likely to be given almost as much credit as if you had intended the result. Similarly, if you had very good intentions, but negative effects, you could not even control, come about, the value of your good intentions will at least be dampened if not ignored or dismissed altogether. You might even be blamed despite the fact that you could not have changed the outcome. The intention and effort to abide by a norm (responsibility) accounts for less or more depending on the result. Smith is saying that in the end, the positive or negative experience is what will count—not your intentions or what he refers to often as the "design."

All these anomalies in Smith fall under the heading of the "irregularities of our moral sentiments." They are "irregular" because "usually" we would assume that good intentions and good results go together, as do bad to bad, and that we should judge them together proportionately. That Smith points to these irregularities is often given a nod by commentators but seldom discussed. For our purposes, however, this phenomenon is of importance. It is important if for no other reason than Smith asserts that such anomalies are a good thing: "nature...

when she implanted the seeds of this irregularity in the human breast, seems, as upon all other occasions, to have intended the happiness and perfection of the species" (TMS II.iii.3.2).

To see why Smith would say this, imagine a world where the reverse held, where we sought to punish or reward actions solely or primarily on their "design." If that were the case, every bad thought we had would be a candidate for punishment, and every good thought for reward. Apart from the fact that we could never get to all the thoughts, actual practice would become extremely unmanageable because a large portion of the incentive to actually do things correctly would be gone. If I get your praise just for my good "design" or positive sentiment, why bother worrying too much about the outcome? One has already secured approval. The following then is what Smith says about what fortune does to us:

> [T]hough the intentions of any person should be ever so proper and beneficent on the one hand, or ever so improper and malevolent on the other; yet if he has failed in producing either the good or the evil which he intended, as one of the exciting causes is wanting in both cases, less gratitude seems due to him in the one, and less resentment in the other. (TMS II.iii.1.7)

And this is so because:

> The effect of this influence of fortune is, first, to diminish our sense of the merit or demerit of those actions which arose from the most laudable or blamable intentions, when they fail of producing their proposed effects; and secondly, to increase our sense of the merit or demerit of actions, beyond what is due to the motives or affections from which they proceed, when they accidentally give occasion either to extraordinary pleasure or pain. (TMS II.iii.2.1)

From what we have seen so far, it is no wonder Smith says it is God's place to judge our intentions, not ours (TMS II.iii.3.2). For if we had that role, "every court of judicature would become a real inquisition." So apart from the unpleasantness of an inquisition, what do these irregularities teach us generally about morality? To answer such questions, we must answer the question of what morality is for? Or to put it another way, what is the purpose of morality?

Smith has an answer to this question, and the answer is that the purpose of morality is human "happiness." As we saw a moment ago, nature "intended the happiness and perfection of the species." Moral norms, if we follow them, exist so that we can, for the most part, live happy lives. Following them generally produces that happiness, for that is what they were "designed" to produce. And what is happiness for Smith? Happiness for Smith is basically peace, enjoyment, and tranquility.

> Happiness consists in tranquility and enjoyment. Without tranquility there can be no enjoyment; and where there is perfect tranquility there is scarce anything which is not capable of amusing. (TMS III.3.30)

Saying moral norms are in the service of happiness does not mean that all moral norms produce or regulate only pleasant events. A person who, out of righteous resentment, demands punishment for a certain injury is not dealing with something pleasant. Nevertheless, maintaining justice in this way does serve the peace and tranquility, and even to some extent the enjoyment, of the society.

Now since "man was made for action" (TMS II.ii.3.3), according to Smith, it is best to concentrate on what one can do to encourage certain positive outcomes and to discourage what would diminish such positive outcomes. Indeed, the essence of morality is "to promote by the exertion of [one's] faculties such changes in the external circumstances both of himself and others, as may seem most favourable to the happiness of all" (TMS II.iii.3.3). What is most favorable to all is what is conducive to peace and tranquility and enjoyment on both the personal and social levels.

But there's an addendum to the idea of happiness for the individual which is to recognize that "the chief part of human happiness arises from the consciousness of being beloved" (TMS I.ii.5.1; III.i.7). We are most, and perhaps only, beloved when we are worthy of being beloved, and sticking closely to the norms of morality is certainly a way to be worthy. From the opening line of TMS onward, socialization has been the focus of Smith's ethics, and he details the various ways we can come together or are torn apart. For example, early on in TMS Smith speaks of "the pleasure of mutual sympathy" and the "correspondence of sentiment" (TMS I.i.2.1–3). We want to share our sentiments with those of others and they to us. The desire for sociality is primitive within us, and Smith goes into great detail about the ways in which we do and do not sympathize with others. We cannot follow him here, but through all that detail, the end remains the same—a peaceful, enjoyable, and tranquil society.

Something similar can be said about one of Smith's other central concepts—the impartial spectator (henceforth IS). Because moral norms are generalized across society, it is important that there be a standpoint of impartiality when assessing the relevance or applicability of a moral norm to certain actions. Yet, the IS is not just ruling impartially. The IS is examining actions based on their *worthiness* of respect.[8] Such an evaluation seems at least one step removed from the ordinary experience of results or outcomes, since the primary purpose is not just to be impartial toward the actions, but to apply to it standards of worthiness. The standards used to judge worthiness do not refer simply or immediately to results but also to attitudes, dispositions, and habits of the actors. Indeed, this is why Smith cannot be called a consequentialist in our modern sense (see below). Worthiness may often have little or nothing to do directly with consequences and more to do with attitude.

Hence, the concept of experience itself is broader than just outcomes. It can include responses, attitudes, evaluations, and the like. Moreover, other explanations might be offered of why worthiness may not present itself simply in terms of what happens. If nature intends our happiness, perhaps the only way to ensure that people will follow the appropriate norms leading to happiness is to present them in rule-like form without reference to the experiences that stand behind the norms and helped formulate them in the first place. The norms may have evolved over time through numerous tests of experience before solidifying themselves as moral norms. And if the norms were laid down by God, as Smith also sometimes suggests, they

---

[8] I argue for this in "Impartial Spectating and the Price Analogy," *Econ Journal Watch*, https://econjwatch.org/articles/impartial-spectating-and-the-price-analogy.

would still be looking toward the experience of happiness being ultimately the standard of value. If man really was made for action, it would make little sense if the norms he was obliged to follow led him away from, rather than toward, happiness. In short, Smith's standard of happiness ensures a bias toward judgments from experience.

Returning to the two moralities of the WN with which we began, it would seem happiness is at some distance from this situation, for the ordinary person is under some tight restrictions on how to act, and persons of rank are continually and happily flaunting the norms. Norms producing happiness seem quite distant. Yet, perhaps this situation is another "irregularity" where the norms, despite appearances, are nevertheless the best ones to have. The apparent unfairness is preferable to abandoning the norms entirely, because we know we cannot lessen the grip of these norms of prudence on the common people without producing bad consequences—consequences which outweigh the consequences of the rich taking liberties with these same norms. Social tranquility is best served by keeping these norms meaningfully and fully in play. Hence, again, there are not two different moralities, but two different behaviors. It is clear from the passage with which we started that Smith holds to keeping the prudential norms in place while chastising deviations from them, even when there is little in negative consequences befalling the individual of rank in her deviations.

We have seen that Smith likes to use a dual contrast approach, then finding the truth somewhere in the middle of letting either rule completely. In this particular case, the common man wants to be more like the person of rank, and the norms of prudence are a help in getting there. In a way, then, there is a mean between holding down the advancement of the common man, on the one hand, and, on the other hand, letting a person flaunt norms that do not have the same impact upon him in their violation as they once did.[9] The norms of prudence do fit in the category of "loose" norms, and this allows individuals to take advantage of openings that, under other circumstances, would be detrimental to their well-being. As we have noticed, in general, it is best to keep the norms of prudence rather tight; but by the same token, one is following those norms to achieve not just basic security but also a position of rank and fortune.

Keeping the norms of prudence tight is suggested by its possible proximity to justice when a person possesses the virtuous character identified as prudence. Consider the following:

> Proper resentment for injustice attempted, or actually committed, is the only motive which, in the eyes of the impartial spectator, can justify our hurting or disturbing in any respect the happiness of our neighbour… The wisdom of every state or commonwealth endeavours,… to restrain those who are subject to its authority, from hurting or disturbing the happiness of one another. The rules which it establishes for this purpose, constitute the civil and criminal law of each particular state or country. The principles upon which those rules either are, or ought to be founded, are the subject of a particular science,… that of natural jurisprudence.

[9] It is interesting that what Smith concentrates on when discussing Aristotle is his doctrine of the mean. (TMS VII.ii.I.12ff)

> A sacred and religious regard not to hurt or disturb in any respect the happiness of our neighbour, even in those cases where no law can properly protect him, constitutes the character of the perfectly innocent and just man; a character which, when carried to a certain delicacy of attention, is always highly respectable and even venerable for its own sake, and can scarce ever fail to be accompanied with many other virtues, with great feeling for other people, with great humanity and great benevolence. (TMS VI.ii.intro.2)

Here is the commutative justice mentioned earlier inscribed in a person's character. One type of character in whom this sort of justice is inscribed is the ordinary prudent person who "in his conduct and conversation…is an exact observer of decency, and respects with an almost religious scrupulosity, all the established decorums and ceremonials of society" (TMS VI.i.10). Later, when discussing "superior" prudence (mentioned below), Smith combines prudence with other virtues such as benevolence and valor to arrive at superior prudence which always has "a sacred regard for the rules of justice" (TMS VI.i.15). All levels, then, of prudence respect most especially the rules of commutative justice and that respect is part of the character of a "prudent man." Perhaps, we could conclude by saying that although there may be sophisticated forms of prudence, with some forms being "looser" than others, they all are similar in having that "sacred regard for the rules of justice."

Smith takes a similar approach in working with loose and strict when discussing moral theory generally. We saw earlier a bit more tolerance of the loose approach to morals generally, although there are times when the strict version is a necessity. From this, we are not entitled to conclude that there are two or three different moralities. Rather, we should be concluding that "happiness" may call for different approaches under different circumstances. For if experience—that is mostly, outcomes—is ruled by the ends of peace and tranquility and enjoyment, one would expect different settings to call for diverse modes or rules of appropriate action.

The picture becomes a bit more complicated when one realizes that there are other more nuanced forms of happiness than peace and tranquility normally understood. There is, for example, something called "superior prudence" in Smith which goes well beyond the kind of prudence applicable to our opening passage. To wit:

> Wise and judicious conduct, when directed to greater and nobler purposes than the care of the health, the fortune, the rank and reputation of the individual, is frequently and very properly called prudence… This superior prudence, when carried to the highest degree of perfection, necessarily supposes the art, the talent, and the habit or disposition of acting with the most perfect propriety in every possible circumstance and situation. It necessarily supposes the utmost perfection of all the intellectual and of all the moral virtues. It is the best head joined to the best heart. It is the most perfect wisdom combined with the most perfect virtue. (TMS VI.i.15)

This superior prudence is not only rare because it is so difficult to attain but also is quite different from ordinary prudence. The first line of this passage dismisses what defined ordinary prudence in the first place, cited earlier. Happiness, in this case, would have to be a different sort of "peace and tranquility" than one gets with ordinary prudence. We might recall Smith's use of "supposed" in the original definition of prudence given above. In using that term, he may have been signaling toward this superior prudence. All this suggests that Smith is not only open to "loose" uses of certain moral concepts but is also doing ethics for the vast majority of ordinary people, rather than the few. He mentions but does not focus upon these rare and superior forms of conduct. Smith is more interested in what can produce peace and tranquility for the middling classes. Individuals of superior prudence are especially absent in the WN as our opening "two morality" passage indicates. WN is governed by ordinary prudence and any deviations from that form that might occur under usual circumstances.

One other point about prudence should be noted here. Ryan Hanley correctly points to the connection between prudence and self-command.[10] Smith's complaint that we witnessed in our opening citation about the two moralities is evidence of this connection. All the vices Smith mentions there are matters of giving in to pleasures rather than controlling them. And the reason we need to judge strongly against pleasure in those cases is to keep from weakening the power of self-command. There may be prudential situations that do not require much in the way of self-command, but those were not part of Smith's examples. Smith instead hints that giving oneself over to profligacy can have the same result for persons of rank as it does to the common man—perhaps just taking much longer for members of the first group to fall into a situation where negative effects make an impact. Sound judgments and the will to follow them are the substance of the procedural part of prudence. The need for self-command then comes up in varying degrees but is applicable to every virtue at every stage—the virtue of prudence being no exception. The difficulty or ease with which one deploys self-command has a lot to do with the degree of positive or negative judgment of moral value we accord to any action or virtue.

This mention of virtue brings up another one of Smith dualisms useful for our purposes here. Smith says that virtue comes in two basic types, the amiable and the respectable. To wit:

> Upon these two different efforts, upon that of the spectator to enter into the sentiments of the person principally concerned, and upon that of the person principally concerned, to bring down his emotions to what the spectator can go along with, are founded two different sets of virtues. The soft, the gentle, the amiable virtues, the virtues of candid condescension and indulgent humanity, are founded upon the one: the great, the awful and respectable, the virtues of self-denial, of self-government, of that command of the passions which subjects all the movements of our nature to what our own dignity and honour, and the propriety of our own conduct require, take their origin from the other. (TMS I.i.5.1)

The opening of this passage points to a process Smith elsewhere describes as a "correspondence of sentiments." I try to enter into your sentiments while you pitch them at a level where I can do so (e.g., neither too strong nor too weak). You also follow the same process toward me. What follows that description in the passage above is a statement of the two types of virtues—namely, the "amiable" and the "respectable." I do not believe the passage should be read as saying the amiable attaches to one side of the correspondence and the respectable to the other. Rather, the two types of virtues are each grounded in the entire process of correspondence

[10] Ryan P. Hanley, *Adam Smith and the Character of Virtue,* (Cambridge University Press, 2009) Chap. 4. Hanley goes a bit too far when he claims, "prudence is itself a species of an account of self-command." It is actually more the reverse; self-command is a tool utilized by the virtue of prudence.

to different effects. Given this, we might plausibly conclude that ordinary prudence falls into the class of respectable virtues. This is because prudence calls for a level of self-command that involves self-government and self-denial. Amiable virtues, on the other hand, tend to fall under the benevolence category. There is always some self-command involved, but of a kind one would want to "indulge."

The distinction between amiable and respectable virtues seems like another "two moralities" problem. Smith even closes the section where these two types of virtues are discussed with another dualism between complete and partial perfection when it comes to assessing an action or character. The distance between the two perfections affects the degree of positive judgment one accords, with the greater distance diminishing accordingly the degree of positive affirmation. But Smith admits that in the real world we mostly live in, partial perfections may predominate.

So just as soon as we think we have nailed down the place for a virtue like prudence, we remember that there are two prudences—one ordinary and one superior. The latter has a kind of self-command simply missing in the former. That "new" form of self-command moves Smith to say the following:

> Virtue is excellence, something uncommonly great and beautiful, which rises far above what is vulgar and ordinary. The amiable virtues consist in that degree of sensibility which surprises by its exquisite and unexpected delicacy and tenderness. The awful and respectable, in that degree of self-command which astonishes by its amazing superiority over the most ungovernable passions of human nature.

From this description, superior prudence might pick up some degrees of amiableness! We cannot indulge this line of inquiry any further here. The main reason for doing so at all is to indicate that Smith has a complex and nuanced moral theory, much of which is unlikely to be manifested in the world of commerce being discussed in WN. Moreover, that complexity that exists in our sentiments is a result of the complexity and diversity of our experiences. The various dualisms Smith puts forward help us see that complexity and its applicability, or lack thereof, to a given set of circumstances. In the commercial world, the level of virtue described in the foregoing passage is not often seen, but fortunately also not often needed for moving an economy forward. If such refinement were called for, wealth would be very hard to come by.

4 Casuistry

A way of supporting our claim that experience rules in Smith is to detour a bit into Smith's view of casuistry. We will not be concerned whether Smith has understood casuistry correctly,[11] only how his view of it helps us understand his reasoning about

[11] There is some reason to believe he has not been completely accurate in his discussion of casuistry. For a bit more balanced view one might consult the following: Albert R. Jonson and Steohan E. Toulmin, *The Abuse of Casuistry: A History of Moral Reasoning*, (Berkeley: University of California Press) 1988. In the secondary literature on Smith not much is made of casuistry. An exception is Eric Schliesser's book *Adam Smith: Systematic Philosopher and Public Thinker*, (Oxford: Oxford University Press) 2017, pp 126–132.

morality elsewhere. Smith's view of the value of casuistry itself is very clear, "casuistry ought to be rejected altogether" (TMS VII.iv.33). But what exactly is casuistry, and what does it do that Smith is so forcefully rejecting? Casuistry, in general, means the imposition of strict rules having moral status upon situations where they either do not apply or cannot apply. The "do not apply" could be taken in a number of ways, but Smith seems to regard it as the propensity to apply strict moral rules to virtually every situation that has a moral dimension to it. The other part of the meaning of casuistry ("cannot apply") is the forcing of strict rules upon particular cases where they are clearly not called for as Smith sees them. That situation could also be described as "should not apply."

The result of seeing casuistry as Smith does gives us a good insight into how he understands the end of morality and how it should function. Consider the following from WN:

> Wherein consisted the happiness and perfection of a man, considered not only as an individual, but as the member of a family, of a state, and of the great society of mankind, was the object which the ancient moral philosophy proposed to investigate. In that philosophy, the duties of human life were treated of as subservient to the happiness and perfection of human life, but when moral, as well as natural philosophy, came to be taught only as subservient to theology, the duties of human life were treated of as chiefly subservient to the happiness of a life to come. In the ancient philosophy, the perfection of virtue was represented as necessarily productive, to the person who possessed it, of the most perfect happiness in this life. In the modern philosophy, it was frequently represented as generally, or rather as almost always, inconsistent with any degree of happiness in this life; and heaven was to be earned only by penance and mortification, by the austerities and abasement of a monk, not by the liberal, generous, and spirited conduct of a man. Casuistry, and an ascetic morality, made up, in most cases, the greater part of the moral philosophy of the schools. By far the most important of all the different branches of philosophy became in this manner by far the most corrupted. (WN V.I.f.30)

Notice first the antipathy to casuistry. Morality and moral theory hold a central place in the various branches of philosophy, but in the hands of the casuists, it becomes thoroughly debased. And what is this debasement? As we noted earlier, Smith regards happiness as the end of morality, but casuistry produces the opposite, at least in this life. Indeed, we see from the passage that morality for Smith is essentially about *this* life. That does not mean that morality stands against the next one. We saw earlier that God intended that following moral norms would lead one to happiness and thus that moral conduct in this life was approved for the next. What was not approved of was the ascetic life demanded by the casuists. There are debates among scholars about Smith's degree of acceptance of religion.[12] Whatever the truth may be about Smith's own commitment to religion, he never gives the impression that virtue is not connected to earthly happiness or that it detracts from attaining

[12] A couple examples of the debate might be: Russell Nieli,"Skepticism, Stoicism, and Providence: The Religious Temper of Adam Smith "*Harvard Theological Review* 79, no. 1–3 (1986): 341–368 on the pro side; and Gavin Kennedy, "Adam Smith and Religion" *History of Economic Ideas* 19, no. 2 (2011): 5–28 on the con side.

happiness in the next life; nor does he suppose one *must* see religion as rejecting happiness.

Another problem Smith has with casuistry allows us to see another feature of Smith's moral philosophy. This is the problem of what might be called the obscuring of sentiment. This problem fits in the category of "what cannot apply"—in this case a rule is unfitted because it would obscure the functioning of sentiment which itself is necessary to arrive at an accurate moral judgment.

> It may be said in general of the works of the casuists that they attempted, to no purpose, to direct by precise rules what it belongs to feeling and sentiment only to judge of. How is it possible to ascertain by rules the exact point at which, in every case, a delicate sense of justice begins to run into a frivolous and weak scrupulosity of conscience? When it is that secrecy and reserve begin to grow into dissimulation? How far an agreeable irony may be carried, and at what precise point it begins to degenerate into a detestable lie? What is the highest pitch of freedom and ease of behaviour which can be regarded as graceful and becoming, and when it is that it first begins to run into a negligent and thoughtless licentiousness? With regard to all such matters, what would hold good in any one case would scarce do so exactly in any other, and what constitutes the propriety and happiness of behaviour varies in every case with the smallest variety of situation. Books of casuistry, therefore, are generally as useless as they are commonly tiresome.

Despite what may be supposed about moral judgements, for Smith they are often nuanced and subtle. The exception to this are judgments of justice which are strict and invariable. To force upon a non-juridical action, a juridical type judgment is to obscure or remove any sentiment that would be involved in correctly assessing the moral act. Many, if not most, moral situations are not matters of justice but of benevolence, or prudence, or gratitude, or sociability, and the like. With respect to these sorts of cases "what would hold good in any one case would scarce do so exactly in any other." Here, we see some of the "looseness" spoken of earlier. Such looseness leaves room for subtlety of judgment and diversity of action. More importantly, this looseness does not obstruct the happiness that can come from proper moral action, since a significant part of producing that happiness is the production of the correct sentiments for Smith. After all, the title of his work on morality is a "theory of moral sentiments" and not a "theory of justice." Happiness and unhappiness are expressed primarily through sentiment.

A third form of perversion found in casuistry is tied to the last one to a large degree. The problem here is again a version of treating moral norms as if they were rules of justice. We find this complaint in the opening line of the passage presented just above from the WN. The treating of moral norms this way actually weakens the effect and recognition of true juridical norms by removing the ability to realize that the need for precision in this area does not transfer over to other types of moral norms and situations. Even more interesting is how the casuists, in some instances through this very strictness, are encouraging movement away from propriety. In law, strictness is a practical necessity, but that does not necessarily mean that it completely and accurately represents what Smith calls "natural jurisprudence." Indeed, it is unlikely to do so.

> Every system of positive law may be regarded as a more or less imperfect attempt towards a system of natural jurisprudence, or towards an enumeration of the particular rules of justice....In no country do the decisions of positive law coincide exactly, in every case, with the rules which the natural sense of justice would dictate. Systems of positive law, therefore, though they deserve the greatest authority, as the records of the sentiments of mankind in different ages and nations, yet can never be regarded as accurate systems of the rules of natural justice. (TMS VII.iv.36)

Hence, even when it comes to justice, strictness, while necessary, may give one a false impression of complete accuracy. It appears inaccurate to say that justice too is "loose." For with justice, the norms of natural justice are likely to be recognized in the same way by various people at various times. That does not make natural justice loose, but rather to various degrees distant from the actual practice of justice. Casuistry does not recognize that distance and thus inhibits the necessary and valuable guidance natural justice could be providing by supposing instead that their rules were complete.

From all of this, one can see that Smith did not encourage the adoption of any moral system that was not fostering happiness in the world we actually live in. The other worldly focus of some approaches to morality result in experiences and forms of practice that either do not help or positively block successful experiences in this life. One more passage should suffice. Notice who and what should be the objects of sound moral advice and experience mentioned in the second sentence of the following citation.

> The alterations which the universities of Europe thus introduced into the ancient course of philosophy were all meant for the education of ecclesiastics, and to render it a more proper introduction to the study of theology. But the additional quantity of subtlety and sophistry, the casuistry and ascetic morality which those alterations introduced into it, certainly did not render it more for the education of gentlemen or men of the world, or more likely either to improve the understanding or to mend the heart. (WN V.i.f.32)

5 Are There Two Moralities?

> "How selfish soever man may be supposed, there are evidently some principles in his nature, which interest him in the fortune of others, and render their happiness necessary to him, though he derives nothing from it except the pleasure of seeing it." (TMS I.i.I.1)

This very famous opening line of TMS sets exactly the tone and setting of the insights to come. Our basic inherent self-interest is recognized and prioritized, but subject to some modifications, namely, a natural interest in others. Neither of these "principles" wipes out the other, so we are called upon to somehow reconcile them. The interest in others turns out to be as powerful, if not at times more powerful, than self-interest for Smith. Notice also that it is not just others we are interested in but the "fortune" of others, meaning broadly what they do and how they do it and the resulting experiences. That of course fits with our narrative here that experience—that is, what happens along with the following reactions and evaluations—is the test of success as determined by what promotes "happiness." Happiness itself usually, if not always, gets expressed in sentiment. Ethics then is the study of norms for, and principles of, actions conducive to happiness. Morality is the embodiment of these norms and principles with immorality being their violation.

Smith's ethics is a thoroughly socialized ethics. We saw this with our "two moralities" opening passage where we stuck with norms which, even when broken without much adverse effect for some, were adhered to for the good of society as a whole. Even more important than the specific norms themselves is the balance Smith insists upon when examining his "principles." The impartial spectator is always needed to counter the perspective of self-interest. But that spectator is not out to obliterate self-interest, but to ensure it remains in its proper place. Indeed, something is just as wrong with the moralist who wants to suppress or abandon self-interest altogether as with the person who thinks every action is all self-interest (TMS III.3.1ff). As Charles Griswold notes about this latter view, "the prudent man is not *homo economicus*."[13] Prudence is, after all, a virtue which suggests at least a modicum of self-command and concern for others. Smith does lean toward the good of society taking precedence over the individual when considering any recommendation for action. What is interesting, and attested to in the first line of TMS, is that we, when all is said and done, may have that bias ourselves. After all, our greatest source of happiness, especially when thought of in terms of tranquility, comes largely from having the approval of others.

What we have examined above also points us to a conclusion that Smith's ethics is not at all like the two main approaches to ethics in our own day, namely, deontologism and utilitarianism. The former, deontology, "is the normative ethical theory that the morality of an action should be based on whether that action itself is right or wrong under a series of rules and principles, rather than based on the consequences of the action."[14] Deontology brings to, rather than proceeds from, experience and posits norms that are not modified or tempered by experience. The rules or norms are often regarded as the commands of reason upon an otherwise morally orderless empirical world. The complete lack of appeal to consequences already distances deontology from Smith's utilization of experience. Furthermore, deontology may call to mind some of Smith's criticisms of casuistry, especially in ignoring the nuances of sentiment. To be fair, Smith's "impartial spectator" does add a deontological dimension to Smith's ethical theory. Nevertheless, suffice it to say that Smith is not a deontologist. But is he a consequentialist?

The other main modern theory, namely, utilitarianism, is broadly "a consequentialist ethical theory holding that the moral worth of actions is determined solely by their contribution to overall utility, defined as maximizing happiness [pleasure] and reducing pain."[15] As the definition implies, utilitarianism is a consequentialist theory that is entirely outcome oriented. Utilitarianism (as is true of deontology) takes

---

[13] Charles L. Griswold Jr., *Adam Smith and the Virtues of Enlightenment,* (Cambridge: Cambridge University Press) 1999, p. 206.

[14] This is the definition to be found in Wikipedia which seemed clearer and more inclusive than some others I examined. All connect deontology to duty and non-consequentialism.

[15] From the *Stanford Encyclopedia of Philosophy*.

many subtle forms which cannot be followed here. But if utilitarianism generally is our consequentialist theory, it would fare no better with Smith than deontology. It supposedly considers happiness like Smith as the end of ethics, denominated through real-world pleasures and pains. Smith, however, does not aggregate pleasures across individuals. It is our *individual* sentiments that matter. For although Smith has a socialized ethics, his ethics does not aggregate the pleasures and pains of individuals to the effective disappearance of the individual altogether. Individuals are the subjects of ethical theorizing in a way that retains that individuality in the circumstances those individuals encounter in living their normal lives.[16] Putting aside Smith's impartial spectator—which would add another non-utilitarian dimension to his moral theory—happiness for Smith is not in any case reducible to pleasure. Recall that peace and tranquility, and enjoyment, also merited approval, and were what Smith meant by happiness. No doubt the pleasures of the utilitarian count in this as well; but those pleasures are significantly less complicated and less subtle than the pleasures of enjoyment and tranquility as suggested above. Hence, Smith is not a consequentialist as the term is used today.

"Consequentialism," then, is more one sided than "experience." Consequentialism is strictly about outcomes, but experience includes both the outcome and the incorporation of that outcome into an attitude, sentiment, or thought. A result or consequence alone does not tell the whole story. We have witnessed many subtleties of attitudes, sentiments, and opinions when considering results in Smith. They all suggest that moral action is not just a matter of aggregating pleasures, no matter how simple or complex those pleasures may be.

We mentioned earlier that Smith's ethics was more like what we would call "virtue ethics" today.[17] Virtue ethics is an ethics which concentrates on developing the sorts of character needed for the execution of worthy actions. We have seen many examples of this focus on character already in what has been discussed above. There is in Smith, however, more focus on the social and sentimental than one typically finds in virtue ethics. Nevertheless, the focus on the appropriate character for a given situation, both in doing and in evaluating actions, remains at the heart of Smith's project. Yet, if we have seen nothing else in our ruminations here, one cannot help but be impressed with Smith's incorporation of many strands of explanations under one moral theory. That is to say that Smith blends in consequences and virtues and duties into our natural quest for happiness. The WN is mostly about ordinary life in a modern commercial state. In that world, the blending of concern for consequences, virtues, and duties manifests itself mainly in the virtue of ordinary prudence.

---

[16] For a contemporary moral theory that is broadly in the Smithean camp, see Schmidtz, David. *Living Together: Inventing Moral Science* (New York: Oxford University Press, 2023).

[17] Wikipedia again gets directly to the point: "virtue ethics…is a philosophical approach that treats virtue and character as the primary subjects of ethics, in contrast to other ethical systems that put consequences of voluntary acts, principles or rules of conduct, or obedience to divine authority in the primary role."

In the end, what we have learned is that there are not two moralities but either many moralities or one, depending on how one understands "morality." If we equate "morality" with a norm of conduct, there are certainly many moralities tied to differing circumstances in Smith. Yet, it seems preferable to think instead of there being just one grand morality whose purpose is human happiness, which in turn involves different categories of action requiring different normative approaches, thus implying different evaluations of actions.[18] As noted above, there are three main categories of actions with normative demands that Smith offers us. They are justice, prudence, and benevolence. These categories have a main virtue as their heading. The first concerns strict rules for setting a workable social context and maintaining it. The second concerns what we owe ourselves and what we should do concerning that; while the third is what we owe and should do with and for others. As we have seen, WN is primarily concerned with the first two, so maybe that's the "two" in "two moralities" that we should keep when thinking about morality in the WN.[19]

Bibliography

Den Uyl, D. J. n.d.-a. Sympathy, sentiment and commerce: Prudence, exchange, and correspondence in the wealth of nations. *Independent Review.*

Den Uyl, D. J. n.d.-b. Impartial spectating and the price analogy. *Econ Journal Watch.*

Griswold, C. L., Jr. (1999). *Adam Smith and the virtues of enlightenment.* Cambridge University Press.

Hanley, R. P., Smith, A. and the character of virtue, (Cambridge University Press, 2009).

Jonson, A. R., & Toulmin, S. E. (1988). *The abuse of casuistry: A history of moral reasoning.* University of Callifornia Press.

Kennedy, G. (2011). Adam Smith and religion. *History of Economic Ideas, 19*(2).

Nieli, R. (1986). Skepticism, stoicism, and providence: The religious temper of Adam Smith. *Harvard Theological Review, 79*(1–3).

Rasmussen, D. B., & Den Uyl, D. J. (2005). *Norms of liberty: A perfectionist basis for a non-perfectionist politics.* Pennsylvania State University Press.

Schliesser, E. (2017). *Adam Smith: Systematic philosopher and public thinker.* Oxford University Press.

Schmidtz, D. (2023). *Living together: Inventing moral science.* Oxford University Press.

Schwarze, M. (2020). *Recognizing resentment: Sympathy, injustice, and liberal political thought.* Cambridge University Press.

Smith, V. L. (1998). The two faces of Adam Smith. *Southern Economic Journal, 65*(1), 1–19.

---

[18] The idea that moral norms function identically we elsewhere label as equinormativity. We oppose this conception of moral norms, as perhaps Smith does as well. See Rasmussen, Douglas B. and Den Uyl, Douglas J. *Norms of Liberty: A Perfectionist Basis for a Non-Perfectionist Politics* (Pennsylvania State University Press, 2005).

[19] I would like to thank Douglas Rasmussen and Teodora Ciobanu for helpful comments on various sections of this essay.

A Violent Attack Against Self-Interest: Harmonies and Tensions in Adam Smith's *Wealth of Nations*

Maria Pia Paganelli

1 Introduction

Adam Smith is famous, among other things, due to two words he uses once in the *Wealth of Nations* ([1776] 1981): invisible hand. He also uses them once in an earlier book, *The Theory of Moral Sentiments* ([1759] 1982), and once before in a juvenile essay on the *History of Astronomy* published posthumously (1982). A lot has been written on the invisible hand, and I shall not attempt to summarize it here, especially given the variety of interpretations. A non-sophisticated possible common definition of invisible hand is that the market somehow allows individual interests to unintentionally benefit society. This is a picture of Smith's view that sees the market as locus of harmonies. Trade after all is a substitute for violently grabbing.

But, in a letter describing the strong negative reactions to his description of the peaceful death of his "infidel" friend David Hume, Smith seems surprised that "[the account of Hume's death gave me] ten times more abuse than the very violent attack I had made upon the whole commercial system of Great Britain" [Adam Smith to Andreas Holt, 26 October 1780 (1987)]. So, Smith defines the *Wealth of Nations* as a "very violent attack against the mercantile system of Britain," not as a description of the harmonies of markets. I thus would like to offer the following reminder on the occasion of the 250th anniversary of the publication of the *Wealth of Nations*. The *Wealth of Nations* is an account of the harmonies as well as the tensions that are present in markets. In a sense, Smith is a very good economist also because he presents us not just with the benefits but also with the costs of markets.

I will offer just a few examples, by no means exhaustive, of the harmonies emerging from markets as well as some non-exhaustive examples of the tensions Smith

M. P. Paganelli (✉)
Department of Economics, Trinity University, San Antonio, TX, USA
e-mail: mpaganel@trinity.edu

J. Ostle et al. (eds.), *Adam Smith's Wealth of Nations After 250 Years*, Contributions to Economics, https://doi.org/10.1007/978-3-032-32299-9_7

sees present in commercial systems. Let me unpack this a little more, starting with the harmony part.

2 Commerce as Aligning Interests

In chapter II of Book I, Smith gives us possibly the second-most famous sentence of the book: "it is not from the benevolence of the butcher, the brewer, or the baker, that we expect our dinner, but from their regard to their own interest" (WN.I.ii.2). There are at least a couple of things worth noticing here, in my view.

First, as Bart Wilson points out (2024), Smith uses "own interest" and not self-interest. For Wilson, this is not an accident. Self-interest, in the eighteenth century as today, implies that one is willing to put their interest above the interest of others, disregarding the interest of others; that an individual would do what is best for them even if that would hurt others, or at the expense of others' wellbeing. If that were the case, if one were to obtain their dinners following their own self-interest, rather than just their own interest, one would possibly steal their dinner, or deceive, with ill-intentions and frauds, the butcher, brewer, and baker to get them the dinner.

But that is not how we get our dinner in Smith's account. We can try to fawn like puppies: "A puppy fawns upon its dam, and a spaniel endeavors by a thousand attractions to engage the attention of its master who is at dinner, when it wants to be fed by him. Man sometimes uses the same arts with his brethren, and when he has no other means of engaging them to act according to his inclinations, endeavours by every servile and fawning attention to obtain their good will" (WN i.ii.2). We can try to beg like beggars (WN I.ii.2). Or we can appeal to the interest of the butcher, brewer, and baker and pay for our dinner. But we do not steal it, we do not beat or kill the butcher, brewer, and baker; we do not threaten them either. We do not disregard their interest and well-being, we appeal to it. This regard for their interest generates harmony because we can obtain our dinner with peace and without harming anyone, and in fact, in the end, we are all better off. That is the magic of markets. As Wilson notes, Smith uses self-interest only once in the entire *Wealth of Nations*, referring to the inferior clergy. Wilson attributes the substitution of own interest with self-interest most likely to the popularity of *The Wordly Philospher*, where self-interest appears in the sentence about the butcher, brewer, and baker within the quotation marks, as if that was the actual word Smith used.

Second, Smith tells us there are these three ways of getting our dinner: frowning like a puppy, begging like a beggar, or engaging in trade. A dog sits under the table and waits for his owner to feed him. A beggar sits on the street and waits for the benevolence of someone to be fed. Both the dog and the beggar are presented in a position of inferiority, depending on someone else, depending on someone superior to them. It is only the buyer who can look in the eyes of the feeder from the same standpoint. The butcher and the buyer of dinner are equal. I have something you want, just like you have something I want. I give you what you want, you give me what I want: "Whoever offers to another a bargain of any kind, proposes to do this.

Give me that which I want, and you shall have this which you want, is the meaning of every such offer" (WN I.i.ii.2). The two are on the same level. They have equal dignity (Paganelli, 2023b). Trade harmonizes also because trade equalizes.

This harmonization of interests works, of course, also at the macro level. There is no need to direct capital one way or another. The owners of capital know what is best for them, and by doing it, they unintentionally allocate resources in the best possible way, without harming anyone, but unintentionally benefiting society. This is the context of the presentation of the invisible hand. We do not need to restrict capital to the domestic markets. Owners of capital would do it themselves, if the returns from other investments are equal. After all, we prefer to keep our things as close to us as possible, under our eyes. We reluctantly invest abroad only when it makes no longer sense to invest at home. We are thus led by an invisible hand to do what is best for society, by doing what is best for ourselves. Bart Wilson would make sure we specify that all this is done while not disregarding the wellbeing of others, while not putting ourselves above others and hurting them. With regard to our own interest, not our self-interest. And it may not be an accident indeed that Smith uses own interest, and not self-interest, here too: "By preferring the support of domestick to that of foreign industry, he intends only his own security; and by directing that industry in such a manner as its produce may be of the greatest value, he intends only his own gain, and he is in this, as in many other cases, led by an invisible hand to promote an end which was no part of his intention. Nor is it always the worse for the society that it was no part of it. By pursuing his *own interest*, he frequently promotes that of the society more effectually than when he really intends to promote it" (WN IV.ii.9, emphasis added).

There is one additional example of the harmonization that markets generate which I would like to emphasize. This becomes more evident when we read the *Wealth of Nations* and Smith's other book, *The Theory of Moral Sentiments*, together. There are two related things from the *Wealth of Nations* relevant to my point: markets create economic growth, which in turn supports (a good) life for more people thus creating happiness.

From his own Introduction of the *Wealth of Nations*, Smith tells us that some nations are so miserably poor that people are forced to abandon their infants, their elderly, and their sick to be devoured by wild beasts: "[some] nations [...] are so miserably poor, that, from mere want, they are frequently reduced, or, at least, think themselves reduced, to the necessity of sometimes directly destroying, and sometimes of abandoning their infants, their old people, and those afflicted with lingering diseases, to perish with hunger, or to be devoured by wild beasts" (Intro 4).

If we think that in *The Theory of Moral Sentiments* Smith tells us that the loss of a child is one of the most tragic events one person can experience, it is hard to imagine what must be going on for a parent to bring their baby to be devoured by a wild beast. Indeed, in *The Theory of Moral Sentiments,* Smith declares: "Can there be greater barbarity, for example, than to hurt an infant? Its helplessness, its innocence, its amiableness, call forth the compassion, even of an enemy, and not to spare that tender age is regarded as the most furious effort of an enraged and cruel conqueror.

What then should we imagine must be the heart of a parent who could injure that weakness which even a furious enemy is afraid to violate?" (TMS V.2.15).

But the need to "destroy" the weakest of society disappears with the presence of wealth. As nations grow richer, they have enough to support all members of society: "Among civilized and thriving nations, on the contrary, though a greater number of people does not labour at all [...] yet the produce of the whole labour of society is so great, that all are often abundantly supplied, and a workman, even of the lowest and poorest order, if he is frugal and industrious, may enjoy s greater share of the necessaries and conveniences of life than it is possible of any savage to acquire" (Intro 4; note that savage is a term of art, not a derogative, to indicate very poor hunter societies). This is surely a reason to rejoice. Smith is quite explicit in the *Wealth of Nations* in saying that growing economies are cheerful economies. Contacting economies, on the other hand, are melancholic. Stagnant ones, even if rich, are dull (WN I.viii.43). And whether an economy is growing or not is demonstrated by its population growth. A growing population is a sign of a growing economy, a declining population of a contracting economy, and a constant population growth a sign of a stagnant economy (Paganelli, 2021).

Smith attributes the cheerfulness of a growing economy to the ability to support more lives, and to have more fulfilling lives. And this ability to support more lives comes from the extension of markets which allows for more division of labor and thus increasing productivity (WN I.1–3). When this is combined with what he says in the *Theory of Moral Sentiments*, the harmonizing powers of markets become more evident.

From the *Theory of Moral Sentiments*, we know we are social creatures. We care about others, and we care that others care about us. We give meaning to our actions and interpret meanings in the actions of others, as Bart Wilson would remind us. We want to be lovely and approvable so that we deservedly receive the love and the approbation of others. We want others to feel like we feel, and we rejoice in feeling like others feel. I do not want to laugh alone. I want you to laugh with me. I would feel miserable if I ended up laughing by myself. Sharing our joys multiplies them, and sharing our pains comfort us: "sympathy [...] enlivens joys and alleviates grief. It enlivens joy by presenting another source of satisfaction; and it alleviates grief by insinuating into the heart almost the only agreeable sensation which it is at the time capable of receiving" (TMS I.i.2.), tells us Smith.

The sharing of our passions with others is what Smith calls humanity. But humanity is only possible in a "mild sunshine." In the middle of a "storm," we need to control our passions and not express them. In a storm, we face the threats of death, in the mild sunshine, we do not think about it: "In the mild sunshine of undisturbed tranquillity, in the calm of retirement of undissipated and philosophical leisure, the soft virtue of humanity flourishes the most, and is capable of the highest improvement. [...] Under the boisterous and stormy sky of war and faction, of public tumult and confusion, the sturdy severity of self-command prospers the most and can be the most successfully cultivated" (TMS III.3.37).

But in a storm, in a battlefield, or, what is relevant here, in severe poverty, we constantly face the risk of death. Under these circumstances, we refrain from expressing our sentiments. In the conform of a mild warm summer day, in peacetime, and in prosperity, we can lift those constraints and express our sentiments more freely (Paganelli, 2017).

Smith insists that "among civilized nations, the virtues which are founded upon humanity are more cultivated than those which are founded upon self-denial and the command of the passions. Among rude and barbarous nations, it is quite otherwise, the virtues of self-denial are more cultivated than those of humanity. The general security and happiness which prevails in ages of civility and politeness, afford little exercise to the contempt of danger [...] to hunger, and pain. [...] The abstinence from pleasure becomes less necessary, and the mood is more at liberty to unbend itself, and to indulge its natural inclinations in all those particular respects" (TMS V.2.8).

And thus, Smith tells us that a savage (which in his context, again, simply means extremely poor, such as people in hunter-gathering societies, without necessarily any disparaging connotations) can be tortured without expressing any agony and can witness torturing without showing any emotions. The same savage would be looked down on, if he expressed any love or affection for his wife (TMS V.2.9). Let me indulge with Smith's own words, as they will show a relevant contrast: "After he [a tortured individual] has been scorched and burnt, and lacerated in all the most tender and sensible parts of his body for several hours together, he is often allowed, in order to prolong his misery, a short respite, and is taken down from the stake: he employs this interval in talking upon all indifferent subjects [...] and seems indifferent about nothing but his own situation. The spectators express the same insensibility; the sight of so horrible an object seems to make no impression upon them" (TMS V.2.9).

But this is how Smith opens the *Theory of Moral Sentiments*, directing himself to readers of a "civilized society". His very first example is the one of the sight of a tortured individual: "Our brother is upon the rack [...] By the imagination we place ourselves in his situation, we conceive ourselves enduring all the same torment, we enter as it were into his body, and become in some measure the same person with him, and thence form some idea of his sensations, and even feel something which, though weaker in degree, is not altogether unlike them. His agonies, when they are thus brought home to ourselves, when we have thus adopted and made them our own, begin at last to affect us, and we then tremble and shudder at the thought of what he feels" (TMS I.1.2).

In a wealthier society, we shiver at the sight of our brother being tortured on the rack (note that here the tortured individual changed into a brother as opposed to an enemy), and a general would even cry in court for not receiving the regiment he hoped for (TMS V.2.10). The expression of emotions which allows the concord of sentiments, which in its turns allows us to grow our humanity is thus possible, for Smith, thanks to the wealth, the "mild sunshine," that trade brings about (Bee & Paganelli, 2019). Markets, and the economic growth they bring with them, bring also equality, dignity, life, cheerfulness, and humanity. Let alone freedom from dependency and good institutions.

After all, for Smith, the hierarchical and oppressive feudal system is brought down by the introduction of trinkets and baubles that commerce allows to have (WN III.iv). For something as trivial as a diamond buckle, feudal lords sold their birthrights, freeing their dependents and unintendedly creating "order and good government" (WN III.iv.4).

For Smith, 250th years ago, and as Wilson reminds us today with a more detailed explanation, humans and only humans are trading animals, and their trading allows for harmonies and growth that no other species has experienced.

3 Tensions

But Bart Wilson reminds us that humans, with wolves and chimpanzees, are the only species who form coalitions to kill other members of their own specie. Smith does not present it this way, but he also recognizes there is a dark side of human beings which also expresses itself in markets. It is true that Smith talks about the own interest of the butcher, brewer, and baker, but that does not mean that there is no self-interest in the *Wealth of Nations*. And, no, I am not meaning self-interest *a la* Stigler meaning that the *Wealth of Nations* is built on the granite of self-interest (Stigler, 1971). I mean self-interest as Wilson means it, putting oneself above others, disregarding others, even hurting others if that brings benefits to the person. The butcher, brewer, baker may not put their interest on top of the interest of their hungry client, but "merchants and manufacturers" do. Their interest is, Smith tells us, "directly opposite to that of the great body of the people" (WN IV.iii.c.10), and they "have generally an interest to deceive and even oppress the publick, and who accordingly have, upon many occasions, both deceived and oppressed it" [WN I.xi.p.10. See also Paganelli (2023a) and Sagar (2021)].

Let's start with what to me is one of the most striking examples of these interests willing and able to oppress others, as opposed to harmonize with each other. This example is, for me, striking because it takes place in the market (almost), without government intervention. In manufactures, the masters always conspire against the public in two ways: by paying workers as little as possible and by trying to raise prices as high as possible.

First thing first: How can they "conspire against the publick?" (WN I.x.c27). Manufacturers are few and concentrated in cities. It is easy for them to get together and form what today we would call a cartel: "The inhabitants of a town, being collected in one place, can easily combine together. The most insignificant trades carried on in towns have accordingly, in some place or another, been incorporated" (WN I.x.c.22). The costs they impose on others are diffused: "The inhabitants of the country, dispersed in distant places, cannot easily combine together. They have not only never been incorporated, but the corporation spirit never has prevailed among them" (WN I.x.c.23). Smith describes the situation in a way that resembles closely today's public choice description of special interest groups (Krueger, 1974; Tullock, 1967; Olson, 1971).

On the one hand, masters are few and concentrated. Smith suggests it would not be just to prevent their getting together, but at the same time he suggests it should not be encouraged (WN I.x.c.27–29). On the other hand, workers are many, and it is more difficult for them to get together, even if it were legal to do so. In Smith's time, it is not legal because the masters influence the legislation and prevent it (WN I.x.c.61). Specifically, Smith tells us that "the masters, being fewer in number, can combine much more easily; and the law, besides, authorizes, or at least does not prohibit their combinations, while it prohibits those of the workmen" (WN I.viii.12) Here is the conflict: Masters want low wages, workers want high wages. A compromise is difficult to obtain because, yes, it is true that the workers have something that the masters want and the masters have something that the workers want, but differently from the butcher, brewer, and baker, which seem to have equal bargaining power, the masters and the workers do not. A mutually beneficial agreement is not something to take for granted because the masters have more bargaining power than the workers. Masters can say, I have what you want and, yes, you have what I want, but if you do not give it to me on the terms that I want, you will get nothing. Masters can say that because they have enough resources to hold out for a very long time. Workers can last only a few days at best. So workers have to cave in to the predation of the masters. For Smith, given their situation, the only bargaining instrument laborers have is violence, and that is not effective because the masters can call the government to suppress it: "to bring the point to a speedy decision, they [the workers] have always recurse to the loudest clamour, and sometimes to the most shocking violence and outrage. They are desperate, and act with the folly and extravagance of desperate men, who must ether starve, or frighten their masters into an immediate compliance with their demands. The masters upon these occasions are just as clamorous on the other side, and never cease to call aloud for the assistance of the civil magistrate, and the rigorous execution of those laws which have been enacted with so much severity against the combinations of servants, labourers, and journeymen" (WN I.viii.13).

Note that here the government is absent, with the exception of preventing workers unionizing, which would not be effective anyway in Smith's account, and the repression of the violent revolts of the workers. Or at least we can think of the government as a passive presence in the background. The problem that Smith identifies is that there are conflicts in the market, absent government, when bargaining powers are significantly different, and significant differences in bargaining powers do not create a harmonious order but fuel self-interested (in Wilson's terms) behaviors.

The problem is further exacerbated if the power of the state backs merchants and manufacturers. Now merchants and manufacturers can pass laws to keep wages low or to eliminate them altogether, institutionalizing and legalizing their predation. In Smith's time, there are indeed maximum wage laws, to prevent wages from rising above a certain level as well as enslaved labor (Martin, 2015). Their justification is the alleged natural laziness of the poor. There are also mandatory apprenticeships where apprentices are to work for free for a specified number of years, allegedly to learn the trade. Allegedly, I say, because Smith condemns both practices. He believes they are the product of the myopic self-interest (my words, not his) of manufacturers. Smith argues that the laboring poor are not naturally lazy. For Smith, there are no natural differences among human beings, as Sandra Peart and David Levy amply demonstrated (Peart & Levy, 2005). Wages are incentives, in today's language. The higher the wages, the more productive a worker would be: "the liberal reward of labor [...] increases the industry of the common people. The wages of labor are an encouragement of industry, which, like every other human quality, improves in proportion to the encouragement it receives. A plentiful subsistence increases the bodily strength of the laborer and the comfortable hope of bettering his condition and of ending his days perhaps in ease and plenty, animates him to exert that strength to the utmost. Where wages are high, accordingly, we shall always find the workmen more active, diligent and expeditious, than where they are low" (WNI. viii.44, p. 99).

Low wages do not incentivize high productivity. Masters would be better off if they paid workers fairly. Apprenticeships, in Smith's account, teach trainees only to be lazy. Paying them for what they produce and detracting from their pay what they break or do not do well would be a much more effective way to teach them the art (WN I.x.c.13–16). The self-interest of the masters backfires, but our love of domineering is too strong to let us take into consideration the wellbeing of the other (WN III.ii.10).

We can start to see how Smith is opening the door to considering the *Wealth of Nations* as a very violent attack against the whole commercial system of Britain. In a sense, this very violent attack that the *Wealth of Nations* is a very violent attack against self-interest. Let's see this in more detail.

Merchants and manufacturers, as Smith introduces them, have an interest that goes against the interest of society. We have already seen that they want to keep wages as low as possible in the attempt to increase their profits. At the same time, to increase their profits, they try to increase the prices at which they sell their products. And higher prices are achieved only through monopolies, granted by state capture. Treaties, subsidies, tariffs, the entire colonial apparatus, are all means that merchants and manufacturers design to restrict access to markets to themselves and thus privilege their position at the expense of others.

Smith goes as far as saying that these special interest groups use the "blood and treasure" of their fellow citizens to better their conditions. They may or may not be aware of the consequences of their actions, but they definitely disregard them. This is self-interest, as Wilson describes it, at its peak.

Smith speaks of "blood and treasure" because in his account, all the recent wars Britain engaged in were meant to establish and defend monopolies for British merchants and manufacturers. As a matter of fact, for Smith, the *entire* British Empire is in fact a construct of merchants and manufacturers. "To found a great empire for the sole purpose of raising up a people of customers, may at first sight appear a project fit only for a nation of shopkeepers. It is, however, a project altogether unfit for a nation of shopkeepers; but extremely fit for a nation whose government is influenced by shopkeepers. Such statesmen, and such statesmen only, are capable of fancying that they will find some advantage in employing the blood and treasure of their fellow citizens, to found and to maintain such empire" (WN IV.vii.c.63). And he continues by saying that "The maintenance of this monopoly has hitherto been the principal, or more properly perhaps *the sole end and purpose* of the dominion which Great Britain assumes over her colonies" (WN IV.vii.c.64. Emphasis added). And again: "A great empire has been established for the sole purpose of raising up a nation of consumers who should be obliged to buy from the shops of our different producers all the goods with which these could supply them. For the sake of that little enhancement of price which this monopoly might afford our producers, the home-consumers have been burdened with the whole expense of maintaining and defending that empire" (WN IV.viii.53).

The power merchants and manufacturers have to bring the country into wars, for Smith, is facilitated by the use of public debt. Debt covers the cost of wars, so that people support wars because they can be entertained by reading the news of them in the newspaper from the comfort of their home [WN V.iii.37, see also Paganelli and Schumacher (2018)].

One way to think about how self-interested merchants and manufacturers are, how much they do put their own interest above the interest of others, and even at the expense not only of the interest but also of the life of others is Smith's commentary on the East India Company.

The East India Company is the worst kind of monopoly for Smith. Merchants and manufacturers have so successfully captured state power that they actually have the same power of the state. The East India Company acts like a sovereign over the territories it monopolizes, or better, it has the same power of a sovereign over those territories. One severe problem that Smith sees is that the Company is not a sovereign, so it has different incentives than a sovereign. For Smith, in theory, a sovereign has long term interest over his kingdom because of the hereditary nature of his role (WN IV.vii.c.102). The East India Company officials, on the other hand, have temporary assignments, which give them only short-term interests (WN IV.vii.c.103). The incentives are such, Smith tells us, that with the military power of a state and temporary assignments, the East India Company officials will grab all they can, not caring about the future, leaving only destruction behind. This distraction is akin to a devastating earthquake. Despite causing this devastating earthquake, the Company officials leave without even looking back, without any concerns about the destruction they caused. They are just concerned about their own immense gains. These are Smith's words: "It is a very singular government in which every member of the administration wishes to get out of the country, and consequently to have done with the government, as soon as he can, and to whose interest, in the day after he has left it and carried his whole fortune with him, it is perfectly indifferent though the whole country was swallowed up by an earthquake" (WN IV.vii.c.106).

This description of self-interested behavior is bad enough, but when combined with how Smith describes the devastation of an earthquake in the *Theory of Moral Sentiments*, the condemnation becomes significantly more serious.

In *The Theory of Moral Sentiments*, Smith asks what one would do if told that the entire population of China would be swallowed by an earthquake. Smith believes that we would feel sorry for the devastation, but we would "snore with the most profound security over the ruin of a hundred millions of his brethren" (TMS III.3.4).

On the other hand, if we were told that tomorrow we would lose our little finger, we would be very anxious and unable to sleep (TMS III.3.4). We care more about things that are close to us than things that are far away from us. Yet, Smith continues, if we were given the choice to save the population of China from that devastating earthquake by giving up our little finger, Smith says, not a villain on earth would choose to keep their little finger at the expense of the life of the population of China. Not a villain on earth would keep their finger and let the earthquake destroy China. Nobody would be able to look at themselves in the mirror the next morning, knowing that they let the population of China be swollen by an earthquake just because they preferred keeping their little finger. His words are strikingly categorical: “Human nature startles with horror at the thought, and the world, in its greatest depravity and corruption, never produced such a villain as could be capable of entertaining it” (TMS III.34). But when Smith describes the East India Company officials, things are different. The East India Company creates those villains. The East India Company officials are the ones *causing* the earthquake so that they can enrich themselves. And they walk away from it, without even looking back, without any concerns or regrets for the devastation they caused. They follow their self-interest, at the expense of the population of the entire subcontinent.

Smith already had told us, earlier in the *Wealth of Nations*, that the monopoly of the East India Company was causing unjustified death. Smith presents Bengal as an example of a contracting economy, as signified by its declining population. But Bengal is a very fertile land which should support the life of many. Instead, Smith tells us, “three or four hundred thousand people die of hunger in a year” (WN I.viii.26). Why? Because of that “mercantile company which oppresses and domineers” which is the East India Company. It cares only about enriching itself, disregarding the life of the people in Bengal.

It is thus difficult to see how the interest of the merchants and manufacturers of East India Company aligns with the interest of society. When a special interest group such as these merchants and manufacturers are willing and able to capture state power to benefit themselves, they do it disregarding the presence of others. They act in their self-interest and not in their own interest, to go back to the distinction that Bart Wilson points out.

4 Virtue and Wealth

But how is it possible, one may ask, to have both the praise of the butcher, brewer, and baker and the condemnation of the East India Company? How is it possible that Smith at the same time lauds the outcomes of markets and violently attacks them?

The butcher is not a monopoly, the merchant in the East India Company is. The brewer faces the competition of many other brewers, the manufacturer of the East India Company has blocked competition with the force of the state. The baker is one among many bakers, and it is impossible for him to cartelize with other bakers, merchants, and manufacturers in colonial trade are few and able to form successful lobbies to obtain privileges.

As Wilson reminds us, we are moral creatures, we care about others, we follow our own interest, and not our self-interest, markets align our interests in a mutually beneficial way. Most of the time. But not always.

As Smith reminds us, we are moral creatures indeed. We are social beings, we do care about the others around us. We want to be lovely and admirable, we want to be the proper object of approbation. At the same time, Smith tells us, we admire the rich and look down on the poor. So, we are presented with two ways to attract the admiration of others: virtue and wealth: "Two different roads are presented to us, equally leading to the attainment of this so much desired object; the one, by the study of wisdom and the practice of virtue; the other, by the acquisition of wealth and greatness. [...] The great mob of mankind are the admirers and worshippers, and, what may seem more extraordinary, most frequently the disinterested admirers and worshippers, of wealth and greatness" (TMS I.iii.3.2).

The majority of us follow a healthy combination of the two. But, Smith continues, virtue is difficult to see. It is not easy to distinguish a virtuous person from a vicious one at first sight. Wealth, on the other hand, is "more gaudy and glittering in its colouring" (TMS I.iii.2). It is visible and easily recognizable. So when we are presented with very large profit opportunities, the temptation to grab them, even if with questionable means, is high. After all, if we gain that large of a profit, we will receive the approbation of many (Levy, 1995). And our wealth will make people forgive and forget the vicious ways we used to get that much wealth: "those exalted stations may, no doubt, be completely degraded by vice and folly. But the vice and folly must be very great, before they can operate this complete degradation. The profligacy of a man of fashion is looked upon with much less contempt and aversion, than that of a man of meaner condition, In the latter, a single transgression of the rules of temperance and propriety, is commonly more resented, than the constant and avowed contempt of them ever is in the former" (TMS I.iii.3.4).

So from the analysis of the *Theory of Moral Sentiments,* we can explain the difference between the butcher, brewer, and baker, and the big merchants and manufacturers. The butcher, brewer, and baker better their condition in the ordinary way, by being honest and respecting their customers, maybe even helped by competitive forces. Big merchants and manufacturers, on the other hand, are presented with very large profit opportunities generated by the opening of new markets in the East and West Indies. They grab the opportunity to seize the power of the state to put themselves in a privileged position, even if that implies using the "blood and treasure" of their fellow citizens.

5 Conclusions

As Bart Wilson teaches us, Smith is very careful in distinguishing between own interest and self-interest. Pursuing one's own interest, pursuing what is best for me while taking into consideration the presence and wellbeing of others, is compatible with moral development and economic development. It can generate a harmonious system of trade and commerce and prosperity. Pursuing one's self-interest, pursuing what is best for me whilst disregarding or even at the expense of others, on the other hand, creates clashes and tensions which are detrimental for both moral and economic development. Adam Smith recognizes the presence of both.

Bibliography

Bee, M., & Paganelli, M. P. (2019). Adam Smith Anti-Stoic. *History of European Ideas, 45*(4), 572–584.

Krueger, A. O. (1974). The political economy of the rent-seeking society. *The American Economic Review, 64*(3), 291–303.

Levy, D. M. (1995). A partial spectator in the wealth of nations: A robust utilitarianism. *European Journal of the History of Economic Thought, 2*, 299–326.

Martin, C. (2015). Equity, besides: Adam Smith and the utility of poverty. *Journal of the History of Economic Thought, 37*(4), 559–581.

Olson, M. (1971). The logic of collective action: Public goods and the theory of groups. In *Second printing with a new preface and appendix*. Harvard University Press.

Paganelli, M. P. (2017). Boys do cry: Adam Smith on wealth and expressing emotions. *Journal of Scottish Philosophy, 15*(1), 1–8.

Paganelli, M. P. (2021). Population as a GDP proxy in Adam Smith. *Journal of Scottish Philosophy, 19*(2), 115–123.

Paganelli, M. P. (2023a). Adam Smith and the morality of political economy: A public choice reading. In P. Sagar (Ed.), *Interprting Adam Smith: Critical Essays* (pp. 111–123). Cambridge University Press.

Paganelli, M. P. (2023b). Smith at 300: The dignity of trade. *Journal of the History of Economic Thought, 45*(2), 193–194.

Paganelli, M. P., & Schumacher, R. (2018). Do not take peace for granted: Adam Smith's warning on the relation between commerce and war. *Cambridge Journal of Economics, 43*(3), 785–797.

Peart, S., & Levy, D. M. (2005). In Project Muse (Ed.), *The "vanity of the philosopher" from equality to hierarchy in postclassical economics* (Vol. Whole Book). University of Michigan Press.

Sagar, P. (2021). Adam Smith and the conspiracy of the merchants. *Global Intellectual History, 6*(4), 463–483.

Smith, A. ([1759] 1982). *The theory of moral sentiments* (Vol. Whole Book). Liberty Classics.

Smith, A. ([1776] 1981). *An inquiry into the nature and causes of the wealth of nations* (Vol. Whole Book). Liberty Classics.

Smith, A. (1982). In I. S. Ross (Ed.), *Essays on philosophical subjects*. Liberty Classics.

Smith, A. (1987). In E. C. Mossner & I. S. Ross (Eds.), *The correspondence of Adam Smith* (Vol. Whole Book). Liberty Classics.

Stigler, G. J. (1971). Smith's travels on the ship of state. *History of Political Economy, 3*(2), 265–277.

Tullock, G. (1967). The welfare costs of tariffs, monopolies, and theft. *Economic Inquiry, 5*(3), 224–232.
Wilson, B. (2024). *Maeaningful economics: Making the science of prosperity more human*. Oxford University Press.

Two Overlapping Readings of *The Wealth of Nations*: Ethics of Identity and Political Economy of Fair Play

Jack Russell Weinstein

1 Introduction

This is an essay about *The Wealth of Nations* but it is framed by elements of my own intellectual autobiography.[1] In it, I present two contrasting but compatible readings of WN: one that I intuited during my first encounters with Smith's work in graduate school and one I have developed over 35 years.

The premise of this chapter is as follows: the first period during which I encountered WN was in service of a deeply focused but decontextualized reading of TMS that made Smith's political economy subservient in revealing but neglected ways. The second was my engagement with WN for its own sake, framed by scholarly debates that dishonestly smuggle in political concerns. The two are complementary but represent very different concerns; the resulting picture is idiosyncratic without being anachronistic.

[1] I have retained Smith's original spelling. While he uses gendered language, I have done my best to make my original writing gender neutral. Please excuse the grammatical awkwardness that sometimes results. My references follow the standardized numbering of *The Glasgow Edition of the Works and Correspondences of Adam Smith*. TMS refers to *The Theory of Moral Sentiments*, sixth edition Smith, *The Theory of Moral Sentiments*. WN designates Smith, *An Inquiry into the Nature and Causes of the Wealth of Nations*. LJ(A) refers to Smith's *Lectures on Jurisprudence*, notes of 1762–1763 and LJ(B) references the 1766 notes in Smith, *Lectures on Jurisprudence*. LRBL refers to his Smith, *Lectures on Rhetoric and Belles Lettres*. *Letter* refers to his "Letter to the Edinburgh Review" in Smith, *Essays on Philosophical Subjects*. Draft refers to "Early Draft of Part of the Wealth of Nations" Smith, *Lectures on Jurisprudence*. Corr. refers to Smith, *Correspondence of Adam Smith*.

J. R. Weinstein (✉)
University of North Dakota, Grand Forks, ND, USA
e-mail: jack.weinstein@und.edu

J. Ostle et al. (eds.), *Adam Smith's Wealth of Nations After 250 Years*, Contributions to Economics, https://doi.org/10.1007/978-3-032-32299-9_8

To put it another way: during the 2000 American presidential election, candidate Ralph Nader snidely referred to future President George W. Bush as a "major corporation disguised as a human being."[2] In this spirit, I consider *The Wealth of Nations* to be the world's most interesting book disguised as the world's most boring. This article recounts my coming to this conviction and is motivated by my frustration with what I consider a "calcification" of the text. TMS is still engaged as forward-looking philosophy; WN is almost exclusively referenced as a document whose time has passed.

The two accounts serve different pedagogical and exegetical purposes but they both inform. I recognize there is tremendous value in experience and expertise. However, I also insist that there is virtue in naivete. Sometimes we become so learned that we disregard what we know. I am happy to use the 250th Anniversary of Smith's text as an excuse to look back at what WN gave me.

2 Autobiographical Interlude 1

I first encountered Adam Smith during a graduate seminar taught by Charles L. Griswold, Jr. at Boston University during the Fall of 1991. It was my first semester as a doctoral student. I was 22 and had just gotten a B.A. I was not in the Philosophy Department yet but was enrolled in BU's University Professors Program, an interdisciplinary department that offered personalized courses of study.

My Ph.D. was going to be on "Philosophy of Social Justice," a mixture of political theory and activism. I had done some direct action organizing as an undergraduate, mostly about voting rights and affordable tuition at public universities. I had also already taught an Honors seminar called *Philosophy of Activism* during my last semester as an undergraduate at the Statue University of New York, Plattsburgh. This made me struggle over whether to begin grad school immediately or spend time as a professional organizer. Jim Miller's *Democracy is in the Streets*, an intellectual history of the 1960s activist group Students for Democratic Society, told me I could do both at the same time. It lied.[3]

The seminar began with *TMS*. I read the book using the perspective from which I experienced most things: immersion in left-wing ideological disputes that framed public policy debates. These included identity politics and the nature of multiculturalism; grassroots citizen action within a democracy; feminist and non-white inclusion, and upward mobility and the legitimacy of counter narratives—one debate in my statewide student union was whether to rename the *Third-World Caucus* the *First World Caucus*. I had worked on AIDS and safer-sex related education, and the cultural normalization of gayness before it was called queer. I helped organize anti Gulf-War protests.

[2] Megan Garvey, "Nader Besieged by Ex-Allies as Race Goes down to the Wire."

[3] Miller, *Democracy Is in the Streets*.

I grew up poor in Washington Heights, a very dangerous, mostly Hispanic neighborhood in Manhattan that was the epicenter of the 1970s and 1980s crack epidemic. There was a part of my neighborhood that my father and I referred to as the demilitarized zone. I was therefore particularly attuned to what Smith would call the "equal and impartial administration of justice" (WN IV.vii.c). Being raised immersed in the so-called war against drugs made racial disparities in criminal sentencing obvious;[4] police brutality was a fact of life.

It was a few years before the surrealistically absurd Super-predator theory would sweep the nation, challenging Smith's contention that there was no "original difference" between people, but it was in the air (LJ(A) vi.47–48).[5] Also, while the false myth of Kitty Genovese's unacknowledged rape was pervasive, it did not resonate.[6] Living in New York City for me was always a mixture of community and competition.

The 1970s and 1980s cultivated a public policy discussion about how self-destructive people were allowed to be, and how realistically or paternalistically social institutions should respond. This coincided with a rise in libertarian thinkers who saw themselves as the descendants of Smith. They added fuel to debates about how much leeway any community had in establishing idiosyncratic rules for themselves, a concern Smith anticipates in his reliance upon social norms for the establishment of virtue, in TMS.

The year 1973 brought the U.S. Supreme Court's definition of obscenity that rested on "community standards." [7] This led to tremendous variation in how transgressive localities were permitted to be. The result was significant variation in neighborhood permissiveness, especially regarding the sex trade. There was a lot of looking away from street prostitution and drug dealing by the New York police, and graffiti was starting to be considered street art rather than vandalism.[8] The AIDS

---

[4] The heightened penalties for crack in the United States as opposed to other forms of cocaine were so transparent as to be laughable. (See: Kilty and Joseph, "Institutional Racism and Sentencing Disparities for Cocaine Possession").

[5] "Super-predator" is a termed coined by John J. Dilulio, Jr., a political scientist housed at Princeton University. He defines them as a "young juvenile criminal who is so impulsive, so remorseless, that he can kill, rape, main, without giving it a second thought." They are "a group of kids that are growing up essentially fatherless, godless, and jobless" and "as many as half of these super-predators could be young Black Males" (Stanley, *How Propaganda Works*, p. 95. See also: Weinstein, "How Does Propaganda Work?").

[6] Kitty Genovese is the subject of an urban legend that many people still believe today. Ms. Genovese was brutally attacked and murdered on March 13, 1964. Media and word of mouth would report for decades that many bystanders with open windows heard the attack and ignored it, making it a central text in a discussion of urban apathy and the bystander effect. The reported story is almost entirely inaccurate, from details about how and where she was murdered, to the fact that many people did, in fact, actively seek to get her help (Gallo, *No One Helped).*

[7] *Miller v. California.*

[8] My neighborhood was the textbook example of what inspired the failed "broken-window" policing policy which accompanied the rise of Rudy Giuliani and the eventual mass-gentrification of New York City (See: Harcourt, *Illusion of Order).*

epidemic inspired interest in syringe service programs that provided needles to intravenous drug users.

Two sets of questions arise. The first involves who is responsible for, in Smith's words, "protecting, as far as possible, every member of the society from the injustice or oppression of every other member" (WN V.i.b.1). It is an irony of the ghetto that the streets with the most illicit behavior are usually the safest. It is in the self-interest of the drug dealers and pimps to make sure that those who carry cash are safe where they ply their trade or customers won't come. It is actually the adjacent streets that are full of desperate addicts and violent thieves; in Washington Heights, a significant number of the users and Johns came from New Jersey by car. The 1972 movie *The Godfather* is a romanticized exploration of this kind of private justice in the face of an inadequate state. The puzzle of the hour was how powerful a sovereign could actually be, let alone a limited one.

The second set of questions ask whether ethnic, racial, sex, or other groups have rights in themselves or whether corporate bodies are only to be regarded as aggregates not collectives, making rights individualistic. I would not have been able to articulate the issue so precisely at the time, but it became a mainstream philosophical concern soon after.[9] 1980s multiculturalism was stymied as to whether race and gender were primary or secondary characteristics of individuals, casting doubt on the ability of one group to understand the plight of another.

This history made my experience in the safety of Boston and the enforced order of rigid graduate work jarring. My childhood was complicated. My parents were avant-garde artists, beatniks really, and I ended up being deeply involved in the punk scene. I was a DJ on the college radio station with a show focused on punk and ska, the Jamaican music genre that developed into reggae. I had a weekly opinion column in the student newspaper called "My Philosophy" and ended up being an activist Editor-in-Chief.

These are not incidentals in my encounter with *The Theory of Moral Sentiments*. A Smithian renaissance had been building since the 1976 publication of the *Glasgow Edition*, which provided not just definitive texts but a consistent paragraph-numbering system that allowed for more sophisticated corpus-wide scholarship. Smith scholars were still fighting about the legitimacy of "The Adam Smith Problem," with many holding tight to the idea that TMS and WN were inconsistent in fundamental ways. Rawls misdescribes Smith in *A Theory of Justice*[10] and

[9] cf. Kymlicka, *Multicultural Citizenship*; Williams, "Justice Toward Groups"; Barry, *Culture and Equality*.

[10] Rawls, *A Theory of Justice*, pp. 22f, 57, 184, 263, 479f, 521f, 525f. One footnote reference, on page 22, is simply a list of names, this time it is those whom Rawls reports Sidgwick to cite as advancing the utilitarian tradition—Sidgwick's definition of utilitarianism is intended to account for all other theories on the list; page 57 contains a one sentence reference to the invisible hand which is to be contrasted with ideas put forth by Bentham; page 184 contains a definition of the ideal-observer theory which Rawls claims is "reminiscent of Hume and Adam Smith"; page 263 is a second reference to the ideal-observer discussion and once again cites Hume and Smith in tandem; page 479f refers to Smith's discussion of the moral sentiments. It cites TMS as the origin of the phrase "self-command" but Rawls uses a secondary work as his main source; page 521f is

MacIntyre does in *After Virtue*,[11] both of whom I would address directly in my dissertation. Virtually every non-specialist treated Smith as both a utilitarian and a clone of Hume. The jury was still out on his place in the canon. No one knew what to do with him and it was still possible to read him as countercultural.[12] Smith offered me an alternative way toward diversity and identity formation that I found intuitive and aligned with many of my values.

While left-wing activism had Marxist sympathies, the United States had not yet started discussing income inequality with the intensity inspired by 2011s Occupy Wall Street protests. It was 10 years before the attacks on The World Trade Center and the resulting Patriot Act that would make ubiquitous surveillance a flashpoint. As such, when the 1991 seminar did arrive at WN, it was possible to compartmentalize the economics and focus on Smith's institutional recommendations. Given my interest in all things underground, I had libertarian sympathies, but these would wax and wane. I was primed for Smith.

---

simply a reference to Hegel's reading of WN; 525f is a parenthetical citation located at the end of an over one-page long list of works that illustrate social cooperation. In this and the next footnote, I follow my dissertation (Weinstein, *Adam Smith and the Problem of Neutrality in Contemporary Liberal Theory*).

[11] MacIntyre, *Three Rival Versions of Moral Enquiry*, 32, 223; Macintyre, *Whose Justice?*, pp. 252, 259, 280, 283, 296, 331, 372; MacIntyre, *After Virtue*, pp. 10, 23 (the index indicates 22), 37, 51, 54, 61, 234–35, 236, 239. The references in TRV are purely ornamental; they make no substantive point. In WJ: page 252 pokes fun at Smith's picture of the progression of history; page 259 contrasts the urgency of economics for Smith as opposed to Hutcheson; page 280 contains two references, both of which seem to equate Hume and Smith and are meant to foreshadow the following chapter which focuses on Hume; page 283 refers to a letter Hume writes Smith about Lord Kames; page 296 states that Hume, as an assimilationist, was second only in influence to Adam Smith; page 331 refers to Stewart's using infanticide, an example as put forth originally by Smith; page 372 refers to English language use by Hume and Smith. In AV: page 10 is a reference to Smith being the grandfather of a particular tradition of a concept of justice; page 23 pairs together Hume and Smith to indicate that they, among others, saw sociology as part of philosophy, page 37 lists the most prominent members of the Scottish Enlightenment, page 51 contains a list of those philosophers who might have failed because they were subject to a "highly specific shared historical background"; page 54 pairs Smith and Hume together as the "least self-questioning" members of the Scottish Enlightenment, "presumably because they are already comfortable and complacent within the epistemological scheme of British empiricism"—MacIntyre does not defend this claim further; page 61 lists Hume, Smith, and Kant as philosophers whose conceptual changes motivated political change; page 234–235 contains a catalog of Smithian virtues. The paragraph which follows immediately after this citation begins with the observation that "Smith's catalogue of the virtues is then not the same as Hume's."; page 236 refers to Smith's stoicism and Republicanism and his stand against casuistry; page 239 explains that when Cobbett speaks of philosophers, he is, among others, referring to WN.

[12] I identified with this and eventually understood him as a fork in the road to Kantian liberalism. Amartya Sen makes a related argument in *The Idea of Justice*, although Fleischacker suggests more similarities between the two in *A Third Concept of Liberty* (Sen, *The Idea of Justice*; Fleischacker, *A Third Concept of Liberty*; See also: Weinstein, "Kant and Smith on Imagination, Reason, and Personhood").

My argument is not that Smith is left-wing. There is scholarship debating whether it is legitimate to understand Smith as partisan.[13] There is even a discussion as to whether he can be considered liberal at all.[14] I am not making any such claims here.

I am reporting instead that Smith's explorations spoke to me personally and that he identified fault lines which I also viewed as essential to the human experience. Perhaps I read him incorrectly; this is irrelevant. It is simply a fact that I responded to him emotionally and I would spend the rest of my professional career engaging either his ideas, or others', filtered through a Smithian lens. My seminar paper for that class was called "Can Men Teach Women's Studies? An Exploration of Adam Smith's Theory of Sympathy."

I would transfer into the Philosophy Department in the middle of that seminar, thanks to Griswold's generous encouragement. I would take many classes with him, including another seminar on the Scottish Enlightenment, and he would direct my dissertation on Smith, Rawls, and MacIntyre on liberal neutrality.[15] It would take me years to grasp and accept that graduate programs in philosophy are vocational efforts designed to socialize professional academics, not communities for entertaining the deep mysteries of life. In many ways, this article constitutes a renewed attack on philosophical sequestration.

Griswold was sometimes patient with my inability to grasp the academic virtues, as he and Smith might call them, and impatient at others. It is beyond question I am in the position to write this essay because of him; I will always be grateful. Yet the "wonder" of philosophy gets lost in the process of writing seminar papers, getting a job, securing tenure, and striving for full professor—"wonder" is Smith's term (HA Intro.1–6). Teaching has helped me preserve that excitement to a certain extent, but the history of ideas is unforgiving. In the next two sections, I hope to reproduce some of the excitement of discovery as I remember it.

2.1 *What I Saw in* The Theory of Moral Sentiments

The Theory of Moral Sentiments book VII begins with Smith arguing that in order to understand "the principles of morals" one must ask two questions: "wherein does virtue consist" and "by what power or faculty in the mind is it, that this character, whatever it be, is recommended to us?" (TMS VII.i.1). In other words, what does it mean to be a good person and how do we access this knowledge? Smith does not list

[13] Fleischacker, *On Adam Smith's "Wealth of Nations"*; Fleischacker, *A Short History of Distributive Justice*; McLean and Brown, *Adam Smith, Radical and Egalitarian.*

[14] Winch, *Adam Smith's Politics*; Harpham, "Liberalism, Civic Humanism, and the Case of Adam Smith"; Letwin, "Was Adam Smith a Liberal?"; Winch, "Adam Smith and the Liberal Tradition"; Khalil, "Is Adam Smith Liberal?" I myself have a forthcoming article on whether Smith is classical liberal, referencing the narrower and more political conscious category (Weinstein, "Is Adam Smith a Classical Liberal").

[15] Weinstein, *Adam Smith and the Problem of Neutrality in Contemporary Liberal Theory.*

the obvious third question "how do we become this person?" He is interested in process more than content; TMS is moral psychology more than metaethics.

There is reason to think these two questions are a summation of TMS itself. However, Smith only enumerates them at the beginning of Part VII, the final section, a historical overview of moral philosophy. By this time, he has already presented his own theory, and these remarks immediately follow his taxonomy of the virtues, a lengthy discussion he only added for the sixth edition. This tells us that Smith had a long journey before he narrowed down the questions and that describing excellence of character is, maybe, not quite an afterthought but something that does not happen automatically.

Smith introduces his section on virtue by claiming that character is judged first, as it affects someone's own happiness, and then second, as it affects others' (TMS VI.intro.1). On its own, this feels Aristotelian in that he is portraying happiness teleologically, but later on, Smith will seem to argue that happiness is tranquility similar to that of "the beggar, who suns himself by the side of the highway" (TMS IV.i.10). This precludes a simplistic contemplative framework for happiness and Griswold argues Smith offers two competing theories, a high and low happiness that mimics Stoicism (TMS VII.ii.1.21, VII.ii.1.42).[16]

It clearly took Smith a while to figure out where he was going and I would suggest he is doing a lot more than he thinks he is. I recognize that such a statement runs counter to history-of-philosophy methodology which aims to interpret texts as their authors intended them to be read. But how could such a forward-thinking philosopher not be on the cusp of what's happening? Smith's lifespan is coextensive with the Scottish Enlightenment. He is writing as forces coalesce to trigger three world-altering revolutions: the American, the French, and the Industrial. Technology and social mores are changing rapidly and England's manufacturing sector is exploding with its access to resources from the Americas.

The case can be made that Smith not only founded modern economics, but also sociology and English as a discipline.[17] TMS inspires both *A Vindication of the Rights of Women*—it is cited twice,[18] and *Uncle Tom's Cabin.*[19] It is noteworthy that not only are these texts of liberation, they are works by women.[20] There was something about TMS that spoke to them in similar ways to how it spoke to me. [21]

---

[16] These are important nuances because if happiness is a synonym for tranquility, then Smith risks being reduced to a hedonist or utilitarian (Griswold, *Adam Smith and the Virtues of Enlightenment*, p. 220; Weinstein, *Adam Smith's Pluralism*, p. 104).

[17] Salomon, "Adam Smith as Sociologist"; Court, "Adam Smith and the Teaching of English Literature."

[18] Leddy, "Grave, Philosophical and Cool Reasoner"; Mokre, "On Adam Smith and Gender Construction."

[19] Camfield, "The Moral Aesthetics of Sentimentality."

[20] Kuiper, "Adam Smith and His Feminist Contemporaries."

[21] Chris Nyland reconstructs Smith's historical approach to women's evolving freedom, although as one would imagine, Smith's writings on women are controversial (Nyland, "Adam Smith: Stage Theory and the Status of Women").

How should we summarize TMS? One sketch is to suggest that Smith is trying to modernize virtue theory for commercial society and the emerging liberalisms. He is confronting the relativism of cultural expectation while attempting to preserve a method of normatively assessing character. Both Plato and Aristotle saw fundamental differences between people and grouped them according to their natures; Smith rejects this. Loosely defined and adjusted for nuance, this is the type of interpretation we find in Ryan Hanley's *Adam Smith and the Character of Virtue.*[22] Substitute the Stoics for Aristotle and we have Gloria Vivenza's *Adam Smith and the Classics.*[23]

A second sketch is that TMS is attempting to create a unified theory of humanity on Newtonian or other grounds.[24] This is the Humean "science of man."[25] It argues that Smith presents an integrated system with TMS at its foundation, relying on future books to describe constants and contrasts of motivation within different spheres of human action.[26] Griswold presents an account like this rooted in the Platonic political agenda in *Adam Smith and the Virtues of Enlightenment,* and in Adam Smith's *Marketplace of Life*, James Ottseon offers an alternative with an eye toward centering human competition from a libertarian perspective. [27]

A third sketch is that TMS is an early attempt at describing the social construction of identity. According to this picture, Smith negotiates cultural difference by investigating the interaction between physical proximity and social connectedness. Here, Smith is struggling with the diminishing sense of responsibility toward others that will eventually be defined by ethnic and political boundaries of the nation state. In essence, he is asking whether globalization is the same as cosmopolitanism while also wondering whether moral obligation is discoverable using the new social science.[28] This is how I interpret him in *Adam Smith's Pluralism*, although I presume the Newtonian sketch as well.[29] It also describes Fonna Forman-Barzilai's *Adam Smith and the Circles of Sympathy*.[30]

---

[22] Hanley, *Adam Smith and the Character of Virtue*.

[23] Vivenza, *Adam Smith and the Classics*.

[24] Hetherington, "Isaac Newton's Influence on Adam Smith's Natural Laws in Economics"; Schliesser, "Some Principles of Adam Smith's Newtonian Methods in the Wealth of Nations."

[25] Hume, *A Treatise of Human Nature*, para. Intro 7. Adam Ferguson's *Essay on the History of Civil Society* is often cited as the first sociology book, but TMS predates it and I think, does every kind of thing Ferguson does, even if their content is different. Furthermore, Smith accused Ferguson of plagiarizing from him, which led to significant tension between the two. (Ferguson, *An Essay on the History of Civil Society*; Weinstein, "The Two Adams").

[26] Griswold, *Adam Smith and the Virtues of Enlightenment*.

[27] Otteson, *Adam Smith's Marketplace of Life*.

[28] This is an interesting analogue to Aquinas whose project was to justify Aristotelean logic by illustrating that it can come to the same conclusions as revelation. Smith is justifying the new social sciences by mapping it onto classical virtue structures. TMS parts from Hume by arguing that one can derive an "ought" from an "is" (Weinstein, *Adam Smith's Pluralism*, pp. 231–32).

[29] Weinstein, *Adam Smith's Pluralism*.

[30] Forman-Barzilai, *Adam Smith and the Circles of Sympathy Cosmopolitanism and Moral Theory*; See also Mokre, "On Adam Smith and Gender Construction."

The third sketch spoke to me as a graduate student particularly because of Smith's emphasis on the imagination as a capacity. I can't think of any cultural conversation I had been exposed to that described thinking in these terms.[31] I experienced a great deal of discussion about creativity growing up among artists, but the imagination was largely associated with children's playtime.[32]

Smith regards the imagination as a primary human capacity, a component of moral judgment. It can be cultivated through experience and education, making it analogous to any other physical or cognitive capacity. It can be better or worse. It can be malnourished by the individual or starved by society; we will revisit this.

The imagination, for Smith, is the foundation of social knowledge, a shocking contrast to what I had been taught. Virtually all left-leaning discourse since the 1960s suggested that political structures needed to overcome the failures and incapacities of the imagination. Injustice and inequality were supported by unbridgeable differences: men could not understand women's experience; White people could not understand Black's.[33]

Pluralist societies were becoming multicultural, not assimilationist.[34] The nineties saw a shift from thinking about diversity in terms of tolerance, which John Grey describes as implicitly disapproving, to a non-begrudging celebration of difference.[35] This led to the somewhat precarious position that someone can value and even participate in other groups' offerings but must always be forthright about their separateness. Multiculturalism, so defined, is an act of assuming the role of guest and of welcoming the stranger, but it also evokes a spectator watching a play, a comparison Smith relies upon throughout TMS.[36] As I will explore with Smith, while this cultivates value pluralism, a liberal good, it also promotes factionalism and instability.

The mechanism Smith uses to describe fellow-feeling with others is sympathy; the word empathy did not yet exist.[37] Smith believes one can use the imagination to

---

[31] This ended up being the topic of my first significant journal article. A draft of which invited the recommendation that I stop "arguing" with Smith (Weinstein, "Sympathy Difference and Education: Social Unity in the Work of Adam Smith").

[32] A well-known discourse about the moral imagination did reach critical mass starting around this time but didn't make it into the seminar. A recent JSTOR search reveals out of 368 articles with "moral imagination" in the title, only 59 were published before 1991, the year I started grad school. Almost all of those were book reviews about literary criticism. This is hardly scientific, but my point is simply that this conversation had not trickled down to me within or outside academia.

[33] Chris Rock makes a joke that illustrates this well. During the initial rise of hip-hop, he remarks that White people often complain about how they "don't get rap." His response is: "that's okay, it's not for you." Unfortunately, I have been unable to track down the original performance of the joke.

[34] I'm talking about theory here. Reality is much more complicated and there still remain fairly consistent patterns of immigrants remaining on the fringes, their children assimilating well, and their grandchildren seeking a return to some traditional manifestations of cultural identity.

[35] Gray, *Enlightenment's Wake*, p. 18.

[36] Marshall, *The Figure of Theater*.

[37] There are a variety of interpretations of what sympathy denotes. Does it just reference the pleasure one gets from having analogous emotions or sentiments? Is it the act of tempering these senti-

reconstruct and relive others' experiences to a certain extent, and then morally judge those actions based on actors' circumstances, not the spectator's own. On the one hand, Smith argues that such sympathy is "what I should suffer if I was really you" (TMS VII.iii.1.4). This allows him to suggest that men can sympathize with women in childbirth and that the living can sympathize with the dead (TMS VII.iii.I.4, I.i.1.13). On the other, sympathy is always "weaker in degree" and imperfect (TMS I.i.1.2). Smith describes the original sentiment as the "substance" and the imagined sentiment as its "shadow" (TMS VI.ii.1.1). He makes use of qualifiers such as "as it were" and "in some measure" to designate that his metaphor should not be taken literally, such as: "we enter as it were into his body, and become in some measure the same person with him" (TMS I.i.1.2). Smith is forthright about the limits of imaginative moral judgment.[38]

Being able to imagine and sympathize over difference is not the same as discovering universal characteristics. One builds pluralism on common humanity while the other integrates inconsistencies. Cosmopolitanism and liberal individualism overlap but are not synonyms. I was and remain skeptical that Kantian liberalisms cultivate true diversity.[39] It may be the case that second-best is all we can do, that the "modus vivendi" compromise Rawls so denigrates is inevitable.[40] The perfect, after all, should not be the enemy of the good. But this doesn't alter the fact that settling on second best is still settling. How aware Smith is that he himself is limited by "the bourgeois virtues" is a matter of debate.[41]

Another aspect of TMS that spoke to me as a graduate student is the way Smith allows individuals to construct their own identities while having a measure of authenticity in their normative self-valuation. Smith is not an existentialist. His theory of freedom is narrow and not metaphysical; he would likely have been baffled at Sartre's observation that he was never freer than when he was in prison. Nevertheless, Smith paints a picture of the self that allows for flexibility and integrity.

---

ments to find concordance between spectator and actor? Is sympathy a capacity like the imagination is? I will pass over this debate, although my interpretation tends toward concordance.

[38] Weinstein, "Adam Smith's Impartial Spectator Is Neither Divine nor an Ideal Observer."

[39] In my doctoral dissertation, I would argue that Rawls's *Political Liberalism* does not have a mechanism for tolerating the intolerant and therefore precludes social change. I elaborate on this in an article comparing Rawls's overlapping consensus and Smith's recommendations for religious competition. I even revisit it in my recent book on Israel and Palestine, questioning whether political partitioning counts as victory. In the recent book, I write: "The liberal individualist insists that if Muslims and Hindus, for example, can't get along in India and require their own states to avoid violence, then it is proof that these religions are 'unreasonable,' and there is more work to be done. Segregation is an unacceptable resolution for diversity-minded modern philosophy" (Weinstein, *Adam Smith and the Problem of Neutrality in Contemporary Liberal Theory*; Weinstein, "Overlapping Consensus or Marketplace of Religions?"; Weinstein, *Israel, Palestine, and the Trolley Problem*, p. 46).

[40] Rawls, *Political Liberalism*, pp. 145–150.

[41] McCloskey, *The Bourgeois Virtues*; Justman, *The Autonomous Male of Adam Smith*.

Again, there is no original difference for Smith and children are largely indistinguishable. People develop capacities, personalities, imagination, and judgment over time. They see themselves through others and learn norms and expectations from society. "I judge of your sight by my sight, of your ear by my ear, of your reason by my reason, of your resentment by my resentment, of your love by my love. I neither have, nor can have, any other way of judging about them" (TMS I.i.3.10). No one raised in isolation could judge themselves either morally or aesthetically (TMS III.i.3).

This begins a process of approval-seeking that helps acculturate and lead to greater understanding of duty to the general rules of conduct. Smith's reliance on social norms opens sympathy to Aristotle's criticism of honor, that it only represents the values of those honoring, not that of the honoree.[42] In response, he argues that people desire to be praiseworthy rather than praised. They therefore develop and cultivate an imagined spectator who acts as their conscience. This construction provides normative evaluation independent of one's society and is the final arbiter of moral judgment.[43]

What stood out to me was the impartial spectator's role in finding individuality and assent in the face of conformity. Creation of an impartial spectator that rejects social norms is difficult because socialization emphasizes the status quo; one of the connections I made in light of my punk-rock background.[44] Sympathy is inherently conservative and resists social change. Self-awareness is also inaccurate. Against all the social forces that influence, the individual has an imperfect mirror: self-deceit is the "fatal weakness of mankind" and "the source of half the disorders of human life" (TMS III.4.6, also ed.2, III.i.5). For Smith, the journey to ethical maturity is a slog; it is not for the faint of heart.

A central villain in Smith's moral psychology is a condition I would call "character dysmorphia"—the distorted perception of self-image that appears accurate and unmediated by the self-spectator.[45] It is one very familiar to all of us but

---

[42] Aristotle, *Nicomachean Ethics*, lines 1095b22–26.

[43] Scholars disagree as to how reliable the impartial spectator is, some see it as an agent of the divine or presenting an Archimedean point of view; others, including myself, understand it to be limited by individual human capacities. At issue is how seriously readers should take Smith's use of theological language in TMS. Is it meant literally or is it just a rhetorical smokescreen protecting him from persecution by the Scottish Kirk? How one interprets the impartial spectator or its accuracy changes depending on whether TMS presumes theism, deism, or atheism (Daniel B. Klein et al., "The Impartial Spectator Rises · Econ Journal Watch"; Weinstein, "Adam Smith's Impartial Spectator Is Neither Divine nor an Ideal Observer").

[44] Punk subcultures of this period saw themselves as making radical statements against social conformity but did so within a subculture with strong esoteric identifiers (See: John Joghead Pierson, *Episode 228*).

[45] I derive the name from body dysmorphia, the popular-culture way of describing Body Dysmorphia Disorder. I chose these terms because those with the disorder actually see themselves as fat, for example, even when they are dangerously thin. "Body dysmorphic disorder (BDD) is defined as a preoccupation with an 'imagined' defect in one's appearance. Alternatively, where there is a slight physical anomaly, then the person's concern is markedly excessive. The preoccupation is associ-

especially the marginalized who learn their social worth through stereotypes and bigotry. If I judge my sight by yours, and you find me ugly or hate me, how can I not but believe this of myself as well?[46]

It's not that Smith had solutions to these problems, per se. Instead, he gave me a language to reflect on them other than the one I had been raised in, which was failing me. He offered me a framework for discussing self-creation in the face of conformity, and a way to consider the virtues without the Greek teleological infrastructure. He felt modern and wasn't horrible. He wasn't racist and offered powerful condemnations of dehumanization, especially of African slaves which he did not own (TMS V.2.9). Nor was he overtly Christian, classist, or anti-woman. He never once concerned himself with "The Jewish Question" or its longstanding anticipations. He told a good story and wrote like a teacher.[47]

Smith was also realistic. The other element of TMS that caught my attention was the juxtaposition of commitments to whom we love with our non-intimates, and those whom we think of abstractly. Smith offers a thought experiment in which an earthquake decimates China and someone back in Scotland, presumably, is contemplating the scale of destructions (TMS 3.3.4). Smith reports that such a person would lament and muse about the cruelty of fate but then go about business as usual. He then contrasts this intellectualized rumination to the person's likely emotional devastation at losing their little finger. The same person who went about their daily lives in the face of the millions who died would be emotionally debilitated by the minor tragedy of a lost extremity. However, rather than suggest hypocrisy, Smith asks whether they would sacrifice all the Chinese people in order to save their finger.[48] "Human nature startles with horror at the thought, and the world, in its greatest depravity and corruption, never produced such a villain as could be capable of entertaining it" (TMS IIII.3.5).

I suspect Smith is overly optimistic; I can imagine half a dozen people who would probably prefer their little finger to the lives of others. What intrigued me most was his follow-up question: "But what makes this difference? When our passive feelings are almost always so sordid and so selfish, how comes it that our active principles should often be so generous and so noble?" (TMS III.3.4).

This is a good question. It is interesting. It is really difficult and while many philosophers have tried to answer it, few succeed. In fact, I only encountered the most persuasive response a few months ago, in Elizabeth Minnich's *The Evil of Banality*.[49] The book explores how everyday individuals can commit grotesque atrocities such as genocide and poses an answer that relies on a bureaucratic trifecta

ated with many time consuming rituals such as mirror gazing or constant comparing" (Veale, "Body Dysmorphic Disorder").

[46] See: E. J. R. David, *Internalized Oppression*.

[47] Smith composed the majority of TMS while holding his two Chairs at Glasgow College.

[48] This is obviously a reference to Hume's famous remark, "Tis not contrary to reason to prefer the destruction of the whole world to the scratching of my finger" (Hume, *A Treatise of Human Nature*, para. 2.3.3.6).

[49] Minnich, *The Evil of Banality*.

of greed, careerism, and status.[50] How this relates to my initial encounter with Smith can be described by a comment she made when I interviewed her in 2025:

> ...how we are thinking about somebody, as you said, in context...matters and bears paying attention to, but we tend to take it out of the calculation for some of the hardest things to understand and some of the most glorious things to experience, like great beauty and love, and people don't think of those as thinking experiences. *We've done something terrible to the notion of thinking. We have shrunk it way down to marching along, to a certain logic that has been prescribed...*[51]

This is not Smith's language, of course, but it presents a message I received from him in 1991. It includes the other aspect of Smith that I found so powerful: that emotion and reason work in tandem, not in opposition. Passions are rational for Smith and reason is emotional.[52]

All of the above is what I was thinking the first time I opened *The Wealth of Nations*.

3 The Wealth of Nations, 1991

Approaching WN from the perspective of pluralistic political cohesion and the social construction of the self requires identifying where WN describes actual individuals. This is surprisingly difficult because the text largely concerns aggregates or collectives. To find true individuality, we need to reverse its trajectory—to invert it, so to speak.[53]

3.1 Inverting the Text

Reading WN inverted involves no longer beginning with Introduction but starting with Book V's discussion of the roles and financing of the sovereign.[54] We then loop around so that Book I, his account of the division of labor, is in the middle, and Book IV, his historical critique of other systems of political economy, is at the end. This makes the structure of WN parallel TMS, which begins by observing the

---

[50] Minnich, *The Evil of Banality*, pp. 209–211.

[51] Elizabeth Minnich, *How Is It That Ordinary People Can Commit Such Overwhelming Evil?, italics are mine.*

[52] Weinstein, *Adam Smith's Pluralism*, Chap. 6.

[53] It is impossible to assert this without noting the irony that WN is almost always read within the liberal individual discourse. The loss of the individual in the face of the collective has been a central problem for the tradition, especially Hobbes, Rousseau, and Rawls.

[54] To be clear, I do not mean to suggest that the insights in this section come from my time as a grad student (if only). I am revisiting WN in that context with my current abilities.

pleasure actors have in witnessing the happiness of others—human connectedness in the face of separation—and ends with a foray through the history of ethics.

If we read WN as printed, our first questions concern national wealth and what would eventually be called human capital: how can a society extract more value from individuals to increase its standard of living? If we start with Book V, however, we begin by asking about the limits of our responsibilities toward others. What is the role of the collective and how much should people contribute to its maintenance? This reframes Smith's full discussion as value-laden rather than utilitarian. To put it polemically, he is now describing a giving rather than an extraction economy.

This is not to suggest that the beginning of WN is morally barren. Smith explicitly articulates an ethical reason for developing his political economy: to manage scarce resources, abjectly poor societies are frequently reduced to killing babies, the elderly, and the sick. Smith wants to build a system of wealth to stop this, a "universal opulence which extends itself to the lowest ranks of the people" (WN I.i.10). However, under this approach, no one steps in to save the condemned. The moral problem is not resolved with intentional action; its solution is systemic and absent of individual accountability.

In Book V, however, the sovereign is made up of real people funded by actual taxpayers. For Smith, taxes are "to the person who pays it a badge, not of slavery, but of liberty… he is subject to government,… he cannot himself be the property of a master" (WN V.ii.g.11). Liberty necessitates responsibility for Smith, but this reciprocal relationship has been obscured by all-against-all libertarianism. I personally did and still do see the world in terms of the first question humanity asks God, in the Abrahamic tradition: am I my brother's keeper? For libertarianism, the answer is no.

There is no theory of political participation in Smith's writing; the fragments of his unfinished treatises on public policy and jurisprudence were burnt upon his death. We can only guess whether he favored democracy, republicanism, or if he was, as Donald Winch argues, a "skeptical whig."[55] Yet, WN does have much to say about the institutions of governance, a fact Smith anticipates in LJ where he reports that commercial society requires more state funding than previous social arrangements. A more expensive sovereign does not designate an "oppressed" people; it is an indication of their wealth (LJB 310).

Smith's economics is built on self-focused people who lack collective agency, but his brief comments on governing suggest an optimism about what people are capable of. For example, he distinguishes between a virtuous legislator "whose deliberations ought to be governed by general principles which are always the same" and "that insidious or crafty animal vulgarly called a statesman or politician, whose councils are directed by the momentary fluctuations of affairs" (WN IV.ii.39).[56] He also regularly uses the phrase "general interest of the society" and its

[55] Winch, *Adam Smith's Politics*, p. 26.

[56] Haakonssen, *The Science of a Legislator*, p. 97.

variants which are analogues to the birds' eye perspective of TMS's impartial spectator (WN I.x.c.25, I.xi.p.8, I.xi.p.10, IV.v.b.12, IV.vii.c.62).[57] Smith's appeals to the public good illustrates that WN is not egoistic.

This is our first foray into WN's contribution to the social construction of the self—the third sketch of TMS that attracted my attention. Economic agency may not necessitate systematic education per se, but wise decision making does, as does political participation. There needs to be a process of economic maturity that parallels moral maturity. In WN: "every individual…can, in his local situation, judge much better than any statesman or lawgiver can do for him" (WN IV.2.10). In TMS: "Every man is, no doubt, by nature, first and principally recommended to his own care; and as he is fitter to take care of himself than of any other person" (TMS II.ii.2.1).

3.2 Virtuous Consumers

As TMS describes, taking care of oneself means developing an identity with accurate self-awareness, countering the negative effects of character dysmorphia. This is necessary because self-conscious commercial agency requires informed consent and tempered rational desire. If agents are incapable of caring for themselves, they can't flourish. In 1991, we might have asked how one knows what is valuable, separable from our social role. Do I buy something because I am a punk rocker or am I a punk rocker because I buy it?

Smith does not offer a theory of consumer choice. Instead, he presents two components in an unrelated fashion that, taken together, anticipate epistemological difficulties. The first is his claim that all people share a "uniform, constant, and uninterrupted effort of every man to better his condition" (WN II.iii.31, II.iii.28). The second is that there is a "natural price" calculated by what it actually costs to bring something to market combined with reasonable profit (WN I.vii.4). This is distinct from "market price," which is "the actual price at which any commodity is commonly sold" (WN I.vii.7).

Smith argues that in a well-functioning market, under conditions of "perfect liberty," the market price tends toward the natural price. Scholars disagree as to whether there is a normative element in pricing (WN V.ii.i.7, WN Vi.i.g.42).[58] This is not unimportant. If there is a moral component to what a merchant can justifiably charge, or a floor to what consumers should pay, then there are serious immoralities

[57] Variations such as "general interest of the whole" and "general interest of the country" (Göçmen, *The Adam Smith Problem Reconciling Human Nature and Society in "The Theory of Moral Sentiments" and Wealth of Nations).*

[58] Fleischacker argues there is not, but I and Jeffrey T. Young see a direct connection to Medieval just price theory (John W. Baldwin, "The Medieval Theories of the Just Price: Romanists, Canonists, and Theologians in the Twelfth and Thirteenth Centuries"; Young, *Economics as a Moral Science*, pp. 7, 27, 68, 144; Weinstein, *Adam Smith's Pluralism*, pp. 148–149).

in rent-seeking or the poor pricing that results from the frequent conspiracies to "deceive and even oppress the public" (WN I.x.c.27, I.x.i, pp. 8–10).

The relationship between natural and market price is intertwined with supply and demand. Low prices are beneficial to the consumer but motivate producers to invest their capital elsewhere.[59] Some people are going to make better, more aware decisions than others. Smith therefore implies what I call elsewhere, an "intellectually virtuous consumer" who knows when the market and natural price align and purchase accordingly, and a "complementary 'intellectually virtuous merchant'" who knows when to sell.[60] In a perfect world, all exchange would happen when natural and market price meet.[61]

WN does not offer an account of how one develops critical commercial judgment, nor does Smith anticipate modern notions of manufactured desire. He also predates the invention of the subconscious and modern discussion of addictive self-destructiveness. He therefore lacked the language to address those moments when someone "falsely" wants something—such as when an addict deeply desires what they should not want, a shortcoming that I was acutely aware of, given my background.

Smith does, however, explain that business success comes from "industry, prudence, and circumspection" which brings us back to the first interpretive sketch of TMS as a modernization of virtue theory for commercial societies (TMS III.5.8).[62] For Smith, economic behavior is a consequence of moral character, which is why he has such harsh words for the rich and greedy.[63]

59 Muller, *The Mind and the Market*, pp. 63–64. Smith predates the modern definition of economics as the study of choice in the face of scarcity, but he clearly anticipates it.

60 Weinstein, *Adam Smith's Pluralism*, pp. 151–153.

61 This equilibrium is the moment of "just price" for Smith. Again, he does not use this term and interpreting it as such is controversial.

62 Weinstein, "Adam Smith's Advice on Living Well in a Commercial Society."

63 Smith divides goods into necessities, conveniences, and luxuries, and mostly reserves his critiques for the third. He observes that the eyes of the rich are bigger than their stomach (TMS IV.1.10) and dismisses their purchases as "baubles" and "trinkets" (TMS IV.i.6, IV.i.10). In WN, he refers to their greed and avarice, and at one point describes their acquisitions as "ornamental," "frivolous," and "trifling." He advises that this will lead to one's fortune being "completely annihilated as if [it] had never existed" (WN II.3.38). As Michael Emmett Brady sums it up, "Smith spent close to 50 pages of the Wealth of Nations…warning against the economic behavior of the members of the Upper Income Class he described as Prodigals, Imprudent risk takers, and Projectors, due to the very negative, detrimental impacts their speculative behavior had on society as a whole" (Brady, "Adam Smith's Analysis of the Good (Sober People) and the Bad (Projectors, Prodigals and Imprudent Risk Takers)," p. 3).

3.3 WN's Educating the Public

There is something else underlying the discussion here. Smith was deeply appreciative of Voltaire whom Muller calls the first "intellectual" because he was the first to try to influence the new phenomenon called "public opinion."[64] MacIntyre and others draw a line between this and Smith's reading public, claiming that Scotland had "that very rare phenomenon, an educated public"[65] How accurate they are is a matter of contention, but there is little doubt that Smith was interested both in addressing general audiences and describing a mechanism through which they could be further educated.[66]

The Voltaire connection emphasizes that Smith's remarks about education address people as individuals and as groups. For example, Smith refers to actors in command of their desires as sober and prudent (cf. WN II.ii.77, II.iii.12, II.iv.15, IV.ii.11, IV.v.a.36) and says of the collective, "an instructed and intelligent people besides are always more decent and orderly than an ignorant" (WN V.i.f.61). This is not insignificant. An educated populace is "more disposed to examine, and more capable of seeing through, the interested complaints of faction and sedition" (WN V.i.f.61).

Here, Smith references another of Voltaire's concerns, fanaticism and factionalism. The *philosophe* was finely attuned to the recent religious wars "when three or four sects were tearing Great Britain asunder with civil wars undertaken in the name of God," wars over trivialities that arose from homogeneity.[67] "Had there been only one religion in England there would be danger of despotism, if there were two they would cut each other's throats, but there are thirty, and they live in peace and happiness."[68] As we will see, Adam Smith will adopt this point of view. For me, it called into question the activist strategy of amplifying the interest group or bloc.

---

[64] Smith calls Voltaire the "most universal genius perhaps which France has ever produced" and "nearly upon a level with the greatest authors of the last age" (Letter 17). He is reputed to have had a bust of Voltaire in his home (Muller, *The Mind and the Market*, 20–21) and to have replied angrily when, late in life, he heard a lesser writer compared to the Frenchman. He reportedly banged his hand on the table and declared "Sir, there is only one Voltaire" (Ross, *The Life of Adam Smith*, p. 429). Phillipson claims Smith "become a disciple of Voltaire's in matters of religion" at Oxford (Phillipson, 2010, p. 58) and visited him several times at home (Pearson, 2008, p. 315). Voltaire appears to have returned this affection, lamenting that in France, "We have nothing to compare with him. I am embarrassed for my dear compatriots" (Ross, *The Life of Adam Smith*, p. 208).

[65] Macintyre, *Whose Justice?*, p. 248; see also: Herman, *How the Scots Invented the Modern World.*

[66] Weinstein, *Adam Smith's Pluralism*, pp. 171–172.

[67] Voltaire wrote that "a doctor named Prynne, scrupulous in the extreme, who would have thought himself damned for ever if he had worn a cassock instead of a short coat, and would have liked one half of the human race to massacre the other for the glory of God and propaganda fide..." (Muller, *The Mind and the Market*, p. 27).

[68] Muller, *The Mind and the Market*, pp. 26–27.

Organizers know that it is easier to mobilize around issues that are deeply rather than widely felt, but strong feelings inspire immoderate behaviors.[69]

For Smith, the government is essential for countering fanaticism. The first three chapters of Book V announce the three duties of the sovereign: protecting the society from invasion (WN V.i.a.); protecting individuals from one another and "establishing an exact administration of justice" (WN V.i.b); and creating and maintaining important public institutions too expensive for individuals or private groups to fund (WN V.i.c). Economists will call these public works natural monopolies;[70] for Smith they include infrastructure and fortifications required to maintain commerce (WN V.I.d, V.i.e).[71]

It is, however, the next two chapters, and the other two forms of public works, that concern us: institutions for "Educations of Youth" and for "Instruction of People of all Ages" (WN V.I.f–g). I have written a great deal about Smith's philosophy of education and his curricular recommendations, so I won't engage in the detail work here.[72] I shall, however, call attention to Smith's change of terminology, calling lessons for the young "education" and lifelong learning "instruction." Here again, we see him distinguishing between the individual and the collective.

The word "instruction" appears more than 100 years before "education"; it's very first use verifies that a sovereign king has made a command official by including his signet.[73] As it evolves up until Smith's day, it largely retains these political undertones while continuing to be about information disseminated informally, almost always authoritatively.[74] "Education" emerges almost exclusively in reference to children, quickly becomes formalized as lessons presented by a teacher to a student, and almost always implies a moral component.[75]

This is consistent with how Smith uses education to describe institutions and instruction to reference larger, more amorphous forces. As the chapters reveal, the young are to be educated by local schools but join adults in receiving instruction

[69] Tempering such sentiments is so central to rhetorical political strategy that the balance between feelings and expression is mentioned in the subtitle of the most influential book on organizing, at the time, Saul Alinsky's *Rules for* Radicals, which calls itself "a pragmatic primer for realistic radicals" (Alinsky, *Rules for Radicals*).

[70] Mill, *Principles of political economy*; Baumol, "On the Proper Cost Tests for Natural Monopoly in a Multiproduct Industry."

[71] Chapter three also includes discussions of the bureaucracy and contributions of different types of trade companies, with special attention to the joint stock company.

[72] Weinstein, "Neutrality, Pluralism, and Education"; Weinstein, "Sympathy Difference and Education: Social Unity in the Work of Adam Smith"; Weinstein, "Introduction"; Weinstein, *Adam Smith's Pluralism*; Weinstein, "Symposium: Adam Smith on Education"; Weinstein, "Adam Smith and the Educative Critique: A Response to My Reviewers"; Weinstein, "The Political Hypotheses of Adam Smith's Pluralism: A Response to My Commentators"; Weinstein, "Adam Smith on Education."

[73] Oxford English Dictionary, *Instruction, n.*

[74] Instruction also becomes a technical legal term. It is first used to describe the directives people pass on to their representatives, the year before Smith's birth.

[75] Oxford English Dictionary, *Education, n.*

from religious organizations and the arts. In my work on education, I make the distinction between education and acculturation where the first denotes intentional lessons for named individuals and the latter references "social pressures arising from influences that are largely passive and always collective in origin."[76] Instruction is a useful third term because it denotes organized intentional persuasion, propaganda, and pressure to move people to specific goals. For Smith, this mainly consists of religious instruction, which prepares people "for another and a better world in a life to come" (WN V.i.g.1).

This reliance on religion, I believe, is a misdirect on Smith's part. Secular or critical comments would trigger the wrath of the Scottish Kirk.[77] Yet, immediately upon announcing the recommendation, Smith initiates a scathing attack on clergy. They appear to be gentlemen but are not (WN V.i.g.1). They gain power by moving society away from justice and fairness, toward fanaticism and superstition (WN V.i.g.1).[78] They support rising political stars then use them for retribution and exclusion of other sects (WN V.i.g.7). Following Voltaire, Smith argues for a society "divided into two or three hundred, or perhaps into as many thousand small sects" so no one can "disturb the publick tranquillity" (WN V.i.g.8).

This would be an undermining move if his goal were to glorify theological indoctrination. However, religion is not all bad. In TMS, Smith explains that adding religious justifications to the "General Rules of Morality" usefully increases their power (TMS (III.5.12). There is for Smith, "scarce any man…who by discipline, education, and example" cannot be taught to follow them and act with "tolerable decency" (TMS III.5.1). Even this optimism is tempered since "false notions of religion are almost the only causes which can occasion any very gross perversion of our natural sentiments" (TMS III.6.12).

Political theory has always struggled with the tension between identity *qua* individual and *qua* citizen. The phrase "liberal education" carries entire ideologies within it. The 1991s multiculturalism expressed skepticism about collective education in the face of difference, especially given the failures of the imagination I described.[79] My question, "Can men teach women's studies?" can be about standpoint epistemology, but also investigates the commensurability of human

---

[76] Weinstein, *Adam Smith's Pluralism*, p. 84.

[77] Smith was reputed to be strategically thoughtful and careful with the Kirk in mind. For example, in a letter to James Hutton, William Robertson suggests that Hutton ought to soften his theological critiques to forestall attack from the Kirk, specifically directing him to "consult our friend Mr. Smith and on following his advice you will be safe" (Kennedy, "The Hidden Adam Smith in His Alleged Theology," p. 39).

[78] Close readers will notice that I omitted Smith's observation that these critiques apply to "every religion except the true." On the one hand, I can understand why this might feel intellectually dishonest. However, first, Smith was not a theocrat, which seems obvious enough to not have to prove. Second, there is no indication of which religion he regarded to be true and how theology would improve Smith's secular system, especially since "true religion" was a sixteenth century rallying cry (Muller, *The Mind and the Market*, p. 24).

[79] I explore this question using a Smithian filter, but not through Smith himself, in Weinstein, "Neutrality, Pluralism, and Education" (See also: Gutmann, *Democratic Education*; Nussbaum,

experience. In WN, this discussion is not about the gender, race, and class fault-lines I found so familiar.[80] It emphasized how religions construct identity.[81]

For Smith, religious worldview is core to how one sees oneself. It provides social connection, recreation, and moral restraint, all public goods for Smith. He describes the poor person who felt seen and tempered in their home village but who moves to the city and is "sunk in obscurity and darkness," with no one against whom to measure their morality—character dysmorphia. This isolation leads to self-neglect and "low profligacy and vice" (WN V.i.g.12). A welcoming sect reverses this alienation. It is usually "austere" with "very severe" punishments, which is good since, echoing Smith's early comment about an educated people, adherents of small sects are more " regular and orderly" than followers of the "established church" (WN V.i.g.12).

Again though, it's not that simple. For Smith, "that which divides us also unites us."[82] Isolated people are attracted to religious communities because "melancholy and gloomy humour" nurse superstition and "enthusiasm" (WN.g.i.15). Adherents are "disagreeably rigorous and unsocial" (WN V.i.hg.12), a danger because "the authority of religion is superior to every other authority" (WN V.i.g.17). Those who seek religious community in the face of isolation can destabilize the state, diminish the power of the sovereign, and trigger the kind of civil war Smith and Voltaire write under the shadow of, because they always choose the most fanatical candidates (WN V.i.g.36). Smith is therefore explicit that the sovereign has no authority over "articles of faith," to "counterbalance the united authority of the clergy of the established church" (WN V.i.g.18).

This is where schooling and other forms of instruction come in. Smith prescribes "science and philosophy… the great antidote to the poison of enthusiasm and superstition," along with frequent and happy "publick diversions" (WN V.g.1.14–15). He offers recommendations for curriculum, how to improve teachers of every level, and strategies to motivate the poor who may not see the long-term benefit of education for their children. It is not exactly the same thing, but this too spoke to me because my own education is what lifted me out of my destructive environment. Upon the death of my undergraduate mentor, I began my published remembrance with the question: "What does one say about the teacher who saved your life?"[83]

Cultivating Humanity; McDonough and Feinberg, *Citizenship and Education in Liberal-Democratic Societies*).

[80] My argument in *Adam Smith's Pluralism* is that gender, race, and class are largely resolvable differences under Smith's system (Weinstein, *Adam Smith's Pluralism*, Chap. 4; Weinstein, "Adam Smith and the Educative Critique: A Response to My Reviewers").

[81] This debate held less weight in 1991. It seems more important now, after the attacks on September 11th and the influence of a revived Christian nationalism in the United States.

[82] Weinstein, *Adam Smith's Pluralism*, pp. 25, 85.

[83] Weinstein, "Requiem for A Philosophy Professor."

3.4 WN's Ethical and Economic Overlap

WN's role in social construction of identity is particularly explicit in Smith's discussion of the conditions of the working class. Recall that all people are fundamentally similar at birth, that there is no original difference. Distinction is the product of the division of labor and "habit, custom, and education" (WN I.ii.4). Dog breeds are more different than people are (WN I.ii.5, V.i.f.50).

Unfortunately, repetitive and thoughtless work drives people to "drowsy stupidity" and "benumb[s] the understanding of almost all the inferior ranks of people" (WN V.i.f.5).[84] This is disastrous for several reasons. First, the national wealth is built on "skills, dexterity and judgment" and a less intelligent labor force will inspire less innovation.[85] Second, it inspires workers to indulge in vices, cause chaos, and lose control of their children: "the people who cloath the whole world are in rags themselves" (LJ(B) 330). Third, it constructs a deformed identity, another case of character dysmorphia. Comparing two individuals who are either physically or mentally "mutilated and deformed," the one with intellectual issues is "the more wretched and miserable of the two" (WN V.i.f.60).

WN's discussion of workers' experience is located in his chapters on "revenue" for and "expense" of the sovereign, another misdirect. He seems to be asking how we pay for government while actually making a moral argument for better working conditions. He does the same in his attack on slavery; he builds a moral critique in TMS but WN presents an economic argument for those who cannot be moved by the dignity of others.[86] Slavery is more expensive than free labor; it is bad business.[87]

Smith does something analogous in education. For the more sophisticated thinkers, he presents a moral case for universal education grounded on character, propriety, and a wide account of human flourishing. For his more myopic financially focused readers, he explains how education makes markets stabler, consumers wealthier, and their private choices an element of the common good.

Smith is explicit as to who these limited readers are. Society is divided into landlords, laborers, and employers (WN I.xi, p. 7). Landlords can glimpse the common good, laborers are too focused on their own needs to see it, and employees are trapped in a conundrum because their wages rise in better economic times and fall

---

[84] Smith rarely sees work as meaningful and satisfying as our modern world often expects it to be. He does not subscribe to what Weber would call a protestant ethic (Weinstein, "Adam Smith on the Meaning of Work, Specialization, and the Division of Labor").

[85] Smith celebrates the intellectual potential of the working classes, arguing that innovation comes from specialization. He offers multiple examples of this throughout WN, including a technological advancement made by a child who wanted to leave his work to play (WN I.i.8, Weinstein, "Adam Smith on the Meaning of Work, Specialization, and the Division of Labor").

[86] Smith virtually rends his garments when he writes of African slaves: "Fortune never exerted more cruelly her empire over mankind, than when she subjected those nations of heroes to the refuse of the jails of Europe, to wretches who possess the virtues neither of the countries which they come from, nor of those which they go to…" (TMS V.2.9).

[87] Weinstein, "Adam Smith's Critiques of Slavery."

in worse.[88] WN addresses what we would now call the business community. Smith is trying to figure out how he can educate the collective, not just individuals.

This brings us back to "'public opinion,' a product of new institutions through which a mass of citizens could become familiar with questions of government." Clubs, coffee houses, lodges, and journals were founded "with the aim of bringing philosophy out of closets and libraries to dwell in clubs and assemblies." This changed the "model of political influence…from the traditional direct appeal to the absolute monarch to the new appeal to the tribunal of 'the public.'"[89] Smith's work should be understood as a major moment in this process.

Smith taught at Glasgow College, well aware that he was educating the ruling class.[90] When he left academia, he shifted his rhetoric to address the world. There is a sense underneath all of his published work that he is writing for everyone. He addresses his audience as "we" throughout TMS,[91] and WN presumes no esoteric knowledge.[92] Smith intended his book to be used, not just read.

Compare this with Mandeville who argued against educating the poor because "bringing them up in ignorance" would keep them unaware of how much better their lives could be.[93] Or, consider, Voltaire's concern that education makes the poor less deferential.[94] Smith had none of these objections because he had faith in a social unity built on individuality. There is a "self-help" element to his work.

I hope it is obvious why a social-justice-oriented political organizer would be so attracted to Smith. Both he and Voltaire claim "man is made for action" (TMS II.iii.3.3).[95] Marx is always presented as someone for whom philosophy is about actual change. Smith presumes the same a century earlier.

4 Autobiographical Interlude 2

I will draw the line between my being a junior and senior scholar at the 2013 publication of *Adam Smith's Pluralism*. It was, in essence, the final version of my graduate paper "Can Men Teach Women's Studies?" which is how I describe it in the acknowledgments.

It goes without saying that a lot happened between then and now: I lived in Vienna, Austria, finished school, then made a circuitous route around the U.S. until

[88] Weinstein, "Is Adam Smith a Classical Liberal?" I will return to the laborers' perspective below.

[89] Muller, *The Mind and the Market*, p. 22.

[90] West, *Adam Smith*, p. 64.

[91] Griswold, *Adam Smith and the Virtues of Enlightenment*, p. 50.

[92] WN certainly references theories and details that require an education, but he explains all of them along the way, bringing his readers along with him. Hence, I would not regard his specialized discussion as exoteric.

[93] Mandeville and Kaye, *Fable of the Bees*, para. I.317.

[94] Muller, *The Mind and the Market*, p. 87.

[95] Muller, *The Mind and the Market*, p. 27.

I landed a job at the University of North Dakota. I earned tenure and promotions, and shifted to public philosophy; I have been on public radio and the Director of the Institute for Philosophy in Public Life for 18 years. I met someone, got married, had a daughter who is now in college, and rescued a few dogs. I matured in my moral and political convictions while living in a very conservative state, in a mostly rural and underpopulated area. My life was very far from what I had imagined it would be as a New York punk rocker or even a starry-eyed graduate student. I often describe the process of job hunting as shifting from fantasizing about where one wants to be to where one hopes to not end up. I'd like to think I have done good work and taught well at UND.

My biggest political shift was a rejection of the ideological model. I probably retain most of the same convictions about morality and justice that I came to grad school with, but I found no book, political party, or moral stance satisfying or adequately justifiable. I experimented with various levels of religious observance. I also went from optimism, to realism, to pessimism. I became conscious of a world that was even less fair, more dangerous, and profoundly more unjust than I perceived it as a 22-year-old.

In other words, I got older.

My old neighborhood changed radically. It became safer and more expensive. Gentrification and investment by private equity firms altered the demographics. Washington Heights went from being the drug-fueled hellscape pictured in the 1990 movie *New Jack City* to the romanticized musical of Lyn-Manuel Miranda's *The Heights.* I go back from time to time but can't relax when I'm there. My intellect knows it's safe, but my nervous system does not, especially when being with my family triggers my fight or flight mechanism. My identity was constructed by urban blight.

Punk rock changed too. Growing up, underground music was built on "scenes," physical communities who knew one another and passed albums around. Even in New York City, the epicenter was still the record store and there was always a distinction between local bands, national acts, and "imported" music. All that disappeared with the internet, Napster, and streaming. Now I can play almost anything I want but independent artists get swallowed up before they find an audience. Genres have replaced subcultures. I can reach out to countless virtual strangers, but social networks have very specific expectations with few role models. There are no more community norms. I've aged out of most of it.

In short, the communities I saw Smith describe in TMS were no longer accessible to me and whatever moral leadership I could offer had to be filtered through the classroom and public philosophy. But UND is a conservative, apolitical school, and North Dakota is a conformist's paradise governed by "Tall Poppy Syndrome"—the social phenomenon of ostracizing or "cutting down" the openly successful in the name of hegemony. Of course, like all American academics, I am hyperaware of being attacked for "bias" in the classroom, whatever that may mean.

The United States changed as well. September 11th moved the culture to one of perennial surveillance, a shift that Smith has little to say about since its advocates frame close scrutiny as safety from foreign hostility and domestic crime, the first two roles of the sovereign. The use of relentless technological scrutiny to promote efficient workers, as Amazon uses, for example, raises quite a few flags, given Smith's criticism of the negative impact of repetitive work, but the United States offers many of his ameliorative tactics, including universal education. There is a fine line between Smith's spectators and the panopticon.

America also saw the rise of a deeply felt debate about income inequality fueled by all the forces that gentrified Washington Heights and lowered real wages, as well as the rise of the global corporations that are now the gatekeepers of my access to punk rock. Shoddy financial instruments that Smith refers to as "stock jobbing" triggered The Great Recession (WN [IV.iii.b.77, IV.iii.b.14, V.i.e.25), and the subsequent bailout concentrated wealth in fewer people, a consolidation exacerbated during the Covid-19 pandemic. All of this inspired formal and informal protests, and widespread criticism of what has come to be called "late-stage capitalism."

The resulting Occupy Wall Street movement's complaints can be framed in two ways: as a Marxist plea for equality of result or a Smithian critique of unrealized universal opulence. This too is a conversation to put off but I will advertise that four of the original 200 Occupiers were my students, one of whom directly credits her involvement to reading Marx in my History of Nineteenth-Century Philosophy class.[96] Regardless of where they and I relate politically, I couldn't be prouder of them.

Another shift in the culture made empathy a political football. This started as a debate over the nomination of Supreme Court justice Sonia Sotomayor but expanded into broader jurisprudence discourse.[97] Eventually, it escalated into rhetoric that any Smithian would find baffling. In 2022, MAGA superstar Charlie Kirk stated "I can't stand the word empathy, actually. I think empathy is a made-up, new age term that—it does a lot of damage."[98] In 2025, billionaire entrepreneur Elon Musk called empathy "the fundamental weakness of Western civilization."[99] Once again, I will pass over substantive debate here other than to recall that part of what initially attracted me to Smith was his counterculture narrative. His outsider status is surprisingly enduring given his role as patron saint of capitalism. It is 2026, and I am even more convinced that the world "needs" Adam Smith.

There are countless other ways in which his work intersects with public debate; how could there not be? What are the rules of the market and upward mobility? What are the downsides of globalization? We were all shaken by the supply-line failures during the Covid pandemic. Perhaps the most amorphous intersection is the

---

[96] That's 1/50th of the original gathering which seems to be an appropriate contribution for North Dakota.

[97] Martha Nussbaum anticipated this debate in 1995. In *Poetic Justice, she explores the role of the* moral imagination in judicial education. The book is explicitly inspired by TMS. Blake, "Analysis | Gorsuch and Sotomayor's Extraordinary Factual Dispute"; Alt, "Senators Must Contest Sotomayor's View That Empathy, Ethnicity Can Overrule Law"; Couzo, "Sotomayor's Empathy Moves the Court a Step Closer to Equitable Adjudication"; Nussbaum, *Poetic Justice*, p. 3.

[98] Yahoo News, "Fact Check."

[99] McCammon, "How Empathy Came to Be Seen as a Weakness in Conservative Circles."

way in which new medicines and technology promote a materialist definition of mind: cognitive psychology won the day. Smith would have no understanding of neurotransmitters or serotonin inhibitors, but he was no fan of Hobbes, whose materialist relativism grounds modern cognitive science. A central concern I have highlighted is the relationship between the imagination and our physical selves. With my focus on TMS, I attended to the former. I now found myself concerned with the latter. What exactly do bodies have to do with all of this?

I am utterly dismissive of the aforementioned popular culture term "late-stage capitalism," which expresses nothing more than dissatisfaction with current political arrangements. It sounds like a critique but isn't; it's an emotive utterance as MacIntyre describes in *After Virtue*.[100] The phrase is rhetorically framed in terms of the history Marx borrowed from Smith but implies an inevitable collapse to the current political order. Plato and Rousseau might have a great deal to say about social decline, but Smith is a philosopher of progress and I am still "an Enlightenment guy" at heart. Late-stage capitalism is too simple and too ambiguous of a phrase to be helpful.

Yet, while dismissive of the rhetoric, I am fully in line with the criticism it represents. I take as given that current levels of income inequality are destructive to societies and the global population;[101] there is research on Smith and income inequality specifically.[102] It is however not clear that limiting trade or understanding the world solely in terms of class or power is as useful as so many of the younger generation presume. Even so, their sense of the game being rigged is justified and needs to be taken seriously.[103] In this environment, how can one not read WN in terms of "fair play"? Fair play is Smith's term (TMS II.ii.2.2).

I will preempt my next section by articulating two philosophical conclusions I came to through Smith. The first, which is the more obvious one, is that nothing is just one thing. No event has a singular cause or meaning. No fact is solely good or bad. Perspective and context are complicated. Contradictions are often true in important ways. As we shall see, Smith's discussion of the butcher, brewer, and baker must be read in this context.

My second more complex conclusion is that Smith's moral psychology is incomplete and inaccurate. Perhaps more precisely, I would argue that what Smith thinks he is doing is not fully representative of what he is actually accomplishing. Sympathy is neither principle-driven nor utilitarian. It isn't a pure virtue ethic either, given that

[100] MacIntyre, *After Virtue*, Chap. 2.

[101] Two particularly good texts on this subject are Wilkinson and Pickett, *The Spirit Level*; Wilkinson and Pickett, *The Inner Level*.

[102] cf. Baum, "Poverty, Inequality, and the Role of Government"; Boucoyannis, "The Equalizing Hand"; Rasmussen, "Adam Smith on What Is Wrong with Economic Inequality."

[103] Two tremendously important articulations of unfair market practices have not yet been adequately dealt with in Smith studies, especially: Klein, *The Shock Doctrine* and Piketty, *Capital in the Twenty-First Century*. An addendum would be Dabid Graeber's critique of Smith which is accurate in some important ways but misrepresents the consequences for Smith's theory (Graeber, *Debt*, Chap. 2).

Smith's agents develop rules for themselves and others. There is a thread of pre-existentialist commitment to authenticity that runs through TMS which deserves more attention. I have therefore come to conclude that the three dominant ethical schools of thought are not contradictory but are hierarchical. Here is how I describe it in my recent book on Israel and Palestine:

> Most of the time, people make moral decisions unreflectively, the way the Greeks described it. They are agents acting according to who they are as people. An honorable person will intuitively tell the truth while a just person will be happiest when they act fairly…
>
> Sometimes, however, people are faced with a complex problem that can't be resolved by habit or intuition, so good people fall back on stated moral principles, as Kant describes it. …When our character fails us, we want to do the right thing for the right reason, but this too can frustrate, because a lot of principled action is obsolete, or simply doesn't apply….
>
> When acting intuitively as good people of good character no longer guides us, and when we have no moral principles to fall back on, the best of us become consequentialists and try to do the greatest good or the least harm. As J.S. Mill puts it in Utilitarianism, the only proof that the greatest happiness principle is true is that in the end, everyone believes it.[104]

I recognize that I am beginning my account by "arguing" with Smith, but this will remain in the background. My intention in this final section is to explore Smith's ideas as I understand them now, in light of the new political realities I bring as a reader. My dissatisfaction with his moral psychology, in particular, makes centering WN all the more productive. I still see it as grounded in TMS—I hold to my published description of WN being "hyperlinked" elaborations of TMS's conclusions.[105] I am, however, more curious about its nuances than I once was.

---

[104] Weinstein, *Israel, Palestine, and the Trolley Problem*, pp. 12–13. In the book, I provide an illustration as to how the hierarchy works, which I present here solely as an explication. I do not intend this current article to provide any substantive claim or contribution to the debate about Israel and Palestine, nor am I making any connections between it and Smith. The passage reads, "When Israelis or their advocates defend themselves against accusations of genocide, they will often assert something akin to 'we are not those kinds of people.' This is ethics of character in action: we are not genocidal therefore we do not commit genocide. But critics will turn around and insist that Israelis (or even Jews as a whole) are, in fact, these kinds of people because mass death is happening before everyone's eyes. The normal psychological response to this is to move down the ladder of ethical theories to the level of principle. Israeli response becomes 'we are not committing genocide because that's not our intention. We are acting in self-defense.' It's a perfectly legitimate Kantian response but it doesn't actually solve the problem because all it does is make people comfortable with killing; it doesn't end it. Intention is redemptive but does not protect the innocent. So, to solve the actual problem, Israel and their advocates are forced to move one more notch down the ladder and say, 'we're doing the best we can,' falling back upon the utilitarian argument that the goal is to lessen the unavoidable pain (Weinstein, *Israel, Palestine, and the Trolley Problem*, 13–14).

[105] Weinstein, *Adam Smith's Pluralism*, p. 58.

5 Wealth of Nations 2026

The conclusion I drew from *Adam Smith's Pluralism* is this: libertarians have it backwards. Just institutions are not the product of a well-functioning market; a well-functioning market is the product of just institutions.[106] Smith did not use this specific language, but it aligns with his conclusions. It also reverses the standard way of considering WN, which is read as an economic text with political recommendations rather than a political text with economic recommendations. This alternative approach echoes my earlier description of reading WN beginning with Book V.

5.1 Natural Equality

A problem for reading WN is that it is regarded as wrong about key ideas, particularly the subjective nature of market value. For Smith, as we have already seen, there is more at play in exchange than simply what the market can bear. This leads to the calcification of the text. If Smith is wrong about subjectivity in exchange—if the final arbiter of the propriety of a purchase is satisfaction—then it becomes easier to discard the entire book, just as the Adam Smith Problem motivated people to dismiss his work as a whole.

The post-*Glasgow-Edition* Smithian renaissance was fortuitous for TMS because it took place alongside the reassertion of history in metaethics and a renewal of interest in the virtues. It offered an attractive alternative to the century-long stalemate between utilitarianism and deontology.[107] It suggested a non-Rawlsian framework to challenge analytic and Kantian ethics.[108] The majority of contemporary Smith scholarship centers TMS, sometimes even attempting to popularize his empathy-based ethics.[109] There is no equivalent to WN. It is studied almost exclusively from the perspective of the history of ideas. In contrast, my intention is to present WN as a living document, albeit a misunderstood one.

Difficulties arise from the fact that Smith does not fit squarely into any narrow ideological camp. His system is neither conservative, libertarian, nor classical

[106] More specifically, my argument is that libertarians argue perfect competition leads to social justice, good education, equity, and minimum standards of thriving. Smith, on the other hand, argues the opposite. Only when we have good universal education, social justice, equity, and minimum standards of thriving, can we move toward perfect competition. In retrospect, one of the failings of *Adam Smith's Pluralism* is that it never spelled out this conclusion as explicitly as I have done here.

[107] The triggering texts of this shift were MacIntyre, *After Virtue*; Nussbaum, *The Fragility of Goodness*; Taylor, *Sources of the Self*.

[108] cf. Fleischacker, *A Third Concept of Liberty*; Sen, *The Idea of Justice*.

[109] cf. Roberts, *How Adam Smith Can Change Your Life*; Fleischacker, *Being Me Being You*; Hanley, *Our Great Purpose: Adam Smith on Living a Better Life*.

liberal narrowly defined.[110] As I discussed above, there is even doubt as to whether he ought to be considered liberal.[111] Given that WN is not any of these things, what is it? I have already presented it in connection with my first sketch of TMS, an account of how political institutions build agency and commercial virtues, and my third sketch, a blueprint diagramming how education and employment contribute to the social construction of identity. I now describe it in terms of the second sketch, the theoretical grounding for a scientific mapping of human behavior.

As I understand it, the starting points of this unified scientific approach are as follows: Smith's system is coherent and consistent. It presumes the Newtonian understanding of the unity of the natural world, that the laws which govern the heavens are the same as those that govern the earth. This means that human nature is describable, predictable in the aggregate, and that social institutions ought to manage people as they are instead of how they should be. While institutions can nudge people in certain ways, they can never control them.

Muller argues that "the conceptual common denominator of Smith's major works was the analysis of the ways in which social institutions tend to pattern character through their appeal to human passions."[112] This is accurate but incomplete. It neglects the role of reason in evaluating and tempering the passions. It also disregards the physicality of human existence.

The latter necessitates the former two. Human beings are physically separate and only understand one another by investigating, imagining, evaluating, and judging observed actions. As we have already seen, Smith observes that separateness traps individuals in their own experience. This leads to, at best, insufficient recognition of others' joy and suffering, and at worst, complete relativism.

In TMS, the shortcomings of empathy are illustrated by Smith's contention that it is easier to empathize with those close in proximity than those further away. The nearer someone is to another, both literally and figuratively, the more accurately

[110] Weinstein, "Is Adam Smith a Classical Liberal?"

[111] My argument against a libertarian-friendly Smith is largely found in my critique of Otteson's approach. He argues that the market is the fundamentally unifying structure for all of Smith's work. I reject this interpretation (See: Otteson, *Adam Smith's Marketplace of Life*; Jack Russell Weinstein, "Review of Adam Smith's Marketplace of Life," *Mind* 113, no. 449 (2004): 202–7; Weinstein, *Adam Smith's Pluralism*, Chap. 2; Jack Russell Weinstein, "Is Adam Smith a Classical Liberal"). To my knowledge, Otteson has never responded to my criticisms, although I have had the significant pleasure of discussing liberty and libertarianism with him on my radio show. The most critical response of *Adam Smith's Pluralism* from the market-centered point of view is probably Craig T. Smith's review (Otteson, James R, "On Liberty and Libertarianism"; Smith, "Review of Jack Russell Weinstein's Adam Smith's Pluralism: Rationality, Education, and the Moral Sentiments").

[112] Muller, *The Mind and the Market*, p. 72.

they can reconstruct their sentiments.[113] This has been referred to as "circles of sympathy," "spheres of intimacy," and "the familiarity principle."[114]

In short, TMS focuses on how people are different, while WN explores how they're the same. In TMS, Smith argues that the imagination is the least effective in reconstructing physical sensations. Entering into bodily appetites of others leads to a "peculiar disgust" and agents even have a hard time sympathizing with themselves because "nothing is so soon forgot as pain" (TMS I.ii.1.3,8). In WN, however, physiology unifies the whole of humanity.

Individual physical capacity is consistent between time and place; ancient and modern peoples have the same basic limitations. Physical effort requires a specific amount of foot pounds to succeed, to use a modern standard, and human beings must coordinate to move beyond this. Without proper machinery, some tasks are simply beyond human abilities.[115] Smith refers to this physical effort as "toil and trouble." It is the "first" or "real" price. It is "what every thing really costs to the man who wants to acquire it" (WN I.v.2).

This leads us down two related paths. The first is descriptive: since all people are fundamentally similar labor-wise, any person or group is a potential trading partner. There is no one who is, in principle, unworthy of exchange, priming humanity for globalization. Similarity also builds common ground for mutual understanding and coordination, from cosmopolitan ethics to the division of labor. People need to understand one another to work with them. Ideally, this progresses toward equal respect and recognition of universal dignity.[116]

The second path is analytic and normative. Smith uses toil and trouble to compare wages over centuries, using labor to calibrate his data. Critics of the labor theory of value misunderstand Smith. Its first job is as a comparative built on the commensurability of the human physique; it is not a rejection of desire. Where Smith and modern economists disagree is how far this subjectivity goes. In contemporary economics, price is not normative, it's an encapsulation of incalculable information. This opens to the door to rent seeking and potential exploitation.

The term "exploitation" is obviously laden. Here, I mean simply getting the better of a trading partner who is not an "intellectually virtuous consumer" or "intellectually virtuous merchant," as described above. It recalls my suggestion to read

---

[113] Smith defines the term "moral sentiments" in LRBL, not TMS. He calls them "moral observations," a definition that incorporates significantly more than just feelings or reactions (LRBL i.144).

[114] Smith's mapping begins with self-consideration, then moves to familial affection he describes as "habitual sympathy," then neighbors, community members, fellow citizens, and eventually those who are so distant that the consideration is motivated by duty, not sentiment (TMS VI.ii.1.16). Duty, involves abiding by "general rules of conduct," and Smith writes that there is "scarce any man" who "by discipline, education, and example" cannot be made to obey them (TMS III.5.1, Griswold, *Adam Smith and the Virtues of Enlightenment*; Otteson, *Adam Smith's Marketplace of Life*; Forman-Barzilai, *Adam Smith and the Circles of Sympathy Cosmopolitanism and Moral Theory*; Fleischacker, *A Third Concept of Liberty*).

[115] Smith often writes as if people are themselves machines, suggesting that investment in laborers and technology is equivalent (WN I.x.b.6).

[116] Weinstein, *Adam Smith's Pluralism*, Chaps. 10–11.

WN beginning with Book V to avoid treating individuals in terms of resource extraction. If we recognize rent-seeking moments in terms of inflated price or insufficient wages—market distortions—we build mechanisms for normative critique.

Economists are certainly free to ignore ethical valuation—models are just simulations of possible worlds. However, the default position that micro- and macroeconomics are value-free science is not defensible. Inventing such a world is a "spectacularly narrow" choice and "quite extraordinary," in the words of Amartya Sen. "Economics is supposed to be concerned with real people. It is hard to believe that real people could be completely unaffected by the reach of the self-examination induced by the Socratic question, 'How should one live?'"[117]

Professional economists meticulously and conscientiously market the discipline as neutral even though it isn't. The nineteenth and early twentieth centuries saw the intentional repackaging of economic inquiry as a social science, and eventually, a hard science.[118] Macroeconomics, at least, is more akin to the humanities.[119] Creating a model that assumes self-interested individuals or value neutral prices is hard to distinguish from literary criticism that chooses a specific interpretive lens, such as psychotherapy or power relations. Hayek's claim that demands for social justice is just "discontent" and "envy" about others' success is rhetoric without philosophical foundation.[120] It neither aligns with Smith nor my presupposition that we are our brothers' keepers.[121] The most generous interpretation is that Hayek is simply doing what I am, reading Smith in terms of his own situatedness.

[117] Sen's welfare economics offers an alternative analytic method, one in which there are "four distinct categories of relevant information regarding a person… 'well-being achievement', 'well-being freedom', 'agency achievement', and 'agency freedom.'" Predictive economics reduces these to one. It regards freedom as "only instrumentally valuable" and agency as "exclusively geared to the pursuit of self-interest." We have already seen enough to understand that Smith could not accept this conflation, although I will return to the question of self-interest shortly. Sen is a paradigmatic example of a Smithian economist (Sen, *On Ethics and Economics*, pp. 1–2).

[118] Weintraub, *How Economics Became a Mathematical Science*. This transition reached its apex with three events: the creation, in 1969, of the Sveriges Riksbank Prize in Economic Sciences in Memory of Alfred Nobel, an award funded by Sweden's central bank to look like a Nobel prize alongside other sciences even thought it was not funded by Alfred Nobel. The other two are the publications of Gary Becker's "A Theory of the Family," in 1974, and his Economic Approach to Human Behavior, in 1976. There, Becker argues that economics could provide a completely unified explanation for all human activity (Becker, *A Theory of Marriage*; Becker, *The Economic Approach to Human Behavior*).

[119] Microeconomics is certainly within the social sciences and provides a kind of reproducibility and verifiability that macroeconomics lack. Micro-economists are excellent at solving distribution problems.

[120] Hayek, *The Constitution of Liberty*, p. 155.

[121] While it is a topic for another time, it seems to me that dismissing a natural moral responsibility for others precludes Hayek's prioritization of liberty and his defense against authoritarianism. The sacredness of liberty or contracts are just first principles. As Maurice Cranston amusingly puts it, "A liberal is a person who believes in liberty as a nudist is a person who believes in nudity" (Cranston 1953 as quoted in Fleischacker, *A Third Concept of Liberty*, p. 3).

Returning to toil and trouble, the phrase is normative in that it points to a common human experience. It signifies the commensurability of history: "Labour…is the only universal" (WN I.v.17). It reveals a floor below which wages cannot fall or workers starve and die. Perhaps this is Smith's Aristotelian roots at work. Subsistence is a moral imperative if we presume a functionalist account of moral obligation.[122] However, Smith's universal opulence differs from Aristotle in its celebration of commercial life, which Aristotle denigrated.[123]

At the moment, however, my concern is with the labor theory of value as an assertion of equality. All people are basically the same, for Smith, and differences, however great, are exaggerated by vanity (WN I.ii.4–5). The moral language of equality permeates Smith's work. He references a "just proportion" to analyze wages (WN IV.vii.c.71, V.ii.i.7) and "equity" to insist that those who "feed, cloath and lodge the whole body of the people" are themselves "tolerably well fed, cloathed and lodged" (WN I.viii.36). As Fleischacker documents, Smith's work is a bridge between classical accounts of distributive justice and the more modern notion articulated during the French Revolution and codified by Rawls.[124]

If people are equal in physical and intellectual abilities, and they are also equal enough in basic material needs such that Smith can strive for universal opulence, how do we know that meeting such needs is possible? This, I suggest, is what the invisible hand actually asserts. If Smith is correct, if nature makes "nearly the same distribution of the necessaries of life…divided into equal portions among all its inhabitants" then there is no global scarcity (TMS IV.1.10). Or, rather, scarcity is a distribution problem as opposed to a supply one. There is direct line between this and Sen's Nobel prize winning work showing that famines are political problems, not supply shortages.[125]

Considering the invisible hand as a Newtonian observation rather than a political aspiration changes it from a prescriptive account of social institutions to a fact of the world. It is another form of equality expressed by the conviction that since there is sufficient food for everyone on earth by nature, then everyone should have enough because there is enough. If people do not have access to their needs, if the invisible hand is not accurately describing the moment, then something terrible has gone wrong.

We are therefore left with an empirical question: does everyone have what they need and if not, why not? Smith's answer is twofold: the invisible hand is prevented by poorly ordered institutions and by individuals who violate "fair play." Both of these are questions of justice.

---

[122] The functionalist argument is as follows: human flourishing requires enough caloric intake to live one's life, which, in turn, creates the obligation for society to ensure its members have enough money to acquire their needs.

[123] Muller, *The Mind and the Market*, p. 5.

[124] Fleischacker, *A Short History of Distributive Justice*, Chap. 1.

[125] Cf. Sen, *Poverty and Famines*.

5.2 Fair Play

My core interest in WN in 2026 is the relationship between fair play and justice, Smith's topic when fair play is mentioned. This emphasizes, yet again, the interwoven nature of his corpus since WN's implicit account of fair play is dependent on its explicit use in TMS. E.C. Mossner puts it best when he writes, "I would charge Smith with an error of literary judgment, the type of error that authors both before and after him have been prone to, that is, the error of assuming that the reader of the second book has also read the first."[126]

Smith's published works present justice as a virtue rather than in terms of the jurisprudence he teaches his students.[127] It incorporates elements of classical "commutative justice"—abstaining from committing physical or reputational harm—with "distributive justice," which, in his time, meant treating people with "love, respect, and esteem" appropriate to the person's role and context (TMS VII.ii.t.10]. The first is a physical requirement, the second a psychosocial. For Smith, all systems of enumerated law are imperfect versions of "natural jurisprudence," and inadequate depictions of "natural justice" (TMS VII.iv.37). Justice as a virtue, however, is "precise, accurate, and indispensable," comparable to the "rules of grammar," as opposed to the other virtues which are more like artistic composition, "loose, vague, and indeterminate" (TMS III.6.11).[128] Injustice requires "real and positive hurt to some particular persons, from motives which are naturally disapproved of."[129] It inspires resentment which endorses punishment which feels, to the sufferer, like social exile (TMS II.ii.1.5, II.ii.2.3).[130]

Justice is "the main pillar that upholds the whole edifice" of society, for Smith (TMS II.ii.4.). It is precise because "upon most occasions" it's a "negative virtue" that "hinders us from hurting our neighbour." It can be met "by sitting still and doing nothing' (TMS II.ii.x.9).[131] Justice is necessary to "social intercourse" and

[126] Mossner, *Adam Smith*, p. 17.

[127] For an overview of the theory of justice in LJ, see David Lieberman (2006).

[128] Nicholas Wolsterstorff argues that Smith "never explicitly tells us what justice is; his theory proves to be, strictly, speaking, a theory of injustice rather than a theory of justice." This is accurate to a certain extent. TMS is a moral psychology so it is concerned with the discovery of and judgments about justice, rather than the robust definitive theory that would likely have been found in his promised but unfinished work. Focusing on the negative consequences is also the common-law legal tradition, at work in LJ (Nicholas Wolterstorff, "Adam Smith on Justice and Injustice," pp. 173–74).

[129] This parallels my division that education provides lessons by individuals to individuals, distinct from socialization and instruction which address the collective.

[130] I do not have the space to engage with Smith's theory of punishment, but it is relevant in that it is a mixture of sentiment-based judgment and common-law tradition. The latter is why he is teaching it in terms of damages to his students of jurisprudence (See: Norrie, "Punishment and Justice in Adam Smith"; Miller, "Sympathetic Exchange, Adam Smith and Punishment"; Stalley, "Adam Smith and the Theory of Punishment").

[131] Note his use of "most occasions." As with self-interest and the butcher, brewer, and baker, Smith makes room for plurality.

therefore, "society cannot subsist" unless its laws are "tolerably observed" (TMS II.ii.3. 6). It falls within the role of the sovereign because injustice is "destructive of all liberty, security, and justice" (TMS II.ii.x.9).

Smith argues that society can exist without beneficence but not without justice (TMS II.ii.3); justice can be compelled but beneficence cannot (TMS II.ii.z.3). However, society without beneficence is "in the most comfortable state." Justice only brings reciprocity or respect of innocence (TMS II.ii.x.9). Nature thus "exhorts mankind to acts of beneficence, by the pleasing consciousness of deserved reward" (TMS II.ii.3–4). For Smith, justice and "the propriety of generosity and public spirit" are "founded upon the same principle" (TMS IV.2.10).[132]

Here we have yet another misdirect on Smith's part. He argues that society requires only justice but his account regularly pairs the term with equity, society, and humanity.[133] Disregarding this results in the thinnest account of justice and identity, undermining TMS's *raison d'être*. It dismisses TMS's recognition of positive liberty[134]—the prerequisites for flourishing, holistically understood, that also requires WN's political economy.[135] However, this thin identity is useful as a marker of where fair play comes in.

---

[132] Smith is using justice as an analytic category but does not conceive of it in isolation.

[133] In TMS alone, justice is paired with "equality of its administration," (TMS Iii.3.4); beneficence (II.ii.VI.concl.3); society, in which he means both political order and companionship (II.iii.2.8); humanity (III.3.37, III.3.38, III.5.8,); truth and humanity (III.5.8); "a proper degree of self-command" (VI.i.15); "perfect prudence" and "proper benevolence" (VI.iii.1, VI.iii.4, VI.iii.11, VI. concl.1]; benevolence (VI.iii.12); prudence and beneficence (TMS VI.concl.2, VI.concl.2), "our duty to others" (VII.ii.1.18), "the most conscientious dread, either of wronging his neighbour, or of violating the integrity of his own character" (VII.4.8). Similar patterns can be found in WN and Lectures on Jurisprudence. However, for the most part, these books use the term justice to refer to the proper function of institutions or the operation of the common-law methodology. An exception is Smith's remark that authoritarian governments (not his term) are less likely to have either interest or inclination to pervert the order of justice, or to oppress the great body of the people" in their own capital cities (WN IV.vii.52). Another is the frequent use of "injustice" in his condemnation of colonialism and his uncertainty about the future of the British Empire: "in what manner the natural system of perfect liberty and justice ought gradually to be restored, we must leave to the wisdom of future statesmen and legislators to determine" (WN IV.vii.c.44). This list is far from exhaustive.

[134] While space prevents me from doing so, it is an instructive experiment to read TMS as an exploration of positive liberty and WN as an account of negative liberty. However, I am not suggesting this is a perfect division, nor am I implying a new Adam Smith Problem. I am only offering it as another way to experience what comes from Smith's misdirect. TMS presents a theory of humanity that grounds WN's political economy; the two can only be separated for analytic purposes.

[135] Smith defines political economy as "a branch of the science of a statesman or legislator, proposes two distinct objects; first, to provide a plentiful revenue or subsistence for the people, or more properly to enable them to provide such a revenue or subsistence for themselves; and secondly, to supply the state or commonwealth with a revenue sufficient for the public services. It proposes to enrich both the people and the sovereign" (WN IV.intro).

Smith only mentions fair play once, the same number of times he cites universal opulence.[136] Individuals may try as hard as they can but may not "justle, or throw down," which would be a "violation of fair play" subject to community sanction (TMS II.ii.2.2).[137] Dugald Stewart quotes a second reference from Smith's burnt manuscripts, that neither politicians nor speculators should violate fair play in any way that stops nature from "the pursuit of her ends, that she may establish her own designs."[138] He then adds another draft citation that argues "little else is requisite to carry a state to the highest degree of opulence from the lowest barbarism, but peace, easy taxes, and a tolerable administration of justice."[139] TMS's reference to fair play describes individuals' behavior, whereas Stweart's version references unfair policy. The first is exploring resentment and remorse within a moral psychology, the second references collective behavior, a component of political economy.

Given that the first is the grounding for the unified science of human beings, it makes sense that normative standards of behavior are attributed to nature. For Smith, nature designates the way history unfolds when it is properly attended to and when nature's standards are not met; this is WN's concern. Philosophy's job is to explain why interfering political structures are "unnatural and retrograde," a notion also expressed in the second Stewart reference (WN III.i.9).[140] Smith puts it this way: while the "the liberal reward of labour" is a "natural symptom of increasing national wealth" the "scanty maintenance of the labouring poor" is a "natural symptom that things are at a stand and their starving condition that they are going fast backwards" (WN I.viii.27).[141]

In TMS, justice is reduced to non-interference because it explores the process by which characters develop to make good economic choices. This is most evident in

---

[136] "Universal opulence" appears in the only extant draft of WN, but its context is the same and its wording is similar (Draft 11).

[137] The full quote is: "In the race for wealth, and honours, and preferments, he may run as hard as he can, and strain every nerve and every muscle, in order to outstrip all his competitors. But if he should justle, or throw down any of them, the indulgence of the spectators is entirely at an end. It is a violation of fair play, which they cannot admit of" (TMS II.ii.2.2).

[138] Stewart, "Account of the Life and Writings of Adam Smith, L.L.D.," para. IV.26. The full quote is: "Man is generally considered by statesmen and projectors as the materials of a sort of political mechanics. Projectors disturb nature in the course of her operations in human affairs; and it requires no more than to let her alone, and give her fair play in the pursuit of her ends, that she may establish her own designs."

[139] Stewart, "Account of the Life and Writings of Adam Smith, L.L.D.," para. IV.26. Here again is the full quote: "Little else is requisite to carry a state to the highest degree of opulence from the lowest barbarism, but peace, easy taxes, and a tolerable administration of justice; all the rest being brought about by the natural course of things. All governments which thwart this natural course, which force things into another channel, or which endeavour to arrest the progress of society at a particular point, are unnatural, and to support themselves are obliged to be oppressive and tyrannical."

[140] Weinstein, *Adam Smith's Pluralism*, Chap. 10.

[141] As a side note, Smith's other uses of the phrase "liberal reward of labor" to refer to how it helps provide for one's children, increase the population, and encourage marriage. This is a direct connection to his moral mission of eradicating infanticide (WN I.viii.42,44, I.iii.40, IV.viii.b.2).

Smith's account of the poor man's son. The young man sacrifices everything of moral value for status and riches, only to recognize at the end of his life that without family, community, and good character, the "enormous and operose machines" of wealth are valueless and destroy those who pursue them (TMS IV.i.8–9).

Non-interference is also the best policy in the face of ignorance or powerlessness. The morality tale of the poor man's son serves as preparation for Smith's reference to the invisible hand. He argues that despite the man making the wrong choice for him personally, the deceptive lure of wealth serves the common good. It "rouses and keeps in continual motion the industry of mankind" (TMS IV.1.10). It "first prompted" humanity to invent, improve, and progress, creating the conditions for the abundance provided by the invisible hand.

For Smith, the invisible hand always denotes human ignorance of inability: in *HA* it explains the unexplained; in WN, it reports the inability to manipulate trade for the common good; here, it is in response to the impossibility of catering to every need.[142] There is a problem, however. The invisible hand advances the collective but often harms individuals.[143] Just because society progresses doesn't mean specific people do: consider the gentrification I experienced in my own life.[144] Smith recognizes that strong economies are often built on workers' suffering and that the most well-off are also the most parasitic. The free market is not a zero-sum affair; it allows for many winners. However, it also results in many losers as well. The invisible hand does not harmonize all interests.[145]

Again, this is where WN comes in. A core purpose is to mitigate the damage of growth including its poor working conditions, income inequality, monopolizing,

---

142 To elaborate: for many obvious reasons, human beings cannot manage global economic systems and distribution cannot scale large enough to attend to all substance needs. All three of Smith's mentions of the invisible hand mitigate human motivation in the face of ignorance. In his HA, "the invisible hand of Jupiter" is an example of primitive mythology explaining natural phenomena (HA III.2). In WN, the invisible hand denotes economic actors' inability to manipulate the market for their or societies' benefit (WN IV.ii.9). Here Smith uses it to make up for the inability to disseminate everyone's needs. According to Smith, people have a "natural hatred of labour" and a love of "present ease and enjoyment" (V.i.b.2). Work seldom has intrinsic value. Job satisfaction is rare and its primary motivation is material gain. Professional employment does not lead to happiness or self-realization (WN I.XI.9). Without false promise, human desire for ease would eclipse personal ambition.

143 Many years ago, I was visiting a sporting goods store with an environmental ethicist friend, Seetha Burtner. The store displayed many taxidermy specimens behind a plaque explaining that hunting was good wildlife management and therefore benefited animals. Seetha talked back to the sign: "it benefits species not animals," underscoring that selectively killing animals did not help those that died. Her point is well taken and it is Smith's point as well.

144 Gentrification benefits a city economically, culturally, and often reduces crime. At the same time, it disproportionately destroys residents' families' homes and livelihood. It erases aspect of the localized culture and commercial relationships that may have been cultivated for generations.

145 I reference harmony as a nod toward the Platonic tradition that considers justice to be the domain of utopian political arrangements that eliminate social conflict (Hampshire 2000). Amartya Sen argues that Smith is best thought of as being part of a counter-lineage which measures justice through comparative improvement over time (Sen 2011, pp. 7–10).

colonization, and the marginalization of the powerless from slaves to women. Smith refuses to distinguish between deserving and underserving poor. He shifts the discussion from the conservative "what should be done about the poor?" to the progressive "how can we raise people out of poverty?"[146] This is why opulence is "universal."

5.3 WN on Moral Motivation

WN offers a policy-based account of what fair play requires: access to education, the arts, religious freedom, exact administration of justice, and the nuanced duties of the sovereign that promote stability. It advocates social arrangements that guarantee profit from one labor, opposing slavery and prohibiting indentured apprenticeships, poor laws, and conspiracies to unnaturally suppressed wages. It promotes free trade and rejects monopolies. It also recognizes that opportunity requires social prerequisites not just *laissez faire* disregard. Smith specifically writes that the concept of necessity should include social essentials such as leather shoes and linen shirts, since they are requisites for employment and self-respect in commercial society (WN V.ii.k.3).

In short, WN offers a massive expansion of subsistence as an economic concept and goal; this is what attracts me to it in 2026. It certainly doesn't meet modern expectations, nor can it address all of our current needs. Smith is a philosopher not a prophet. But taken seriously, it opens the door to a philosophically consistent approach to social welfare that recognizes the socially constructed and policy-supported nature of individual identity, while leaving free trade and policies of fair play still on the table. Late stage or not, capitalism isn't going anywhere. We might as well try to improve it.

There is one final issue: the thin conception of identity that results from a society that operates without beneficence. Smith rejects this simplicity during his discussion of the butcher, brewer, and baker (WN II.ii.2). For generations, readers have claimed that Smith's agents are solely motivated by self-interest. This is just wrong.

Smith's agents are driven by two sets of distinct natural principles we have already encountered. The first contains the perpetual desire to better one's own condition and the "desire of the welfare and preservation of society" (TMS II.i.5.10), along with individuals being better judges of their needs than lawmakers and their being recommended to their own care (WN IV.2.10, TMS II.ii.2.1). These principles are individualistic and self-focused.

The second set, however, is other-oriented. People have "an original desire to please, and an original aversion to offend their neighbors" (TMS III.2.6). They have a "natural love for society" (TMS II.ii.3.6) and "can subsist only" in one (TMS

[146] Fleischacker, *A Short History of Distributive Justice*, p. 64.

II.ii.3.1).[147] The first sentence of TMS, his Newtonian grounding principle for his entire corpus, explains that the happiness of others is "necessary" even to those who derive no pleasure from it (TMS I.i.1.1).[148]

Therefore, Smith's agents are both self-interested and other-oriented at the same time. Recall that Smith taught me that nothing is just one thing. This is the paradigmatic example. Smith's agents have multiple motivations and can be concerned with themselves *and* others. He is clear in these passages that the "charity of well-disposed people" does "indeed" supply the beggar with "the whole fund of his subsistence." While "nobody but a beggar chuses to depend chiefly upon the benevolence of his fellow-citizens" only the needy "depend upon it entirely" (WN I.ii.2). Smith's grammar is plural.

The problem for Smith is not that people aren't beneficent or benevolent; it's that they are neither predictable nor controllable. Charity works but not according to a preferred schedule. The needy receive food when they're thirsty and drink when they're hungry. Smith's discussion is about control, not self-interest.[149] Commercial exchange supplies people with what they want when they want it; benevolence is sporadically successful. In short. exchange is a form of persuasion: "Give me that which I want, and you shall have this which you want, is the meaning of every such offer" and while it provides people "the far greater part" of what they require, it is not exclusive. Self-interest is a rhetorical strategy for Smith, not a philosophical shibboleth. Justification is hierarchical.

The freedom to exchange is part of fair play for Smith; so is the liberty to change one's trade "as often as he pleased" (WN I.vii.6, I.x.a.1).[150] Yes, of course, Smith's system of perfect liberty is a proposal for what a commercial society might look like and a call for limited government, whatever that might mean. But these are just some components visible though certain sets of filters. WN is also a document that attends to those for whom the game is rigged, who are marginalized and disregarded, and who lack the economic or political power to inspire change.

Smith tells us this. He describes the workers and their invisibility:

> His condition leaves him no time to receive the necessary information, and his education and habits are commonly such as to render him unfit to judge even though he was fully informed. In the publick deliberations, therefore, his voice is little heard and less regarded, except upon some particular occasions, when his clamour is animated, set on, and supported by his employers, not for his, but their own particular purposes (WN I.xi, p. 9).

---

[147] Smith rejects the social contract, postulating a progressive stadial system in its place (cf. Berry, *Social Theory of the Scottish Enlightenment*, pp. 30–33; Khalil, "Is Justice the Primary Feature of the State?")

[148] See: Weinstein, *The First Sentence of Adam Smith's Theory of Moral Sentiments, Explained.*

[149] I have mapped out this chapter paragraph by paragraph to elucidate both Smith's language and how few consequential claims there actually are in it (Weinstein, "What My Dog Can Do: On the Effects of WN I.Ii.2").

[150] One of Smith's many critiques of slavery is that the enslaved are denied their right to exchange and change professions (Weinstein, "Adam Smith's Critiques of Slavery").

In this penultimate paragraph of the first book of WN, at the culmination of the theoretical grounding of what Smith himself called "the very violent attack I had made upon the whole commercial system of Great Britain" (Corr., p. 208), Smith remarks this: everyday workers are too busy, too tired, kept too ignorant to participate in political deliberations, and too wracked with character dysmorphia to self-judge, and the only time their employers pay attention to them is to rile them up as an angry mob that acts against its own interests. I find it wholly unbelievable that the brilliant philosopher who is so forthright about the alienation of the downtrodden would come to the conclusion that the best thing society can do for these people is stand back and let nature take its course.

In summary, I transitioned into my second discussion of WN by asking how, in the current moment, anyone could avoid reading WN in terms of fair play. My answer is that we can't because it was never intended to be read as such.

6 Conclusion

I am confident it is transparent that Smith's system as I read it in 1991 coheres with and elucidates his work as I am reading it in 2026. I hope this retrospective persuasively illustrates that whatever disagreements modern day economists have with Smith pale in comparison to what all of us can still learn from him.

I conclude by suggesting this: at the 250th anniversary of Smith, it is not enough to glorify what WN has meant to people in the past. With apologies for taking the metaphor beyond clarity, it is time to deliquesce the calcified tome whose fragments adorn the political agenda of Economics 101. None of Smith's work is an artifact.

I would suggest instead that his political economy does what it has always done, establishes an agenda for attending to the suffering of those who are victims of poverty. Of course, what follows from this is and will remain the subject of complex, deeply felt debate. As long as such engagement continues and Smith is an authentic part of it, *The Wealth of Nations* will remain what it ought to be: a living document to inspire those who regard themselves as their brothers' keepers.

Bibliography

Alinsky, S. D. (1989). *Rules for radicals: A practical primer for realistic radicals*. Vintage Books.

Alt, R. (2026). *Senators must contest Sotomayor's view that empathy, ethnicity can overrule law*. The Heritage Foundation. Retrieved from March 9, 2026, from https://www.heritage.org/political-process/commentary/senators-must-contest-sotomayors-view-empathy-ethnicity-can-overrule

Aristotle. (1999). *Nicomachean ethics* (M. Ostwald, Trans.). Library of Liberal Arts. Prentice Hall.

Baldwin, J. W. (1959). The medieval theories of the just price: Romanists, canonists, and theologians in the twelfth and thirteenth centuries. *Transactions of the American Philosophical Society, New Series, 49*(4), 1–92.

Barry, B. M. (2002). *Culture and equality: An egalitarian critique of multiculturalism* (2. print). Harvard University Press.
Baum, S. (1992). Poverty, inequality, and the role of government: What would Adam Smith say? *Eastern Economic Journal, 18*(2), 143–156.
Baumol, W. J. (1977). On the proper cost tests for natural monopoly in a multiproduct industry. *The American Economic Review, 67*(5), 809–822.
Becker, G. S. (1974). *A theory of marriage*. NBER Chapters. National Bureau of Economic Research.
Becker, G. S. (1978). *The economic approach to human behavior*. University of Chicago Press.
Berry, C. J. (1997). *Social theory of the Scottish enlightenment*. Edinburgh University Press.
Blake, A. (2022, June 29). Analysis|Gorsuch and Sotomayor's extraordinary factual dispute. *The Washington Post*. Retrieved from https://www.washingtonpost.com/politics/2022/06/29/gorsuch-sotomayor-praying-coach/
Boucoyannis, D. (2013). The equalizing hand: Why Adam Smith thought the market should produce wealth without steep inequality. *Perspectives on Politics, 11*(4), 1051–1070.
Brady, M. E. (2017, December 22). *Adam Smith's analysis of the good (sober people) and the bad (projectors, prodigals and imprudent risk takers): The proper role of the central bank in generating the Wealth of Nations using the visible hand to empower the sober people by using targeted bank policy*. SSRN Scholarly Paper No. 3092045. Social Science Research Network.
Camfield, G. (1988). The moral aesthetics of sentimentality: A missing key to uncle tom's cabin. *Nineteenth-Century Literature, 43*(3), 319–345.
Court, F. E. (1985). Adam Smith and the teaching of English literature. *History of Education Quarterly, 25*(3), 325–340.
Couzo, V. (2013). Sotomayor's empathy moves the court a step closer to equitable adjudication. *Notre Dame Law Review, 89*(1), 403.
David, E. J. R. (2013). *Internalized oppression: The psychology of marginalized groups*. Springer Publishing Group.
de Mandeville, B., & Kaye, F. B. (1988). *Fable of the bees: Or, private vices, publick benefits*. Liberty Fund.
Ferguson, A. (1980). *An essay on the history of civil society*. Transaction Publishers.
Fleischacker, S. (1999). *A third concept of liberty*. Princeton University Press.
Fleischacker, S. (2004). *On Adam Smith's "Wealth of Nations": A philosophical companion*. Princeton University Press.
Fleischacker, S. (2009). *A short history of distributive justice*. Harvard University Press.
Fleischacker, S. (2019). *Being me being you: Adam Smith and empathy*. The University of Chicago Press.
Forman-Barzilai, F. (2010). *Adam Smith and the circles of sympathy cosmopolitanism and moral theory*. Cambridge University Press.
Gallo, M. M. (2015). *No one helped: Kitty Genovese, New York City, and the Myth of Urban Apathy*. Cornell University Press.
Garvey, M. (2000, October 31). Nader Besieged by Ex-Allies as race goes down to the wire. *Los Angeles Times*. https://www.cnn.com/2000/ALLPOLITICS/stories/10/31/latimes.nader/index.html
Göçmen, D. (2007). *The Adam Smith problem reconciling human nature and society in "the theory of moral sentiments" and Wealth of Nations*. Tauris Academic Studies [Imprint].
Graeber, D. (2010). *Debt: The first 5,000 years*. Melville House.
Gray, J. (1995). *Enlightenment's wake: Politics and culture at the close of the modern age*. Routledge.
Griswold, C. L. (1999). *Adam Smith and the virtues of enlightenment*. Modern European Philosophy. Cambridge University Press.
Gutmann, A. (2001). *Democratic education*. Princeton Paperbacks. Princeton University Press.
Haakonssen, K. (1989). *The science of a legislator: The natural jurisprudence of David Hume and Adam Smith*. Cambridge University Press.

Hanley, R. P. (2009). *Adam Smith and the character of virtue* (1st ed.). Cambridge University Press.
Hanley, R. P. (2019). *Our great purpose: Adam Smith on living a better life*. Princeton University Press.
Harcourt, B. E. (2001). *Illusion of order: The false promise of broken windows policing*. Harvard University Press.
Harpham, E. J. (1984). Liberalism, civic humanism, and the case of Adam Smith. *The American Political Science Review, 78*(3), 764–774.
Hayek, F. A. (2011). In R. Hamowy (Ed.), *The constitution of liberty: The definitive edition*. University of Chicago Press.
Herman, A. (2007). *How the Scots invented the modern world: The true story of how Western Europe's poorest nation created our world and everything in it*. Crown/Archetype.
Hetherington, N. S. (1983). Isaac Newton's Influence on Adam Smith's Natural Laws in Economics. *Journal of the History of Ideas, 44*(3), 497–505.
Hume, D. (2009). A treatise of human nature. In D. F. Norton & M. J. Norton (Eds.), *Oxford philosophical texts*. Oxford University Press.
Justman, S. (1993). *The autonomous male of Adam Smith*. University of Oklahoma Press.
Kennedy, G. (2011). The hidden Adam Smith in his alleged theology. *Journal of the History of Economic Thought, 33*(3), 385–402.
Khalil, E. L. (1998). Is justice the primary feature of the state? Adam Smith's critique of social contract theory. *European Journal of Law and Economics, 6*, 215–230.
Khalil, E. L. (2002). Is Adam Smith liberal? *Journal of Institutional and Theoretical Economics (JITE)/Zeitschrift Für Die Gesamte Staatswissenschaft, 158*(4), 664–694.
Kilty, K. M., & Joseph, A. (1999). Institutional racism and sentencing disparities for cocaine possession. *Journal of Poverty, 3*(4), 1–17.
Klein, N. (2008). *The shock doctrine: The rise of disaster capitalism*. Picador.
Klein, D. B., Swanson, N. R., & Young, J. T. (2025). The impartial spectator rises. *Econ Journal Watch, 22*(2), 296–326.
Kuiper, E. (2006). Adam Smith and his feminist contemporaries. In *New voices on Adam Smith*. Routledge.
Kymlicka, W. (1995). *Multicultural citizenship: A liberal Theory of minority rights. Oxford political theory*. Clarendon Press.
Leddy, N. B. (2013). Grave, philosophical and cool reasoner: Mary Wollstonecraft on the use of gender in Adam Smith. *The Adam Smith Review, 7*(7), 8–17.
Letwin, W. (1988). Was Adam Smith a liberal? In K. Haakonssen (Ed.), *Traditions of liberalism: Essays on John Locke, Adam Smith, and John Stuart Mill*. Centre for Independent Studies.
Lieberman, D. (2006). Adam Smith on justice, rights, and law. In K. Haakonssen (Ed.), *The Cambridge companion to Adam Smith*. Cambridge University Press.
MacIntyre, A. C. (1984). *After virtue: A study in moral theory* (2nd ed.). University of Notre Dame Press.
Macintyre, A. (1989). *Whose justice? Which rationality?* University of Notre Dame Press.
MacIntyre, A. (1990). *Three rival versions of moral enquiry: Encyclopaedia, genealogy, and tradition*. University of Notre Dame Press.
Marshall, D. (1986). *The figure of theater: Shaftesbury, Defoe, Adam Smith, and George Eliot*. Columbia University Press.
McCammon, S. (2025, March 22). How empathy came to be seen as a weakness in conservative circles. Religion. *NPR*. Retrieved from https://www.npr.org/2025/03/22/nx-s1-5321299/how-empathy-came-to-be-seen-as-a-weakness-in-conservative-circles
McCloskey, D. N. (2006). *The bourgeois virtues: Ethics for an age of commerce*. University of Chicago Press.
McDonough, K., & Feinberg, W. (Eds.). (2005). *Citizenship and education in liberal-democratic societies: Teaching for cosmopolitan values and collective identities*. Oxford University Press.
McLean, I., & Brown, G. (2007). *Adam Smith, radical and egalitarian: An interpretation for the 21st century*. Palgrave Macmillan US.

Mill, J. S. (1891). In J. Laurence Laughlin (Ed.), *Principles of political economy.*
Miller, J. (1994). *Democracy is in the streets: From port Huron to the Siege of Chicago.* Harvard University Press.
Miller, E. (1996). Sympathetic exchange, Adam Smith and punishment. *Ratio Juris, 9*(2), 182–197.
Miller v. California. (1973). No. 70-73 (S. Ct June 21, 1973).
Minnich, E. K. (2017). *The evil of banality: On the life and death importance of thinking.* Rowman & Littlefield.
Minnich, E. (2025). *how is it that ordinary people can commit such overwhelming evil?* Episode 191. Hosted by Jack Russell Weinstein. Why? Philosophical discussion about everyday life. Institute for Philosophy in Public Life, November 9, 2025. MP3, 1:23:40. Retrieved from https://philosophyinpubliclife.org/2025/11/10/how-is-it-that-ordinary-people-can-commit-such-overwhelming-evil-with-guest-elizabeth-minnich/.
Mokre, M. (2002). On Adam Smith and gender construction. In C. Gerschlager & M. Mokre (Eds.), *Exchange and deception: A feminist perspective.* Springer US.
Mossner, E. C. (1969). *Adam Smith: The biographical approach* (The David Murray lectures) (Vol. 30). University of Glasgow.
Muller, J. Z. (2002). *The mind and the market: Capitalism in modern European thought.* Alfred A. Knopf.
Nicholas, W. (2016). Adam Smith on justice and injustice. In R. P. Hanley (Ed.), *Adam Smith: His life, thought, and legacy.* Princeton University Press.
Norrie, A. (1989). Punishment and justice in Adam Smith. *Ratio Juris, 2*(3), 227–239.
Nussbaum, M. C. (1987). *The fragility of goodness: Luck and ethics in greek tragedy and philosophy.* Cambridge University Press.
Nussbaum, M. C. (1995). *Poetic justice: The literary imagination and public life.* The Alexander Rosenthal lectures. Beacon Press.
Nussbaum, M. C. (2003). *Cultivating humanity: A classical defense of reform in liberal education* (7. print). Harvard University Press.
Nyland, C. (1993). Adam Smith: Stage theory and the status of women. *History of Political Economy, 25*(4), 617–640.
Otteson, J. R. (2002). *Adam Smith's marketplace of life.* Cambridge University Press.
Otteson, J. R. (2011). On liberty and libertarianism. *Why? Philosophical discussions about everyday life.* Performed by Weinstein, Jack Russell. Aired May 8, 2011, on Prairie Public radio.
Oxford English Dictionary. (2025a). *Education, n.* Oxford University Press.
Oxford English Dictionary. (2025b). *Instruction, n.* Oxford University Press.
Pierson, J. J. (2026). *Dr. Jack Russell Weinstein of Why? Philosophical Discussions Abo...* Episode 228. Jughead's Basement. March 11, 2026. 2:00:03. Retrieved from https://www.podomatic.com/podcasts/jugheadsbasementtnh/episodes/2026-03-11T06_00_00-07_00
Piketty, T. (2014). *Capital in the twenty-first century* (A. Goldhammer, Trans.). Belknap Press.
Rasmussen, D. C. (2016). Adam Smith on what is wrong with economic inequality. *American Political Science Review, 110*(2), 342–352.
Rawls, J. (1971). *A theory of justice.* Harvard University Press.
Rawls, J. (1993). *Political liberalism.* Columbia University Press.
Roberts, R. D. (2014). *How Adam Smith can change your life: An unexpected guide to human nature and happiness.* Portfolio/Penguin.
Ross, I. S. (2010). *The life of Adam Smith* (2nd ed.). Oxford University Press.
Salomon, A. (1945). Adam Smith as sociologist. *Social Research, 12*(1), 22–42.
Schliesser, E. (2005). Some principles of Adam Smith's Newtonian methods in the Wealth of Nations. In W. J. Samuels, J. E. Biddle, & R. B. Emmett (Eds.), *Research in the history of economic thought and methodology.* Emerald Group Publishing.
Sen, A. (1983). *Poverty and famines: An essay on entitlement and deprivation.* Oxford University Press.
Sen, A. (1987). *On ethics and economics.* Royer Lectures. Basil Blackwell.
Sen, A. (2011). *The idea of justice* (Reprint edn.). Belknap Press.

Smith, A. (1981). An inquiry into the nature and causes of the Wealth of Nations. In R. H. Campbell & A. S. Skinner (Eds.), *Glasgow edition of the works and correspondence of Adam Smith*. Liberty Fund.

Smith, A. (1982a). Essays on philosophical subjects. In J. C. Bryce & W. P. D. Wightman (Eds.), *Glasgow edition of the works and correspondence of Adam Smith*. Liberty Fund.

Smith, A. (1982b). Lectures on jurisprudence. In R. L. Meek, D. D. Raphael, & P. G. Stein (Eds.), *Glasgow edition of the works and correspondence of Adam Smith*. Liberty Fund.

Smith, A. (1982c). The theory of moral sentiments. In D. D. Raphael & A. L. Macfie (Eds.), *The Glasgow edition of the works and correspondence of Adam Smith*. Liberty Classics.

Smith, A. (1985). Lectures on Rhetoric and Belles lettres. In J. C. Bryce (Ed.), *Glasgow edition of the works and correspondence of Adam Smith*. Liberty Fund.

Smith, A. (1987). Correspondence of Adam Smith. In E. C. Mossner & I. S. Ross (Eds.), *Glasgow edition of the works and correspondence of Adam Smith*. Liberty Fund.

Smith, C. (2014). Review of Jack Russell Weinstein's Adam Smith's pluralism: Rationality, education, and the moral sentiments. *Erasmus Journal for Philosophy and Economics, 7*(2), 162–169.

Stalley, R. (2012). Adam Smith and the theory of punishment. *Journal of Scottish Philosophy, 10*(1), 69–89.

Stanley, J. (2017). *How Propaganda Works*. Princeton University Press.

Stewart, D. (1982). Account of the life and writings of Adam Smith, L.L.D. In J. C. Bryce & W. P. D. Wightman (Eds.), *Essays on philosophical subjects*. Liberty Fund.

Taylor, C. (1989). *Sources of the self: The making of the modern identity*. Harvard University Press.

Veale, D. (2004). Body dysmorphic disorder. *Postgraduate Medical Journal, 80*(940), 67–71.

Vivenza, G. (2001). *Adam Smith and the classics: The classical heritage in Adams Smith's thought*. Oxford University Press.

Weinstein, J. R. (1998). *Adam Smith and the problem of neutrality in contemporary liberal theory*. Boston University.

Weinstein, J. R. (2004a). Neutrality, pluralism, and education: Civic education as learning about the other. *Studies in Philosophy and Education, 23*(4), 235–263.

Weinstein, J. R. (2004b). Review of Adam Smith's marketplace of life. *Mind, 113*(449), 202–207.

Weinstein, J. R. (2006). Sympathy difference and education: Social unity in the work of Adam Smith. *Economics and Philosophy, 22*, 79–111.

Weinstein, J. R. (2007). Introduction: Adam Smith's philosophy of education. In V. Brown (Ed.), *The Adam Smith review* (Vol. 3). Routledge.

Weinstein, J. R. (2012). Overlapping consensus or marketplace of religions? Rawls and Smith. *Philosophia, 40*(2), 223–236.

Weinstein, J. R. (2013). *Adam Smith's pluralism: Rationality, education, and the moral sentiments*. Yale University Press.

Weinstein, J. R. (2014a). Symposium: Adam Smith on education. In V. Brown (Ed.), *The Adam Smith review* (Vol. 3). Routledge.

Weinstein, J. R. (2014b). The two Adams: Ferguson and Smith on sympathy and sentiment. In E. Heath & V. Merolle (Eds.), *Adam Ferguson: Philosophy, politics and society*. Pickering & Chatto.

Weinstein, J. R. (2014c). What my dog can do: On the effects of WN I.Ii.2. In D. F. Hardwick & L. Marsh (Eds.), *Propriety and prosperity*. Palgrave Macmillan.

Weinstein, J. R. (2015a). Adam Smith and the educative critique: A response to my reviewers. *Studies in Philosophy and Education, 34*(5), 541–550.

Weinstein, J. R. (2015c). The political hypotheses of Adam Smith's pluralism: A response to my commentators. *Cosmos and Taxis, 2*(3).

Weinstein, J. R. (2017). Kant and Smith on imagination, reason, and personhood. In E. Robinson & C. W. Surprenant (Eds.), *Kant and the Scottish enlightenment*. Taylor & Francis.

Weinstein, J. R. (2019a, December 18). Adam Smith on education: Socialization and acculturation. *Adam Smith Works*. Retrieved from https://www.adamsmithworks.org/documents/adam-smith-on-education-socialization-and-acculturation

Weinstein, J. R. (2019b, April 21). Requiem for a philosophy professor: Remembering David N. Mowry—PQED: Philosophical questions every day. *PQED: Philosophical Questions Every Day*. Retrieved from https://pqed.org/2019/04/requiem-for-a-philosophy-professor-remembering-david-n-mowry-1941-2019/

Weinstein, J. R. (2020, December 1). *'How does Propaganda work?' Why? radio with guest Jason Stanley*. The Institute for Philosophy in Public Life. Retrieved from https://philosophyinpublicl-ife.org/2020/11/30/how-does-propaganda-work-with-guest-jason-stanley/

Weinstein, J. R. (2021). *The first sentence of Adam Smith's theory of moral sentiments, explained*. Adam Smith Works. Liberty Fund. 00:05:57. https://youtu.be/Dr5JpZd4aVM?si=VSrpWc9gIrfRvSr3

Weinstein, J. R. (2024). *Israel, Palestine, and the Trolley problem: On the futility of the search for the moral high ground*. The Digital Press at the University of North Dakota.

Weinstein, J. R. (2026a). Adam Smith on the meaning of work, specialization, and the division of labor. In J. Jonker & G. Rozeboom (Eds.), *Oxford handbook of philosophy and work*. Oxford University Press.

Weinstein, J. R. (2026b). Adam Smith's critiques of slavery. In J. Mascat & L. Mercier (Eds.), *Out of sight: Slavery in modern European philosophy*. Edinburgh University Press.

Weinstein, J. R. (2026c). Adam Smith's impartial spectator is neither divine nor an ideal observer. *Econ Journal Watch*.

Weinstein, J. R. (2026d). Is Adam Smith a classical liberal? In L. Marsh, M. Novak, & M. Pennington (Eds.), *The Palgrave handbook of classical liberalism*.

Weinstein, Jack Russell. "Adam Smith's advice on living well in a commercial society." In Handbook of virtue ethics in business and management, Alejo José G. Sison. Springer Science + Business Media, 2015.

Weintraub, E. R. (2020). In B. H. Smith (Ed.), *How economics became a mathematical science*. Duke University Press.

West, E. G. (1977). *Adam Smith: The man and his works*. Liberty Fund.

Wilkinson, R. G., & Pickett, K. (2011). *The spirit level: Why greater equality makes societies stronger* (Paperback edn.). Bloomsbury.

Wilkinson, R. G., & Pickett, K. (2019). *The inner level: How more equal societies reduce stress, restore sanity and improve everyone's well-being*. Penguin Press.

Williams, M. S. (1995). Justice toward groups: Political not juridical. *Political Theory, 23*(1), 67–91.

Winch, D. (1978). *Adam Smith's politics: An essay in historiographic revision*. Cambridge University Press.

Winch, D. (1988). Adam Smith and the liberal tradition. In K. Haakonssen (Ed.), *Traditions of liberalism: Essays on John Locke, Adam Smith, and John Stuart Mill*. Centre for Independent Studies.

Yahoo News. (2025, September 11). *Fact check: Charlie Kirk once said empathy was 'made-up, new age term.'* Retrieved from https://ca.news.yahoo.com/fact-check-charlie-kirk-once-001900786.html

Young, J. T. (1997). *Economics as a moral science: The political economy of Adam Smith*. Edward Elgar.

Pragmatism, Optimism, and Improvement in the Wealth of Nations

Craig Smith

Adam Smith's *An Inquiry into the Nature and Causes of the Wealth of Nations* has reached its 250th birthday. The book has become a classic of world importance, read (or more often referred to) down to our own day. That a book is held to be a classic that has shaped the course of thinking about commerce and spawned an academic discipline (Economics) is quite an achievement, more so as it still speaks to us today and has interesting lessons for us in how we think about our own world. But neither of these things, impressive as they are, tells us much about what Smith himself set out to do in his monumental work. This is the topic that I wish to explore in what follows: I want to outline what I think that Smith thought that he was doing with his *Inquiry* and explore the message that he hoped that his audience would take from his book. In doing so I want to suggest that Smith was optimistic, yet pragmatic, in what he hoped to achieve with the book, and that ultimately we can see this in how he explores the overarching concept of 'Improvement'.

Adam Smith lived in a time of rapid social change. The Great Britain of his day was on the way to becoming the most developed and modern economy in Europe. Eighteenth century Scotland has been described as the 'Age of Improvement' (Phillipson & Mitchison, 1970) a time when leading thinkers like Smith tried to understand how to make their society better. The seventeenth century had been a period of civil and religious war that culminated in a series of famines in the 1690s. The attempt to set up a trading colony at Darien in Central America went disastrously wrong with the loss of a significant part of the limited amount of capital held by the Scots, and this in turn set the scene for the Union of Parliaments with England allowing access to its larger home market and colonial trade.

Once the Union of Parliaments had been secured in 1707, Scottish society lost its political elite to London. Nicholas Phillipson (1981) has argued that this created the

C. Smith (✉)
The University of Glasgow, Glasgow, UK
e-mail: Craig.Smith@glasgow.ac.uk

J. Ostle et al. (eds.), *Adam Smith's Wealth of Nations After 250 Years*, Contributions to Economics, https://doi.org/10.1007/978-3-032-32299-9_9

space in which the spectacular outpouring of intellectual achievement known as the Scottish Enlightenment took form. The Scots were now 'North Britons' but acutely conscious that Scotland was far behind in terms of economic growth. Through the course of the eighteenth century, the growing political stability experienced by Scotland led to a process of very rapid economic development. Along with this was a pronounced growth in Scotland's towns and cities as the population moved off the land and into them to seek employment.

The changes that Smith saw around him caught his attention, and his developing fascination with how these social and economic changes were brought about is what prompted his *Inquiry*. The simple, and obvious, observation that some societies were better off than others is where Smith starts the book. In the short introduction (WN Int. 4, p. 10) he is clear that a society where the 'dreadful violation of humanity' (TMS V.2.15, p. 210) involved in infanticide and geronticide is no longer necessary is a society that is an 'improvement' on one where they are everyday occurrences and accepted as necessary by a large part of the population. Smith had no truck with the flimsy rhetoric of figures such as Rousseau who saw nobility in poverty. Poverty was grim, poverty made you have to accept the unacceptable, poverty had to be ended. To the extent that the new commercial society that Smith observed around him was reducing poverty, it was obviously a good thing and a cause for optimism.

Wealth is the difference that allows this improvement to take place, and so we need to understand what wealth is and where it comes from, if we are to encourage such improvements. This observation on the improvement that comes with wealth also provided Smith with his idea of the *Nature* of Wealth. Wealth lies not in the splendour of gold and silver, the national treasury, the palaces of the nobility, or even in the bank accounts of the leading merchants. Instead, it lies in the capacity that the inhabitants of a society have to secure a standard of living that banishes want. He is absolutely clear that 'Every man is rich or poor according to the degree in which he can afford to enjoy the necessaries, conveniencies, and amusements of human life' (WN I.v.1, p. 47). Smith's project then is to inquire into the nature of wealth with a view to working out where it comes from, or to put it in more scientific terms, what *Causes* it.

Smith was not alone in his fascination with social change. His friends in the Scottish Enlightenment, David Hume, Adam Ferguson, Lord Kames, James Hutton, Joseph Black, William Cullen, and others, formed a peculiarly Scottish subset of the wider European movement of Enlightenment (Berry, 1997). A movement characterised by the belief that science, education, and public debate could dispel superstition, ignorance, and tyranny. The Enlightenment optimism that freedom and progress were possible took root, but it also took on a peculiarly Scottish dimension: a dimension that might best be captured by a sense of pragmatism, or careful prudence and practical application of ideas. An idea that we will return to later.

Smith's conception of *Inquiry* is shaped by the understanding of science that we find in his *Essays on Philosophical Subjects* (1795). The *Essays* were published posthumously and include those which Smith felt worthy of retaining when he burned the rest of his unpublished papers. Here Smith defends the modern, Newtonian method of induction—generalisation from evidence and experiment to provide simple and clear systems of knowledge that explain the causal process behind phenomena. But he also explains how science advances, and how one system of explanation comes to supplant earlier systems of explanation by leading the imagination more easily through causal connections that account for apparently disjointed phenomena.

In the essay *The Principles which lead and direct Philosophical Enquiries illustrated by the History of Astronomy* Smith explores the nature of philosophy and science. He argues that our understanding of the world is a pattern of connections that exist in the imagination. The 'natural career of the imagination' (Astronomy, p. 41) flows smoothly and allows us to make sense of the world until it comes across something that does not fit with our established understanding drawn from experience. This creates an emotional unease (surprise) and prompts a desire to make sense of the inexplicable (wonder).

Philosophy is the modern response to this unease and represents the 'science of the connecting principles of nature' (Astronomy, p. 45). Its success depends on its ability to render things 'familiar to the imagination' (Astronomy, p. 96). As he puts it:

> Philosophy, by representing the invisible chains which bind together all these disjointed objects, endeavours to introduce order into this chaos of jarring and discordant appearances, to allay this tumult of the imagination, and to restore it, when it surveys the great revolutions of the universe, to that tone of tranquillity and composure, which is both most agreeable in itself, and most suitable to its nature. (Astronomy, p. 46)

Smith considers the development of science through an account of the move from one system of thought to another. For Smith a system is an 'imaginary machine invented to connect together in the fancy those different movements and effects which are already in reality performed' (Astronomy, p. 66). To explain the shift from one system to another Smith points to two principles that lead us to prefer one system of thought to another, and which provide increasingly satisfactory explanations. The first of these is that if our imagination is to be led smoothly, then there must be as few 'gaps' (Astronomy, p. 42) as possible in a theory. If a theory fails to account for observed phenomenon, then we will notice the gap and anxiety will develop prompting us to seek a new explanation. The system with the fewest such gaps at any one time is the one most likely to be favoured. Theories arise in response to dissatisfaction at the gaps in existing accounts. To succeed they must not only account for the gap, but also for all that the preceding theory had explained. A theory must be 'more completely coherent' (Astronomy, p. 74) than its predecessors.

Smith's second principle is the Newtonian preference for identifying a few simple generalisations from observation that explain a multiplicity of phenomena. Explanatory simplicity not only makes it easier for the mind to follow the theory, but it also avoids the danger of a convoluted account producing additional gaps. If the theory necessary to explain a complex phenomenon is as complex as the phenomenon itself, then it will fail to relieve the 'embarrassment' (Astronomy, p. 59) that we find ourselves in.

Our desire for a satisfying explanation can mean that we tend to run too quickly into the belief that our system accounts for everything: over ambition leads to over complexity and eventually to unease that we are overreaching such that 'the curiosity of mankind, grasping at an account of all things before it had got full satisfaction with regard to any one, [it] hurried on to build, in imagination, the immense fabric of the universe' (Ancient Physics, pp. 107–108).

The point is that Smith was committed to the twin ideas of empirical observation and systematic and methodical explanation. The test of his own theories would be whether they could account for all of the elements of the observed phenomenon and do so in a more straightforward and persuasive fashion that his rivals.

Smith's presentation of his *Inquiry* is also influenced by his discussion of the construction of literary arguments in his *Lectures on Rhetoric* where he notes that:

> When the sentiment of the speaker is expressed in a neat, clear, plain and clever manner, and the passion or affection he is possessed of and intends, *by sympathy*, to communicate to his hearer, is plainly and cleverly hit off, then and then only the expression has all the force and beauty that language can give it. (Rhetoric, p. 25)

In presenting his arguments, Smith hit upon a particular rhetorical technique that placed the central explanatory idea at the very start of the work. The first page of *The Theory of Moral Sentiments* starts with the idea of sympathy, and the first sentence of the first page of the *Wealth of Nations* starts:

> The greatest **improvement** in the productive powers of labour, and the greater part of the skill, dexterity, and judgment with which it is any where directed, or applied, seem to have been the effects of the division of labour. (WN i.i.1, p. 12, my emphasis)

These are the central explanatory ideas of each book, advertised to the reader at the very beginning. In the *Wealth of Nations* improvement is explained by the division of labour. What follows is a study of the operation of the division of labour which demonstrates that it is the force behind the growth of wealth that facilitates improvement.

The *Wealth of Nations* provides us with an analysis of the features of the division of labour (dexterity, time saved, the invention of machines) that generate increased output that has proven so effective that it remains the basis of Intro to Econ lectures to this day. Sadly, that is often all that students hear of Smith. This is a shame because it is the subsequent analysis of the features necessary for the division, and hence the increase in wealth, that is the heart of his work.

He traces the development of the division of labour to the human propensity to truck, barter, and exchange. This propensity allows the interdependence necessary for the unfolding of specialisation and the development of commercial societies. In a commercial society 'every man becomes in some measure a merchant' (WN I.iv.1, p. 37) and this changes how we interact with each other in a whole range of ways beyond economic exchange.

The first chapter of Book I also sees Smith stake out his understanding of the nature of wealth in very clear terms. The example that Smith uses to illustrate the complex system of interdependency involved in a commercial society is the woollen coat of an ordinary worker (WN I.i.11, pp. 22–23). The vast number of interconnections that lie behind the production of this good illustrate the power of the division of labour, but they also illustrate that such complex co-operation can only be achieved through trade; and that the increase in production provides more of the 'necessaries and conveniences of life' (WN Intro.4, p. 10) to ordinary people. Indeed, at the end of the chapter, Smith suggests a startling image for his readers when he points out that the ordinary labourer is materially better off than an African king (WN I.i.11, pp. 23–24). Rhetorical as this point may be, it indicates to the reader that Smith's understanding of wealth is a radical departure from that of many of his peers. The idea that wealth could be illustrated by a worker's coat must have seemed startling counter-intuitive to those used to imagining wealth in terms of piles of treasure.

Smith also underlines the social impact of the division and describes how trade and specialisation shape the manners and the legal and political institutions of a commercial society, creating a new form of human life. Trade requires stable expectations and this leads to a gradual introduction of the rule of law expanding from the cities to the countryside (as Scotland and the Highlands showed). Smith's point was that specialisation required legal and political stability, but it also generated it in ways that have transformed the way we live.

If the division of labour depends on trade, then it is limited by the extent of the market. The greater the market, the greater the opportunity for specialisation. This leads Smith to an analysis of the features that extend or restrict markets and hence prevent specialisation and retard improvement in living standards. Some of these are obvious, such as the isolation of the Highland villages where the size of the market precludes the specialisation as butcher, brewer, and baker. Geographically isolated communities will only become wealthier when transport and communication are improved. Others are less obvious and are man-made, such as tariffs, colonial monopolies, guilds, and apprenticeships. Showing these to be misguided and actively harmful to the improvement in living standards was the applied object of Smith's theoretical inquiry.

In such cases Smith's basic argument is almost always the same: that the interests of the ordinary people in attaining as high a standard of comfortable living as possible is harmed by a faulty understanding of the economy advanced by self-interested merchants or mistaken theorists who exploit the ignorance of politicians to secure income for themselves. The guild system, for example, is defended on the basis that the sort of skill that is required to engage in the trade in question can only be acquired through a long apprenticeship, but the reality, as Smith sees it, is rather that these are designed to prevent entry to the market, to reduce competition, and to artificially maintain prices. Smith is unsparing in his unmasking of such arguments as harming the interests of society at large.

This, then, was Smith's conception of *Inquiry* and what made his theory of improvement an improvement on the theories that had gone before. To be judged a success the *Wealth of Nations* had to provide the following:

- A systematic account that explained the observed phenomena
- An account that fits with our wider thinking without leaving gaps
- A clear and simple statement so that the imagination is led smoothly and easily and
- A single, or a very few, central principles

If these were in place then, according to Smith's theory of the progress of science, the system would supplant pre-existing systems or rival systems, even if there was a struggle to maintain the existing systems on behalf of their partisans.

Smith's intention for the book can also be seen if we look at the way in which he structures it. Books I and II outline his theory of the economy, Book III demonstrates the historical evolution of the political institutions that make commercial society possible, in Book IV he turns to the failure of alternative theories and then concludes with Book V where he develops his own understanding of the role of government and how it should be funded. The policy prescriptions in Book V are made in the light of the success of his own theory over that of his rivals.

Smith's aim in writing the *Wealth of Nations* was to supplant the alternative theories found in the work of Sir James Steuart, the physiocrats, and mercantile thinkers such as Thomas Mun. Smith mentions such writers along the way, but he does not engage in polemic or provide extensive critiques of their systems. His style of argument was to provide a system of his own that showed the weakness of alternative accounts and explained more than they were able to explain.

In this sense, then, the *Wealth of Nations* is a contribution to existing debates in political economy, one which demonstrates the failings of rival theories while proposing an alternative account that explains what they explain and more than they can. Smith did not mention Sir James Steuart in the *Wealth of Nations*, but in a letter to William Pulteney in September 1772, he wrote: 'I have the same opinion of Sir James Stewart's book as you have. Without once mentioning it, I flatter myself, that every false principle in it, will meet with a clear and distinct confutation in mine' (Smith Corr. No. 132, pp. 163–164). Smith's aim was to provide a systematic account of the economy whose persuasiveness lay in its capacity to lead the reader through a series of clear analyses to a better understanding of what generated wealth.

The same strategy is displayed towards the Physiocrats, where the short chapter at the end of Book IV on agricultural systems is a brief, direct engagement with the main tenets of the French economists, but one which rests on the system of ideas as outlined from the preceding three books where they are not directly engaged. For example, the analysis in Book III is an unintended consequences account of the impact of foreign trade on the agricultural system, an account that shows that the development of a market in consumer goods undermined the power basis of the landowning class at the same time as it introduced a consistent legal system across the country. The analysis of the relationship between town and country has elements which are conceptualised abstractions, but it also includes a wealth of historical detail. The wider point that Smith is making is that the Physiocratic stress on agriculture is understandable, 'natural' even, in terms of theory, but it does not accurately account for the actual path of development in Europe. In addition to being a criticism of the Physiocratic analysis, Smith is also making a deeper observation about method. Physiocracy works in theory but fails to account for the observable data of the historical record. The tendency to view agriculture as the only truly productive activity, again a perfectly 'natural' assumption, fails to account for the role of trade in finished goods as the driver of economic improvement in towns which then spread to the countryside.

Far more time in Book IV is spent directly criticising the various mercantile restrictions and showing how, on both the level of theory and on a practical cost/benefit analysis, they fail to secure their goals. However, as Maria Pia Paganelli (2022) has shown, these direct criticisms are a follow up to the long digression on the historical value of silver in Book I (often skipped by modern readers as dull historical detail), which actually represents a carefully assembled body of data that directly refutes the mercantile attitude to precious metals. Smith's presentation of his own theory is his argument against other theories.

Given his understanding of the progress of science, Smith's view of his own system in the *Wealth of Nations* was that it was an improvement on what went before. He would never, and does never, claim that it is perfect and all encompassing. Instead, the more modest claim is that it works better than the alternatives and thus provides a new starting point for the next generation of political economists to seek gaps or problems of over complexity that will eventually build until a new system replaces his'. A system whose success will be judged by whether it can explain everything that Smith's system can explain and do so in a simple fashion while explaining things that Smith cannot.

Comparing Smith's approach to political economy with that of Steuart reveals another important difference in attitude to what might be achieved by economic theories. Steuart's approach to political economy includes a significant guiding role for a government informed by the ideas developed in his writings. The difference between Smith and Steuart's overall view of how economic improvement was to be secured is stark. As Andrew Skinner noted: 'In the case of Smith there is a clear presumption against interference by government—although that is not to be taken to mean that Smith saw a limited role for the state. But in Steuart's work "the science of domestic policy" is consistently directed to the "statesman." His government is "continually in action"'. Steuart was far more confident in government and central direction. (Skinner, 1990, p. 181; See also Rutherford (2012, pp. 111–114)).

Smith, it is fair to say, did not share this view on the likely success of the deliberate organisation of the economy to map onto the dictates of a theory. In a late addition to *The Theory of Moral Sentiments,* he criticised political reformers whose zeal for an idealistic philosophical system leads them to seek to remodel society. He famously observed that:

> The man of system, on the contrary, is apt to be very wise in his own conceit; and is often so enamoured with the supposed beauty of his own ideal plan of government, that he cannot suffer the smallest deviation from any part of it. He goes on to establish it completely and in all its parts, without any regard either to the great interests, or to the strong prejudices which may oppose it. He seems to imagine that he can arrange the different members of a great society with as much ease as the hand arranges the different pieces upon a chess–

> board. He does not consider that the pieces upon the chess–board have no other principle of motion besides that which the hand impresses upon them; but that, in the great chess–board of human society, every single piece has a principle of motion of its own, altogether different from that which the legislature might chuse to impress upon it. (TMS VI.ii.17, pp. 233–234)

Here Smith cautions against well-meaning men of public spirit who design plans for social improvement. The danger of the man of system is that he can only impose his own plan by preventing the individuals from pursuing their own plans of improvement. The result would be a near constant need to intervene, to direct, and to suppress individual initiative and knowledge of particular circumstances. In the end this would undermine the very engine of improvement that Smith identifies in individual initiative where 'the study of his own advantage naturally, or rather necessarily, leads him to prefer that employment which is most advantageous to the society' (WN IV.ii.4, p. 454).

Two very stark statements indicate the difference in approach he saw between his theory and that of Steuart and highlight one of the most important lessons that Smith hoped his readers would take on board:

> The stateman, who should attempt to direct private people in what manner they ought to employ their capitals, would not only load himself with a most unnecessary attention, but assume an authority which could safely be trusted, not only to no single person, but to no council or senate whatever, and which would nowhere be so dangerous as in the hands of a man who had the folly and presumption enough to fancy himself fit to exercise it. (WN IV.ii.10, p. 456)

> All systems either of preference or restraint, therefore, being thus completely taken away, the obvious and simple system of natural liberty establishes itself of its own accord. Every man, as long as he does not violate the laws of justice, is left perfectly free to pursue his own interest his own way, and to bring both his industry and capital into competition with those of any other man, or order of men. The sovereign is completely discharged from a duty, in the attempting to perform which he must always be exposed to innumerable delusions, and for the proper performance of which no human wisdom or knowledge could ever be sufficient; the duty of superintending the industry of private people, and of directing it towards the employments most suitable to the interest of society. (WN IV.ix.51, p. 687)

This system succeeds because 'the law ought always to trust people with the care of their own interest, as in their local situation they must generally be able to judge better of it than the legislator can do' (WN IV.v.b.16, p. 531), and this in turn provides a better explanation for the development and success of commercial society in driving forward improvement than alternative accounts that give a privileged role to the deliberate actions of politicians or the interests of particular orders within society. Indeed, such improvement as has been attained has been secured in spite 'both of the extravagance of government, and of the greatest errors of administration' (WN II.iii.31, p. 343). Provided with tolerable security, individuals will seek to improve their condition and to secure 'the necessaries, conveniencies and elegancies of life' (WN III.iii.12, p. 405).

Passages like this are direct challenges to the general approach of those economists who see the task of political economy as the implementation of policy to direct economic agents in a programme of improvement aimed at economic development. This was clearly not what Smith hoped for his own *Inquiry*. Instead, he adopted a more pragmatic view of what his work could achieve and a more indirect approach to achieving it. He hoped that the convincingness of his system would make it intellectually embarrassing for the advocates of alternative systems to advance their foolish or interested arguments. His *Inquiry* does not provide an alternative blueprint for the economy, instead it provides a set of principles through which we can analyse a policy and the likelihood of its success in attaining improvement.

Smith's concern about the ability of theory to provide a direct guide to policy is compounded by his worries about the incentives at play in the newly developing politics of commercial societies. Clear examples of this are Smith's worries about the nature of politics itself. Flattery and lobbying quickly and inevitably become the chief means of advancement in the new centralised political systems and this process corrupts any original noble image of the statesman pursuing the public good. The suspicion that politics can be a corrupting process is confirmed by Smith's views about the character of those who hold public office—of whom he is almost uniformly dismissive. Of all the 'political speculators' it is 'sovereign princes' (TMS VI.ii.2.18, p. 234) who pose the greatest danger. He notes: 'It is the highest impertinence and presumption, therefore, in Kings and ministers, to pretend to watch over the oeconomy of private people' when 'they are themselves always, and without any exception, the greatest spendthrifts in society' (WN II.iii.36, p. 346). Or even more strongly: 'All for ourselves, and nothing for other people, seems, in every age of the world, to have been the vile maxim of the masters of mankind' (WN III.iv.10, p. 418), and 'The violence and injustice of the rulers of mankind is an ancient evil, for which, I am afraid, the nature of human affairs can scarce admit of a remedy' (WN IV.iii.c.8, p. 493). Government and the enforcement of legal norms are clearly necessary for the stability of society and the operation of economic life, but the political processes that characterise the institution of government are viewed with suspicion by Smith.

Sometimes the language that Smith uses to make his point against government intervention in the ordinary operation of trade and industry suggests that such interventions represent an injustice. That they would be: 'a manifest violation of the most sacred rights of humanity' (WN IV.vii.b.44, p. 582). This appearance of rights talk may at first lead us to read Smith as adopting a doctrinaire ideological position that deals in absolutes and rules out government intervention, but that is not the kind of argument that he makes. If we look a little closer at the actual reasons Smith offers for his opposition to intervention, we find that talk of the violation of rights gives way to an analysis of the inefficiency of such interventions. Smith deploys his theoretical insights and marshals the empirical evidence to show his reader that these policies do not work in practice. In this his argument, as well as his general outlook, is pragmatic.

Once we have understood what wealth is, where it comes from, and the limitations of theorists and governments in advancing it, the next question is how are we to encourage further improvement? At this point Smith moves from systematic theorist to policy analyst. Political economy became a particularly Scottish concern because of the practical problems that Scotland faced. This was not idle speculation, rather it was an intensely practical project. Systematic inquiries, like Smith's *An Inquiry into the Nature and Causes of the Wealth of Nations*, were intended to inform policy. It is here that we see Smith develop a two-level cost/benefit analysis. The first level is the likelihood of any systematic application of a theory being possible given the reality and power of the interests of individuals. The second level is the likelihood of any given policy achieving its ends without generating unintended consequences that created additional problems for society.

When it comes to the first level, that of the application of theory, Smith did not believe that the account provided in the *Wealth of Nations* could be deliberately enforced by central direction. Instead, he hoped that the principles outlined in his work would inform the thinking of individuals. We can see something of the sort of thing that Smith had in mind if we look at some of the policies for improvement that he witnessed first-hand in the Scotland of his day.

The Scotland of Smith's time had seen its government withdraw to London to be replaced by a sort of 'administrative vacuum' (Campbell, 1982, p. 19) where powerful politicians managed Scotland from a distance on behalf of Westminster. As we noted above, Nicholas Phillipson has argued that this created the space for the Scottish Enlightenment, but it also created the space for innovations in the pursuit of improvement. The government of Scotland was undertaken at a local level in county and burgh councils and at a national level by a set of commissions or boards set up for specific purposes, or by a set of voluntary associations and clubs. This system created a society where national government was largely absent or inattentive. The authority of the representatives of the state in any given locality—the church minister, the schoolmaster, the taxman, and the sheriff was potentially fragile. Scotland's emerging middle class was given the space to self-organise rather than become dependent on the central government.

From this emerged two distinct visions of how to promote improvement. The first of these we might call the enlightenment model, typified by the activities of the societies set up by Smith and his fellow literati.

The Honourable Society of Improvers in the Knowledge of Agriculture in Scotland (1723–1745) was one such. The Improvers wanted to spread knowledge of modern scientific agriculture around Scotland. They were an elite society, but one which was dedicated to sharing knowledge and experimentation (Smout, 2012, p. 277). They sought to foster a desire for investment of thought, time, and effort, in the practical application of new techniques and discoveries to improve the security of food supply. An obvious example of this tradition is Smith's friend Henry Home, Lord Kames. Kames was an active improver on his estate at Blair Drummond. His book *The Gentleman Farmer* (1776) shared his experience of attempted improvement with a view to providing practical suggestions to other farmers. In addition to advice on new crops such as potatoes, crop rotation, and the use of manure as a fertiliser, Kames gives a detailed account of the importance of offering long term leases on medium sized farms. The argument here was that tenant farmers have an incentive to invest in improving their farms. This was a view that Adam Smith shared and, as Brian Bonnyman (2014) has shown, formed part of his advice to his former pupil the Duke of Buccleuch as he reformed his estates.

The spirit of improvement continued in the Edinburgh Society for Encouraging Arts, Sciences, Manufactures, and Agriculture founded in 1754, which would eventually become the Royal Society of Edinburgh, Scotland's national academy (its motto is *Knowledge made Useful*). Adam Smith was an early member and took an active part in the main activities of the Society. Its aim was to spread knowledge of the latest scientific and technological advances to the wider public. It did this through public meetings and through prize competitions to encourage innovation.

This model of encouraging improvement was through the discussion of ideas, their application in a practical setting by informed individuals, and the experimentation and learning that flowed from this. This was the enlightened pursuit of improvement, and one can see how Smith might have hoped that armed with the principles drawn from the *Wealth of Nations* and the better understanding of the operation of commerce, those who read and explored his ideas might learn to apply them for themselves.

An alternative vision for promoting improvement, perhaps best named the activist model, can be found in the activities of the Commissioners of Forfeited and Annexed Estates (1716–1721/1755–1782). This was a body set up to manage the estates in the Highlands that were confiscated from those who took part in the Jacobite Rebellions in 1715 and 1745–1746. Unlike the voluntary societies this was a state sanctioned development Board. The personnel were drawn from establishment Scotland and included Smith's friend Lord Kames. Their task was not simply to manage these estates, but to do so as part of a wider deliberate economic and social transformation of the Highlands: a sort of early version of regional development policy. The violent suppression that followed the defeat of the Jacobites at Culloden in 1746 included their disarming and the attempted suppression of their culture. This stick was to be accompanied by the carrot of a programme of road building, town improvement, and agricultural reform that was intended to free the clansmen from dependence on their chiefs and provide them with a better quality of life. The two-edged and quite deliberate attempt to civilise the Highlands became a key medium for the pursuit of improvement. One of the chief innovations favoured by the Commissioners was the development of new industries in fishing and kelp gathering (for use in glass manufacturing). These coastal industries were seen as a more secure living than the traditional small-scale farming of the Highlands. Deliberate attempts were made to encourage the population to move to new towns on the coast—such as Ullapool—where bounties were offered to encourage fishing and kelp gathering.

Smith directly addresses this in his discussion of the Herring Bounty (WN IV.v.a.31–35, pp. 519–522) added to the third edition of the *Wealth of Nations* in 1784. It is an empirical illustration of his wider point about how bounties disrupt the natural flow of capital and labour, even to the extent that an industry is raised up to secure the bounty itself. This was a direct reference to the attempts to encourage fishing as a means to economic improvement in Scotland by offering a subsidy based on the fish caught. Smith could see that such policies were ineffective and, moreover, that they enriched some rather than leading to general improvement for all. Smith was a pragmatist and he could see very well that he lived in a society where political loyalty was bought through pensions, sinecures, and jobs—where advancement meant loyalty to 'the people above' (Murdoch, 1980), where it mattered what was subsidised and who got the subsidy, and he could also see that in cases like the Herring Bounty this was a barrier to effective and long-term economic improvement.

Adam Smith was intimately familiar with the work of these different strategies to encourage improvement, one driven by central government largesse and directed from above through favoured intermediaries, and the other driven by individual initiative informed by the dissemination of the latest knowledge. In the *Wealth of Nations* he explains how, under conditions of 'regular government' (WN III.iii.8, p. 402), the legal enforcement of property rights, and a secure system of capital circulation through the 'judicious operation' (WN II.ii.86, p. 321) of private banking, the division of labour and commerce directed by individual initiative are a surer path to improvement.

It is obvious that Smith saw an important role for the state. He lists a number of areas where it can act with advantage on particular issues (Kennedy, 2005), but these are always assessed on a pragmatic and contextual basis when they move beyond defence and the provision of justice. When it comes to the surest path to general improvement, Smith felt that he had provided a theory that demonstrated the superiority of individual initiative.

Improvement is a suitably reserved term for a careful Scotsman to adopt. It points to a gradualism and a pragmatism in what can be achieved both in theory and in practice. I think Alexander Broadie captures this when he observes that improvement is central to the enlightenment project, but that the Scots had the 'guarded or qualified optimism' (Broadie, 2001, p. 38) of practical men who did not expect too much from grand projects for improvement.

Smith was an optimist when it came to the potential for commercial society to improve the lives of the population. When people point to the discussion of the negative impact of the division of labour on individual workers in Book V (WN V.i.f.50, p. 782) as an example of Smith's pessimism about commercial society and his awareness of a deterioration in living conditions, they tend to over-egg the pudding. Smith tells us of the ill effects of commercial society and offers us solutions to them through education and entertainment, but these are, as we might say today, first world problems. There are reasons to be cheerful, and actions that can be taken to respond to the potential drivers of deterioration. Stable government, the rule of law, and modern freedom have led to rising living standards and higher wages in a growing economy. These are good things, and a careful analyst should be willing to celebrate them and to acknowledge the potentially negative unintended consequences that might go along with them. On balance Smith's optimism about commercial society outweighs his pessimism about these potential problems.

Smith's optimism lay in the benefits that he saw arising from commercial society. His book was intended to make those benefits clear, to outline a convincing account of the causes from which they followed, and to supplant alternative accounts. He was both optimistic about the potential for future improvement, both of economic theory and living standards, but he was pragmatic and under no illusions that the system that he advocated for stood any chance of becoming a reality in its entirety. As he put it:

> To expect, indeed, that the freedom of trade should ever be entirely restored in Great Britain, is as absurd as to expect that an Oceana or Utopia should ever be established in it. Not only the prejudices of the publick, but what is more unconquerable, the private interest of many individuals, irresistibly oppose it. (WN IV.i.43, p. 471)

In a letter to his friend Andreas Holt, Smith described the *Wealth of Nations* as a 'very violent attack' on 'the whole commercial system of Great Britain' (Corr, p. 251). The violence of the attack did not lie in the rhetorical delivery of the criticism, but rather in the brutality of his demonstration of the failings of alternative accounts. He saw the *Wealth of Nations* as a systematic inquiry into the principles of the economy that might influence policy and advise political leaders not as a blueprint to be applied, but as a way of thinking about economic matters. By making his argument in a clear, coherent, and evidence backed fashion so that it supplanted rival theories, it would become increasingly difficult for those who sought to enrich themselves at the expense of their fellow citizens to be able to make their arguments without public embarrassment. It would be much harder for an interested producer to convince a politician that particular regulations, restraints, privileges, or subsidies were necessary for the wealth of the nation if Smith had demonstrated that there was an alternative system to foster improvement that required no such interventions and which benefitted all consumers rather than a few producers.

The reality of politics is that the interests of the interested can trump even the best of available systems of ideas, and read with hindsight the history of subsequent centuries, from the long campaign to abolish the corn law, to the spread of colonialism and imperialism, the rise of economic planning, and the neo-mercantilism of more recent times, suggests that the example of the *Wealth of Nations* did not entirely inoculate public debate against the bad ideas that it took aim at. It is in this sense that Smith was both optimistic and pragmatic about the potential for the *Wealth of Nations*, and that might be just the frame of mind for a thinker intent on improvement rather than perfection. Adam Smith was an optimistic Scotsman, if that is not too difficult an image for people to conjure. His hope for the book was for the pragmatic pursuit of improvement through careful evidence-based analysis guided by general principles derived from scientific inquiry. Modest in what he hoped to achieve, but confident that he had the means to do so with the power of his theory. Smith, then, gives us an optimistic path to improvement, one which is both realistic about what it can achieve and realistic about the vested interests that it would face. This, perhaps, is why we are still reading it 250 years later.

Bibliography

Berry, C. J. (1997). *Social theory of the Scottish enlightenment*. Edinburgh University Press.

Bonnyman, B. (2014). *The third duke of Buccleuch and Adam Smith: Estate management and improvement in enlightenment Scotland* (Scottish historical review monographs). Edinburgh University Press.

Broadie, A. (2001). *The Scottish enlightenment*. Birlinn.

Campbell, R. H. (1982). The enlightenment and the economy. In R. H. Campbell & A. S. Skinner (Eds.), *The origins and nature of the Scottish enlightenment* (pp. 8–25). John Donald.

Kames, H. H. L. (1776). *The gentleman farmer*. In W. Creech and T. Cadell (Eds.).

Kennedy, G. (2005). *Adam Smith's lost legacy*. Palgrave Macmillan.

Murdoch, A. (1980). *The people above: Politics and administration in mid-eighteenth century Scotland*. John Donald.

Paganelli, M. P. (2022). Adam Smith's digression on silver: The centrepiece of the *Wealth of Nations*. *Cambridge Journal of Economics, 46*(3), 531–544.

Phillipson, N. T. (1981). The Scottish enlightenment. In R. Porter & M. Teich (Eds.), *The enlightenment in national context* (pp. 19–40). Cambridge University Press.

Phillipson, N. T., & Mitchison, R. (1970). *Scotland in the age of improvement*. Edinburgh University Press.

Rutherford, D. (2012). *In the shadow of Adam Smith: Founders of Scottish economics 1700–1900*. Palgrave Macmillan.

Skinner, A. S. (1990). Sir James Steuart: Economic theory and policy. In D. Mair (Ed.), *The Scottish contribution to modern economic thought* (pp. 174–196). Aberdeen University Press.

Smith, A. (1976a [1759]). In D. D. Raphael & A. L. Macfie (Eds.), *The theory of moral sentiments*. Oxford University Press.

Smith, A. (1976b [1776]). In R. H. Campbell & A. S. Skinner (Eds.), *An inquiry into the nature and causes of the Wealth of Nations* (2 Vols.). Oxford University Press.

Smith, A. (1980). In W. P. D. Wightman (Ed.), *Essays on philosophical subjects*. Oxford University Press.

Smith, A. (1983). In J. C. Bryce (Ed.), *Lectures on Rhetoric and Belles lettres*. Oxford University Press.

Smith, A. (1987). In E. C. Mossner & I. S. Ross (Eds.), *The correspondence of Adam Smith* (Rev. edn.). Oxford University Press.

Smout, T. C. (2012). A new look at the Scottish improvers. *The Scottish Historical Review, XCI, I*(231: April 2012), 125–149.

Smith in Practice and Applied

Thinking Like Adam Smith: Character, Psychological Institutionalism, and Unintended Consequences

Jerry Z. Muller

1 Introduction

To explore the present timeliness of Adam Smith's work is to run the risk of anachronism, of wrenching his views out of their historical context. But to ignore its possible timeliness is to consign the study of past thought to antiquarianism. Those most inclined to make Smith into a patron saint often fail *to think like Adam Smith* because they are satisfied to *like what Adam Smith thought* (or more often, what they suppose him to have thought). Trying to find the timely in Smith by thinking as Smith thought is a less certain, but potentially more rewarding enterprise.

In the popular mind—and not only in the popular mind—capitalism is more often than not associated with unleashed greed and the pursuit of pleasure. Max Weber was voicing a most Smithian sentiment when, in criticism of this view, he wrote that:

> The impulse to acquisition, the pursuit of gain, of money, of the greatest possible amount of money, has in itself nothing to do with capitalism. This pursuit exists and has existed among waiters, physicians, coachmen, artists, prostitutes, dishonest officials, soldiers, brigands, crusaders, gamblers, and beggars—one can say that among "all sorts and conditions of men," in all times and in every land on earth, where the objective possibility of it has existed or exists. This conception of capitalism ought to be given up once and for all in the nursery school of cultural history. Unbridled avarice is not in the least the equivalent of capitalism, still less of its "spirit." Capitalism may actually amount to the restraint, or at least the rational tempering, of this irrational impulse.[1]

[1] Max Weber, *Gesammelte Aufsätze zur Religionssoziologie*, 2nd edition (Tübingen, 1922), p. 22.

J. Z. Muller (✉)
Catholic University of America, Silver Spring, MD, USA

J. Ostle et al. (eds.), *Adam Smith's Wealth of Nations After 250 Years*, Contributions to Economics, https://doi.org/10.1007/978-3-032-32299-9_10

One need not accept Weber's conception of the spirit of capitalism to appreciate Adam Smith's characterization of the restraining, disciplining effect of the market economy, or the ways in which it guides self-interest toward fulfilling the needs of others. As, in the last generation, large parts of the world have attempted the great leap forward into capitalism, they are increasingly reminded of the social discipline and work-orientation it demands.

The link of self-interest to mutual concern expressed in the commercial query "Can I help you?" and in the sales clerk's perfunctory "Have a nice day" is often scorned—except by those who have lived in societies where sales clerks, for lack of institutional incentives, habitually ignore potential customers. Seen from the heights of moral rigorism, such commercially motivated solicitude is evidence of a lack of true charity and altruism. Seen historically and comparatively, the market's ability to create a self-interested regard for others may be preferable to the more brutal means by which self-interest has been pursued, or the explicit indifference that most often characterizes the relations of morally imperfect individuals toward one another.

2 Smith's Intellectual Project

From his first book, *The Theory of Moral Sentiments* of 1759 (which he continued to revise throughout his life), to his most famous book, *The Wealth of Nations* of 1776, the overarching concern of Smith's writings was the design of social institutions that would bring about the greatest public good. Since Smith's day, however, the various parts of his intellectual project have fragmented into discrete disciplines and sub-disciplines. The gains in the precision of analysis have been great; but the loss in overall understanding has been substantial.

The bulk of the subject matter of *The Wealth of Nations* has been absorbed by the discipline of economics, which benefited hugely from Smith's efforts to systematize economic knowledge. Smith's exploration of the influence of social institutions on personality (in both TMS and WN) has become the subject matter of sociology and social psychology. In their efforts to become "value-neutral" social sciences, all three disciplines have increasingly eschewed the vocabulary of character and virtue—a vocabulary that implies that some modes of behavior are more laudable than others, a question now often regarded as beyond the purview of social science. Smith's assumption that even a modern commercial society—perhaps *especially* such a society—requires the promotion of "superior prudence" in its governing elites smacks of anti-democratic heresy, at least to those more swayed by democratic dogma than by reflection on successful democratic practice.

Smith was critical of "the propensity to account for all appearances from as few principles as possible," a tendency "natural to all men, but which philosophers in particular are apt to cultivate with a peculiar fondness, as the great means of displaying their ingenuity" ("History of Astronomy," I.i).

This propensity has led to the simplification and distortion of Smith's vision by various academic disciplines and political ideologies. Economists, for example, long tended to assume that economic behavior could be accounted for by treating all individuals as rational profit-maximizers, an assumption they often ascribe to Smith.

In so doing, they overlook the many departures from this model in *The Wealth of Nations* as well as *The Theory of Moral Sentiments*, or else dismiss them as irrelevant to economic analysis.

A major recent contribution of economists to transdisciplinary social scientific thought has taken the form of a methodological imperialism in which the language and assumptions used to analyze economic behavior in the market are now applied to other institutions and fields, such as the family and politics. To conceive of children as "consumer durables," the quantity and quality of which vary with the psychic gains they provide, would likely have been viewed by Smith as an ingenious curiosity. But instead of contributing to the explanation of human behavior, it seems merely to extend to new areas the tautological premises of the many economists who "assume that individuals attempt to maximize utility, and [then] define utility as that which the individual attempts to maximize".[2] It is similarly ingenious to explain voters as utility maximizers and politicians as mere aggregators of economist interests. But so narrow a view of human motivation does little to explain the frequency with which citizens vote against their economic self-interest or on the basis of non-economic values, or why ideology and the process of legislative deliberation often determine the votes of elected legislators.[3]

Smith did not try to develop a science of economics free of moral judgments or ethical considerations. His policy recommendations were shot through with moral purposes—above all, to improve the material and moral welfare of the great mass of the population—what he called "universal opulence". But his science of political economy was not a moralistic science: he tried to bring about improvement not by preaching, but by designing institutions that would strengthen incentives to act in socially beneficial ways. Smith's attention to the gap between intentions and consequences provides a powerful antidote to the tendency of cultural critics to substitute moral indignation for social analysis. Many other social thinkers have tried their hands at using institutions to direct human passions, often with results that were futile when they were not nightmarish. Smith's success as a psychological institutionalist can be attributed in large part to his insistence on understanding the workings of existing institutions rather than attempting to design entirely new institutions on the basis of purported social scientific knowledge.

---

[2] David M. Winch, *Analytical Welfare Economics* (Hammondsworth, 1971), p. 25.

[3] For a critique of the empirical validity of "public choice" theory, see Jeffrey Friedman, "The Democratic Welfare State," *Critical Review*, Vol. 4, no. 4 (1990), pp. 672–74.

3 Smith as Psychological Institutionalist

Smith saw one of his tasks as that of the traditional moral philosopher, to reflect on the nature of moral excellence.

But, like many Enlightened intellectuals, Smith prided himself on describing man as he really was, not as we might want him to be. His conception of man was not as an intrinsically good creature corrupted by society, nor was it man as irredeemably evil except by the grace of God. His project was to take man as he actually was and to make him more like what he should be, not by the power of government and not primarily by preaching, but by discovering the institutions that made men tolerably decent and might make them more so.

Smith wrote brilliantly about the psychological basis of scientific inquiry in his early essay on "The Principles which Lead and Direct Philosophical Inquiries" and in his lectures on rhetoric, he discussed the psychology of theoretical exposition.

Though he never explicitly formulated his own method of investigating social life, its elements are clear enough. It included the specification of widely shared psychological propensities—such as the propensity to seek the attention and approval of others—and the attempt to explain the regularities of human action accordingly.

A second element was the inductive attempt to discover regularities in social life through observation and comparison, for which history provided much of the raw data.

A third element involved an examination of the ways in which basic human propensities were shaped and molded into particular character types by historically changing social, political, cultural, and economic structures.

In this strategy of exploring human nature and the institutional arrangements through which character could be shaped in morally positive directions, Smith drew upon more than a century of renewed reflection on the role of the passions.

A widespread if diffuse intellectual trend in the seventeenth and eighteenth centuries sought to analyze the passions in order to channel them into morally beneficial directions through social institutions. This tradition of reflection, which we might call "the institutional direction of the passions" (or, in the interest of conciseness, "psychological institutionalism"), formed the bridge between the recovery of classical philosophy by the humanists and the rise of modern social science.

The Smithian solution, drawing upon the tradition of the institutional direction of the passions, looked to the structure of emotional incentives provided by social institutions to channel, cultivate, and dampen human passions so as to improve human character. The quality of character which was necessary for the realization of any virtue, Smith emphasized, was the ability to control oneself. "Self-command is not only itself a great virtue," Smith asserted, "but from it all the other virtues seem to derive their principal lustre" (TMS 241). Without self-command, the virtues of prudence, propriety, or benevolence could not be brought to bear.

Man's psychological make-up included "malevolent and unsocial passions," such as anger and resentment, which Smith sought to subdue through self-control, using the other passions. The superior virtues, for Smith, grew out of our "benevolent and social affections," passions which he sought to develop and cultivate through proper social institutions and through moral philosophy (TMS 172). His complaint against previous philosophers and moralists was that they had devoted too little attention to a third category of affections—the selfish passions. These passions, such as the desire for attention and praise, were not intrinsically anti-social, Smith argued. Indeed, they could even be admirable when pursued according to the rules of justice, so that they did not involve injury to others (TMS 173). It was these passions which Smith felt it necessary to legitimate, as long as they were properly channeled. For while God might act from benevolence alone, there was need for man as an imperfect creature to act from many motives aside from benevolence (TMS 305). Because our beneficent passions are "very limited" (TMS, 218), they form an insufficient basis to motivate decent conduct toward the many people outside the range of our benevolent feelings.

Smith took the ancient Stoic notion that "images" or "semblances" of perfect virtue were attainable by the many through adherence to moral conventions, and wedded it to the early-modern discoveries that self-love enlightened by the passion for approbation might produce human decency, and that self-interest could be channeled to produce socially beneficent behavior.

A good deal of virtuous behavior, Smith wrote, was actually prompted by self-interest, such as the worthy habits of "economy, industry, discretion, attention, and application of thought," and related "inferior virtues" such as "prudence, vigilance, circumspection, temperance, constancy, firmness" (TMS, 304–305). In Smith's judgement, it was these virtues which commercial society was better suited than previous social arrangements to promote. His *Wealth of Nations* was devoted primarily to showing how self-interest, when properly channeled by law and other, less formal social institutions, could produce socially beneficent effects and behavior. In *The Theory of Moral Sentiments*, he focused upon the role of the desire for approbation in producing propriety and virtue. In both works, as well as in his lectures on jurisprudence, he explored the institutional direction of the passions toward morally and socially beneficent ends. For although persuaded by earlier seventeenth and eighteenth-century writers that self-love and self-interest *could* lead to socially positive effects, he was eminently aware that whether or not they *actually* had such effects depended upon the institutions through which they were channeled and directed.

"Natural liberty" was possible, Smith thought because man's natural "sociability"—his desire for the sympathy, attention, and approval of others—made men capable of subordinating their egoistic desires to the demands of shared social rules.

A main focus of *The Theory of Moral Sentiments* therefore is on the social processes by which the egoistic passions are channeled, moderated, and redirected, so that men can live peaceably with others, pursue their happiness with foresight, and act altruistically.

The psychological precondition for the practice of any of these virtues is self-command, the ability to control our own passions. In itself, self-command is not sufficient to rank as moral, since it can be put to immoral uses. But it is the psychological prerequisite for any sort of positive moral achievement. Smith approves of commercial society because of the increase of self-control it makes possible; but he believes that commercial society requires a degree of self-control that the market by itself cannot provide.

4 Anticipating Unintended Consequences

Smith's great analytic motif was the unanticipated consequences of human action. In *The Wealth of Nations*, this theme is pervasive. Indeed, the book is almost an encyclopedia of the role of unintended consequences in human affairs, a phenomenon (or analytic perspective) which fascinated Smith.

In calling attention to the gap between intentions and results, Smith was not attempting to demonstrate that deliberate attempts to better the human condition were futile. In *The Theory of Moral Sentiments*, he praised that "superior reason and understanding, by which we are capable of discerning the remote consequences of all our actions, and of foreseeing the advantage or detriment which is likely to result from them" (TMS IV 2. 6, p. 189). Smith's science of a legislator was devoted to improving the ability of the legislator to anticipate the previously unanticipated consequences of his actions. The reform of human institutions demanded an awareness that the *consequences* of human actions were often different from the *intentions* which motivated the actors.

This was no recipe for the revolutionary replacement of existing institutions by new ones designed by the social scientist. On the contrary, Smith believed that many existing institutions were already highly functional, that others could be made to function better through the influence of the intellectual or of the legislator, and that yet others provided models for institutional innovation.

Many of the institutions which had historically provided the greatest benefit had come about in an unplanned fashion, without deliberate human foresight (WN IV iv 17, p. 422). But Smith did not intend this as a call to quietism: the purpose of social science as he conceived it was to aid the legislator in anticipating the consequences of his proposed actions.

The visible hand was that of the legislator, who usually preserved, sometimes reformed, and occasionally designed new institutions which channeled the motives of individuals toward socially beneficent ends "as if by an invisible hand".

The theme of the unintended and unanticipated consequences of human action appears with many variations in *The Wealth of Nations*, and in additional mutations in *The Theory of Moral Sentiments*. Smith explores the many ways in which the outcomes of intentional actions are different from those anticipated, in directions sometimes positive and sometimes negative, or positive from the perspective of society but not from that of the actor.

Smith is perhaps best known for his explication of unintended consequences which are beneficial for the actor and for society at large. The most striking version of this theme comes in this passage:

> Every individual is continually exerting himself to find out the most advantageous employment for whatever capital he can command. It is his own advantage, indeed, and not that of the society, which he has in view. But the study of his own advantage naturally, or rather necessarily leads him to prefer that employment which is the most advantageous to the society. (WN IV ii. 4, p. 454)

Were it not for legislative attempts to direct the flow of investment, Smith argues, individuals would prefer to invest in domestic industries, where they can supervise their investments, and will direct their investments into those industries where there are the greatest profits to be made, that is where the effective demand for any commodity outruns its supply. Smith concludes that:

> As every individual, therefore, endeavours as much as he can both to employ his capital in the support of domestic industry, and so to direct that industry that its produce may be of the greatest value; every individual necessarily labours to render the annual revenue of the society as great as he can.
>
> He generally, indeed, neither intends to promote the publick interest, nor knows how much he is promoting it. By preferring the support of domestic to that of foreign industry, he intends only his own security; and by directing that industry in such a manner as its produce may be of the greatest value, he intends only his own gain, and he is in this, as in many other cases, led by an invisible hand to promote an end which was no part of his intention. Nor is it always the worse for the society that it was no part of it. By pursuing his own interest he frequently promotes that of the society more effectually than when he really intends to promote it. (WN IV ii 9, p. 456)

The image of the "invisible hand" in this passage (the only place in *The Wealth of Nations* in which the image appears) is a metaphor for the socially positive unintended consequences of the institution of the market, which through the profit motive and the price mechanism channels the self-interest of individuals into collective benefits. There is nothing mysterious about the "invisible hand"—at least once its functions have been made manifest by social science. And yet, because of the gap between the explicit intentions of the actor and the ultimate result of his action, the notion that the social outcome of the market process is benevolent is counter-intuitive, or contrary to common sense.

The customer knows from his experience that the merchant sells him a commodity for more than the merchant paid for it.

Not only that, but after having tried to purchase it as cheaply as possible, the merchant tries to sell it for the most he can get! How the customer may benefit from a system made up of many such merchants he is at a loss to explain.

The legislator knows from his experience that merchants, manufacturers, and laborers are typically self-seeking, at least in their economic relations. Smith's claim that the ultimate outcome of all of this self-seeking can further the common good is, at first, puzzling.

Yet Smith goes on in the very next paragraph to offer his most important justification for the superiority of the market in allocating resources, a justification based upon the distribution of knowledge in society.

> What is the species of domestic industry which his capital can employ, and of which the produce is likely to be of the greatest value, every individual, it is evident, can, in his local

> situation, judge much better than any statesman or lawgiver can do for him. The statesman who should attempt to direct private people in what manner they ought to employ their capitals, would not only load himself with a most unnecessary attention, but assume an authority which could safely be trusted, not only to no single person, but to no council or senate whatever, and which would nowhere be so dangerous as in the hands of a man who had folly and presumption enough to fancy himself fit to exercise it. (WN IV ii 10, p. 456)

The legislator, then, is not in a position to have adequate knowledge of the myriad interactions of supply and demand that occur in a sophisticated economy. Nor does anyone else. But individuals have both the motive (of economic gain) and the ability to gather knowledge of the supply and demand for any single commodity in a particular market. Thus the legislator concerned with the common economic good should, in general, refrain from exercising direct control over prices and production. Much of that can be left to the "invisible hand" of the market, though maintaining, perfecting, protecting, and compensating for the negative effects of the market will require the visible hand of government.

Smith believed that individuals were better judges of local economic opportunities than the distant legislator, and he began from the premise that they were motivated to engage in economic activity by their perceived self-interest. But he never maintained that they correctly perceived their true self-interest, much less than they acted "rationally." In *The Wealth of Nations*, Smith explored at length the human propensity to overrate the likelihood of gain and underestimate the likelihood of failure in a variety of professions and economic activities, from soldiering to smuggling (WN I x b 26–34, pp. 124–128). In the *Theory of Moral Sentiments*, when Smith used "the invisible hand" as a metaphor for the unanticipated and unintended social consequences of action, it was to portray unintended outcomes which are negative from the point of view of the individual actor, but positive from the perspective of society. The intention in this case is the desire to get rich.

The Wealth of Nations also provides numerous instances of unanticipated outcomes which are negative from the perspective of the interests of both the actor and society at large. Smith argued, for example, that the quality of education at the great English universities had been eroded by the unanticipated effects of philanthropy. The philanthropists who endowed professorships intended to improve the quality of learning. Yet the assured income from these endowments freed the professors from the need to depend upon student fees, an independence, Smith argued, which had destroyed the incentive for professors at Oxford and Cambridge to devote themselves to teaching (WN V i f 5–9, pp. 760–761). Similarly, pious donors motivated to strengthen the established church had provided endowments for the higher education of its ministers. Yet the donors had unwittingly succeeded in producing clergymen unsuited by their higher education to appeal to the common man, thereby preparing the ground for evangelical sects (WN V i g 1, pp. 788–789; also V i g 29, pp. 805–806). In economic policy, Smith showed that time and again legislation intended to boost the production or price of some commodity through government bounties had failed, or had even produced the opposite of the intended effect, because its framers had misjudged its impact (WN IV iv, pp. 499–543). The attempts by government to increase revenue by raising customs duties could have the opposite of the intended effect, Smith showed, by discouraging the consumption of the commodity in question, or by encouraging smuggling. In such cases, Smith advised the legislators, government might increase its revenue by lowering the level of excise taxes (WN V ii k 33–34, p. 884). By taking into account the experience of past legislative errors, the government could adjust and improve regulations so as to bring about the desired effect.

Smith's most effective demonstration of the role of social science in anticipating the unanticipated consequences of social action came in the long chapter devoted to the theories of the French physiocrats. Here Smith showed how a proposal for economic improvement could be scrutinized to reveal the gap between its claims and its anticipatable results. The intention of the physiocrats was to promote agricultural production, and they urged placing restrictions on domestic manufacture and foreign trade in order to achieve their goal. But the result of implementing the physiocratic system, Smith argued, would be to retard agricultural growth. By discouraging the production of manufactured goods made in the towns, he reasoned, the measures suggested by the physiocrats would remove the stimulus for the landlords and farmers to boost their production. (WNIV, ix, 48–49, pp. 686–687). Proper policy analysis showed that the anticipatable results of physiocratic proposals would yield results opposite to those intended.

Smith's emphasis on unintended consequences gives portions of *The Wealth of Nations* an ironic tone which many moralists find disturbing because it seems to mock the fitness of the relationship between motivation and result, while those who pride themselves on their worldliness often find it congenial. It is possible that this tone was intentional. It may have been part of Smith's rhetorical strategy for converting the reflections of the philosopher into the maxims of the legislator, for it recommended the book's prescriptions to those worldly men of affairs who in the cynical world of Georgian politics were unlikely to heed more directly moral appeals. By calling attention to the unanticipated consequences of human intentions, Smith makes the reader aware of formerly hidden connections in the social world. This awareness may promote a highly self-flattering sense of intellectual superiority and perspicacity which makes the doctrine all the more attractive.

The motif of anticipating the unintended consequences of social action has been parceled out among diverse academic disciplines and competing political ideologies.

For some economists, there is one great unintended but quite foreseeable consequence of human action: the socially beneficial outcome of market competition. It is among sociologists that the theme of unanticipated consequences of human action has been most explicitly treated, along with its corollary of the "latent" (unintended or unstated) functions of social institutions that exist alongside their "manifest" (intended or stated) purposes. When the actual consequences of government social policy fall short of expectations, it is often because legislators have failed to recognize the latent functions of existing social institutions. Libertarians (and some conservatives) have adopted Smith's belief in the unintended, socially positive outcomes of the market as their guiding maxim, along with the belief that the unanticipated consequences of government action tend to be negative. Conversely, many liberals and leftists tend to overlook the negative unanticipated consequences of *government* action, often accepting good intentions as a substitute for good policy.

As a result, those who are most attuned to the unintended positive consequences of the market and to the unintended negative consequences of government action are least inclined to participate in government, either as civil servants or elected legislators. Those, on the other hand, who are most willing to serve as civil servants or legislators tend to be more conscious of the negative consequences of the market and the positive consequences of government action. Both camps depart from Smith's program of cultivating men of public spirit who would be moved to participate in government—men who, with the help of social scientific knowledge, would recognize both the role of market mechanisms in securing the greatest public good and the importance of an extensive framework of public services and non-governmental organizations in helping markets perform that function.

5 Smith and the Visible Hand of Government

Smith predicted that the costs of government would increase as it undertook functions that were essential to the public welfare—not only defense, justice, education, and transportation, but other projects that were in the collective interest but unprofitable for individuals or corporations to undertake.

The number and scale of such projects have indeed increased with the development of capitalism and, under the heading "public goods," have become a subject of both economic theory and public policy.

Smith also suggested the manner in which public goods should be provided. In providing universal education, the government should not involve itself in running the schools, paying the teachers, or directing students to particular schools and particular teachers. That approach would deny the consumers of public services the ability to choose, and so destroy the incentives of the providers of such services to provide them efficiently. Smith instead advised government to set standards; provide the better part of the costs of education to those least able to afford it; and, whenever possible, to allow citizens to choose how they acquire the education necessary to meet those standards.

Smith's preference is for public goods to be provided through the market, even when government provides its citizens with the means to purchase such goods in the marketplace.

One contemporary example of this strategy would be the market provision of universal education through the use of school vouchers, provided by government for use at private schools. If this strategy proved politically unacceptable on one or another grounds (including grounds of entrenched interests), a second-best Smithian solution would be the provision of choice within a public school system. For when the market is judged to be an inadequate mechanism, the Smithian predisposition is to design structures with incentives that create some of the disciplining effects of consumer choice upon the providers of public services.

6 "Externalities" and the Role of Regulation

Perhaps the most important updating of Smith's thought was Arthur Cecil Pigou's theory of "social costs," first suggested in his Economics of Welfare of 1920 and refined by subsequent analysts. Pigou pointed out that the real costs of a commodity include not only the "private costs" reflected in the market price, but also the costs of negative "externalities". These are negative byproducts of commercial activity that, in the absence of effective laws and regulation, are not reflected in market prices, but are borne by people with no role in the production or consumption of the commodity. One might say that Smith's failure to recognize this problem indicates the irrelevance of his work to contemporary industrial societies.

Or one might say that since Smith did not view it as a problem, there is no reason for us to do so (This would be a sign of Smithian "fundamentalism"). A third approach—one most in keeping with the spirit of Smith's work—would be to recognize the reality of such disharmonies of private and social costs, and then attempt to use law to restructure the private costs in such a way that the total costs are borne by those who make and consume the commodities that create the negative byproducts (This is what economists call "internalizing the externalities"). One contemporary application of this method is the imposition of a tax on polluters equal to the cost imposed by the polluter on others.

When government regulation of private economic activity is judged to be necessary, it can also be done in a more and a less Smithian manner. One approach is for the government to set standards and to specify how they are to be met. This is the approach usually favored by activists who lobby the government to impose regulation and by the lawyers who write the legislation. In a more Smithian approach, the government sets the standards to be met and leaves it to the ingenuity of diverse actors in the market to provide the most economically efficient means of meeting them. This approach creates a structure of incentives to guide private interests toward a socially desirable outcome.

Take the example of environmental pollution. The moralistic response to pollution is that it is reprehensible and that the government should forbid it regardless of the costs.

Smith would probably agree that pollution is reprehensible, but would try to control it in a way that would allow the market to minimize the costs of achieving this social goal. In one fairly recent application of this Smithian approach, the government has set permitted levels of air pollution, along with a system of "pollution permits" that can be bought and sold, allowing different firms to optimize their costs by spending more on either permits or pollution-control devices, or by shutting down the sources of pollution.

Smith objected to excessive government intervention in economic and social life because laws are often enacted to serve private interests at the expense of the public interest, and because legislators do not have the information necessary to coordinate economic activity. On these issues he was persuasive, but not dogmatic. Neither of these problems could ever be eliminated, he realized, but they could both be ameliorated. Only recently have economists devoted attention to gauging the actual effectiveness of various governmental measures instead of applauding or condemning such measures on ideological grounds. Psychological Institutionalism Beyond the Market Smith was far from believing that even well-functioning market institutions would produce a society of decent men and women. That task required other institutions that socialized the individual, taught him to control his passions, and fostered benevolence. The beginning—though not the end—of a Smithian approach to contemporary social policy would exhibit a certain prejudice in favor of those socializing institutions that Smith thought had demonstrated their indispensability. But it would also demand a continual reevaluation of the effectiveness of such institutions in light of changing historical circumstances and the possibility of adapting such institutions to provide incentives for morally desirable and socially necessary behavior. Last but not least, a Smithian approach would consider how government public policy might ameliorate the negative effects of market processes on such institutions.

Smith regarded the family as the first and most effective socializing institution, since it is there that children take their first steps toward self-command. First under the influence of parental authority and then out of the habitual sympathy that arises from frequent interactions with siblings, children learn to curb their passions and accommodate their desires to those of others.

Smith was concerned that processes within commercial society might tend to undermine those very qualities of character which are its greatest achievement and on which its success depends. In arguing against monopoly profits, he noted that wealth acquired too quickly and easily made "sober virtue" seem superfluous. Elsewhere, he argued that the lower ranks of society were threatened by their tendency to emulate the "loose" lifestyle of the rich and powerful, a lifestyle that Smith found morally abhorrent in the upper classes, and socially disastrous when imitated by the lower. In his time and place, Smith regarded these trends more as a potential danger than as an acute threat to the character type he sought to promote. We can readily imagine how Smith would view an entertainment industry in which "lifestyles of the rich and famous" have become a staple of mass culture that competes with family, schools, and religion for moral influence.

Unlike thinkers from Plato to Rousseau, Smith did not disparage public amusements, nor did he demand that they promote virtue. He did, however, suggest that the law should prohibit "scandal or indecency" in an otherwise free market for public entertainment. And he spoke of the role of government in "promoting the prosperity of the commonwealth, by establishing good discipline, and by discouraging every sort of vice and impropriety". But, as Smith also warned, the role of legislators requires "the greatest delicacy and reserve to execute with propriety and judgement. To neglect it altogether exposes the commonwealth to many gross disorders and shocking enormities, and to push it too far is destructive of all liberty, security, and justice" (TMS, VI, ii.2.18).

7 Liberty and the Public Good

Smith's views have often been distorted by being associated with the tendency of nineteenth-century liberalism and twentieth-century libertarianism to regard the individual's pursuit of his perceived interests as intrinsically good and government as intrinsically evil. This tradition was quite foreign to Smith and other representatives of the Scottish Enlightenment. Smith's moral and political philosophy might serve as a corrective to contemporary neo-liberal theory which conceives of liberty as nothing more than the individual's capricious indulgence of one's passions and holds that any effort by government to restrain such behavior leads inevitably to tyranny. Smith's many comments on the evil and folly of politicians and legislators were no more a condemnation of government than his many criticisms of merchants were a condemnation of commerce. The right to indulge one's passions was not what he meant by "natural liberty". He assumed that some degree of governmental prohibition of immoral action is necessary, but tried to minimize the need for such restraint by encouraging the cultivation of social control and individual conscience. If government policy abandons the support of the institutions that foster decency, citizens will be obliged to choose between an all-powerful state to ensure a modicum of security and a Hobbesian war of all against all.

Smith contended that the greatest happiness comes from acting in a manner we know to be virtuous, while the greatest misery comes from knowing we have violated moral laws.

For Smith, this was a result of the constitution of the human mind. Like the propensity to truck, trade, and barter to improve our fortune, the satisfaction of acting according to moral law, and the inner pain that comes from violating it, can be inferred from human experience.

Smith believed that one of the important roles of the intellectual was to draw moral distinctions between modes of behavior. Much of contemporary social science—especially economics—champions the opposite view. While Smith devoted much of The Theory of Moral Sentiments to demonstrating how and why we become benevolent, contemporary economists who turn to questions of public policy sometimes seem to agree with one of Smith's intellectual foils, Bernard de Mandeville, that benevolence and altruism are illusory. According to one acute observer of the discipline, Economists of the past thought it was part of their task to remind their readers that there are high and low pleasures, that many of the high ones require reason and the sometimes painful acquisition of knowledge, that we aspire to tastes better than our current ones, and that such aspirations are sometimes hindered by profit-seeking businesses that cater to vices and overemphasize the importance of what money can buy. Today's economists are more likely to feel a professional obligation to combat such sentiments than to support them. Here again, Smith's work helps provide a corrective to the unanticipated negative consequences of the discipline he helped spawn.

Within other academic disciplines descended from moral philosophy, it has become fashionable to treat all moral codes as merely functions of systems of power. The need for the institutional direction of the passions is implicitly discounted, social control is treated as intrinsically suspect, and the preference for some standards of behavior over others is assumed to be ultimately arbitrary. In questioning the premises of such fashionable assumptions, a re-examination of Smith's works would indeed be timely.

8 Capitalism, Democracy, and the Prospects for a Decent Society

Perhaps the greatest institutional transformation that has taken place since Smith's day is the diffusion of political influence brought about by the spread of voting rights. Political representation is much broader than in Smith's day. And democracy, despite its poor historical record, as recounted by Smith in his lectures, has become the norm, albeit in a form much attenuated from the ideals of classical republicanism—and perhaps more successful for that very reason. To a degree rarely articulated in democratic theory, representative democracy may well owe its success to its ability to exercise some control over the governors while safeguarding against an excessively expressive citizenry—a fact appreciated by the framers of the American Constitution.[4] For reasons that remain to be fully analyzed, capitalism seems to be a necessary (though by no means sufficient) prerequisite for representative democracy. Smith wrote The Wealth of Nations, to encourage politicians to resist the pressures of economic groups attempting to use political power to advance their own interests. The combination of representative democracy and commercial society does not so much eliminate this problem as transform it, as more interests come to exert political influence.

One role for the intellectual, Smith suggested, was to serve as a member of what Hegel was to call "the universal class"—a professional bureaucracy devoted to the common good. To be sure, Smith's conception of this role was far more modest than Hegel's. For Hegel, the function of the universal class was nothing less than to bring about the "moralization" of society. For Smith, that goal could be achieved only partially and indirectly by creating a legal framework in which non-governmental institutions could channel the passions toward socially desirable outcomes. Smith himself took such a government post during the last decade of his life, and similar roles have been filled by his intellectual successors.

Smith was remarkably prescient in identifying the promise of capitalism, and his work contributed in no small measure to the fulfillment of that promise. The difficulties and dangers to which Smith pointed remain with us. That he did not solve them may reflect the fact that they are incapable of resolution. But some insoluble

[4] Joseph Schumpeter, *Capitalism, Socialism, and Democracy* (1942), chapters 21–23. Albert O. Hirschman, *Shifting Involvements: Private Interest and Public Action* (Princeton, 1982), p.106. Steven E. Rhoads, *The Economists View of the World* (Cambridge, 1985), pp. 201–202.

problems are more benign than others, and it was Smith's judgment that the problems posed by commercial society are preferable to the alternatives.

As we have seen, Smith believed that such a society is better suited to advance what the stoic philosophers had called the "inferior virtues"—in other words, it was more likely to be morally decent. But he realized that a decent society would not come about through the market alone, nor were even the best-designed institutions adequate to the task. That task demanded that moralists like himself offer an intellectually coherent and emotionally compelling account of the standards of virtue and vice, and of the sources of shared respectability.

The fulfillment of the promise of a decent society depended as well on the willingness of some to pursue the public good, and on the knowledge, wisdom, and prudence of those so motivated. In this sense, too, an awareness of Smith's work in the context of his time may help us appreciate both its timelessness and its timeliness.

Bibliography

Hanley, R. P. (Ed.). (2016). *Adam Smith: His life, thought, and legacy*. Princeton University Press.

Muller, J. Z. (1995). *Adam Smith in his time and ours: Designing the decent society*. Princeton University Press.

Rasmussen, D. C. (2017). *The infidel and the professor: David Hume, Adam Smith, and the friendship that shaped modern thought*. Princeton University Press.

Rosenberg, N. (1960). Some institutional aspects of the Wealth of Nations. *Journal of Political Economy, 18*(6), 557–570.

250 Years After *The Wealth of Nations*: Adam Smith and the Foundations of Modern Entrepreneurship

Max Rangeley and Daniel Lacalle

1 Introduction: Smith, Entrepreneurship, and Capitalism

In 1776, Adam Smith published *An Inquiry into the Nature and Causes of the Wealth of Nations*, a work that fundamentally reshaped the study of economic life (Smith, 1776; Viner, 1927). Two and a half centuries later, the questions Smith addressed remain central to debates about prosperity, institutions, and innovation. How do societies generate sustained economic growth? What kinds of institutions encourage productive enterprise? And how do individual efforts to improve one's condition translate into broader social progress?

Although Smith did not employ the modern term "entrepreneur", his analysis offers a remarkably rich framework for understanding entrepreneurial activity. Throughout *The Wealth of Nations* and *The Theory of Moral Sentiments*, Smith examined the behavioural motivations, institutional conditions, and social mechanisms that enable individuals to create value through exchange, specialisation, and investment (Smith, 1759, 1776; Otteson, 2002). His account of economic development therefore extends far beyond a simple defence of markets. Instead, Smith presents a complex system in which moral norms, institutional arrangements, and competitive processes interact to channel individual initiative towards productive outcomes (Rothschild, 2001; Griswold, 1999).

In contemporary economic discourse, entrepreneurship is widely recognised as a central driver of innovation, structural transformation, and long-term growth (Acs et al., 2009; Shane, 2003). Entrepreneurs identify new opportunities, mobilise resources under conditions of uncertainty, and reorganise production in ways that

M. Rangeley (✉)
Cobden Centre, Plymouth, UK

D. Lacalle
Tressis, Madrid, Spain

J. Ostle et al. (eds.), *Adam Smith's Wealth of Nations After 250 Years*, Contributions to Economics, https://doi.org/10.1007/978-3-032-32299-9_11

expand the range of goods and services available to society. Yet these activities do not occur in isolation. As Smith emphasised, economic behaviour is embedded within social relationships and institutional frameworks that shape incentives, coordinate expectations, and enable cooperation among individuals who possess dispersed knowledge and divergent interests (Smith, 1759; North, 1990).

Seen through this perspective, Smith's work can be read as an early analysis of the foundations of entrepreneurial economies. His writings illuminate several mechanisms that remain essential to modern innovation systems: the moral foundations of trust that enable cooperation, the human propensity to exchange that underlies market activity, the productivity gains arising from the division of labour, and the institutional arrangements that sustain open and competitive economic systems (Smith, 1776; Wilson & Farese, 2022). These mechanisms collectively explain how individual initiative can generate broader prosperity when embedded within appropriate social and legal structures.

This chapter revisits Smith's insights in order to explore their relevance for modern entrepreneurship. Rather than treating Smith solely as a historical figure in the development of economic thought, we interpret his ideas as a conceptual framework for understanding the dynamics of contemporary entrepreneurial economies. In doing so, we draw on both scholarly research and practical experience. The authors have worked across several domains—including academic research, public policy institutions and think tanks, and entrepreneurial ventures and investment environments. This combination of perspectives informs the approach taken in this chapter. Smith himself wrote not only as a philosopher but also as a keen observer of commercial society, and examining his work through both analytical and practical lenses helps illuminate how his insights continue to resonate within modern economic life (Rothschild, 2001).

Building on this framework, the chapter develops a series of lessons from Smith's work that are particularly relevant for entrepreneurs and for the environments in which they operate.

First, Smith's theory of moral sentiments highlights the importance of trust, reputation, and ethical conduct in sustaining economic cooperation under conditions of uncertainty (Smith, 1759; Griswold, 1999). Entrepreneurial ventures often depend on incomplete contracts, evolving relationships, and reputational signals, making moral credibility a critical component of long-term success.

Second, Smith's observation of humanity's "propensity to truck, barter, and exchange" reveals the social foundations of entrepreneurship as a process of discovering and organising mutually beneficial exchanges (Smith, 1776). Entrepreneurs create value not merely by producing goods but by identifying opportunities for cooperation and aligning the interests of multiple stakeholders.

Third, Smith's analysis of the division of labour emphasises the role of specialisation, learning, and coordination in driving productivity and innovation (Smith, 1776; Wilson & Farese, 2022). Modern entrepreneurial firms frequently operate within complex networks of specialised actors, making the effective organisation of complementary capabilities a central entrepreneurial task.

Fourth, Smith's institutional analysis highlights the importance of legal, political, and social frameworks in shaping economic incentives. Secure property rights, predictable rules, and open competition create the environment within which entrepreneurial experimentation and investment become possible (Smith, 1776; North, 1990; Baumol, 1990).

Fifth, Smith's discussion of the "invisible hand" illustrates how decentralised economic activity can generate socially beneficial outcomes when individual initiative operates within competitive institutional settings (Smith, 1776; Viner, 1927). Rather than functioning as an automatic guarantee of optimal outcomes, market processes coordinate dispersed knowledge through competition, experimentation, and feedback.

Finally, Smith's broader critique of privilege, monopoly, and political interference in markets offers an enduring warning about the risks that arise when institutional incentives become distorted (Smith, 1776; Baumol, 1990). When economic success depends less on value creation and more on regulatory privilege or financial protection, the entrepreneurial energies that Smith associated with economic progress can be diverted towards less productive activities.

Taken together, these lessons suggest that entrepreneurship is not simply an individual attribute but a systemic phenomenon emerging from the interaction between human motivations, institutional structures, and market processes. Smith's work therefore provides a powerful lens through which to analyse the conditions under which entrepreneurial activity becomes a driver of prosperity rather than stagnation or rent-seeking.

As we mark the 250th anniversary of *The Wealth of Nations*, revisiting Smith's insights is more than an exercise in intellectual history. The global economy continues to confront questions that Smith himself recognised: how to foster innovation, design institutions that reward productive enterprise, align private incentives with broader social prosperity, maintain open and competitive markets in the face of concentrated economic and political power, and ensure that economic systems encourage value creation rather than rent-seeking (Smith, 1776; North, 1990; Baumol, 1990). Smith also recognised the importance of sustaining the moral and institutional foundations of commercial society—trust, justice, and stable rules—without which entrepreneurial activity and long-term prosperity cannot flourish (Smith, 1759; Haakonssen, 1981). By examining these questions through a Smithian framework informed by both scholarly analysis and practical experience, this chapter seeks to illuminate enduring lessons for entrepreneurs, policymakers, and scholars concerned with the foundations of economic progress.

2 Moral Sentiments and Sympathy: Long-Term Enterprise Requires Trust and Ethical Conduct

Adam Smith's *The Theory of Moral Sentiments* (1759) is often overshadowed by the canonical status of *The Wealth of Nations*. Yet for Smith the moral foundations of social life were not peripheral but essential to understanding economic behaviour. Modern entrepreneurship, particularly in environments characterised by uncertainty, incomplete contracts, reputation effects, and long-time horizons, is deeply shaped by mechanisms Smith identified in his moral philosophy—most notably sympathy, the impartial spectator, and the internalisation of moral norms. Rather than portraying market actors as purely self-interested maximisers, Smith argued that individuals are inherently social beings whose economic decisions are embedded in networks of trust, reciprocal expectations, and ethical commitments (Smith, 1759; Griswold, 1999). For entrepreneurs these insights offer a clear lesson: durable enterprise requires more than innovation and risk-taking. It also depends on moral conduct, the cultivation of trust and the accumulation of reputational capital. One of the most famous quotations from Smith (1776 p. 26) is:

> It is not from the benevolence of the butcher, the brewer, or the baker, that we expect our dinner, but from their regard to their own interest; and we address ourselves, not to their humanity but to their self-love.

Yet he also wrote, earlier, that (1759, p. 9):

> How selfish soever man may be supposed, there are evidently some principles in his nature, which interest him in the fortune of others, and render their happiness necessary to him, though he derives nothing from it except the pleasure of seeing it.

Smith's concept of sympathy—the capacity to imaginatively project oneself into the situation of others—serves as a central mechanism of social coordination. Through sympathy individuals learn how their actions appear from another person's perspective, giving rise to what Smith calls the impartial spectator, an internal moral judge that disciplines behaviour by aligning it with shared social expectations (Smith, 1759). Sympathy is not merely an emotional fluctuation, it is a cognitive process that enables people to anticipate reactions, coordinate actions, and sustain cooperation in situations where formal enforcement is limited, or as he phrased it:

> By the imagination we place ourselves in his situation, we conceive ourselves enduring all the same torments, we enter as it were into his body, and become in some measure the same person with him, and thence form some idea of his sensations. (Smith, 1759, p. 9)

Entrepreneurship often takes place precisely under such conditions. Early ventures rely on informal agreements, uncertain promises, and evolving relationships. Co-founders must trust one another, customers must believe claims about quality or delivery and employees must exert effort despite uncertain future rewards. Research in entrepreneurship shows that perceptions of integrity, fairness, and trustworthiness strongly influence entrepreneurial success (Acs et al., 2009; Boudreaux et al.,

2019), reinforcing Smith's insight that moral character supports economic coordination.

For Smith, commercial society depends on a moral infrastructure because markets do not function in isolation. Although *The Wealth of Nations* highlights the efficiency of the division of labour and the coordinating role of the invisible hand, Smith's earlier work emphasises that these mechanisms presuppose shared norms of conduct (Rothschild, 2001). Markets are therefore social and moral achievements. Entrepreneurs who ignore this dimension may generate short-term gains but undermine long-term viability. Studies of entrepreneurial ecosystems demonstrate that trust reduces transaction costs, facilitates knowledge exchange, and encourages investment flows (Isenberg, 2011). These findings echo Smith's emphasis on moral sentiments as stabilising forces within economic systems. Reputation functions as a form of capital: it accumulates gradually through consistent behaviour but can be destroyed quickly through opportunism. This brings to mind one of Warren Buffett's most famous quotes, from his 1989 Berkshire Hathaway letter to shareholders:

> In looking for people to hire, you look for three qualities: integrity, intelligence, and energy. And if they don't have the first, the other two will kill you.

The importance of reputation becomes particularly visible during the process of resource mobilisation. New ventures rarely possess extensive collateral, audited track records, or institutional guarantees. Instead they rely heavily on the perceived character of the founder when attracting investors, partners, and early employees. Venture capital research consistently shows that assessments of founder integrity weigh heavily alongside evaluations of technology or market potential (Zott & Huy, 2007). Smith's framework helps explain this pattern. When entrepreneurs behave in ways that appear trustworthy and consistent, others can sympathetically identify with their intentions. This identification reduces perceived information asymmetries and allows cooperative relationships to form despite uncertainty.

Smith's theory also clarifies why ethical conduct must be habitual rather than strategic. The impartial spectator does not approve of behaviour that appears virtuous only when convenient. Moral approval arises when conduct reflects stable character traits and internalised norms rather than opportunistic signalling (Smith, 1759; Hanley, 2009). Entrepreneurship involves repeated interactions across time with investors, employees, customers, and suppliers. In such environments consistency matters. Even small acts of misrepresentation or unfairness can cause disproportionate damage because they undermine expectations of honesty and reciprocity that cooperation depends upon.

Sympathy also shapes relationships with customers. Smith observed that individuals seek the approval of others and are troubled by their disapproval. Entrepreneurs who recognise this dynamic understand that customers evaluate more than price and utility; they also judge fairness, honesty, and intention. Evidence from behavioural economics and marketing suggests that customers value transparency, procedural fairness, and authentic communication even when outcomes are imperfect (Fehr & Falk, 2002). Firms that communicate openly, honour commitments, and treat customers respectfully accumulate reputational capital that can buffer them against competitive shocks. By contrast, firms that erode trust may struggle to recover credibility regardless of pricing strategies.

Importantly, Smith does not view morality as a constraint on economic success. Instead moral conduct facilitates prosperity by enabling cooperation under conditions of uncertainty. Entrepreneurial environments, characterised by experimentation, innovation, and rapid change, cannot be fully governed by contracts or regulation. Informal norms therefore act as the connective tissue of entrepreneurial ecosystems. When entrepreneurs behave in ways consistent with the impartial spectator—demonstrating fairness, prudence, and beneficence—others become more willing to participate in risky but mutually beneficial ventures. Trust reduces the need for costly monitoring, lowers risk premiums demanded by investors, and stabilises relationships throughout supply chains.

Smith's perspective also highlights the importance of ethical leadership inside entrepreneurial firms. The impartial spectator develops through social interaction, and leaders often function as a local embodiment of that moral standard. When entrepreneurs model honesty, humility, and fairness they shape expectations within their organisations, encouraging employees to internalise similar norms. Research in organisational behaviour supports this idea: ethical leadership increases engagement, discourages opportunistic conduct, and fosters cultures of reciprocity (Brown & Treviño, 2006). In Smithian terms, the entrepreneur's behaviour becomes a benchmark against which employees evaluate their own conduct.

Finally, Smith's framework encourages a broader understanding of entrepreneurial purpose. While self-interest remains an important motivator, Smith emphasised that individuals also desire to be worthy of admiration and indeed get satisfaction from the wellbeing of others. This aspiration moderates narrow self-interest and aligns individual ambition with social benefit (Smith, 1759). Entrepreneurship therefore represents both a pathway to private gain and also a social role involving responsibilities: creating value, treating partners fairly, contributing to communities, and demonstrating integrity in economic life. Smith's emphasis on virtues such as prudence, justice, and beneficence offers entrepreneurs a moral compass for navigating complex strategic decisions.

3 The Propensity to Truck, Barter, and Exchange: Entrepreneurship Is Fundamentally About Value Exchange

> People were doing business with one another through the Internet already, through bulletin boards. But, on the Web, we could make it interactive, we could create an auction, we could create a real marketplace. Pierre Omidyar, Founder of eBay

Adam Smith famously argues in *The Wealth of Nations* that the foundation of economic life lies in a natural human disposition: "the propensity to truck, barter, and exchange one thing for another" (Smith, 1776). Although the phrase is widely cited, its relevance for entrepreneurship is often underexplored. For Smith, this propensity reflects neither pure self-interest nor simple calculation. Instead, it expresses a distinctively human capacity for reciprocal cooperation, communication, and imaginative understanding of others' wants. Viewed through this broader Smithian framework, entrepreneurship appears as both an act of ingenuity and also a practice of value exchange: discovering, articulating, negotiating, and delivering value in ways that align the interests of multiple parties.

Smith's account of exchange begins with the observation that humans, unlike animals, cannot satisfy their needs through self-sufficiency or dominance but must rely on persuasion. Individuals obtain the cooperation of others not by appealing to benevolence alone but by appealing to their self-love and demonstrating the possibility of mutual benefit (Smith, 1776). This argument is often misunderstood. Smith does not claim that individuals are motivated only by self-interest. Rather, he emphasises that in market contexts persuasion must take the form of value alignment. Entrepreneurs, as initiators of new exchanges, must therefore understand the desires, constraints, and aspirations of others. Entrepreneurship becomes a process of matching problems with solutions and showing stakeholders why a proposed exchange is worthwhile.

This insight has important implications for entrepreneurial practice. Contemporary research on opportunity recognition suggests that successful entrepreneurs identify unmet needs, latent preferences, or inefficiencies and transform them into viable products or services (Shane, 2003; Eckhardt & Ciuchta, 2008). This perspective closely reflects Smith's proposition that economic development arises from individuals' capacity to discover possibilities for mutually advantageous exchange. Entrepreneurs make the human propensity to exchange productive by identifying new opportunities where value can be created and negotiated. In Smith's language, they are "projectors" who reconfigure patterns of exchange in ways that expand mutual benefit (Smith, 1776; Hirst, 2012).

Smith also emphasises that exchange requires communication and trust—conditions that cannot be reduced to self-interest alone. Markets depend on shared understandings about the value of goods, the reliability of promises and the norms governing transactions. Entrepreneurs must therefore cultivate persuasive communication, relational intelligence, and contextual awareness. Whether pitching to investors, negotiating with suppliers, or engaging early adopters, entrepreneurs are fundamentally involved in persuasion: presenting a vision of mutual gain and framing it in ways that resonate with the priorities of others. In this respect Smith's analysis anticipates modern theories of entrepreneurial effectuation, which emphasise how entrepreneurs co-create opportunities with stakeholders through iterative commitments and negotiation (Sarasvathy, 2001). Exchange is not simply a transfer of goods but an evolving social process.

Another important element of Smith's account is the idea that markets function as discovery processes. Exchange reveals information about preferences, technological possibilities, and social needs. Entrepreneurs contribute to this process by initiating exchanges that test hypotheses about what others value. Their activities generate feedback that reshapes economic understanding. This insight parallels later Austrian perspectives—particularly Hayek's description of markets as systems for communicating dispersed information (Hayek, 1945). Yet Smith's analysis also retains a richer social dimension: entrepreneurial discovery depends not only on analytical insight but also on the ability to understand other people's perspectives and respond to them creatively.

Smith's framework also sheds light on innovation. Innovation is often associated with technological breakthroughs, but it frequently arises from new ways of organising exchange. Digital platforms, for example, create multi-sided markets in which value is co-produced by users, developers, and advertisers. Their success depends on orchestrating large networks of exchange while reducing transaction frictions. From a Smithian perspective, platform entrepreneurs harness the natural propensity to exchange by designing infrastructures that enable vast numbers of mutually beneficial transactions. The entrepreneurial challenge is therefore not only technological but institutional: creating structures that facilitate cooperation and value creation at scale.

Smith further recognised that the desire to better one's condition plays a central role in motivating exchange (Smith, 1776; Brown, 1994). This desire is not purely material; it also involves recognition, status, and approval. Entrepreneurs often leverage this motivational structure by offering consumers products that satisfy both functional and symbolic needs. Modern marketing theory supports this interpretation, showing that consumers derive value not only from practical utility but also from identity, status, and narratives of self-improvement (Vargo & Lusch, 2004). The propensity to exchange is therefore connected to broader human aspirations for advancement and social recognition.

Equally important is Smith's emphasis on fairness and reciprocity. While individuals seek advantageous exchanges, long-term cooperation depends on perceptions of equity and proportionality. Exchanges perceived as exploitative undermine trust and damage reputational capital. Modern entrepreneurial ecosystems illustrate this principle clearly. Access to partnerships, funding and collaborative opportunities often depends on reputational networks and norms of fair dealing (Stam, 2015). Entrepreneurs who repeatedly pursue one-sided gains may achieve short-term success but risk exclusion from future opportunities. Sustainable entrepreneurship therefore requires maintaining exchange relationships that participants perceive as mutually beneficial.

Smith also emphasised that exchange enables the division of labour, which increases productivity and economic growth. However, the relationship is reciprocal: the division of labour expands because exchange opportunities grow. For entrepreneurs, this highlights the importance of designing business models that coordinate specialised actors. Start-ups frequently rely on external partners for manufacturing, logistics, or technological development. The entrepreneur's task is to organise these relationships into coherent value chains that benefit all participants. This requires structuring incentives and agreements so that each party perceives participation as worthwhile. In this way Smith's theory anticipates modern discussions of value chains and entrepreneurial coordination, and indeed the importance of common rules, both formal and informal, including on modern digital platforms like eBay:

> We can never expect to see the members of the same society so disposed towards each other as to cooperate freely and efficiently unless they are instructed, not only in the common rules of justice, but in the ways in which mutual accommodation may be beneficial to all. (1759)

Lastly, Smith recognised that although the propensity to exchange is universal, its expression varies across institutional and cultural contexts. Social norms, legal systems and political institutions shape how exchanges occur and which entrepreneurial activities are feasible. When institutions protect property rights, enforce contracts, and encourage open competition, opportunities for exchange expand dramatically. Conversely, restrictive or unstable institutional environments limit the scope of entrepreneurial activity. Thus while the underlying human propensity is constant, the institutional framework determines how fully it can be realised.

4 Division of Labour: Focus and Specialisation Drive Entrepreneurial Growth

> Great things in business are never done by one person. They're done by a team of people.
> Steve Jobs, in *Steve Jobs: The Lost Interview* (1995)

The division of labour is one of the most influential concepts in *The Wealth of Nations*, serving as Adam Smith's primary explanation for economic development. Smith's famous opening example—the pin factory in which ten workers performing specialised tasks produce far more pins than if each worker made pins independently—illustrates a principle that has shaped economic thought for centuries.

> One man draws out the wire, another straights it, a third cuts it, a fourth points it, a fifth grinds it at the top for receiving the head; to make the head requires two or three distinct operations; to put it on is another; and the important business of making a pin is, in this manner, divided into about eighteen distinct operations. (1776)

Although this example originates in eighteenth-century manufacturing, its relevance extends well beyond that context. For modern entrepreneurs, Smith's analysis offers a powerful framework for understanding how focus, specialisation, and the coordination of complementary capabilities generate innovation, scalability, and competitive advantage. Entrepreneurship rarely depends on isolated generalists; instead it involves mobilising and coordinating specialised knowledge within firms and across wider ecosystems.

Organisational behaviour is now a core part of all business school education, for instance Nelson and Winter wrote in their seminal 1982 work *An Evolutionary Theory of Economic Change*:

> Organisational routines are the primary means by which firms accumulate knowledge and scale their operations efficiently.

Yet many of the core elements of modern organisational analysis were prefigured by Smith some 250 years ago. Smith argues that the division of labour increases productivity through three main mechanisms: increased dexterity, reduced switching between tasks, and the invention of machines that facilitate specialised work (Smith, 1776). Each mechanism remains highly relevant to contemporary entrepreneurship. Increased dexterity reflects the accumulation of tacit knowledge—skills refined through repetition and experience. Entrepreneurs who focus on specific capabilities, whether in product design, customer segments, or technological expertise, benefit from similar learning effects. Empirical research shows that start-ups with clearly defined competencies or markets often outperform those pursuing diffuse strategies (Helfat & Peteraf, 2003; Winter, 2000). Concentrated effort allows knowledge to accumulate more rapidly, and accumulated knowledge becomes a source of competitive advantage. In this sense, Smith's insight closely aligns with modern theories of dynamic capabilities and organisational learning.

The second mechanism identified by Smith—the reduction of switching costs—highlights the cognitive and temporal efficiencies generated by specialisation. Entrepreneurs often begin by performing many different roles, from product development to marketing and financial management. While this generalism may be unavoidable at early stages, it becomes inefficient as ventures grow. Constantly shifting between tasks consumes time and attention, reducing overall effectiveness. Sustainable growth therefore requires entrepreneurs to reduce switching costs through delegation, role differentiation, and structured processes. Designing an organisation in which individuals can concentrate on well-defined tasks becomes a central entrepreneurial responsibility. Smith's reasoning anticipates modern organisational theory, which emphasises the importance of clear responsibilities, workflow design, and operational focus in high-growth firms (Burton & Obel, 2018). Entrepreneurship, in this sense, often involves replacing improvised multitasking with coordinated specialisation.

The third mechanism—the invention of machines—is perhaps Smith's most forward-looking observation. Smith argued that the division of labour stimulates innovation because workers who repeatedly perform specialised tasks become particularly capable of identifying inefficiencies and proposing improvements (Smith, 1776). Individuals closely engaged with a specific process often recognise opportunities for innovation that outsiders overlook. This idea remains highly relevant in contemporary knowledge economies. Many entrepreneurial opportunities emerge when individuals with deep expertise encounter persistent problems within their fields and develop solutions to address them. Scholars of innovation describe this phenomenon as user-driven innovation, in which those closest to a problem generate new ideas for improvement (von Hippel, 2005). Entrepreneurs who cultivate domain-specific knowledge—whether in biotechnology, software engineering, or renewable energy—are therefore well positioned to identify opportunities that arise from practical experience.

At the same time, Smith recognised that extreme specialisation could produce disadvantages. He warned that highly repetitive labour might narrow intellectual development and limit broader capacities (Smith, 1776; Sen, 2010). For entrepreneurs, this observation highlights an important tension between depth and breadth.

Firms require specialised expertise to operate efficiently, but founders must retain an integrative perspective that allows them to coordinate specialised contributors:

> Firms require specialised expertise to operate efficiently, but founders must retain an integrative perspective that allows them to coordinate specialised contributors. (Helfat & Peteraf, 2003)

The entrepreneurial role therefore involves synthesising diverse forms of knowledge rather than mastering every domain personally. Scholars sometimes describe this capacity as boundary-spanning cognition—the ability to connect insights from different fields and translate them into coordinated action (Weick, 1995). From this perspective, entrepreneurship reflects a division of labour not only in tasks but also in knowledge and judgment.

Smith's analysis also emphasises that specialisation depends on the scale and connectivity of markets. He famously observed that "the division of labour is limited by the extent of the market" (Smith, 1776). Specialisation becomes viable only when markets are large enough to support it. This insight anticipates modern theories of clusters and entrepreneurial ecosystems. Research shows that firms specialising in narrow domains often thrive when embedded in dense networks of complementary organisations (Porter, 1998; Stam, 2015). Such ecosystems provide specialised suppliers, skilled labour, professional services, and knowledge spillovers that reinforce productivity. Regions such as Silicon Valley, Shenzhen, and Bangalore illustrate this Smithian dynamic: extensive markets and dense networks allow firms to specialise deeply while benefiting from collaboration and knowledge exchange.

Smith also recognised that the division of labour interacts with natural variations in human talents and inclinations. Individuals differ in abilities, preferences, and experiences, and these differences encourage specialised roles within economic life (Smith, 1776; Otteson, 2002). Modern entrepreneurship reflects this pattern. Many founders emerge from professional or educational environments where they develop specialised expertise—engineers launching technology ventures, scientists commercialising research, or designers building creative enterprises. Entrepreneurial opportunities often arise when individuals recognise how their distinctive capabilities can be applied to solve particular problems. In this sense, specialisation is not only organisational but also personal. Entrepreneurial identity—the sense of what one is uniquely equipped to do—frequently shapes the direction of venture creation (Fauchart & Gruber, 2011).

Another implication of Smith's theory concerns the entrepreneur's role in designing and managing the division of labour within growing firms. As organisations expand, founders must shift from performing tasks themselves to constructing systems that enable others to perform specialised roles effectively. This transition involves creating workflows, defining responsibilities, and establishing routines that coordinate activity. Organisational routines become repositories of shared knowledge and allow production or service delivery to scale efficiently (Nelson & Winter, 1982). Entrepreneurs who successfully make this transition demonstrate careful judgment in allocating responsibilities and balancing efficiency with flexibility.

Smith's emphasis on specialisation also illuminates modern developments in modular and platform-based entrepreneurship. Digital platforms create architectures in which many specialised actors contribute complementary innovations. For example, platforms such as Amazon Web Services or the Apple App Store allow thousands of developers and firms to build specialised services while relying on shared infrastructure. These systems extend the division of labour beyond the boundaries of individual firms to entire ecosystems. Entrepreneurs participating in such platforms must understand how to position their capabilities within these modular structures, focusing internally on distinctive expertise while leveraging external specialisation.

5 Institutions Matter: Entrepreneurship Thrives in Supportive Ecosystems

> The sovereign has only three duties to attend to; three duties of great importance, indeed, but plain and intelligible to common understandings. First, the duty of protecting the society from the violence and invasion of other independent societies; secondly, the duty of protecting, as far as possible, every member of the society from the injustice or oppression of every other member of it; and, thirdly, the duty of erecting and maintaining certain public works and certain public institutions, which it can never be for the interest of any individual, or small number of individuals, to erect and maintain; because the profit could never repay the expense to any individual or small number of individuals, though it may frequently do much more than repay it to a great society. (Smith, 1776)

> Institutions are the rules of the game in a society or, more formally, are the humanly devised constraints that shape human interaction. They structure incentives in human exchange, whether political, social, or economic. In consequence, they shape the direction of economic activity and, more generally, the way the human game is played. (North, 1990, p. 3)

> "Americans have combined human ingenuity, a market system, a tide of talented and ambitious immigrants, and the rule of law to deliver abundance beyond any dreams of our forefathers." Warren Buffett, shareholder letter of Berkshire Hathaway (2017)

Although Adam Smith is often portrayed as a champion of laissez-faire markets, his writings reveal a nuanced understanding of the institutional foundations required for economic development. For Smith, markets do not always arise spontaneously, nor do they function universally without some level of governance, justice, and public infrastructure. In *The Wealth of Nations*, he repeatedly emphasises that economic activity depends on "peace, easy taxes, and a tolerable administration of justice" (Smith, 1776), highlighting the role of institutions in securing property rights, enabling exchange, and reducing uncertainty. Entrepreneurs, whose activities are inherently forward-looking and uncertain, rely heavily on these institutional supports. Understanding entrepreneurship through a Smithian lens requires recognising that ventures flourish not in vacuums but in ecosystems providing stability, coordination, and opportunities for specialisation.

Perhaps the best example of extraordinary economic growth in modern history is Singapore. Upon independence, Singapore had roughly the same GDP per capita as

Kenya, Nigeria and Ghana; it now has a GDP per capita of more than $90,000, double that of most countries in Western Europe. Lee Kuan Yew, the patriarch of Singapore, phrased it best when he said that:

> The task of the leaders must be to provide or create for them a strong framework within which they can learn, work hard, be productive and be rewarded accordingly. And this is not easy to achieve.

Yet Smith's institutional thought extends beyond formal legal frameworks. He emphasises the importance of norms, trust, and moral conventions—elements elaborated in *The Theory of Moral Sentiments*—as preconditions for market functioning (Smith, 1759). These informal institutions reduce transaction costs, facilitate cooperation, and align expectations among actors with incomplete information. Modern institutional economics echoes these insights. Scholars such as North (1990) argue that institutions—formal and informal—structure incentives, shape opportunities, and guide entrepreneurial activity. Where institutions reward innovation, fairness, and productive risk-taking, entrepreneurship flourishes; where they reward rent-seeking, corruption, or extraction, talent is diverted into unproductive activity (Baumol, 1990). Smith anticipates this distinction in his critique of monopolies, mercantilist privileges, and political capture.

Some 40 years after the publication of the *Wealth of Nations* and the *Declaration of Independence* (both in 1776), as debates took place about the types of institutions that should grow in the United States—such as central banks—Thomas Jefferson wrote a letter to Samuel Kercheval, on July 12, 1816:

> Laws and institutions must go hand in hand with the progress of the human mind. As that becomes more developed, more enlightened, as new discoveries are made, new truths disclosed, and manners and opinions change with the change of circumstances, institutions must advance also to keep pace with the times.

As the human mind has progressed through the centuries, our understanding of the nature of justice has progressed accordingly. Indeed, a central institutional requirement for entrepreneurship is a well-functioning system of justice. Smith regarded justice as a foundational public good, establishing the rules under which contracts are enforced, property secured, and disputes adjudicated. Without it, society would collapse into disorder, making commerce impossible (Smith, 1759; Haakonssen, 1981). Entrepreneurs depend critically on an environment where agreements can be trusted and rights protected. Contemporary evidence confirms that entrepreneurial activity is higher in countries with efficient, transparent, and predictable legal systems (Djankov et al., 2002). In Smith's framework, the rule of law is not external to markets; it is the institutional scaffold enabling entrepreneurial action.

Smith also emphasises the state's role in providing public works and infrastructure that private actors (arguably) cannot supply profitably. Roads, harbours, and canals reduce transaction costs, extend market reach, and enlarge the "extent of the market", which determines possibilities for specialisation (Smith, 1776). For entrepreneurs, such infrastructure shapes opportunity, reducing distribution costs, enabling access to new customers, and connecting them to specialised suppliers. In the modern economy, digital infrastructure—broadband connectivity, data standards, cybersecurity—performs a similar role, although when private actors can provide such services, for instance Starlink, it is generally more cost-effective and efficient.

Regulatory frameworks are another crucial institutional factor. Smith criticised regulations that entrenched privilege or restricted market entry, such as guild monopolies or politically granted corporate charters, because they protect incumbents at the expense of innovation and consumer welfare (Smith, 1776; Viner, 1927). Modern entrepreneurship research observes similar patterns: regulatory capture inhibits entrants and reduces competition. Yet Smith also recognised the need for regulations that address market failures, protect consumers, and preserve fair competition. Effective entrepreneurship depends on a balance: rules should safeguard the public without stifling experimentation, fostering openness, competition, and accountability.

Institutions also influence human capital. Smith stressed that widespread education enhances workforce productivity, social cohesion, and entrepreneurial capacity (Smith, 1776; Winch, 1978). Educated populations supply skilled labour, scientists, and innovators, essential to high-growth ventures. Education also strengthens moral awareness and civic virtue, supporting informal institutions of trust and cooperation. Modern evidence confirms that regions with strong educational systems—universities, vocational training, research centres—experience higher start-up activity and innovation (Audretsch & Lehmann, 2005). From a Smithian perspective, education is a public investment expanding collective entrepreneurial capability.

Smith anticipates modern cluster theory and innovation hubs. Although he did not use this terminology, his analysis of market expansion, specialisation, and coordination reflects agglomeration dynamics. Dense networks of specialised firms, suppliers, financiers, and skilled workers amplify productivity and innovation. As Porter would write in the 1990s in *The Competitive Advantage of Nations*:

> Clusters are geographic concentrations of interconnected companies and institutions in a particular field. They increase the productivity with which companies can compete, they drive innovation, and they stimulate new business formation by fostering interaction, competition, and knowledge spillovers. (Porter, 1998, p. 78)

Entrepreneurs in these ecosystems benefit from knowledge spillovers, shared norms, and complementary capabilities. Smith's observation that the division of labour is limited by the extent of the market implies that the size, diversity, and connectivity of local ecosystems determine which ventures can emerge and scale (Smith, 1776; Porter, 1998). Silicon Valley, Boston's biotech cluster, and Berlin's digital start-up scene exemplify this dynamic: legal, infrastructural, educational, and cultural institutions combine to support entrepreneurial experimentation.

Another critical institutional factor is limiting rent-seeking. Baumol summarised this problem directly and concisely in *Entrepreneurship: Productive, Unproductive, and Destructive*:

> Where entrepreneurial activity is rewarded with productive gains, economies prosper; where it is diverted into rent-seeking, societies stagnate. (Baumol, 1990)

Smith warned against concentrated economic and political power—merchants, guilds, or monopolies—lobbying for advantages that distort markets, suppress competition, and harm consumers (Smith, 1776; Fitzgibbons, 1995). For entrepreneurs, rent-seeking institutions create entry barriers, reduce innovation incentives, and channel creativity into lobbying rather than productive activity. Comparative studies show that economies dominated by political favouritism or oligarchic control experience lower rates of innovative entrepreneurship and slower growth (Acemoglu & Robinson, 2012). Smith's critique of mercantilism remains relevant for discussions of market concentration, antitrust, and regulatory capture.

Lastly, prefiguring many modern institutionalist analyses, Smith emphasises the moral and cultural dimensions of institutions. Institutions shape incentives and social values. Societies rewarding experimentation, tolerating failure, and celebrating innovation foster entrepreneurial cultures. Conversely, cultures prioritising stability over risk inhibit entrepreneurial emergence. Smith understood that norms such as industriousness, prudence, and fairness matter as much as laws in shaping behaviour (Smith, 1759; Otteson, 2002). Modern research confirms that cultures supporting autonomy, creativity, and achievement correlate strongly with entrepreneurial activity (Hayton et al., 2002). Institutions thus provide not just rules but environments of meaning, influencing how individuals pursue opportunities.

6 The Invisible Hand: Self-Interest with a Referee, Not a Miracle

The idea of the "invisible hand" appears only once in *The Wealth of Nations*, yet many people see it as Smith's main argument about market coordination (Smith, 1776; Adam Smith Institute, n.d.). In Book IV, Chapter II, Smith writes: "He intends only his own gain, and he is in this, as in many other cases, led by an invisible hand to promote an end which was no part of his intention" (Smith, 1776). Smith is saying that self-interest generates socially beneficial outcomes when it happens in an environment where competition, enforceable property rights, and independent regulation create a platform for prosperity.

Entrepreneurs, workers, and consumers all seek to achieve their own welfare. An entrepreneur wants to earn more, reduce risk, and gain recognition but also wants a sustainable, long-term business that provides goods and services that most stakeholders value. Employees want security and a better salary, but they also want a healthy and nurturing work environment. Customers want quality products at a good price. That part does not change (Smith, 1776; Adam Smith Institute, n.d.).

An independent institutional environment is essential to achieve prosperity. Institutions can help self-interest manifest as value creation or as value extraction. In competitive markets with independent and simple regulations that facilitate open, fair, and transparent transactions with low barriers to entry, entrepreneurs can achieve their interests by offering better products at competitive prices. When the environment is of open competition, clear and transparent, and facilitating regulation, self-interest is inevitably aligned with general society interests (Smith, 1776; Adam Smith Institute, n.d.).

Sustainability and environmental, social and governance investment are not imposed by governments. These are characteristics of an open and transparent free-market system where customers and investors are aligned to support those investments that generate the best products and services for citizens. Despite what many politicians say, monopoly privilege, regulatory capture, or information asymmetry are traits of heavily intervened markets with excessive regulation and government control.

Monopolies can only exist if governments elevate them and suppress competition through legislation, taxation, and regulation. In such an unhealthy environment of interconnected political motives, the outcome is rent-seeking and wealth transfers rather than wealth creation. Think of the Argentina tyre manufacturers who benefitted from government intervention and competition limitations to impose prices of $400 per tyre, compared to international prices of $100 to allegedly save jobs (iProfessional, 2024).

Competition and open markets are the most valuable tools to avoid corruption. Competition functions as a feedback mechanism that continuously reallocates resources towards their most valued uses (Smith, 1776).

Governments are notoriously poor at choosing losers but even worse at picking winners. The examples in energy are plentiful. Germany's mistake in closing its nuclear terminals and sending billions in subsidies to solar only to increase dependency on Russian gas and coal is a clear example. This is not capitalism; it is interventionism thinly disguised as free markets.

7 The Visible Hand of the State and Zombie Firms

Central planning never works. No central authority has sufficient local knowledge to allocate resources optimally. Instead, prices, profits, and losses function as information signals in a decentralised discovery process. Rising profit margins indicate that an entrepreneur has transformed undervalued inputs into valued outputs, while non-cyclical losses show the risk of asset misallocation and the need to change strategy (Smith, 1776). Hayek (1945) called it the "knowledge problem".

If your business model only works when your customer is trapped, misinformed, or subsidised, you are building on sand. You are hiding behind the visible hand of the state. Furthermore, as you grow, the system will tempt you to play the same game. It will be easier to hire a lobbyist than a better engineer. Easier to ask for a new regulation than to improve (Smith, 1776; Lacalle, 2020).

The European Union is a clear case of Smith's logic, working with the wrong institutional signals. On paper, the single market should provide a continental extent like the United States. It has become a legislative machine of tax rules, excessive regulations, and barriers to competition that limit the effective market they can serve. The result is that companies find enormous barriers to growth and capital prefers to invest in US entities that face lower burdens (DevDiscourse, 2026). European policymakers often mention the need for "strategic autonomy" and "industrial champions" to justify protectionist measures and subsidies. These policies hinder the innovation they claim to promote. When the European Union restricts cross-border data flows, imposes divergent tax regimes across member states, or channels subsidies towards established firms in traditional sectors, it creates an environment in which scale-intensive digital businesses struggle to compete globally (DevDiscourse, 2026). The result is a chronic underperformance in technology compared to the United States and China.

Policymakers decide to "pick winners" through industrial policy, directing capital towards sectors they call strategic. However, innovation is unpredictable; it emerges from decentralised experimentation, failure, and iteration. Centralised planning never works because it systematically misses disruptive innovations that redefine markets (Lacalle, 2017; DevDiscourse, 2026). The entrepreneurs best positioned to succeed are those who navigate around regulatory constraints.

We have said many times that central banks can print money but they cannot print jobs (Lacalle, 2020). They can, however, print the illusion of prosperity by keeping unproductive firms alive. These zombie companies use up credit, talent, and political attention that should go to new ventures. They are the opposite of Smith's invisible hand: they are an invisible tax on innovation.

The consensus narrative suggests that expansionary monetary policy and fiscal stimulus drive growth by boosting aggregate demand. This confuses cause and effect. Demand is a consequence of wealth creation, not its source. When governments and central banks artificially inflate demand through monetary expansion or deficit spending, they do not create new wealth; they redistribute existing wealth and distort price signals (Lacalle, 2017, 2020).

Artificial money creation is never neutral. It benefits the first recipients of money, the state and crony sectors, and disproportionately hurts independent small businesses, savers, and real wages, whose purchasing power erodes through inflation. This shows why, with unprecedented monetary expansion over the past 15 years, median real wages in many advanced economies have stagnated and productivity growth has stalled while asset prices have surged. Monetary inflation is the reason. Smith would recognise this pattern immediately: it is the modern equivalent of mercantilist privilege, operating through the monetary system rather than through trade monopolies (Smith, 1776).

In *The Wealth of Nations*, Smith is explicit that money is a means of circulation, not the substance of wealth (Smith, 1776, 2023). Wealth, for him, consists in the productive stock—machines, buildings, infrastructure, knowledge, and skills—that allows a society to generate future income. Growth occurs when a significant share of current output is saved and invested in this productive stock rather than consumed.

The post-crisis period has been characterised by unprecedented monetary expansion, negative real rates, and repeated interventions designed to protect firms and sectors from insolvency (Lacalle, 2020). While these policies have reduced short-term financial stress, they have also encouraged the survival of "zombie firms" and misallocated capital towards low-return projects. High concentrations of such firms depress investment, productivity, and innovation by tying up resources that could otherwise flow to more dynamic enterprises (Aghion et al., 2005).

The accumulation of zombie firms—entities whose earnings do not cover interest expenses over the business cycle—represents one of the most damaging consequences of ultra-loose monetary policy. In Japan, this phenomenon lasted for decades following the asset bubble collapse of the early 1990s, contributing to stagnation and lost productivity growth. Europe and, to a lesser extent, the United States replicated similar dynamics after 2008 (Lacalle, 2020).

Zombie firms impose multiple costs on the economy. They tie up capital, labour, and managerial attention in low-productivity uses, reducing the resources available for high-growth ventures. They suppress competition by undercutting prices, made possible by subsidised financing, making it harder for more efficient entrants to gain market share. They distort market signals, as their continued survival suggests profitability where none exists, leading to malinvestment by others observing the same sector. And they create political constituencies opposed to reform, as workers, creditors, and suppliers all have short-term interests in preventing insolvency even when long-term interests point towards reallocation (Lacalle, 2020).

These "zombie firms" often belong to sectors that are politically sensitive or considered strategic, and they benefit from a combination of low financing costs, repeated refinancing, and implicit or explicit guarantees (Lacalle, 2020). In this environment, competition is not eliminated, but it is manipulated: productive entrants must compete not only with the market but with political coalitions that have strong incentives to avoid acknowledging sunk costs.

From a Smithian perspective, this represents a double failure. First, it prevents the reallocation of capital from low-productivity uses, thereby depressing overall growth and innovation (Smith, 1776). Second, it corrodes the legitimacy of markets, as citizens observe that success appears to depend more on connections than on competence. For entrepreneurs genuinely engaged in value creation, this erosion of trust is not an abstract political problem; it directly affects their operations, their ability to attract talent, and the regulatory risks they face.

When central banks keep artificially low interest rates, they do not stimulate productive investment; they subsidise the least efficient actors. The firms that should exit the market, freeing resources for more innovative competitors, are instead kept alive through repeated refinancing at near-zero rates. This creates what has been described as a "survival of the most indebted" rather than survival of the fittest (Lacalle, 2017, 2020). The result is lower productivity growth, diminished innovation, and a transfer of wealth from savers and new entrants to legacy firms with political connections.

Financial repression—negative real interest rates combined with capital controls and regulatory pressure on banks to hold government debt—operates as a hidden tax on the productive economy. Savers are penalised and banks become almost government fiscal agents rather than efficient allocators of capital (Lacalle, 2017, 2020). For entrepreneurs, this environment means competing not just against better ideas, but against subsidised incumbents whose survival depends on monetary accommodation rather than market validation.

Free money is very expensive in the long term. Markets do not fail when they allow unprofitable firms to close and reallocate resources; they fail when political intervention prevents this reallocation. Inequality of outcomes is not problematic when it reflects differences in effort, innovation, and value creation; it becomes intolerable when it reflects differences in political access. The solution is not more subsidies and protection, but more competition and transparency—the institutional framework Smith proposed (Smith, 1776).

8 Conclusion: Adam Smith's Enduring Lessons for Entrepreneurial Economies

Two hundred and fifty years after the publication of *The Wealth of Nations*, Adam Smith's analysis continues to provide a remarkably powerful framework for understanding the conditions under which entrepreneurial activity contributes to economic prosperity (Smith, 1776; Viner, 1927). Although the modern vocabulary of innovation ecosystems, venture finance, and technological entrepreneurship would have been unfamiliar in Smith's time, the underlying mechanisms he identified remain strikingly relevant. His work offers a coherent account of how individual initiative, institutional design, and social norms interact to generate sustained economic development (Rothschild, 2001; North, 1990).

This chapter has revisited several key elements of Smith's thought and examined their implications for contemporary entrepreneurship. The first lesson arises from Smith's moral philosophy. In *The Theory of Moral Sentiments*, Smith emphasised that economic life is embedded in systems of trust, reputation, and reciprocal expectations (Smith, 1759; Griswold, 1999). Entrepreneurial ventures frequently operate in environments characterised by uncertainty, incomplete contracts, and evolving relationships. Under such conditions, credibility and moral conduct become essential forms of capital. Trust reduces transaction costs, facilitates cooperation, and allows entrepreneurs to mobilise resources and partnerships even in the absence of formal guarantees.

A second insight emerges from Smith's famous observation that human beings possess a natural "propensity to truck, barter, and exchange" (Smith, 1776). Entrepreneurship can be understood as an extension of this fundamental social capacity. Entrepreneurs identify opportunities for mutually beneficial exchange, align the interests of diverse participants, and develop new forms of cooperation that generate value. Markets are therefore not merely mechanisms for allocating existing goods; they are dynamic processes through which new combinations of resources and new forms of exchange are discovered.

Smith's analysis of the division of labour provides a third lesson for modern entrepreneurial systems. Productivity and innovation arise when individuals and organisations specialise, accumulate expertise, and coordinate complementary capabilities (Smith, 1776; Wilson & Farese, 2022). Contemporary entrepreneurial firms operate within networks of specialised suppliers, skilled workers, financiers, and knowledge institutions. The task of the entrepreneur increasingly involves orchestrating these specialised actors into productive systems that allow knowledge to accumulate and innovation to scale.

A fourth lesson concerns the institutional environment in which entrepreneurial activity takes place. Smith repeatedly emphasised that markets depend on a framework of justice, secure property rights, and public infrastructure that enables individuals to cooperate under predictable rules (Smith, 1776; Haakonssen, 1981). Modern research on entrepreneurial ecosystems echoes this insight: productive entrepreneurship flourishes where institutions reward innovation, protect competition, and provide stable expectations about the rules of economic interaction (North, 1990; Acs et al., 2009).

Fifth, Smith's concept of the "invisible hand" helps explain how decentralised economic activity can produce socially beneficial outcomes when embedded within an appropriate institutional framework (Smith, 1776; Viner, 1927). Individual actors pursuing their own objectives—entrepreneurs seeking opportunity, investors allocating capital, and consumers expressing preferences—collectively generate patterns of coordination that no central authority could deliberately design. Competition, experimentation, and feedback allow markets to function as discovery processes that reveal information about preferences, technologies, and opportunities, enabling entrepreneurial initiative to contribute to broader economic progress.

Sixth, Smith was equally clear that these dynamics are not automatic or guaranteed. Throughout *The Wealth of Nations*, he warned that economic systems can become distorted when institutional incentives encourage privilege, monopoly, or political favour rather than productive competition (Smith, 1776; Baumol, 1990). When resources are directed towards protecting incumbents or sustaining inefficient structures, entrepreneurial energy may be diverted away from innovation and towards rent-seeking. Smith's critique of mercantilist privileges therefore remains relevant for contemporary debates about regulatory capture, financial distortions, and barriers to market entry.

Taken together, these insights reveal a broader lesson: entrepreneurship is not simply the result of individual talent or ambition. It is the outcome of a complex system in which moral norms, institutional frameworks, and competitive processes interact to channel human initiative towards productive ends. When these elements are aligned, entrepreneurial activity becomes a powerful driver of innovation, growth, and rising living standards. When they are misaligned, the same energies may be diverted towards less productive, or even counter-productive, forms of economic behaviour (Baumol, 1990; North, 1990).

Revisiting Smith in the twenty-first century therefore provides more than historical perspective. It offers a conceptual foundation for understanding how entrepreneurial societies emerge and how they can be sustained. In an era characterised by rapid technological change, global competition, and evolving institutional arrangements, Smith's insights remind us that prosperity ultimately depends on the interaction between human creativity, ethical conduct, and institutional design (Smith, 1759; North, 1990).

As the world marks the 250th anniversary of *The Wealth of Nations*, Smith's work continues to illuminate the conditions under which individual initiative can generate collective prosperity (Smith, 1776). For entrepreneurs, policymakers, and scholars alike, the enduring relevance of Smith's analysis lies in its recognition that economic progress arises not from isolated innovation but from systems that allow enterprise, cooperation, and competition to flourish together. Two and a half centuries after Smith first described the dynamics of commercial society, the central challenge remains the same: to build institutional and moral frameworks that allow entrepreneurial creativity to generate prosperity not only for individuals, but for society as a whole.

Bibliography

Acemoglu, D., & Robinson, J. A. (2012). *Why nations fail: The origins of power, prosperity, and poverty*. Crown.

Acs, Z. J., Desai, S., & Hessels, J. (2009). Entrepreneurship, economic development and institutions. *Small Business Economics, 31*(3), 219–234.

Adam Smith Institute. (n.d.). *The Wealth of Nations*. Retrieved from https://www.adamsmith.org/the-wealth-of-nations

Aghion, P., Bloom, N., Blundell, R., Griffith, R., & Howitt, P. (2005). Competition and innovation: An inverted-U relationship. *The Quarterly Journal of Economics, 120*(2), 701–728.

Audretsch, D. B., & Lehmann, E. E. (2005). *Entrepreneurship and economic growth*. Oxford University Press.

Baumol, W. J. (1990). Entrepreneurship: Productive, unproductive, and destructive. *Journal of Political Economy, 98*(5), 893–921.

Boudreaux, C. J., Nikolaev, B. N., & Klein, P. (2019). Socio-cognitive traits and entrepreneurship: The moderating role of economic institutions. *Journal of Business Venturing, 34*(1), 178–196.

Brown, V. (1994). *Adam Smith's discourse: Canonicity, commerce and conscience*. Routledge.

Brown, M. E., & Treviño, L. K. (2006). Ethical leadership: A review and future directions. *The Leadership Quarterly, 17*(6), 595–616.

Buffett, W. (2017). Berkshire Hathaway shareholder letter (for fiscal year 2016).

Burton, R. M., & Obel, B. (2018). *The science of organizational design: Fit between structure and coordination*. Springer.

DevDiscourse. (2026, March 1). *Inside Europe's AI capital network: How finance is driving tech sovereignty*. Retrieved from https://www.devdiscourse.com/article/technology/3820041

Djankov, S., La Porta, R., Lopez-de-Silanes, F., & Shleifer, A. (2002). The regulation of entry. *The Quarterly Journal of Economics, 117*(1), 1–37.

Eckhardt, J. T., & Ciuchta, M. P. (2008). Selected variation: The population-level implications of multistage selection in entrepreneurship. *Strategic Entrepreneurship Journal, 2*(3), 209–224.

Fauchart, E., & Gruber, M. (2011). Darwinians, communitarians, and missionaries: The role of founder identity in entrepreneurship. *Academy of Management Journal, 54*(5), 935–957.

Fehr, E., & Falk, A. (2002). Psychological foundations of incentives. *European Economic Review, 46*(4–5), 687–724.

Fitzgibbons, A. (1995). *Adam Smith's system of liberty, wealth and virtue: The moral and political foundations of the Wealth of Nations*. Clarendon Press.

Foss, N. J., & Klein, P. G. (2012). *Organizing entrepreneurial judgment: A new approach to the firm*. Cambridge University Press.

Griswold, C. L. (1999). *Adam Smith and the virtues of enlightenment*. Cambridge University Press.

Haakonssen, K. (1981). *The science of a legislator: The natural jurisprudence of David Hume and Adam Smith*. Cambridge University Press.
Hanley, R.P. (2009) Adam Smith and the Character of Virtue. New York: Cambridge University Press.
Hayek, F. A. (1945). The use of knowledge in society. *American Economic Review, 35*(4), 519–530.
Hayton, J. C., George, G., & Zahra, S. A. (2002). National culture and entrepreneurship: A review of behavioural research. *Entrepreneurship Theory and Practice, 26*(4), 33–52.
Helfat, C. E., & Peteraf, M. A. (2003). The dynamic resource-based view: Capability lifecycles. *Strategic Management Journal, 24*(10), 997–1010.
Hirst, P. Q. (2012). Adam Smith and the "Projectors". *Political Studies, 30*(4), 545–558.
iProfesional (2024). 'Los neumáticos Michelin son más baratos en Chile que en Argentina', iProfesional, 28 April.
Isenberg, D. J. (2011). *The entrepreneurship ecosystem strategy as a new paradigm for economic policy: Principles for cultivating entrepreneurship*. Babson Entrepreneurship Ecosystem Project, Babson College (working paper).
Jobs, S. (2003) 60 Minutes interview with Lesley Stahl, CBS News, December 2003.
Lacalle, D. (2017). *Interview on technological and economic development*. Retrieved from https://www.youtube.com/watch?v=1uTMygk9DRI
Lacalle, D. (2020). Central banks cannot print jobs: Understanding real economic recovery. *The Breakdown Podcast*. Retrieved from https://podscripts.co/podcasts/the-breakdown
Nelson, R. R., & Winter, S. G. (1982). *An evolutionary theory of economic change*. Harvard University Press.
North, D. C. (1990). *Institutions, institutional change and economic performance*. Cambridge University Press.
Otteson, J. R. (2002). *Adam Smith's marketplace of life*. Cambridge University Press.
Porter, M. E. (1998). *Clusters and the new economics of competition*. Harvard Business School Press.
Rothschild, E. (2001). *Economic sentiments: Adam Smith, Condorcet, and the enlightenment*. Harvard University Press.
Sarasvathy, S. D. (2001). Causation and effectuation: Toward a theoretical shift from economic inevitability to entrepreneurial contingency. *Academy of Management Review, 26*(2), 243–263.
Sen, A. (2010). *The idea of justice*. Allen Lane.
Shane, S. (2003). *A general theory of entrepreneurship*. Edward Elgar.
Smith, A. (1759). *The theory of moral sentiments*. A. Millar.
Smith, A. (1776). *An inquiry into the nature and causes of the Wealth of Nations*. W. Strahan and T. Cadell.
Smith, M. (2023). Adam Smith on growth and economic development. *History of Economics Review, 86*(1), 2–15.
Stam, E. (2015). Entrepreneurial ecosystems and regional policy: A sympathetic critique. *European Planning Studies, 23*(9), 1759–1769.
Vargo, S. L., & Lusch, R. F. (2004). Evolving to a new dominant logic for marketing. *Journal of Marketing, 68*(1), 1–17.
Viner, J. (1927). Adam Smith and laissez-faire. *Journal of Political Economy, 35*(2), 198–232.
von Hippel, E. (2005). *Democratizing innovation*. MIT Press.
Weick, K. E. (1995). *Sensemaking in organizations*. Sage.
Wilson, B. J., & Farese, G. M. (2022). A universally translatable explication of Adam Smith's famous proposition on "the extent of the market". *Journal of the History of Economic Thought, 44*(3), 343–364.
Winch, D. (1978). Adam Smith's Politics: An Essay in Historiographic Revision. Cambridge: Cambridge University Press.
Winter, S. G. (2000). The satisficing principle in capability learning. *Strategic Management Journal, 21*(10–11), 981–996.
Zott, C., & Huy, Q. N. (2007). How entrepreneurs use symbolic management to acquire resources. *Administrative Science Quarterly, 52*(1), 70–105.

Adam Smith, Human Capital, and the Wealth of Nations

Constantine Yannelis

Adam Smith is celebrated today for publishing *The Wealth of Nations* in 1776, which many Britons like to cheekily claim was the most important thing to happen globally in that year. The contribution cemented Smith's reputation as the founder of classical economics, and today he is rightly well known for his theory of the division of labor, productivity, and the benefits of free markets and the rule of law. What is often neglected in even hagiographic discussions of Smith's contributions is the fact that he can also be considered the first economist to clearly articulate the idea of human capital. While the term human capital was not coined in 1776, and certainly no formal theory in the area exists, Adam Smith still managed to articulate many of the key principles that would be formalized centuries later by his successors.[1]

Economists today recognize that human capital is a key component of the wealth of nations, and many such as myself would argue that it is the single most important factor contributing to growth and general societal progress. Human capital is defined as the collective stock of knowledge, skills, experience, health, and other attributes that individuals possess, which make them productive and creates economic value for themselves, businesses, and nations. Human capital is an intangible asset, meaning that unlike oil or car factories, we can't directly see or touch the knowledge that

[1] It is worth noting two studies in the past which have studied the relationship between Adam Smith and human capital theory. Spengler (1977) and Schultz (2005) both discuss how Adam Smith's thinking shaped modern human capital theory. This essay provides a needed reminder after several decades, a quarter millennium following the publication of Smith's best known book.

C. Yannelis (✉)
University of Cambridge, Cambridge, UK
e-mail: cny21@cam.ac.uk

J. Ostle et al. (eds.), *Adam Smith's Wealth of Nations After 250 Years*, Contributions to Economics, https://doi.org/10.1007/978-3-032-32299-9_12

allows humans to build jetliners or computers. But in today's knowledge-driven economy, it is difficult to argue against the idea that the education and skills that workers possess are a key component of societal wealth. Today human capital theory is at the forefront of modern economics, and we can thank Adam Smith for first putting some of these important ideas to posterity.

Admittedly, the first recorded use of the precise term human capital was from Irving Fisher in 1897 (Goldin, 2019),[2] and the modern field was largely developed beginning with Becker (1962) and with his and others' early contributions synthesized in his seminal textbook *Human Capital: A Theoretical and Empirical Analysis*. While the specific term was not coined in 1776 and a formal theory did not yet exist, Smith managed to outline key principles that would not be formalized until the mid-twentieth century. Today, economists recognize human capital—the collective stock of knowledge, skills, experience, and health possessed by individuals—as the single most important factor contributing to societal progress. It is an intangible asset; unlike a car factory or an oil well, one cannot touch the knowledge required to build a jetliner. Yet, in a knowledge-driven economy, it is undeniable that worker education and skill are the primary components of national wealth.

But it was Adam Smith writing in 1776 who was the first economist to note the similarity between physical and human capital. This comparison reveals several key insights. First, education and training are described as requiring costs—time, effort, and tuition—just like physical capital does in terms of material or resources. Second, capital yields returns over its useful life after an initial upfront investment. Third, skills are not sui generis; they are created through investment. Smith noted an early version of the concept of depreciation. Like machines that wear out over time, skilled workers have a working life during which their training yields returns. This introduces the idea that human capital, like physical capital, can depreciate through obsolescence of skills or lack of use.

Adam Smith's contribution to human capital theory also extends to his nuanced understanding of incentives and individual decision-making. Throughout *The Wealth of Nations*, Smith repeatedly emphasizes that individuals respond to economic incentives when choosing whether to invest in education and training. He recognized that the decision to undertake costly and time-intensive education depends critically on the expected future returns. If wages do not sufficiently compensate for the initial investment, rational individuals will forgo acquiring specialized skills. This insight lies at the heart of modern human capital theory, where individuals are modeled as forward-looking agents who weigh costs and benefits

[2] The Cambridge educated economist J.S. Nicholson (1891) coined the term "living capital" slightly before Fisher, and he credited Smith in the first paragraph of his essay on the topic: "*Adam Smith boldly places under 'fixed capital' the acquired and useful abilities of all the inhabitants or members of the society on the grounds: first, that the acquisition of such talents' by the maintenance of the acquirer during his education, study, or apprenticeship always costs a real expense, which is a capital fixed and realised as it were in his person'; and, secondly, because the improved dexterity of a work-man may be considered in the same light as a machine or instrument of trade 'which facilitates and abridges labour, and which, though it costs a certain expense, repays that expense with a profit*".

over time. Smith's discussion anticipates later formalizations of investment behavior, including the role of expected earnings, uncertainty, and time horizons in shaping educational choices.

While Smith did not use the precise term, he clearly noted the similarities between physical and human capital noting that: "*When any expensive machine is erected, the extraordinary work to be performed by it before it is worn out, it must be expected, will replace the capital laid out upon it, with at least the ordinary profits. A man educated at the expense of much labour and time to any of those employments which require extraordinary dexterity and skill, may be compared to one of those expensive machines*." Smith foreshadowed the concept of human capital by treating education not as a moral or metaphysical attribute, but as a key input into productivity.

The passage begins with a familiar economic idea: when someone builds an expensive machine, the capitalist expects that the machine's output over time will not only replace the initial investment cost, but also generate a profit. Capital thus yields returns over its useful life, after an initial upfront investment. The key insight into human capital comes when Smith compares a man, who is educated at the expense of much labor and time, to one of these expensive machines. Education and training are described as requiring costs (time, effort, tuition) just like physical capital does in terms of material or resources. By emphasizing "*extraordinary dexterity and skill*," the passage frames human abilities as things that increase productivity in specialized employments, which is key to Smith's theory of the division of labor. These skills are not innate gifts alone; they are *produced* through investment in human capital. Implicit in the analogy is the idea that skilled workers must earn higher wages to recoup investments, just as machines must generate profits to recover physical capital investments. Otherwise, the investment in education would not be valuable. This anticipates later human capital theory that wages partly reflect returns on investments in education and training. Like machines that wear out over time, skilled workers have a working life during which their training yields returns. This subtly introduces the idea that human capital, like physical capital, can depreciate through obsolescence of skills, or lack of use.

While not using the term human capital directly, Smith comes tantalizingly close when he makes a direct comparison between the acquisition of talents and machines. He uses the phrase capital in discussing the acquisition of talents through education or apprenticeships: "*The acquisition of such talents, by the maintenance of the acquirer during his education, study, or apprenticeship, always costs a real expense, which is a capital fixed and realized, as it were, in his person*." Smith notes that the stock of talents—we might call them human capital—make up a part of societal wealth—which we might call the human capital stock: "*Those talents, as they make a part of his fortune, so do they likewise that of the society to which he belongs*." Smith goes on to directly compare the increase in workers' productivity to physical capital in the form of machines. "*The improved dexterity of a workman may be considered in the same light as a machine or instrument of trade which facilitates and abridges labour, and which, though it costs a certain expense, repays that expense with a profit*." In making this comparison Smith notes a key insight that will form the basis of later models of human capital investment, formulated by Becker (1962) and Ben-Porath (1967). Like investments in physical capital, investments in human capital can increase productivity and pay for themselves over the long term.

Indeed, writing nearly two centuries before Becker and Ben Porath, Smith even understood that investment in human capital, like investment in physical capital, is key to labor productivity: "*The work which he learns to perform, it must be expected, over and above the usual wages of common labour, will replace to him the whole expense of his education, with at least the ordinary profits of an equally valuable capital.*" In the same paragraph, he even hinted at the importance of discounting the future appropriately in determining the returns to human capital. Modern models of human capital investment account for the fact that individuals discount the future—in other words, a pound earned today is preferred to a pound far in the future. Smith anticipated the concept of a discount rate by centuries, again using his own terminology. "*It must do this too in a reasonable time, regard being had to the very uncertain duration of human life, in the same manner as to the more certain duration of the machine.*" In noting that time preferences depend on uncertainty, or risk, Smith captured key intuition of financial models that would arrive centuries later, like the Capital Asset Pricing Model in which the discount rate used is a function of risk.

Smith understood that the productivity increases from education, or human capital investment as economists like to say, results in higher wages. The increase in education and credentials stemming from the investment leads to greater trust for professionals: "*We trust our health to the physician, our fortune, and sometimes our life and reputation, to the lawyer and attorney. Such confidence could not safely be reposed in people of a very mean or low condition.*" Human capital is incident on wages, resulting in higher earnings once trainings are completed: "*Their reward must be such, therefore, as may give them that rank in the society which so important a trust requires.*" Smith also understood that the increase in wages must compensate for the "great expense" or investment that must be laid out to undertake investments in education. Many will not go through years of training to become doctors or lawyers if they cannot recoup the expenses. "*The long time and the great expense which must be laid out in their education, when combined with this circumstance, necessarily enhance still further the price of their labour.*" In other words, an investment in human capital must be recouped by future returns through labor earnings.

Adam Smith's early observations regarding human capital were not a mere digression, or a casual observance. These lie at the core of the central argument made in the wealth of nations, that specialization and division of labor in a free market leads to increased growth and prosperity. The division of labor at the heart of *The Wealth of Nations* refers to the practice of breaking production into smaller tasks, with each worker specializing in one specific job. This increases productivity by improving efficiency, skill, and speed while reducing wasted time and effort.

At the core of division of labor lie differences in the productive abilities of individuals. Indeed, Smith notes human capital differences as a key driver in talent differences among workers: "*The difference of natural talents in different men, is, in reality, much less than we are aware of; and the very different genius which appears to distinguish men of different professions, when grown up to maturity, is not upon many occasions so much the cause, as the effect of the division of labour*." Smith argues that these differences stem less from natural ability, but rather from habit, custom, or education. He takes the example as the difference between a philosopher and a porter: "*The difference between the most dissimilar characters, between a philosopher and a common street porter, for example, seems to arise not so much from nature, as from habit, custom, and education.*"

Smith argues that the differences between skilled (philosophers) and unskilled workers (the porter) are not innate,[3] but diverge over time. Differences arise after they begin apprenticeships and training. "*When they came in to the world, and for the first six or eight years of their existence, they were, perhaps, very much alike, and neither their parents nor playfellows could perceive any remarkable difference. About that age, or soon after, they come to be employed in very different occupations.*" Adam Smith even notes that human capital continues to develop over time, and that productivity grows with experience. "*The difference of talents comes then to be taken notice of, and widens by degrees, till at last the vanity of the philosopher is willing to acknowledge scarce any resemblance*." This was a remarkably progressive view for the time, when birth largely determined one's social class and when mobility was difficult. But Smith recognized that it was, at least to a very large extent, education and training that led to differences between social groups. Smith further noted that the differences between a porter and a philosopher were not solely due to education, but also habit and custom. While school is a large determinant of human capital accumulation, families, peers, and communities also play a large role in developing human capital.

These differences in talents—driven by education and custom—are key to the gains in productivity stemming from division of labor. Division of labor increases productivity by allowing workers to specialize in specific tasks where they have greater talent, which improves efficiency and output. In Adam Smith's classic pin factory example, the process of making pins was divided into several distinct steps, such as drawing out the wire, cutting the wire, sharpening the point, and attaching the head to the pin. In essence, this was the precursor of the assembly line a century and a quarter before Henry Ford. The idea is the same as that of a car factory. Instead of one worker performing all the necessary tasks alone and producing only a few pins per day, each worker focused on just one step of the process. This specialization made workers faster and more skilled at their individual tasks, reduced the time lost switching between different activities, and encouraged the use of simple tools designed for each step. As a result, a small group of workers could produce thousands of pins in a single day, demonstrating how division of labor greatly increases productivity. And this productivity increase is even greater when workers

[3]Indeed, I only call porters unskilled relative to philosophers in Smith's analogy, which is likely based off of his experience at Oxford. The porters that I have interacted with in Cambridge are tremendously skilled individuals, and they clearly have accumulated a great deal of human capital.

are attached to tasks where they have the greatest talent, or task-specific human capital.

Smith not only understood that human capital affects productivity, but also that changes in the supply of workers affect wages. During the period, in which *The Wealth of Nations* was written, guilds were adept at restricting the supply of high-skilled workers: "*The bye-laws of the corporation regulate sometimes the number of apprentices which any master is allowed to have, and almost always the number of years which each apprentice is obliged to serve. The intention of both regulations is to restrain the competition to a much smaller number than might otherwise be disposed to enter into the trade. The limitation of the number of apprentices restrains it directly. A long term of apprenticeship restrains it more indirectly, but as effectually, by increasing the expense of education.*" Smith, like the associations of workers in his day, understood that restricting the numbers of those entering professions reduced the supply of labor, and creates artificial scarcity. Today we see similar scarcity in many professions like medicine, where the American Medical Association and similar organizations in other countries restrict the number of new doctors who can be trained, keeping wages high.

High wages for professionals can attract more investment in education, and similarly a glut of workers can lead to an exodus of trainees in skilled fields. Smith described how an oversupply of skilled workers can reduce wages, and in some cases even render investments in human capital unprofitable: "*In professions in which there are no benefices, such as law and physic, if an equal proportion of people were educated at the public expense, the competition would soon be so great as to sink very much their pecuniary reward. It might then not be worth any man's while to educate his son to either of those professions at his own expense.*" Smith continues that "*They would be entirely abandoned to such as had been educated by those public charities, whose numbers and necessities would oblige them in general to content themselves with a very miserable recompence, to the entire degradation of the now respectable professions of law and physic.*" His argument parallels modern academic literature such as Katz and Murphy (1992), who argue that much of the variation in wages can be explained by changes in the supply and demand of skilled workers.

Smith's discussion of the supply of skilled workers is still relevant to many modern discussions of policy. New Labour under Blair famously set the goal of half of Britons completing university. This target was reached in 2019, but at the same time the college wage premium, or the amount that graduates earn in excess of their peers who did not attend university, has fallen in Britain over the past 20 years. Adam Smith would not have been surprised by this fact. In the United States a vigorous debate rages regarding admitting more skilled immigrants under the H1B Visa program. In a seminal study, Doran et al. (2022) use visa lotteries to show that firms that are awarded skilled worker visas see lower wages for native workers. The invisible hand determines not only the price of goods, but also allocates the price of labor for skilled and unskilled workers in accordance with the laws of supply and demand.

Indeed, Smith was also aware that not all investments led to great increases in wages. Even in 1776, academic scholars struggled. Smith refers to academics as an "unprosperous race of men." Like today, in 1776 the number of scholars seeking employment greatly exceeded the number of positions available. Although unlike today, most of these positions were in holy orders rather than universities. "*That unprosperous race of men, commonly called men of letters, are pretty much in the situation which lawyers and physicians probably would be in, upon the foregoing supposition. In every part of Europe, the greater part of them have been educated for the church, but have been hindered by different reasons from entering into holy orders.*"

It is important to put Smith's views on scholars in personal context, as his views were likely shaped by personal experience. After studying at the University of Glasgow at the age of 14, the prodigy left his native Scotland and at the age of 17 undertook postgraduate studies at Balliol College in Oxford. Smith generally had a low opinion of his studies in Oxford, writing in the *Wealth of Nations* that "*In the university of Oxford, the greater part of the public professors have, for these many years, given up altogether even the pretence of teaching.*" Surely, had Smith read at Pembroke College in Cambridge rather than Balliol, his unflattering views on academics would likely have differed greatly.[4]

Again, Smith points to supply and demand as the cause of misfortune for the unprosperous race of scholars. This imbalance of learned scholars and positions echoes the modern day, when PhD programs produce far more graduates each year for the number of available academic positions. "*They have generally, therefore, been educated at the public expense; and their numbers are everywhere so great, as commonly to reduce the price of their labour to a very paltry recompence.*" University administrations would do well to reread the *Wealth of Nations* to better understand the dynamics of academic employment, and why so many graduates with advanced degrees cannot find employment commensurate to their skills.

Smith goes beyond calling academics simply unprosperous men, and compares them to mendicants, calling scholars and beggars "nearly synonymous." But in doing so Smith makes an important point about complementarities between human capital and technology, meaning that technology can be a boost to skills in creating productivity: "*Before the invention of the art of printing, a scholar and a beggar seem to have been terms very nearly synonymous. The different governors of the universities, before that time, appear to have often granted licences to their scholars to beg.*" Rather than viewing machinery solely as a substitute for labor, he recognized that technology often acts as a supplement to existing skills to boost productivity. Using the example of the printing press, Smith pointed out that this invention provided a new source of revenue for scholars by allowing the cheap reproduction of books, but crucially, this innovation only held value because of the scholars' pre-existing education and literary abilities. This observation closely mirrors the modern economic concept of skill-biased technical change, illustrating his belief that improvements in methods and machinery inherently complement educated labor to

[4] Of course, this comment is in jest. Despite Adam Smith's misgivings, Oxford has had a sterling reputation for centuries, and it is well known that for centuries Oxford has been the second-best university in the British Isles, and indeed globally.

raise overall economic output. Smith points out that printing allowed scholars to generate returns on their writing, but that printing created a source of revenue, allowing scholars and universities to sell books. But this new innovation only had value because of scholars' education and literary abilities. Thus technology can serve to supplement existing skills.

Printing is of little use to an illiterate, but a scholar can create books or pamphlets and sell and suddenly cheaply reproduce and sell these. We see similar effects with inventions today: artificial intelligence and large language models can assist skilled programmers by automating relatively simple tasks. But utilizing these tools, which can hallucinate and generate errors, requires a deep understanding of underlying processes and goals. In other words new technologies complement existing human capital, a point made nearly 250 years later by Acemoglu and Autor (2011). Economist Daron Autor and others have summarized this pattern: over the past 60 years the U.S. saw a large increase in educated workers *and* rising returns to education. In Smith's day, technical change was slower, but he understood that "improvements in machinery and methods" complement skilled labor in raising output. In short, Smith's framework foreshadows the modern skill-biased technical change view.

While the *Wealth of Nations* and the legacy of Adam Smith are often celebrated in defense of free markets and liberal economic thought, his work showed careful consideration for the limits of markets. Today only the most extreme libertarians would not be in support of some public support for education, given the large externalities associated with an educated population and workforce. Smith discussed public investment in education, which was common during his life if not universal. Smith notes that: "*It has been considered as of so much importance that a proper number of young people should be educated for certain professions, that sometimes the public, and sometimes the piety of private founders, have established many pensions, scholarships, exhibitions, bursaries, etc. for this purpose, which draw many more people into those trades than could otherwise pretend to follow them.*" Smith acknowledged the limits of universal public education at the time, but noted that early childhood interventions could have significant effects on occupational productivity later in life. "*But though the common people cannot, in any civilized society, be so well instructed as people of some rank and fortune; the most essential parts of education, however, to read, write, and account, can be acquired at so early a period of life, that the greater part, even of those who are to be bred to the lowest occupations, have time to acquire them before they can be employed in those occupations.*"

While Smith is correctly known today as a champion of the market, he was not a caricature and understood that in some areas, such as education, public intervention was not only beneficial but essential. Smith proposed a system of parish or district schools where children could be taught for a moderate reward. Indeed, Smith suggested that universal primary education could be imposed on the population: "*For a very small expense, the public can facilitate, can encourage and can even impose upon almost the whole body of the people, the necessity of acquiring those most essential parts of education*" This came nearly a century before the Education Act of 1870 established a framework for the education of all elementary school age children in England and Wales. Smith proposed a system that would look similar to that created by the Education Act, in which local authorities create schools: "*The public can facilitate this acquisition, by establishing in every parish or district a little school, where children may be taught for a reward so moderate, that even a common labourer may afford it; the master being partly, but not wholly, paid by the public.*" Smith grappled deeply with questions of who finances higher education, which can be paid for directly by the public or the individual. Smith also worried about moral hazard, arguing that if the public pays fully for education this could lead to sloth: "*if he [the student] was wholly, or even principally, paid by it [the public], he would soon learn to neglect his business.*" One is reminded of the stereotype of the elderly graduate student, two centuries before Bart Simpson famously said "*Look at me, I'm a graduate student! I'm 30 years old and made $600 last year.*" Studies have confirmed the hypothesis of both Smith and Simpson, for example Garibaldi et al. (2012) found that when an Italian private university introduced tuition fees, students graduated in a shorter amount of time.

Smith's interest in public education may come from experiences in his native Scotland, which educated a great number of common people to read and write. Smith writes that: "*In Scotland, the establishment of such parish schools has taught almost the whole common people to read, and a very great proportion of them to write and account.*" Smith himself benefitted from the ubiquity of Scottish education, he attended the Kirkcaldy Burgh school before attending university. Smith notes that England had a similar system of charity schools but which was not as universal in its provision of education as the Scottish system: "*In England, the establishment of charity schools has had an effect of the same kind, though not so universally, because the establishment is not so universal.*"

Smith also lamented the fact that schools focused on more arcane academic subjects such as Latin, and suggested a more vocational education focusing on maths and mechanics: "*If, in those little schools, the books by which the children are taught to read, were a little more instructive than they commonly are; and if, instead of a little smattering in Latin, which the children of the common people are sometimes taught there, and which can scarce ever be of any use to them, they were instructed in the elementary parts of geometry and mechanics.*" As a frequent attendee of high table, having been forced to take several years of the Cambridge Latin Course during elementary school turned out to have some use for me personally, but I can sympathize with Smith in that most people may not readily benefit from memorizing declensions relating to fellows named Caecilius living in Pompeii. Debates about the extent to which scholars should pursue academic versus vocational tracks remain as relevant today as they were in 1776, with many American universities today cutting humanities programs in favor of engineering and sciences and dwindling enrollment in British humanities programs.

Smith highlighted that recognition was a key component of a successful education system: "*The public can encourage the acquisition of those most essential parts of education, by giving small premiums, and little badges of distinction, to the children of the common people who excel in them.*" Today educational and academic prizes abound, ranging from children winning small tokens of recognition for reading to grand prizes such as the Nobel and the Fields Medal. Smith also understood the virtues of licensing, common in many professions today ranging from accounting to teaching. "*The public can impose upon almost the whole body of the people the necessity of acquiring the most essential parts of education, by obliging every man to undergo an examination or probation in them, before he can obtain the freedom in any corporation, or be allowed to set up any trade, either in a village or town corporate*." Smith related licensing to the supply and demand for labor, which he correctly noted was key in determining wages, and concerns about guilds artificially driving up the price of labor. But he did not directly articulate a key benefit of licensing, namely that this could solve an information asymmetry when the public is unaware of which practitioners are informed, and which are charlatans adopting a masquerade of expertise.

While it would take more than a century for Cambridge economist and St. John's fellow Alfred Marshall to coin the terms "external economies" and "diseconomies," Smith understood conceptually that economic decisions could affect society as a whole. Externalities are economic costs that are not borne by the agent making a decision. Marshall's successor Arthur Pigou developed a rigorous theory and study of externalities in economics. Externalities can be negative, such as a factory creating air pollution, or positive such as an individual obtaining a vaccination leading to health benefits for others.

Today, while we may quibble about their size or beneficiaries, it is widely recognized that education has significant externalities. A more educated population creates more innovation, is healthier and has a better functioning society. I directly benefit from having educated neighbors and peers. Despite there being no term for externality in 1776, Adam Smith instinctively recognized that externalities were important in human capital provision. In *the Wealth of Nations* he writes that: "*The expense of the institutions for education and religious instruction, is likewise, no doubt, beneficial to the whole society, and may, therefore, without injustice, be defrayed by the general contribution of the whole society*." The fact that higher education generates significant externalities is a primary reason why societies have significant government intervention in education markets, as economic theory shows that the proper response to positive (negative) externalities is a subsidy (tax).

Some use the significant externalities associated with education to argue for making higher education free or publicly provided. However, this has significant distributional issues given that highly educated individuals tend to earn more than others, as noted in my own work including Catherine and Yannelis (2023) and Catherine et al. (2026). Smith realized that, while the whole of society benefits from an educated population, individuals themselves could pay for the private benefits that they accrue from their studies: "*This expense, however, might, perhaps, with equal propriety, and even with some advantage, be defrayed altogether by those who receive the immediate benefit of such education and instruction, or by the voluntary contribution of those who think they have occasion for either the one or the other*." Today we still have vigorous debates about whether higher education should be financed by society through higher taxes, or by individuals through paying tuition. Smith does not provide an answer to this debate, and policymakers and economists still argue about the right level and approach regarding government intervention in education markets.

This ongoing debate is most relevant in the debate regarding whether to organize education through an Anglo-American system, where students pay tuition to universities, or through the continental model in which taxpayers pay directly for higher education. The advantage of the former approach is that those who "*receive the immediate benefit of such education and instruction*" directly pay for their education. Carpenters and plumbers rightly wonder why they should pay for the education of higher-earning doctors and lawyers.

Along with the invisible hand, Smith is perhaps best known for his parable of the pin-maker. At the heart of this story lies education, or as economists would say human capital investment: "*To take an example, therefore, from a very trifling manufacture, but one in which the division of labour has been very often taken notice of, the trade of a pin-maker: a workman not educated to this business (which the division of labour has rendered a distinct trade, nor acquainted with the use of the machinery employed in it (to the invention of which the same division of labour has probably given occasion), could scarce, perhaps, with his utmost industry, make one pin in a day, and certainly could not make twenty*".

In this passage, Adam Smith uses the humble pin-maker to illustrate a foundational insight about productivity: education and task-specific training are indispensable complements to the division of labor. Smith emphasizes that without being educated into a particular trade, and without familiarity with the machinery that specialization itself brings forth, even the most diligent worker would produce almost nothing. Industry alone is insufficient. What matters is *directed* effort—effort informed by training, experience, and the accumulated knowledge embedded in tools and techniques. The division of labor does not merely slice production into smaller tasks; it transforms those tasks into distinct skills that must be learned. Productivity gains arise not from working harder, but from working with the right human capital in the right institutional and technological context.

The quote also reveals Smith's deeper point that technology and human capital evolve together. The machinery used by the pin-maker is itself a product of specialization, suggesting a feedback loop in which division of labor generates tools, and those tools in turn raise the returns to specialized training. An uneducated worker cannot benefit from machinery, just as machinery is useless without skilled hands to operate it. Smith thus anticipates a modern idea: productivity depends on complementarities between skills and technology. Education enables workers to take advantage of new tools, while technological progress increases the payoff to acquiring those skills. The pin factory is not merely a story about efficiency; it is an early model of how learning, specialization, and innovation jointly determine economic output.

Perhaps the biggest critique inherent in Adam Smith's theory of the division of labor comes from human capital depreciation: the idea that skills may atrophy and decay if they are not used. Human capital depreciation has been a core component of many models of human capital such as that of Ben-Porath, and the magnitude of these decays is a parameter that I estimated in my own research (Dinerstein et al., 2022). Smith wrote that individuals specializing in specific tasks will not develop other skills. In other words, a man whose whole life is spent performing a few simple operations has no occasion to exert his understanding: "*But the understandings of the greater part of men are necessarily formed by their ordinary employments. The man whose whole life is spent in performing a few simple operations, of which the effects, too, are perhaps always the same, or very nearly the same, has no occasion to exert his understanding, or to exercise his invention, in finding out expedients for removing difficulties which never occur.*" Smith continues that the specialized worker "*naturally loses, therefore, the habit of such exertion, and generally becomes as stupid and ignorant as it is possible for a human creature to become.*" The pin factory in which each worker specializes in a different small task might be the most efficient model for producing pins, but small repetitive tasks will not create new skills or opportunities for workers on the line. Indeed, if workers become "*stupid and ignorant,*" and skills depreciate, then the effects of the specialization of labor may undo many of the positive externalities of education. This lesson is particularly relevant in today's rapidly changing economy with the advent of machine intelligence, workers need to be able to adapt and learn new tools to avoid skill obsolescence.

Human capital depreciation, and the necessity of learning, of being able to acquire versatile skills is especially important in today's rapidly changing economy, as it was in Britain on the cusp of the industrial revolution. At any point in time where progress is rapid, there is tremendous uncertainty regarding which skills will be relevant in the future. In hindsight today it seems obvious that the internet would massively transform the economy, but even brilliant economists missed the mark when this new technology was emerging. Paul Krugman famously exhorted that the internet would have no more impact on the economy than the fax machine. For every economist or prognosticator who missed a major trend, we can point to numerous speculative bubbles and fads that passed. It was only a few years from the quarter-millennial anniversary of the *Wealth of Nations* that Non-Fungible Tokens, or NFTs commanded high valuations, with wealthy speculators paying millions for online pictures of "Bored Apes."

The uncertainty surrounding the future utility of skills highlights the importance of accumulating versatile and broad human capital and continuous learning. Five years ago, I would tell young undergraduates that they should learn to code. My view was that anyone with basic coding skills would be employable, and at the time Silicon Valley tech firms were desperate to hire competent programmers. This advice turned out to be roughly as accurate as Krugman's forecast of the impact of the internet. Today tech firms only seem interested in junior programmers named Claude, as Artificial Intelligence continues to improve in basic coding.[5]

[5]Artificial Intelligence replacing junior workers leads to new concerns about human capital accumulation. While it is difficult for junior and semi-skilled programmers to find positions, the returns have never been higher for very skilled coders. But many top-level computer scientists were once rookie programmers, and today we face very real concerns that the human capital accumulation

In the coming years Artificial Intelligence may transform the labor market. Or it may not. Workers will need to be able to adapt to a constantly changing labor market and learn new tools. We should not overly fear new technologies. The words "*The increase of technical efficiency has been taking place faster than we can deal with the problem of labour absorption… this means unemployment due … outrunning the pace at which we can find new uses for labour*" would not seem out of place in the opinion pages of one of our major newspapers today, bemoaning the labor market effects of new computing technologies. But they were written almost a century ago in 1930, by John Maynard Keynes regarding the effects of new technologies on the workforce. Since the plow and the steam engine, economic thinkers have raised concerns about technology displacing labor.

We should not fear new technologies, and like electricity and the steam engine, many jobs in the future will be replaced by new invention. In their place many new professions will be created which we cannot yet even fathom. Even at King's College Cambridge, where Keynes worked along the brightest minds of his generation such as Alan Turing, no one could imagine professions that would exist a century later such as graphic designers, cloud architects, AI champions or driverless car software engineers. Even the early founders of computer science could not dream up the professions that their innovations would one day create, just as James Watt, a Scotsman like Adam Smith and his friend, likely could not imagine that his Watt steam engine would usher in the Industrial Revolution. Coincidentally, Watt commercialized his engine in 1776, a momentous year in intellectual history, not only with Smith's seminal work and the American Declaration of Independence, but also marking the publishing of Gibbon's *Decline and Fall of the Roman Empire*.

Crucially it was the technologies that displaced labor which created new professions. Making predictions is hard, especially about the future, but let me offer that the past is likely our best guide to the future. Smith pointed out in 1776 that technology and labor can be complementary, and increase productivity, writing that: "*a workman not educated to this business (which the division of labour has rendered a distinct trade), nor acquainted with the use of the machinery employed in it (to the invention of which the same division of labour has probably given occasion), could scarce, perhaps, with his utmost industry, make one pin in a day, and certainly could not make twenty.*" Crucially, Smith realized the key to unlocking the relationship between labor and technology is education, or human capital investment. Society needs to be well equipped to train the next generation of leaders if we are to take advantage of new innovations.

Adam Smith is rightly recognized as the progenitor of many ideas in economics, but he is due more credit than is sometimes offered. In particular, Smith is not only the founder of free market economics, the division of labor and the doctrine of the invisible hand, but we can view his ideas as the early antecessor of human capital theory. Adam Smith arguably was the first to come up with the analogy between

---

pipeline may become broken. Given current models, it seems unlikely that Large Language Models could fully replace humans in terms of innovation, given their reliance on human-generated training data.

human and physical capital. Smith also had other important insights, namely that human capital depreciates and that education raises productivity and wages. He also tackled deeply with the question of whether the public or the private purse should finance higher education, and offered glimmers of the concept of externalities in education: the idea that a generally educated populace benefits all of society.

Despite being a staunch advocate of markets, Smith had the intellectual maturity to recognize that these had limits. Smith did not believe markets alone would deliver optimal education outcomes. He saw a role for government in correcting market failures related to education, incentives, and access. At the same time, he recognized that there were great private benefits to education, and that in many cases it made sense for individuals to shoulder costs where they reaped benefits. Perhaps most importantly, Smith may have been the first to articulate that supply and demand ultimately determine both wages and the investments in skills that create productivity to support those wages. In summary, Adam Smith's observations about knowledge and productivity laid an early foundation for what became human capital theory. By linking his analysis to the formal work of later economists, we see a consistent narrative: investing in skills benefits both individuals and society.

Taken together, these insights in *The Wealth of Nations* make a strong case that Adam Smith deserves recognition not only as the father of classical economics, but also as the intellectual progenitor of human capital theory. Long before the language of investment, depreciation, discounting, and externalities entered the economist's toolkit, Smith articulated their underlying logic with remarkable clarity. He treated education and training as costly, purposeful investments that raise productivity, shape wages, interact with technology, and generate benefits that extend beyond the individual to society at large. He understood that skills are accumulated over time, can decay if neglected, and are shaped by incentives and institutions. In short, Smith saw that the wealth of nations depends not merely on machines or markets, but on the cultivation of human abilities themselves. Modern human capital theory did not so much overturn Smith as give formal structure and mathematical precision to ideas he had already placed at the center of political economy.

References

Acemoglu, D., & Autor, D. (2011). Skills, tasks and technologies: Implications for employment and earnings. In *Handbook of labor economics* (Vol. 4, pp. 1043–1171). Elsevier.

Becker, G. S. (1962). Investment in human capital: A theoretical analysis. *Journal of Political Economy, 70*(5, Part 2), 9–49.

Becker, G. S. (1975). *Human capital: A theoretical and empirical analysis*. National Bureau of Economic Research.

Ben-Porath, Y. (1967). The production of human capital and the life cycle of earnings. *Journal of Political Economy, 75*(4, Part 1), 352–365.

Catherine, S., & Yannelis, C. (2023). The distributional effects of student loan forgiveness. *Journal of Financial Economics, 147*(2), 297–316.

Catherine, S., Ebrahimian, M., & Yannelis, C. (2026). How do income-driven repayment plans benefit student debt borrowers? *Journal of Financial Economics, 178*, 104253.

Dinerstein, M., Megalokonomou, R., & Yannelis, C. (2022). Human capital depreciation and returns to experience. *American Economic Review, 112*(11), 3725–3762.

Doran, K., Gelber, A., & Isen, A. (2022). The effects of high-skilled immigration policy on firms: Evidence from visa lotteries. *Journal of Political Economy, 130*(10), 2501–2533.

Garibaldi, P., Giavazzi, F., Ichino, A., & Rettore, E. (2012). College cost and time to complete a degree: Evidence from tuition discontinuities. *Review of Economics and Statistics, 94*(3), 699–711.

Goldin, C. (2019). Human capital. In *Handbook of cliometrics* (pp. 147–177). Springer.

Katz, L. F., & Murphy, K. M. (1992). Changes in relative wages, 1963–1987: Supply and demand factors. *The Quarterly Journal of Economics, 107*(1), 35–78.

Nicholson, J. S. (1891). The living capital of the United Kingdom. *The Economic Journal, 1*(1), 95–107.

Schultz, T. W. (2005). Adam Smith and human capital. In *Adam Smith's legacy* (pp. 147–158). Routledge.

Spengler, J. J. (1977). Adam Smith on human capital. *The American Economic Review, 67*(1), 32–36.

Sun, S. T., & Yannelis, C. (2016). Credit constraints and demand for higher education: Evidence from financial deregulation. *Review of Economics and Statistics, 98*(1), 12–24.

Yannelis, C., & Tracey, G. (2022). Student loans and borrower outcomes. *Annual Review of Financial Economics, 14*(1), 167–186.

Micropolitics: Applying Adam Smith's Ideas to Changing Policy

James Lawson

1 Introduction

Adam Smith was the first to systematise the study of political economy. He explained why markets generate prosperity and why monopolies undermine it. He showed why the statesman who tries to direct the decisions of private individuals will know less than the individuals themselves. These insights, set down 250 years ago in The Wealth of Nations, remain as relevant to the challenges of today as they were to the mercantilist system Smith dismantled in 1776. The societies that embraced his ideas became rich. Those that ignored them remained poor, or became so.

Yet there is a puzzle at the heart of Smith's legacy. If the intellectual case for markets was won over two centuries ago, why has it proved so difficult to translate that victory into lasting reform? Governments have been elected on explicit mandates to cut the state, deregulate, boost trade, and enable competition. They entered office with conviction and left having changed remarkably little. The ideas were sound. The mandate was clear. The levers of power, once grasped, appeared to be connected to nothing.

The answer lies in a distinction Smith himself would have recognised, though he did not frame it in these terms. There is a difference between the science of how an economy works and the engineering of how to reform one. Smith gave us economic science. He showed us that individuals acting in their own interest generate outcomes no planner could design, that producers will always seek to rig the market in their favour, and that intervention reliably produces consequences opposite to those intended. What he did not provide, because it was not his task, was a manual for dismantling the structures that stand between his principles and their application.

J. Lawson (✉)
Adam Smith Institute, London, UK
e-mail: james@adamsmith.org

J. Ostle et al. (eds.), *Adam Smith's Wealth of Nations After 250 Years*, Contributions to Economics, https://doi.org/10.1007/978-3-032-32299-9_13

Smith's core insights can be distilled into a handful of propositions that remain the essential foundation for any serious policy maker:

1. *Self-interest as the universal motivator.* Self-interest is a universal motivator, as operative in the corridors of Whitehall as in the marketplace. Policy must be designed for humans as they are, not as we might wish them to be.
2. *The conspiracy against the public.* Producers will conspire against the public interest, seeking privileges, protections, and monopolies at the consumer's expense. "People of the same trade seldom meet together, even for merriment and diversion, but the conversation ends in a conspiracy against the public".
3. *The limits of central knowledge.* The individual can judge far better than any statesman how to deploy his own resources. Central direction will always be defeated by the dispersal of knowledge across millions of actors.
4. *The man of system.* The planner imagines he can arrange the members of a great society as easily as the hand arranges pieces on a chessboard. He forgets that every piece has a principle of motion of its own.
5. *Unintended consequences.* Intervention produces unintended consequences, not by accident but by the structural logic of the systems it creates.
6. *Competition and the possibility of exit.* Competition and the possibility of exit are the only reliable disciplines against inefficiency and capture. Without the threat that the consumer can go elsewhere, any organisation, public or private, will stagnate.
7. *The division of labour and specialisation.* The greatest improvements in productivity arise from specialisation. The state that attempts to do everything itself will do everything badly. The case for contracting out, and for allowing the private sector to do what it does best, begins here.
8. *Taxation, spending, and the limits of the state.* Taxes should be equitable, certain, convenient, and efficient. The state is structurally profligate because it spends other people's money, raiding capital budgets to satisfy immediate demands. Smith identified clear duties for the sovereign in defence, justice, and essential public works, but was equally clear that beyond these duties, it exceeds its competence.

The manual for applying these insights had to be written by others. Two centuries after the Wealth of Nations, the public choice theory of James Buchanan and Gordon Tullock emerged. They applied the Smithian insight about self-interest to the behaviour of politicians, bureaucrats, and interest groups within the state itself. Public choice theory is diagnostic. Once you accept that public servants are motivated by the same forces as private ones, the failures of government reform become not mysterious but predictable. The interest groups that benefit from the status quo will fight to preserve it. The bureaucracy that administers the system has every incentive to expand it. The dispersed public that pays for it all has neither the information nor the motivation to resist. Smith diagnosed the tendency of producers to conspire against the public. Public choice theory showed that this tendency operates with even greater force inside the state than outside it.

If public choice is the diagnosis, the creative counterpart is a discipline known as micropolitics. Where conventional policy advice tells governments what they ought to do, micropolitics concerns itself with how to get it done. It begins with the Smithian recognition that people respond to incentives, not exhortation. It proceeds by analysing the specific interest groups that will oppose a reform, mapping the benefits they currently enjoy, and constructing policies that offer them something they value more in exchange. It does not confront; it trades. It does not impose grand plans; it engineers incremental changes that accumulate, irreversibly, in the direction of greater freedom and competition.

Out of the crises of the 1970s in the United Kingdom, the Adam Smith Institute was founded explicitly to apply Smith's ideas to the challenges of that era. It was established by Madsen Pirie and brothers Eamonn and Stuart Butler, who had studied together at the University of St Andrews in Scotland, Smith's own country. Where the think tanks and academics of the post-war period had fought the battle of ideas, the ASI set out to do the policy engineering. Over four decades, it developed and applied the toolkit of micropolitics: the practical methods by which Smithian principles could be made to work in a world of entrenched interests, bureaucratic resistance, and political markets that operate by rules quite different from economic ones.

This chapter examines that toolkit and its intellectual foundations. It begins by setting out the specific insights from the Wealth of Nations that bear most directly on public policy today. It then presents the theory of micropolitics, showing how these Smithian concepts, filtered through public choice analysis, generate a practical method for policy design. It illustrates that method through case studies drawn from four decades of the Institute's work, from the privatisations and contracting out of the 1980s to the education reforms and housing innovations of the 2010s and 2020s. Finally, it considers where Smith's insights must be applied next.

2 Self-Interest as the Universal Motivator

Perhaps the most famous passage in Smith's work is also the most consequential:

> It is not from the benevolence of the butcher, the brewer, or the baker that we expect our dinner, but from their regard to their own interest. We address ourselves, not to their humanity, but to their self-love, and never talk to them of our own necessities but of their advantages.[1]
>
> This is sometimes read as a celebration of greed. It is nothing of the sort. It is an observation about the mechanism by which cooperation occurs among strangers. The butcher does not sell us meat because he only cares about our hunger. He sells it because he wishes to earn a living, with which he can buy other goods, pay his rent, feed his own family, and provide for his future. We do not appeal to his compassion. We appeal to his advantage. The transaction benefits both parties, and no altruism is required to make it work.

[1] Smith (1776, Book I, Chapter II, p. 26).

Smith was making a deeper point still. The sentence immediately preceding the famous passage is often overlooked:

> Whoever offers to another a bargain of any kind, proposes to do this. Give me that which I want, and you shall have this which you want, is the meaning of every such offer; and it is in this manner that we obtain from one another the far greater part of those good offices which we stand in need of.[2]

Self-interest, properly understood, is not selfishness. It is the engine of exchange. It requires each party to consider what the other wants and to offer something of value in return. It is a social mechanism, not an antisocial one. The market works precisely because it forces the self-interested individual to attend to the interests of others.

The implications for public policy are profound. If self-interest drives behaviour in the marketplace, it drives behaviour everywhere else too. The politician seeking re-election, the civil servant protecting his department, the union leader expanding his membership, the regulator justifying his existence: all are acting on the same principle as the butcher. They are pursuing their own advantage within the system as they find it.

This is not a counsel of despair. It is the starting point for realism. Policy that assumes public servants will act against their own interests out of duty will fail. It will fail not because public servants are wicked, but because they are human. The minister who demands efficiency savings from a department whose senior officials gain status from larger budgets is asking those officials to act against the very incentives the system has placed before them. He might as well ask water to flow uphill.

The corollary is just as important. If we are to radically change policy, be it privatising an institution, removing a restrictive union practice, or transforming failing schools, we cannot simply impose the change and expect compliance. We need to buy off the existing interest groups. We need to make reform a mutually beneficial exchange, one where those affected serve the cause of policy change not due to their humanity, not because of their love of the public good, but due to their self-love, because they benefit from it as well. The council tenant accepts the loss of a subsidised rent because she gains ownership of her home at a discount. The unionised worker drops his opposition to privatisation because he receives discounted shares in the new company. The headteacher embraces academy status because she gains control of her own budget. In each case, the mechanism is identical to the one Smith described: give me that which I want, and you shall have this which you want.

[2] Ibid.

3 The Conspiracy Against the Public

Smith was no sentimentalist about the private sector either. He understood that the same self-interest which drives productive exchange also drives the attempt to rig the game:

> People of the same trade seldom meet together, even for merriment and diversion, but the conversation ends in a conspiracy against the public, or in some contrivance to raise prices.[3]

Producers, left to their own devices, may seek to restrict competition, raise barriers to entry, and secure privileges from the state. Smith saw this in the mercantile system of his day, where merchants and manufacturers lobbied for tariffs, monopoly charters, and colonial trading rights, all at the expense of the consumer. This is what is sometimes now called crony capitalism, and it unfairly undermines the argument for free markets, because it is the abuse of state power that is required to enable it. The merchant who competes fairly in the marketplace is a benefactor. The merchant who lobbies Parliament for protection against his rivals is a parasite. The free marketeer's quarrel is not with the critic who points to crony capitalism, but with the crony capitalist himself. Smith was blunt about their motives:

> The proposal of any new law or regulation of commerce which comes from this order, ought always to be listened to with great precaution, and ought never to be adopted till after having been long and carefully examined, not only with the most scrupulous, but with the most suspicious attention. It comes from an order of men, whose interest is never exactly the same with that of the public, who have generally an interest to deceive and even oppress the public, and who accordingly have, upon many occasions, both deceived and oppressed it.[4]

Smith established a principle that should be carved above the door of every government department:

> Consumption is the sole end and purpose of all production; and the interest of the producer ought to be attended to, only so far as it may be necessary for promoting that of the consumer.[5]

This principle has been systematically inverted in the modern public sector. State monopolies in health, education, and housing have been "captured" by their producers: the administrators, the unions, and the professional bodies whose convenience the service increasingly serves. The National Health Service does not wake patients at dawn because patients prefer it, but because staff rotas are arranged for the convenience of the workforce. Schools do not resist measurement of their results because measurement harms children, but because it exposes failure among teachers and administrators. The Post Office did not end Saturday collections because consumers demanded fewer deliveries, but because it made life easier for postal workers.

---

[3] Smith (1776, Book I, Chapter X, Part II, p. 145).

[4] Smith (1776, Book I, Chapter XI, Conclusion, p. 267).

[5] Smith (1776, Book IV, Chapter VIII, p. 660).

The same inversion of priorities manifests in how services are measured. Consider the cleaning of the London Underground. Transport for London can record the input: how many times each carriage was cleaned, how many hours of labour were deployed, how many litres of disinfectant were consumed. But the relevant question for the consumer is different. Is the train actually clean? Does the passenger perceive it to be so? A service measured by the effort of its producers rather than the experience of its consumers will always optimise for the wrong thing. The carriages may be cleaned three times a day and still feel filthy to the commuter. The distinction between the producer's metric and the consumer's reality is at the heart of what Smith identified.

The pattern extends beyond the traditional public services. Wherever the state creates a system of benefits or entitlements, an infrastructure of providers grows up around it whose interests become entangled with the continuation and expansion of the system. The hotels housing migrants at public expense serve not only the migrants but the hotel operators who depend on the contracts. The Motability scheme, designed to help disabled people access transport, generates a surrounding ecosystem of dealerships, insurers, and administrators with a direct financial interest in the scheme's generosity. In each case, a programme created to serve a vulnerable group acquires a penumbra of commercial interests whose livelihood depends on the programme's persistence and growth. These interests will lobby for its expansion and resist its reform with the same tenacity as any eighteenth century guild. They are not the intended beneficiaries, but they become the most effective defenders.

In every case, the Smithian pattern holds. The producers form a concentrated, self-conscious interest group. They know what they stand to lose from reform and are prepared to fight. The general public consumers are dispersed, disorganised, and bear only a fractional share of the cost. The result is that services nominally provided for the benefit of the public are increasingly geared to the benefit of those whose livelihood is gained within them.

The eighteenth century mercantilist and the twenty-first century public sector union are separated by 250 years of history, but the operating logic is much the same.

4 The Limits of Central Knowledge

The Smithian case against state direction rests not merely on incentives but on information. The individual, he argued, possesses knowledge that the central authority cannot:

> What is the species of domestic industry which his capital can employ, and of which the produce is likely to be of the greatest value, every individual, it is evident, can, in his local situation, judge much better than any statesman or lawgiver can do for him.[6]

[6] Smith (1776, Book IV, Chapter II, p. 456).

He went further, warning against the presumption of those who believe otherwise:

> The statesman who should attempt to direct private people in what manner they ought to employ their capitals would not only load himself with a most unnecessary attention, but assume an authority which could safely be trusted, not only to no single person, but to no council or senate whatever, and which would nowhere be so dangerous as in the hands of a man who had folly and presumption enough to fancy himself fit to exercise it.[7]

The statesman fails not because he is malicious but because he is ignorant. He does not know, and cannot know, the thousands of local circumstances that determine whether a particular decision is wise or foolish. The farmer knows his soil. The shopkeeper knows his customers. The factory manager knows his supply chain. The minister in Whitehall, however intelligent, however well-briefed, knows none of these things with the intimacy that the person on the ground possesses.

Smith also touched upon a puzzle that would prove central to the later development of economic thought. In his famous diamond-water paradox, he observed:

> Nothing is more useful than water: but it will purchase scarce any thing; scarce any thing can be had in exchange for it. A diamond, on the contrary, has scarce any value in use; but a very great quantity of other goods may frequently be had in exchange for it.[8]

Smith could not fully resolve this paradox himself. He remained broadly committed to a labour theory of value, which held that the cost of production determined the price of goods. It fell to later thinkers to provide the answer. In the 1870s, Carl Menger in Vienna, William Stanley Jevons in Manchester, and Leon Walras in Lausanne arrived independently at the theory of marginal utility: the insight that value is determined not by the total usefulness of a class of goods, but by the usefulness of the next unit available. Water is cheap not because it is unimportant but because it is abundant; the marginal glass adds little to what we already have. Diamonds are expensive not because they are more useful in total but because they are scarce; each additional diamond commands a high price because so few exist.

This was more than an academic refinement. It was a revolution in how we understand value, and it demolished the intellectual foundation on which Marx would build his entire system. If value is subjective, determined by the assessments of millions of individuals in their particular circumstances, then no central authority can calculate it. Ludwig von Mises (1920) drove this point home with his economic calculation argument: without market prices generated by genuine exchange between private owners, a socialist planning board has no national basis on which to allocate resources. It is not that the planners are too stupid. It is that the information they require does not exist in a form they can use. Prices are not data to be collected and fed into a model. They are signals generated by the dispersed, subjective valuations of countless individuals, each responding to circumstances that only they can observe.

[7] Smith (1776, Book IV, Chapter II, p. 456).

[8] Smith (1776, Book I, Chapter IV, p. 44).

Friedrich Hayek extended the argument further in his essay "The Use of Knowledge in Society".[9] The knowledge required to coordinate a complex economy is not scientific or technical knowledge that can be written down and transmitted to a central office. It is knowledge of "the particular circumstances of time and place": which supplier is reliable, which route is quickest, which customer is likely to pay. This knowledge is held by the individual on the spot, and it changes constantly. No statistical aggregate can capture it. No planning committee can replicate it. The price mechanism aggregates this information automatically, without anyone needing to understand the whole. Central planning destroys this mechanism and replaces it with the guesswork of officials who possess a tiny fraction of the relevant knowledge.

The Austrian tradition, from Menger through Mises to Hayek, thus completed the argument that Smith began. Smith saw that the individual knows his own circumstances better than the statesman. Menger showed that value itself is subjective and individual. Mises demonstrated that without private ownership and market exchange, rational economic calculation is impossible. Hayek explained that the knowledge on which a functioning economy depends is dispersed, tacit, and irreducible to central collection.

The implications for public sector reform are direct. Every centralised target imposed on a hospital, every national curriculum prescribed for a school, every planning regulation drafted in Whitehall for application in localities the drafter has never visited, is an act of the same presumption Smith identified 250 years ago. The case for devolving power to headteachers, GPs, and local communities rests on this foundation. The people closest to the problem possess knowledge the centre does not have and cannot acquire. Policy that overrides their decisions does not merely offend liberty. It destroys the very information on which good outcomes depend.

5 The Man of System

Though drawn from the Theory of Moral Sentiments rather than the Wealth of Nations, Smith's portrait of the "man of system" is crucial for those concerned with the practice of reform:

> The man of system is apt to be very wise in his own conceit; and is often so enamoured with the supposed beauty of his own ideal plan of government, that he cannot suffer the smallest deviation from any part of it. He goes on to establish it completely and in all its parts, without any regard either to the great interests, or to the strong prejudices which may oppose it. He seems to imagine that he can arrange the different members of a great society with as much ease as the hand arranges the different pieces upon a chess-board. He does not consider that the pieces upon the chess-board have no other principle of motion besides that which the hand impresses upon them; but that, in the great chess-board of human society,

[9] Hayek, F.A., "The Use of Knowledge in Society," *The American Economic Review*, Vol. 35, No. 4, 1945, pp. 519–530.

> every single piece has a principle of motion of its own, altogether different from that which the legislature might choose to impress upon it.[10]

This is the definitive critique of holistic, top-down reform. The planner who designs a grand scheme for society treats people as objects to be moved according to his will. He forgets that they have wills of their own, interests of their own, and the capacity to resist, evade, or subvert any plan that ignores those interests.

The passage is remarkable for its precision. Smith does not say that the man of system is wicked. He says he is enamoured. He is in love with the beauty of his own plan. This is a psychological observation as much as a political one. The reformer who has spent years devising a comprehensive programme for the transformation of society cannot bear to see it compromised, trimmed, or adapted to the messy realities of implementation. He would rather see it fail in its purity than succeed in a modified form.

Many failed government programmes in modern history can be understood through this lens. The reorganisation of local government in the early 1970s, which produced larger, more remote, and less accountable authorities. The comprehensive education reforms that ignored the preferences of parents. The housing targets imposed from above that unite every local interest group in opposition. The "dash for growth" under Liz Truss, which attempted to bypass every institutional constraint simultaneously and collapsed within weeks. In each case, the man of system drew up his blueprint, moved his chess pieces, and watched as they moved back.

The alternative, as Smith implies and as micropolitics makes explicit, is to work with the principle of motion that each piece already possesses. Rather than commanding people to behave differently, alter the circumstances so that their natural pursuit of advantage leads them where you want them to go. This is not a counsel of timidity. It is a counsel of realism. The reformer who works with human nature will always outperform the reformer who works against it.

Smith contrasted the man of system with a different kind of reformer:

> "Whose public spirit is prompted altogether by humanity and benevolence" and who "will respect the established powers and privileges even of individuals, and still more those of the great orders and societies, into which the state is divided"[11]

This second figure does not abandon the goal of reform. He pursues it by accommodation rather than by force. He is, in the language of this chapter, the micropolitician.

---

[10] Smith (1759, The Theory of Moral Sentiments, Part VI, Section II, Chapter II, pp. 233–234).

[11] Smith (1759, Part VI, Section II, Chapter II, pp. 232–233).

6 Unintended Consequences

Smith documented, case after case, how interventions designed to achieve one outcome produced the opposite. The Corn Laws, intended to secure the food supply, raised the price of bread and impoverished the labourer. The apprenticeship statutes, intended to ensure quality, restricted competition and entrenched guilds that served no one but their own members. Colonial trade restrictions, intended to enrich the mother country, misallocated capital on a colossal scale by forcing it into channels less productive than those it would naturally have found.

These were not accidents. They were the predictable result of interfering with a complex system whose workings the legislator did not fully understand. Smith showed that when you block one channel of trade, capital flows into another, often less productive one. When you grant a monopoly to one group, you tax every consumer who must deal with it. When you subsidise an activity, you create a constituency that will fight to keep the subsidy long after its original purpose has passed.

The pattern repeats with mechanical regularity in the modern state. Rent controls, introduced to make housing affordable, destroy the incentive to build or maintain rental properties and create the very shortage they were intended to prevent. Agricultural subsidies, introduced to support struggling farmers, become entrenched entitlements that persist decades after the original crisis, distorting land use and inflating food prices. Employment regulations, introduced to protect workers, raise the cost of hiring and price the most vulnerable out of the labour market entirely.

In each case, the intervention creates a new interest group with a stake in its continuation. The subsidy recipients lobby to keep their subsidy. The regulators lobby to keep their regulatory power. The compliance industry that grows up around the regulation lobbies to keep the regulation complex. What begins as a temporary response to a specific problem becomes a permanent feature of the landscape, defended by groups whose existence depends upon it.

Smith saw this dynamic with perfect clarity 250 years ago. The mercantilist regulations he attacked had been in place for generations, defended by precisely the interest groups they had created. The modern regulatory state is his mercantilist system in new clothing.

7 Competition and the Possibility of Exit

Smith's case for competition is often reduced to an argument about efficiency: that rival firms, competing for custom, will drive down prices and drive up quality. This is true, but it understates the point. Competition is not merely a mechanism for lower prices. It is the only reliable discipline against the tendency of every organisation, public or private, to serve its own interests at the expense of those it is supposed to serve.

> In general, if any branch of trade, or any division of labour, be advantageous to the public, the freer and more general the competition, it will always be the more so.[12]

Where competition exists, the consumer has the power to leave. This power of exit, the ability to take one's custom elsewhere, is the most potent force in economics. It is the force that keeps the butcher honest, the baker attentive, and the brewer solvent. It requires no regulator, no ombudsman, no consultative committee. It operates automatically, silently, and with ruthless efficiency. The firm that fails to serve the customer loses the customer. The firm that loses enough customers ceases to exist. No government inspector achieves a fraction of this disciplinary effect.

Remove the possibility of exit, and the slow rot of producer capture begins. The service deteriorates. The queues lengthen. The complaints are met with indifference, because the complainant has nowhere else to go.

The economist Albert Hirschman (1970) formalised the distinction in his celebrated work Exit, Voice, and Loyalty. When dissatisfied with an organisation, people can either leave (exit) or complain (voice). In competitive markets, exit dominates. The customer who dislikes a restaurant does not write to its management committee; he goes to a different restaurant. The restaurant, observing the loss of custom, either improves or closes. The feedback loop is immediate and inescapable.

In the public sector, exit has been abolished by design. The citizen cannot choose a different tax authority. The patient cannot, in most cases, take the NHS funding allocated to their treatment and spend it at a rival provider. The parent, until the academy reforms of the 2010s, could not escape the catchment area of a failing school. Without exit, voice is all that remains: consultative committees, ombudsmen, citizens' panels, public consultations. Decades of experience have demonstrated that these mechanisms achieve little. The producers sit on the committees. The ombudsmen lack enforcement power. The consultations are rituals of participation that change nothing.

A watchdog, as Smith's intellectual descendants observed, is less effective if it has dined for years at the same table as the intruder it is supposed to guard against.

The reintroduction of exit, or mechanisms that simulate its effect, is the thread that connects nearly every successful reform discussed in this chapter. Contracting out introduced competition into local services. The Right to Buy gave council tenants the ultimate exit from state housing. The academy programme allowed schools to leave local authority control. Street Votes give residents the power to opt in to development on their own terms. In every case, the mechanism works because it restores to the individual the power that Smith identified as the foundation of all market discipline: the power to go elsewhere.

[12] Smith (1776, Book II, Chapter II, p. 329).

8 The Division of Labour and Specialisation

The very first sentence of the Wealth of Nations announces one of the most consequential ideas in the history of economic thought:

> The greatest improvement in the productive powers of labour, and the greater part of the skill, dexterity, and judgement with which it is any where directed, or applied, seem to have been the effects of the division of labour.[13]

Smith illustrated the point immediately with what has become perhaps the most famous passage of industrial description ever written:

> A workman not educated to this business, nor acquainted with the use of the machinery employed in it, could scarce, perhaps, with his utmost industry, make one pin in a day, and certainly could not make twenty. But in the way in which this business is now carried on, not only the whole work is a peculiar trade, but it is divided into a number of branches, of which the greater part are likewise peculiar trades. One man draws out the wire, another straights it, a third cuts it, a fourth points it, a fifth grinds it at the top for receiving the head; to make the head requires two or three distinct operations; to put it on is a peculiar business, to whiten the pins is another; it is even a trade by itself to put them into the paper.[14]

In such a factory, Smith reported, ten men could between them produce upwards of 48,000 pins in a day. Each man, by specialising in a narrow task, was effectively producing 4800 pins, compared with the one or perhaps 20 he could have managed alone. The gain did not come from working harder. It came from working differently: each worker perfecting a narrow task, developing dexterity through repetition, and saving the time otherwise lost in switching between activities.

The principle extends far beyond the factory floor. Smith argued that specialisation is the engine of economic progress. It is the reason that a modern labourer enjoys comforts that a medieval king could not command. The woollen coat on the worker's back is the product of the combined efforts of the shepherd, the wool sorter, the spinner, the weaver, the dyer, the fuller, the dresser, and dozens of others, each contributing a specialised skill to a process no single individual could replicate alone.

> It is the great multiplication of the productions of all the different arts, in consequence of the division of labour, which occasions, in a well-governed society, that universal opulence which extends itself to the lowest ranks of the people.[15]

Smith also observed that the division of labour is limited by the extent of the market. A village cannot support a specialist pin maker because the demand is too small. Only when the market is large enough to absorb the output of a specialist can specialisation occur. This is the fundamental argument for trade: by extending the market beyond the borders of the parish, the county, or the nation, trade permits a degree of specialisation that a closed economy could never sustain. It is also the

---

[13] Smith (1776, Book I, Chapter I, p. 13).

[14] Smith (1776, Book I, Chapter I, pp. 14–15).

[15] Smith (1776, Book I, Chapter I, p. 22).

argument against autarky and protectionism, which shrink the market and force producers back towards the inefficiency of generalism.

The relevance to public policy is direct. The state, by its nature, is a generalist. A single government department is expected to design policy, draft legislation, manage procurement, administer services, handle complaints, and evaluate its own performance. It does all of these things, and it does most of them badly, for the same reason that Smith's solitary pin maker produced only one pin a day: it is attempting to perform too many distinct operations with the same people and the same skills.

The case for contracting out, which became one of the most powerful micropolitical tools of the 1980s, rests squarely on this Smithian foundation. When a local authority invites private firms to bid for the provision of refuse collection, street cleaning, or building maintenance, it is applying the division of labour. The authority retains the role of specifying and monitoring the service. The private firm takes on the role of delivering it. Each does what it is best equipped to do. The result, confirmed repeatedly in practice, is that the same service is delivered at 20–40% lower cost, not because private workers are more virtuous but because specialist firms organise the work more efficiently than a bureaucracy attempting to manage dozens of unrelated functions simultaneously. It is the pin factory applied to the public sector.

The principle applies equally to the argument for open markets and international trade. Smith demolished the mercantilist case for self-sufficiency with a characteristically pointed analogy:

> It is the maxim of every prudent master of a family, never to attempt to make at home what it will cost him more to make than to buy. What is prudence in the conduct of every private family, can scarce be folly in that of a great kingdom.[16]

He illustrated the absurdity of protectionism with the example of Scottish wine. Using greenhouses and heated walls, it is perfectly possible to grow grapes in Scotland and produce wine from them, at perhaps 30 times the cost of importing it from France. The fact that something can be done domestically does not mean it should be. The resources squandered on Scottish viticulture could be deployed in industries where Scotland holds a genuine advantage. Every government procurement decision, every "buy British" mandate, every insistence on domestic production where an international supplier offers better value, repeats the error Smith identified. The logic of specialisation and exchange applies between nations just as it applies between individuals, and the gains from trade are no less real for being dispersed across millions of transactions that no single observer can see.

[16] Smith (1776, Book IV, Chapter II, pp. 456–457).

9 Taxation, Spending, and the Limits of the State

Smith identified three essential duties of the sovereign: the defence of the nation from external threat, the administration of justice to protect citizens from one another, and the provision of certain public works and institutions that private enterprise could not profitably maintain, such as roads, bridges, and basic education. This framework remains the most useful starting point for any discussion of what government should do, and by implication, where it has overreached.

On the question of how the state should fund its legitimate activities, Smith laid down four maxims of taxation in Book V of the Wealth of Nations. They remain as relevant today.

The first maxim is equity. Subjects of the state should contribute to its support in proportion to their respective abilities, that is, in proportion to the revenue they enjoy under its protection. The second is certainty. The tax which each individual is bound to pay should be certain and not arbitrary:

> The time of payment, the manner of payment, the quantity to be paid, ought all to be clear and plain to the contributor, and to every other person.[17]

Smith regarded certainty as so important that he considered even a considerable degree of inequality less harmful than a small degree of uncertainty.

The third maxim is convenience. Every tax ought to be levied at the time and in the manner most likely to be convenient for the contributor to pay it. Taxes on rent are best collected when rent is due; taxes on goods are best collected at the point of sale.

The fourth maxim is efficiency:

> Every tax ought to be so contrived as both to take out and to keep out of the pockets of the people as little as possible, over and above what it brings into the public treasury of the state.[18]

Smith identified four ways in which a tax can fail this test: by requiring a great number of officials to collect it, whose salaries consume much of the revenue; by obstructing the industry of the people and discouraging them from engaging in the activities that might employ and maintain them; by imposing penalties and forfeitures that ruin those who attempt to evade it; and by subjecting the people to frequent visits and examinations by the tax collector, exposing them to unnecessary trouble, vexation, and oppression.

By these standards, the modern British tax system is a disgrace. It is complex beyond comprehension, with thousands of pages of legislation riddled with exemptions, reliefs, and special provisions that serve the interests of accountants and lobbyists more than those of taxpayers. It is uncertain: individuals and businesses routinely discover retrospective liabilities they could not have anticipated. It is inconvenient: the administrative burden falls disproportionately on small firms and

---

[17] Smith (1776, Book V, Chapter II, Part II, p. 825).

[18] Smith (1776, Book V, Chapter II, Part II, p. 826).

the self-employed, who lack the resources to navigate the labyrinth. And it is grossly inefficient: HMRC's own estimates of the "tax gap" run to tens of billions of pounds annually, while the compliance costs borne by businesses represent a deadweight loss to the economy that Smith would have found scandalous.

Smith also understood that the state is structurally inclined to spend more than it should. He drew a sharp distinction between the habits of private individuals and those of public authorities:

> It is the highest impertinence and presumption, in kings and ministers, to pretend to watch over the economy of private people, and to restrain their expense. They are themselves always, and without any exception, the greatest spendthrifts in the society. Let them look well after their own expense, and they may safely trust private people with theirs.[19]

The logic is straightforward. Private individuals spend their own money and bear the consequences of waste. Public authorities spend other people's money and bear no personal cost when it is squandered. Capital is accumulated by private parsimony and destroyed by public prodigality. This asymmetry produces a systematic bias towards overspending, particularly on the current account. Politicians face constant pressure to fund immediate services and satisfy the wage demands of public sector workers. Capital investment, which serves future voters who have no voice in today's political market, is always the first to be cut.

The result is the phenomenon Smith's successors would recognise as private affluence and public squalor: a prosperous private sector alongside a shabby, under-capitalised public sector where buildings crumble, equipment is obsolete, and infrastructure is made to serve long past its useful life. The state has plenty of money for salaries and pensions. It never has enough for maintenance, renewal, or modernisation. This is not bad luck. It is the predictable consequence of the incentive structure Smith described.

The implications for reform are clear. Taxes should be simplified, lowered, and made as transparent as possible, so that citizens can see what they are paying and judge whether they are receiving value in return. Public spending should be subjected to the same discipline of competition and consumer choice that operates in the private sector. And the boundary of the state should be drawn around the functions that only the state can perform best.

10 Micropolitics: The Theory

The eight Smithian insights set out above explain why markets work and why states fail. They do not, by themselves, explain how to reform a state that has failed. For that, a second body of thought is required: one that applies Smith's observations about self-interest not to the economy but to the political process itself.

---

[19] Smith (1776, Book II, Chapter III, p. 346).

There is a widespread and seductive assumption among those sympathetic to markets that winning the battle of ideas is sufficient to change reality. It is comforting for intellectuals to believe that they are the real rulers, that once the case for free markets has been made and accepted, events will follow naturally in its wake. This is the Keynesian illusion: that "madmen in authority, who hear voices in the air, are distilling their frenzy from some academic scribbler of a few years back".[20] It flatters the intellectual class by telling them that ideas are the ultimate determinants, and that to win the battle for ideas is to win thereby the battle for events.

The battle of ideas is necessary but not sufficient. Ideas do not implement themselves. Governments do not simply read the Wealth of Nations and apply its conclusions. Between the seminar room and the statute book lies a political market populated by interest groups, bureaucratic incentives, and institutional resistance. Without the engineering to navigate that market, the finest ideas in the world will remain confined in books.

Public choice theory, developed by James Buchanan, Gordon Tullock, and others from the 1960s onwards, provided the diagnostic framework. Its central insight was simple. People behave in political life in a very similar fashion to their behaviour in economic life. The politician, the bureaucrat, the union leader, and the voter are not transformed into selfless servants of the public good the moment they enter the political arena. They continue to maximise their advantage, trade for support, and protect their interests, just as they do in the marketplace.

Previously, scholars had supposed there was a dichotomy: that people acted for private gain in economics but for the public good in politics. Public choice shattered this illusion. It revealed a political marketplace in which votes are traded, coalitions are built from minorities who agree to support each other's special interests, and the will of governments is a feeble reed against the pressures imposed by organised groups.

The theory explains why the public sector over-produces, why it is captured by its producers, why it resists reform, and why the bureaucracy fights to expand. It explains why minorities are so often benefited at the expense of majorities: because small groups with concentrated interests will trade their support to secure benefits, while the dispersed majority, facing only a fractional cost per head, offers little resistance. It explains why capital budgets are raided to fund current spending, why consumer watchdogs are captured by the industries they monitor, and why every attempt to impose private sector discipline on the public sector washes away like a tide, leaving the rocks exactly where they were.

Armed with this analysis, we can see why conservative programmes have laboured under such difficulties. The essence of the conservative formula, curbing the role of government, reducing regulation, and cutting spending, runs counter to the interest of almost every group involved in the process. These policies might indeed benefit society as a whole. None of this is sufficient to take them into the

---

[20] Keynes (1936, p. 383).

realm of practical politics, because the groups that stand to lose are concentrated, organised, and vocal, while those who stand to gain are dispersed and silent.

This is the socialist ratchet. State power and spending are extended rapidly under collectivist administrations and more slowly under conservative ones. If a conservative government manages a brief holding action, preventing an increase while it holds office, this is regarded as the best that can be hoped for. Public choice explains why. Bureaucrats fight to expand their empires. Beneficiaries fight to retain their subsidies. The pressures are unidirectional.

It was this analysis that explained the great puzzle of the 1970s. Both Richard Nixon in the United States and Edward Heath in Britain were elected on platforms hostile to collectivism, pledging to roll back the state. Both failed. Not because the ideas were wrong, not because they lacked conviction, and not because the intellectual community opposed them (it opposed Reagan and Thatcher just as fiercely). They failed because they did not know how to do it. They had won the battle of ideas. They had secured the mandate. But they lacked the policy engineering to turn either into results. They knew what they wanted but not how to achieve it against a system designed to resist precisely this kind of change.

A decade later, the Reagan and Thatcher administrations succeeded where their predecessors had failed. The difference was not in the ideas, nor the times, nor the mandate. It was policy technique. The later governments were equipped with the detailed mechanics of implementation. They had moved beyond the strategy of simply inflicting pain and hoping for the best.

11 From Critique to Creativity

If public choice theory tells governments what not to do, micropolitics tells them what they can do instead. It is the creative counterpart to the diagnostic critique. If the prevailing political system acts to thwart certain types of policy, perhaps others can be constructed which work with the pressures it imposes, instead of trying to override them.

The starting point is Smith's insight about exchange. If self-interest is the universal motivator, then reform must be structured as a transaction. Instead of facing head-on the opposition of groups which perceive value in their state benefits, the new policies seek to trade in the political market, offering where possible something of greater perceived value which nonetheless makes possible a reduction in the size and scope of government.

The mechanics of this trade draw on all of the Smithian insights we have identified: self-interest, producer capture, the limits of central knowledge, the danger of holistic planning, the power of competition and exit, and the logic of specialisation. No single insight generates the method. It is their combination, applied to the specific circumstances of each case, that produces workable policy. The forms this trade takes include:

- *Substitution of benefit*. People might surrender a state benefit if an alternative benefit is available to compensate them. The council tenant gives up subsidised rent because she receives ownership of her home at a discount. The state benefit is eroded not by abolition but by the substitution of a superior private benefit in exchange.
- *Capitalising the benefit*. People will often give up a continuing, long-term gain in return for a substantial, immediate one-off gain. The miner accepts the closure of his pit because he receives the most generous voluntary redundancy payment in British history. The employee of a state industry accepts privatisation because he receives free shares whose value he can see rising. Such transactions are routine in economic markets; yet policies which embody them have seemed novel in politics.
- *Creating new players*. Sometimes a group enjoys a position of such power that no reasonable offer can buy them off. In these cases, the strategy shifts to altering the balance of forces in the political market. A new group is established and built up which will outweigh the first. Two million new shareholders, created by the privatisation of British Telecom, constitute a powerful constituency for private ownership that did not exist before the sale. The new homeowners created by the Right to Buy form a political force that no subsequent government dares to confront.
- *Eroding power*. Policies can be constructed to circumvent and neutralise the power of a group before attempting to deal with the benefit they enjoy. The Thatcher trade union reforms did not attack union power head-on, as Heath's Industrial Relations Act had tried and failed to do. They devolved power from the leaders to the members through secret ballots, used civil law rather than criminal law to enforce compliance, and introduced each measure gradually so that no single step was large enough to provoke a mass confrontation. Each measure seemed calculated to fall short of anything which would arouse a major outcry. It was the cumulative effect which added up to real reform.

12 Characteristics of the Method

Several features distinguish micropolitics from conventional policy advice:

- *It is non-confrontational*. Conventional free market policy regards state benefits as illegitimate and seeks their removal. This arouses resentment. Micropolitics accepts that the benefit is there and will be defended, whether or not it has any claim to legitimacy. The status quo itself is regarded as a source of legitimacy by those who enjoy it. The micropolitician does not dispute this. He offers a better deal.
- *It is piecemeal rather than holistic*. It does not seek to implement a vision all at once. There are no ideological formulae which automatically produce the correct

answers. The interest groups, the character of their benefit, and its past operation vary from one section of society to another. If the problems are different in each area, then so must be the solutions.

- *It is gradual, but not gradualist*. There is a clear distinction. Gradualism involves taking small steps against the grain of society, hoping they are small enough to be tolerated. Micropolitics takes steps with the grain. The policies created within its framework are not designed to be tolerated, but to be preferred to the prevailing state of affairs.
- *It is less coherent, by design*. It produces different policies in almost every area, because every area presents different problems with different interest groups. The unity lies not in the policies themselves but in the method by which they are generated. The methods are all designed to work in the world of interest group pressures, and all to give individual preferences primacy in the political process.

The public sector presents many aspects, all different, and all sustained by different groups and different forces. To the micropolitician these aspects are like a series of locked doors. The objective is to open them up in order to let in consumer choices and responsiveness to individual need. The instruments are the keys which each of the micropolitical techniques constitute. No two keys are identical, but information learned about the opening of one door can be used to help unlock others.

13 The Connection to Smith

The thread connecting Smith to micropolitics is not a matter of applying any single insight mechanically. It is that the entire method is Smithian in its logic. It assumes self-interest. It analyses producer capture. It respects the limits of central knowledge by devolving decisions to individuals. It rejects the man of system's chessboard in favour of piecemeal, incremental change. It reintroduces competition and the possibility of exit where the state has abolished them. It applies the division of labour by separating the specification of services from their delivery. And it recognises, as Smith did with the mercantilist system, that every intervention creates its own defenders, and that the only way to overcome them is to offer a better bargain.

The method is not a list of policies. It is a means of generating policies. It starts not with a blueprint for the ideal society but with a technique for changing the one that exists. Whatever society emerges as a result of that process will be one resulting spontaneously from the interplay of different decisions and actions, not one decided by planners to be superior. In this respect, micropolitics is the most Smithian of all approaches to reform. It trusts the process of exchange, applied to politics, to produce outcomes superior to those any single mind could design.

14 Applying Micropolitics in Practice

The theory of micropolitics was not developed in a library. It was forged in practice, tested against the resistance of real interest groups, and refined by the trial and error of actual implementation. The Adam Smith Institute, founded in 1977, served as the principal workshop for this engineering. What follows are the highlights of four decades of micropolitical policy, selected for the diversity of techniques they illustrate and the scale of their impact.

14.1 The Right to Buy

Of all the micropolitical victories, the Right to Buy remains the most vivid illustration of the method. By 1979, some 35% of the British population lived in publicly owned homes at highly subsidised rents. Council estates formed a vast block of opposition to any reform that threatened their subsidy. The old approach, advocated for years by Conservatives, was to bring rents up to economic levels. It failed repeatedly, because those in receipt of the benefit valued it more highly than others resented paying for it.

The new policy did not abandon the objective, but it changed the offer. Instead of taking away a subsidy, it offered something tenants valued even more: ownership. Council tenants were given the right to buy their homes at discounts ranging from 20 to 70% depending on length of tenure. The calculation was pure Smith: address yourself not to their humanity but to their self-love, and never talk to them of your necessities but of their advantages.

The result was a transfer of property and power on a massive scale. By 1986, over one million tenants had bought their homes. A new class of homeowners had been created, a political force with a direct stake in the continuation of property-owning capitalism. The Labour Party, which had furiously opposed the policy, was forced into a U-turn and pledged to keep it. Council officials watched their empires crumble. Elected councillors saw their captive voting blocs slipping away.

The Right to Buy succeeded because it offered a better deal. The old approach tried to override the interests of council tenants. The new method sought to offer an exchange with something of greater value. It created new players in the political market whose interests were permanently aligned with private ownership.

14.2 Privatisation

The word "privatisation" did not appear in the 1979 Conservative manifesto. The concept emerged through practice, and the technique was learned by doing. The contrast between two attempts to privatise the gas industry illustrates the learning curve perfectly.

In 1981, the government attempted to separate the profitable gas showrooms from the rest of British Gas and sell them. The management, led by the formidable Sir Dennis Rookes, fought to keep his empire intact. The workforce threatened strikes. Scare stories circulated about "cowboys" fitting dangerous appliances. The proposal was withdrawn, having alienated every significant interest group. It was a textbook example of how not to do it.

Five years later, the privatisation of British Gas as a whole was a triumph, because the policy had changed. Management were offered something they valued more than running a public enterprise: the prospect of heading a powerful private corporation. Workers who had previously threatened strikes now received free shares and priority purchasing; over 90% bought in. The gas-using public received preferential share allocations and vouchers towards their bills. Every interest group that had been alienated by the first attempt was bought off by the second.

The privatisation of British Telecom in 1984 broke further ground as the first major utility sale. The government sold it intact, winning management support. It went over the heads of the union leadership, which had campaigned fiercely against the sale, by offering free shares directly to employees. 96% of the workforce bought shares. Two million members of the public became shareholders through easy instalment terms and bill vouchers. The sale attracted criticism for "underpricing", but the premium was deliberate. A share price that fell on the first day would have created a constituency disillusioned with capitalism. A price that rose created two million new capitalists with a personal stake in the success of the private sector.

Not every privatisation required a giant flotation. The National Freight Corporation demonstrated what could happen when workers were not merely bought off but made the owners. In a management-worker buyout, the drivers, loaders, checkers, and sorters of a road haulage federation bought into the new company. Some mortgaged their homes. Others pooled their life savings. The results were spectacular. The company proved highly profitable in the private sector, and the share-owning workers saw the value of their investment increase 54-fold. The old division between "us and them" dissolved. Workers identified with the company because they owned it. This was Smith's insight about dispersed knowledge in action: the people on the ground knew the potential of the business far better than any Whitehall official, and given ownership, they had every incentive to act on that knowledge.

British Airways illustrated a different lesson: that the mere preparation for privatisation could itself be transformative. In 1983 the airline was making huge losses and was grossly overmanned. By its sale in 1987, it was profitable and popular. The transformation was achieved through micropolitical technique: generous voluntary redundancy reduced the workforce from 59,000 to 39,000, and employees were offered lump sum cash inducements to surrender their inflation-proof, index-linked pensions in favour of standard funded schemes. The looming sale concentrated minds. Staff realised that in the private sector, their jobs would depend on satisfying the customer, not the minister.

The purpose of privatisation was not principally to create perfect competition. Academic economists complained that replacing a public monopoly with a private monopoly yielded no benefit. They missed the point. A state industry cannot raise capital on commercial terms, cannot site its factories based on efficiency, and cannot close its loss-making operations without a political crisis. Its investment decisions are determined not by projected returns but by the political map of marginal constituencies. A private company, even an imperfect monopoly, is subject to technological innovation, independent regulation, and the disciplines of the capital market. Whereas public monopolies are sustained indefinitely by new laws brought in to protect them from new threats, private monopolies are eroded over time. The priority was to move the asset out of the political market and into the economic one. Competition could follow; the transfer of ownership was the essential first step.

14.3 Trade Union Reform

The reform of trade union law provides the most vivid contrast between the macropolitical and micropolitical approaches. In the 1960s and 1970s, both the Wilson and Heath governments attempted comprehensive reform through single, sweeping Acts of Parliament. Both failed, because they united the entire union movement in defiance.

The Thatcher reforms succeeded because they were constructed differently. They came in a series of small steps rather than a single confrontation. Each measure seemed limited, perhaps calculated to fall short of anything which would arouse a major outcry. It was the cumulative effect which added up to transformation. Instead of taking power from unions and giving it to the government, the reforms devolved power from union leaders to their members through mandatory secret ballots. The members were hardly likely to rally against measures that gave them more say. The reforms used civil law rather than criminal law, removing the opportunities for union leaders to cast themselves as martyrs.

This strategy was vindicated in the 1984–1985 miners' strike. Where the 1974 strike had brought down the Heath government, this one failed. The government had neutralised the central grievance by guaranteeing that no miner would be forced out of a job. Relocation grants, retraining, and the most generous voluntary redundancy payments in British history were offered. The dispute was reduced to a fight over the future size of the industry, a matter of great interest to the union leadership but of little concern to individual miners being offered large cash sums to leave. The micropolitical insight that the leaders of interest groups do not necessarily represent the views of their members proved decisive.

14.4 Contracting Out

Contracting out applied Smith's division of labour to local government. Instead of councils producing services in-house, private firms were invited to bid for the work. The council retained the role of specifying and monitoring the service. The contractor delivered it.

The beauty of the policy lay in how it managed the political market. The public feared a decline in quality; this was met by tightly drawn contracts with penalty clauses. The bureaucracy feared loss of status; this was addressed by moving management up to the higher-status work of contract oversight. The workforce was offered first refusal on jobs with the new provider or reabsorption elsewhere in the council.

Savings of 20–40% were achieved consistently, not because private workers were exploited but because specialist firms organised labour more efficiently than a generalist bureaucracy. While purists complained that it fell short of a full free market, the micropoliticians had meanwhile taken the approach to such a stage of success that the government felt confident enough to mandate local authorities to seek outside bids. The advocates of the total solution were still arguing about the ideal; the engineers had built the machine and set it running.

14.5 The Citizen's Charter

As the great privatisation programme ran its course in the 1990s, micropolitics turned to the services that remained within the state. The question was simple: if a defective pullover from Marks and Spencer could be returned for a refund, why was there no equivalent recourse when the state failed to deliver the health treatment or education a citizen had paid for through taxation?

The Citizen's Charter, championed by Prime Minister John Major but driven intellectually by figures including Madsen Pirie, sought to introduce the ethos of consumer rights into the public sector. It was not imposed from above. The specific standards had to come from the services themselves, through a process of negotiation that ensured ownership. The critical distinction was between the producer's view ("we cleaned the train three times today") and the consumer's view ("is the train clean?"). Services were to be measured by results experienced, not effort expended.

The Charter demanded that public bodies publish their standards, transforming vague commitments into specific, measurable promises. The Charter Mark scheme introduced reputational competition between departments. In the rail industry, the principle was established that passengers were entitled to refunds for late or cancelled trains, creating a direct financial incentive for improvement.

The policy achieved real gains, but it also exposed a fundamental limitation. The Schools Charter promised parents information but not education. If a child left school unable to read, there was no redress. The Department of Education successfully blocked any mechanism that would have imposed a genuine cost on failure. The Charter taught a lasting lesson: measurement and the threat of apology can raise standards, but without the permanent pressure of competition, without the ability to exit, the internal forces of the bureaucracy will eventually reassert themselves.

14.6 2010 Education Reforms

If privatisation was the grand project of the 1980s, the school reforms initiated by Michael Gove in 2010 were a textbook micropolitical project of the next generation. The intellectual architecture traced directly to the Adam Smith Institute. In the original Micropolitics, Pirie had proposed a three-legged stool for education: open entry, school independence, and per capita funding. The ASI's Omega Report developed the concept of a "virtual voucher", designed to achieve the market discipline of a voucher system without the political toxicity of the word itself. Funding would follow the pupil. If a parent chose School A over School B, the money would flow to School A.

Michael Gove recognised that the "Academy" concept, originally introduced by Andrew Adonis under Tony Blair, was the vehicle through which these ideas could finally be delivered. He moved it from a niche solution for failing schools to a systemic revolution. By allowing good and outstanding schools to convert to academy status, he unleashed a wave of voluntary exit from local authority control. Schools that converted received the funding that local authorities had previously held back for central services. The incentive was financial as much as philosophical.

The technique was micropolitical throughout. Gove weaponised precedent: by expanding a mechanism Labour had invented, he made it ideologically difficult for opponents to attack the core principle. He relied on voluntary opt-out rather than compulsion, creating a coalition of the willing that eroded the local authority's power base from within. And he moved fast. By 2012, half of all secondary schools had converted. Once thousands of schools had become independent legal entities with their own contracts and assets, it became administratively impossible to reverse the reform.

Academies now constitute nearly half of all schools in England. The local authority monopoly has been broken. It is arguably the most significant legacy of 14 years of Conservative government, and it was achieved not by grand design but by the patient application of micropolitical technique to the specific interest groups and incentive structures of the English education system.

14.7 Street Votes: Turning NIMBYs into YIMBYs

The most recent and perhaps most vividly micropolitical reform addresses the housing crisis. By the 2010s, it was widely accepted that Britain needed to build far more homes, but the planning system had been captured by local homeowners, the most reliable voting bloc, who blocked development to protect their property values and amenity. This is the phenomenon of NIMBYism ("Not In My Back Yard").

In 2017, the Adam Smith Institute published "Yes In My Back Yard" by John Myers, applying micropolitical logic to the problem. The insight was that opposition to development was not ideological but transactional. People opposed building because they bore the costs (noise, disruption, strain on services) without sharing the rewards. The solution was to flip the incentive. Under the Street Votes proposal, individual streets could vote to grant themselves permitted development rights. If a supermajority of residents voted yes, every homeowner on that street would see the value of their property rise immediately, as they now possessed the right to extend upwards or develop gaps. The neighbours captured the economic value of development. NIMBYs became YIMBYs.

Separately, the ASI's polling confirmed that opposition to Green Belt development, which ran at a net margin of −31%, swung to +13% when a "community dividend" was offered. The 44-point swing proved that the obstacle was not ideological but structural. People were not against building. They were against building that enriched developers while imposing costs on residents.

The concept moved from think tank paper to statute. It was enacted through the Levelling Up and Regeneration Act 2023, with a consultation in 2024 closely mirroring the original ASI design. It is a textbook case of the micropolitical method: a specific analysis of the interest groups, a policy constructed to offer them a better deal, and a mechanism that works with self-interest rather than against it.

14.8 The Cautionary Tale of Truss

The brief premiership of Liz Truss as Prime Minister serves as the negative proof of the micropolitical method. While her supporters characterise it as a failure of nerve and her opponents as a failure of ideology, it was fundamentally a failure of political engineering.

The administration declared war on the institutional architecture rather than managing it. By bypassing the Office for Budget Responsibility and dismissing the Permanent Secretary to the Treasury, it united the bureaucratic establishment against it without first securing alternative bases of support. This was the man of system in action: so enamoured with the beauty of the plan that he cannot suffer the smallest deviation.

The sequencing of announcements compounded the error. The government committed to a massive Energy Price Guarantee costing between £70 billion and £140 billion, paired with significant tax cuts, before any corresponding spending reductions or supply-side reforms had been secured. Markets assess risk on the probability of implementation. Spending increases and tax cuts are politically easy to deliver. Spending cuts and structural reform are politically hard. The markets correctly calculated that the former was guaranteed while the latter was speculative, and priced accordingly.

The resulting spike in gilt yields directly increased mortgage rates, imposing tangible financial pain on the aspirational middle class, the bedrock of any conservative project. No amount of rhetoric about a 2.5% growth target could compensate for hundreds of pounds added to monthly mortgage payments. The government had alienated its own core constituency through the unintended consequences of its own sequencing.

The Truss experiment demonstrated that fiscal credibility is a prerequisite for radicalism, not a constraint upon it. The Thatcher government of 1981 raised taxes to establish credibility before cutting them later. It rolled the pitch. It built alliances. It banked fiscal trust before spending it. The Truss government attempted to bypass this sequencing entirely and collapsed within weeks. It confirms the central thesis of this chapter: being right is not enough. The engineering matters as much as the idea.

15 The Future of Smithian Policy-Making

Smith's ideas have been vindicated by 250 years of evidence. The question for the next generation of reformers is how to apply them against a state that has learned new ways to resist. The danger is that reformers become the very thing Smith warned against: the man of system, so enamoured with his plan that he forgets every chess piece has a principle of motion of its own. When the mandate arrives, it will not be enough to know what needs to change. The reformer must know how to change it.

The challenges are different in form from those that Smith confronted in the mercantilist system or those that the Adam Smith Institute confronted in the bloated state of the late 1970s, but they are identical in structure. The state no longer owns the car factories and the airlines. It controls through regulation, compliance, and the proliferation of arm's-length bodies whose budgets have tripled even as their numbers have been cut.

The temptation in deregulation is to sweep away the regulatory accumulation of the last 30 years in one "Great Repeal Act". This is the man of system at his most seductive: one clean, elegant stroke that restores liberty in a single afternoon. It would unite every vested interest into a single coalition of resistance and collapse under its own ambition. The micropolitical approach is to target specific, indefensible regulations where the public benefit of removal is immediate and visible. Win small battles. Build momentum. Let each success create the constituency for the next.

In planning, the ambition to rebuild the physical economy is strangled by a system designed to say "no". Smith would have recognised the dynamic instantly: a conspiracy against the public by those who already own homes against those who wish to. The micropolitical solution is not to override local objections from above, but to dissolve them with direct incentives, as Street Votes have begun to demonstrate. The obstacle is not purely ideological but transactional. The logic is identical to that of the butcher: address yourself not to their humanity but to their self-love.

In energy, British costs are among the highest in the developed world, not for lack of technology but because every project is treated as a unique commission rather than a manufacturing process. South Korea's KEPCO builds nuclear reactors for a fraction of the cost of Hinkley Point C by constructing fleets of identical stations. The micropolitical solution is regulatory mimeticism: automatically approving designs already operating safely in allied jurisdictions rather than insisting on a bespoke British standard. This is the division of labour applied to nations. Smith demolished the case for making Scottish wine when French wine could be imported at a thirtieth of the cost. The same logic applies to reactors.

The method extends well beyond these examples. In pension reform, grandfathering the Triple Lock for current pensioners while adjusting terms for future retirees would neutralise the most powerful opposition without threatening a single existing beneficiary. In tax reform, Smith's own maxims of equity, certainty, convenience, and efficiency provide the template. The same approach applies to the welfare system, to immigration, to procurement, to the courts. In every case the work is the same: analyse the interest groups, map the conspiracy against the public, identify what each group values, construct the trade, and move fast enough that the new arrangements become irreversible before the old interests can regroup.

The physics of the problem has not changed since 1776. People respond to incentives. Producers can conspire against the public. The statesman who attempts to direct private people in what manner they ought to employ their capitals loads himself with a responsibility for which no human wisdom is sufficient. The man of system fails because he forgets that every chess piece moves of its own accord.

What has changed since 1776 is that we now possess the engineering to work with these forces rather than against them. The micropolitical method, developed over four decades by the Adam Smith Institute and tested against the most entrenched of interests, offers a proven means of turning Smithian principles into practical results. It does not promise a revolution. It promises progress that is incremental, irreversible, and built on the choices of millions of individuals pursuing their own advantage.

> The natural effort of every individual to better his own condition, when suffered to exert itself with freedom and security, is so powerful a principle that it is alone, and without any assistance, not only capable of carrying on the society to wealth and prosperity, but of surmounting a hundred impertinent obstructions with which the folly of human laws too often incumbers its operations.[21]

[21] Smith (1776, Book IV, Chapter V, Part II, p. 540).

The task of the micropolitician is to remove those obstructions, one by one, and let that natural effort do its work.

Bibliography

Buchanan, J. M., & Tullock, G. (1962). *The calculus of consent: Logical foundations of constitutional democracy*. University of Michigan Press.
Hayek, F. A. (1945). The use of knowledge in society. *The American Economic Review, 35*(4), 519–530.
Hirschman, A. O. (1970). *Exit, voice, and loyalty: Responses to decline in firms, organizations, and states*. Harvard University Press.
Keynes, J. M. (1936). *The general theory of employment, interest and money*. Macmillan.
Lawson, J., & Pirie, M. (2026). *Micropolitics revisited*. Adam Smith Institute.
Myers, J. (2017). *Yes in my back yard*. Adam Smith Institute.
Pirie, M. (1988). *Micropolitics*. Wildwood House.
Smith, A. (1759 [1976]). In D. D. Raphael & A. L. Macfie (Ed.), *The theory of moral sentiments*. Clarendon Press.
Smith, A. (1776 [1976]). In R. H. Campbell, A. S. Skinner, & W. B. Todd (Eds.), *An inquiry into the nature and causes of the Wealth of Nations*. Clarendon Press.
von Mises, L. (1920 [1935]). Economic calculation in the socialist commonwealth. In F. A. Hayek (Ed.), *Collectivist economic planning*. Routledge.

The manufacturer's authorised representative in the EU is Springer Nature Customer Service Centre GmbH, Europaplatz 3, 69115 Heidelberg, Germany. If you have any concerns regarding our products, please contact ProductSafety@springernature.com

Printed and bound by CPI Group (UK) Ltd, Croydon, CR0 4YY
20/10/2026
02236451-0020